W9-DJI-241

# The Urban World

# The Urban World

J. John Palen
University of Wisconsin
Milwaukee

**McGraw-Hill Book Company**
New York St. Louis San Francisco Düsseldorf
Johannesburg Kuala Lumpur London Mexico
Montreal New Delhi Panama Paris São Paulo
Singapore Sydney Tokyo Toronto

The Urban World



1 2 3 4 5 6 7 8 9 0 D O D O 7 9 8 7 6 5 4

This book was set in Times Roman by Black Dot, Inc. The editors were Lyle Linder, Helen Greenberg, and Susan Gamer; the designer was Rafael Hernandez; the production supervisor was Judi Frey.
R. R. Donnelley & Sons Company was printer and binder.

Library of Congress Cataloging in Publication Data

Palen, J John.
The urban world.

1. Cities and towns. 2. Cities and towns—United States. 3. Underdeveloped areas—Urbanization.
I. Title.
HT151.P283 301.36'0973 74-10730
ISBN 0-07-048088-5

For Joseph, Beth, and Ellen,
who are growing up in an urban world

# Contents

# Preface

Today urbanism has become the American way of life; residence in an urban area is the norm. The overwhelming majority of those reading this book have been lifelong residents of either central cities or surrounding suburbs and are now in college studying for urban professions and occupations. We can thus predict with reasonable certainty that their future lives will be spent in, and intimately bound up with, urban areas. Both intellectual and practical concerns thus demand that we know as much as possible about the nature of our cities and how urban areas have changed and can be expected to change over time.

This book is written for undergraduate students enrolled in courses on urbanization and the nature of urban life. Its goal is to give the student having little formal exposure to urban sociology or related areas a coherent overview of the field. Of course, in an area as broad as the urban scene, selectivity is both inevitable and necessary. The topics included and the emphases they receive reflect in part the state of the discipline, in part my own interests, and in part a conscious effort to provide for the needs of students with different backgrounds and interests. Although I myself am an urban sociologist with a strong interest in human ecology, I have made every attempt to avoid a parochial or sectarian reliance on any one orientation or discipline.

The book consists of eighteen chapters divided into four parts. Part One, "Focus and Development," consists of two chapters. Chapter 1, "Introduction," will acquaint the student with the recency and magnitude of urbanization and provide some basic definition of the field. Chapter 2, "The Emergence of Cities," provides a sociological framework for describing and analyzing the early growth and development of cities. The influence of natural environment, technology, and population growth on developing urban social organizations are stressed in order to make the reader aware of the background of contemporary urban life and the extent of social change. Preindustrial cities are described to provide a perspective for viewing the many changes in our own society.

Part Two, "The American City," consists of seven chapters on the development and nature of urbanism and urbanization in the United States today. Chapter 3 details factors of the environment, population, and technology that have contributed to the growth of the American city and the development of our present urban way of life. This chapter emphasizes long-term national trends as an aid to understanding current conditions. Chapter 4, "Developing Ecology of American Cities," concentrates on current patterns of urbanization and on theories developed to account for changes in urban structure. Particular attention is given to how physical patterns reflect social organization. Chapter 5, "Metropolitan Region," examines America's expanding metropolitan areas and how the trend toward decentralization reflects a new technology that has outgrown earlier city-hinterland patterns.

Chapter 6, "Life-Styles: The City," focuses on the social and psychological aspects of different urban ways of life. The city is seen as a milieu in which diversity is tolerated and often rewarded, and in which people of different ethnic backgrounds, races, and social classes can coexist. Chapter 7 examines suburbanism as a way of life and the growing differentiation of suburbs. The suburbs now contain a larger percentage of our national population than do the central cities, and the implications of this fact are explored.

Who has the power in the city—and who doesn't—is the topic of Chapter 8, "Urban Stratification and Power." Various theories and studies on community power structures are discussed, and research on the relative powerlessness of blacks and women is presented. Finally, Chapter 9 details the particular problems and social structures of four urban minorities: blacks, Mexican-Americans, American Indians, and Japanese-Americans.

Part Three, "Urban Planning and Redevelopment," takes up planning and the social questions related to it. Chapter 10 is concerned with housing problems in the United States—in particular, the pros and cons of urban renewal and other government housing programs. Chapter 11 discusses the development of urban planning in the United States and Europe. The planning experience in America is examined and compared with that in the Netherlands and Scandinavia; and the different traditions of government policy and public land ownership are detailed. Chapter 12 focuses on "new town" experiments, particularly in Great Britain.

Part Four, "Urbanization in the Third World," consists of five chapters on the urban explosion in Latin America, Africa, the Middle East, and Asia—a dimension largely ignored by urban texts in the past. The patterns of urbanization and spatial organization in developing countries, as distinct from those of North America, are emphasized. The effects of urbanization on traditional life-styles are also discussed—especially in the chapters on Latin America and Africa.

The conclusion, "Toward the City's Future," is a potpourri of plans and speculations about what the city should or will be like in the future. The focus is not only on the plans themselves, but also on how and why we plan as we do. A plea is made for starting with the social needs of people and then planning in such a way as to fulfill them—as opposed to the more common approach of designing the physical structures first and then attempting to adjust people to them.

I would like especially to thank a number of colleagues for their careful and critical reading of the manuscript—in particular, Edgar Borgatta, Scott Greer, George Hesslink, and Ephraim Mizruchi. The final version owes much to their contributions. I am, of course, solely responsible for all errors of omission or commission.

I would also like particularly to thank Dianne Berg for her research aid and her cheerfulness in typing much of the manuscript from rough copy. The invaluable assistance of Helen Greenberg and Lyle Linder, my editors; Susan Gamer, editing supervisor; and Juanita James, photo editor, is also most gratefully acknowledged.

**J. John Palen**

Part One

# Focus and Development

Chapter 1

# Introduction

*The men who dwell in the city are my teachers, and not the trees or the country.*

Socrates
In Plato's *Phaedrus*

Men and women have been on this globe at least a million years, and for almost all of those millenia they have lived in a world without cities. In our preoccupation with contemporary urban problems we tend to forget that cities are a relatively new social invention, having existed for a scant 7,000 years. These 7,000 years, however, although they represent only an instant in the eye of history, encompass almost the entire period we like to call "civilization." Man's social and cultural development during these years is in great part the story of the cities he has built and the life that he has lived within them. Our history is to a substantial degree the description of the triumph of cities and city life. Much of what we call "ancient history" is, more precisely, the saga of the rise and fall of dominant cities. Western civilization is almost unimaginable without a Babylon, an Athens, a Carthage, or a Rome.

## THE URBAN EXPLOSION

Although a number of strategically located—and sometimes magnificent—cities dominate our view of the past, it is well to keep in mind that these cities all existed in lands which were over 90 percent rural. As recently as 150 years ago even Europe was still overwhelmingly rural. Most contemporary urban dwellers are not aware that urbanization on the scale we are familiar with is an extremely recent phenomenon. As late as 1800, only 1.7 percent of the world's population lived in cities of 100,000 or more; 2.4 percent lived in communities of 20,000 or more; and only 3 percent lived in places of 5,000 or more.[1] Even a little over 100 years ago only about 5 percent of the world's population lived in cities of 20,000 or more.[2] We can put the rate of world urbanization in perspective by noting that if Milwaukee, Wisconsin had had the same population 200 years ago that it does today, it would have been the largest city in the world; in fact, the urbanized-area population of Milwaukee, 1.4 million, would have made it by far the largest urban population concentration in the world. Today the United States is one of the most urbanized nations in the world, with over three-quarters of its 210 million residents living in urban places.

During the last 200 years urbanization has accelerated until today, for the first time, we are on the threshold of living in a world that is numerically more urban than rural: some twenty years from now, the majority of the world's population will be living in urban rather than rural places. This rapid transformation from a rural to a heavily urbanized world and the development of urbanism as a way of life have been far more dramatic and spectacular than the much better known population explosion.

Urban growth, which began to explode during the latter part of the eighteenth century, cumulatively accelerated during the nineteenth and twentieth centuries. By 1800 the population of London had reached 1 million; Paris exceeded 500,00; and Vienna and St. Petersburg had each reached 200,000. A century later, ten cities had reached or exceeded 1 million: London, Paris, Vienna, Moscow, St. Petersburg, Calcutta, Tokyo, New York, Chicago, and Philadelphia. Today the people living in cities outnumber the entire population of the world 150 years ago. This urban explosion, which will be discussed in greater detail in Chapter 2, occurred for a number of reasons; among the more important were: (1) a rapidly growing population; (2) enclosure of farmlands and scientific management

[1]Philip Hauser and Leo Schnore, *The Study of Urbanization,* Wiley, New York, 1965, p. 7.

[2]Based on Kingsley Davis, "The Origin and Growth of Urbanization in the World," *American Journal of Sociology,* **60:**433, March, 1955.

of agriculture; (3) improved transportation and communication systems; (4) stable political governments; and (5) the development of the industrial revolution. While details differ from country to country, the pattern has been similar. Agriculture raised the surplus above previous subsistence levels. Then in rather short order this extra margin was transferred by entrepreneurs, and later by governments, into the manufacturing sector.[3] The result was urban expansion and growth fed by a demand by the burgeoning manufacturing, commercial, and service sectors for a concentrated labor force.

## SIZE OF CITIES

In discussing the size of cities it should be kept in mind that urbanization and the growth of cities are not the same thing. In the Western world the two things happened at the same time, but it is quite possible to find extremely large cities in essentially rural countries. Some of the world's largest cities—for example, Shanghai, Bombay, and Cairo—exist in nations that are still largely rural.

Urbanization, described by the percentage of a nation's total population living in urban areas, is a process that clearly has a beginning and an end. For instance, three-quarters of the United States' population of 215 million is now urban; the maximum level of urbanization is probably somewhere around 90 percent. However, even after a nation achieves a high level of urbanization, its cities and metropolitan areas can continue to grow. This is clearly the case in North America and Western Europe. While there is a limit to the percentage of urbanization possible, we as yet do not know what the practical limit is on the size of cities or metropolitan areas.

The latest figures from China indicate that Shanghai, with almost 11 million people in the city proper, is now the world's largest city. As Table 1-1 indicates, Tokyo, with almost 9 million, and New York, with almost 8 million, are not far behind. These figures count only those living in the city proper. The data for New York, for example, were limited to its five boroughs, Queens, Brooklyn, Manhattan, Staten Island, and the Bronx. The total populations of metropolitan areas are far larger. The Tokyo-Yokohama metropolitan area, for example, has a population in excess of 20 million. Note that today five of the world's ten largest cities are in Asia; only one is in North America, and only two are in Europe.

[3] *Urbanization in the Second United Nations Development Decade,* United Nations, New York, 1970, p. 6.

**Table 1-1 World's Most Populous Cities, 1970**

| City | Size |
|---|---|
| 1. Shanghai | 10,820,000 |
| 2. Tokyo | 8,841,000 |
| 3. New York | 7,895,000 |
| 4. Peking | 7,570,000 |
| 5. London | 7,379,000 |
| 6. Moscow | 7,050,000 |
| 7. Bombay | 5,969,000 |
| 8. Seoul | 5,536,000 |
| 9. Sao Paulo | 5,187,000 |
| 10. Cairo | 4,961,000 |

*Source:* United Nations *Demographic Yearbook,* 1972.

## "URBANISM" AND "URBANIZATION" DEFINED

Before going further, let us clarify two of the basic terms we will be using in the remainder of this book, "urbanism" and "urbanization." The use of these terms in sociological literature is at best confusing since they are sometimes used as synonyms and sometimes used to represent entirely different concepts. As one author has put it: "It is instructive, but hardly encouraging, to note that distinguished books in the field of urban sociology use them in exactly opposite senses."[4] In fact, Meadows and Mizruchi maintain that "urbanism" and "urbanization" as conceptual tools cannot be adequately defined.[5]

In this book the concept "urbanization" will be used to connote the proportion of a population living in urban places, and the changes in social organization that result from such population concentrations. Urbanization is thus a process—the process by which rural areas become transformed into urban areas. In demographic terms, urbanization is an increase in population concentration; organizationally, it is an alteration in structure and functions. Demographically, urbanization involves two elements: the multiplication of points of concentration, and the increase in the size of individual concentrations.[6] Organization is more difficult to define since it includes changes in the internal spatial structure of cities,

[4]Robert Bierstedt, *The Social Order,* McGraw-Hill, New York, 1970, p. 417.

[5]Paul Meadows and Ephraim Mizruchi (eds.), *Urbanism, Urbanization, and Change: Comparative Perspectives,* Addison-Wesley, Reading, Mass., 1969, p. 4.

[6]Hope Tisdale Eldridge, "The Process of Urbanization," in J. J. Spengler and O. D. Duncan (eds.), *Demographic Analysis,* Free Press, Glencoe, Ill., 1956, pp. 338–343.

changes in economic and social structures, and other related questions that are generally treated in a special area of urban sociology known as "human ecology" (see Chapter 4).

"Urbanism," on the other hand, connotes a condition of life rather than a process. It refers to the behavioral aspects of urban life—to the particular ways of life that are typical of city living. Under the conceptual label "urbanism" is found research concerned with the social-psychological aspects of urban life, urban personality patterns, and the behavioral adaptations required by city life. Urbanism as a way of life will receive detailed treatment in Chapters 6 and 7, on city and suburban life-styles, as well as in later chapters, particularly those on developing areas.

Note that it is quite possible for an area to have a high degree of urbanization and a low level of urbanism. Cairo, the world's tenth-largest city, houses many people who are still basically rural. A place such as Addis Ababa, a city of 1 million, is largely an agglomeration of villagers. Some developing cities do not possess the urban character of older European or American cities one-tenth their size (for example, see Chapter 15 for a detailed description of Addis Ababa). On the other hand, urbanism as a way of life has moved far beyond urbanized areas. The cultural patterns of most of the supposedly rural areas of the United States are today clearly dominated by urban values, urban attitudes, and

Harvesting wheat in the United States is a national business dependent on heavy mechanization.

urban life-styles. Rural dairy farmers, wheat growers, and cattlemen, with their professional lobbies and subsidies, are all part of a complex and highly integrated economic and social system which is essentially urban.

## EMERGENCE OF THE FIELD

The scientific study of urbanism and urbanization is a relative newcomer to the academic scene. The perceptive student will quickly note that almost all the empirical study is the product of the last fifty years, with the bulk of the research having been done in the last twenty years. Many of the early systematic studies of cities and the life lived within them are associated with a remarkable group of scholars connected with the University of Chicago in the 1920s and 1930s. The American city at this time was experiencing rapid transformation and change in terms of industrialization, heavy immigration from rural areas and foreign countries, and changing social patterns and customs. To many observers the city, at least implicitly, represented social disorganization, depersonalization, and the breakdown of older traditional ways of life.

A typical view of urban life, given in an anonymous poem of 1916 called "While the City Sleeps," goes in part:

Stand in your window and scan the sights,
On Broadway with its bright white lights.
Its dashing cabs and cabarets,
Its painted women and fast cafes.
That's when you really see New York.
Vulgar of manner, overfed,
Overdressed and underbred.
Heartless and Godless, Hell's delight,
Rude by day and lewd by night.

The impact of the city, with its emphasis on rationality, division of labor, and diversity, on simpler, traditional ways of life was also reflected by the sociologists of the day. Since most of these sociologists were themselves the products of rural or small-town backgrounds, it is not surprising that they placed heavy emphasis on differences between the rural and the urban, and on the effect of the city as a transformer of rural life. Significantly, "of the 19 presidents of the American Sociological Society who had been born prior to 1880, who had completed their graduate studies before 1910, and who had achieved some prominence before 1920, not one had experienced a typical urban childhood."[7]

[7]Roscoe C. Hinkle, Jr., and Gisela J. Hinkle, *The Development of Modern Sociology*, Doubleday, Garden City, New York, 1954, p. 3.

Fortunately, the newly emerging discipline of urban sociology did not calcify on explaining differences between the rural and the urban, but rather began to examine the urban scene empirically and systematically. Eventually, the original dichotomy was abandoned, and limited hypotheses began to be developed on the basis of empirical research.

As urban researchers began to define urban communities sociologically, they focused on three major sets of community characteristics or variables: (1) the city as a unique demographic structure and an ecological community; (2) the city as a characteristic form of social organization, with related social structures; (3) the city as a set of characteristic values, attitudes, and subjective perceptions. Research from all three perspectives is presented in the following chapters: the earlier chapters place relatively greater emphasis on the relationships between physical spatial features and forms of social organization; later chapters treat the social-psychological aspects of urbanism and the life-styles associated with it.

Chapter 2

# The Emergence of Cities

*Men come together in cities for security; they stay together for the good life.*
Aristotle

This chapter outlines the growth of urban life from the first tentative agricultural villages of Kurdistan to the industrial cities of the nineteenth century. Largely archeological and historical material is included, not because there is anything sacred about beginnings as such, but because having some understanding of the origin and function of cities helps us to better understand contemporary cities and how and why they got to be what they are today. Thus our interest is not so much in the chronology of historical events as the patterns and processes of urban development.

Our knowledge of the spatial structure of ancient cities and the social life lived within them comes mainly from the research of archeologists and historians. Theirs is a difficult task, for there is very little verifiable information upon which to make firm statements regarding urban life of earlier centuries. As a result, relatively little of a cumulative sociological nature is known about early patterns of urbanization. Lewis Mumford has aptly stated the problem:

> Five thousand years of urban history and perhaps as many of proto-urban history are spread over a few score of only partly explored sites. The great urban landmarks Ur, Nippur, Uruk, Thebes, Heleopolis, Assur, Nineveh, Babylon, cover a span of three thousand years whose vast emptiness we cannot hope to fill with a handful of monuments and a few hundred pages of written records.[1]

## PRECONDITIONS FOR CITIES

What we know is that before cities could emerge and grow a number of preconditions had to be met.[2] Before the urban revolution could take place, an agricultural revolution was necessary. Only when the agricultural system was capable of producing a surplus was it possible to withdraw labor from food production and apply it to the production of other goods. The size of the urban population was thus directly related to the efficiency of agricultural workers; and agriculture remained primitive for millennia.

When the agricultural, or Neolithic, revolution began is lost in the dimness of prehistory, but it was a momentous event, for it made the emergence of permanent settlements possible. Perhaps as early as 15,000 years ago, during the Mesolithic period, there were hamlets from India to the Baltic area that based their culture on the use of shellfish and fish.[3] Within these Mesolithic hamlets possibly were seen the earliest domestic animals, such as pigs, ducks, geese, and man's oldest companion, the dog. Mumford suggests that the practice of reproducing food by plant cuttings—as with the date palm, the olive, the fig, and the grape—probably derives from Mesolithic culture.[4]

This process of settlement entered a second stage between 10,000 and 8,000 B.C. with the systematic gathering and planting of certain seeds.

[1]Lewis Mumford, *The City in History, Its Origins, Its Transformations and Its Prospects,* Harcourt, Brace, and World, New York, 1961, p. 55.

[2]Not everyone agrees with an implicit evolutionary typology such as is used in this chapter. Bruce Trigger, for instance, strongly argues against an evolutionary approach in explaining the emergence and growth of cities and argues that "what seems to be required is a more piecemeal and institutional approach to complex societies." [Bruce Trigger, "Determinants of Urban Growth in Pre-industrial Societies," in Peter Ucko, Ruth Tringham, and G. W. Dimbleby (eds.), *Man, Settlement, and Urbanism,* Schenkman, Cambridge, Mass., 1972, p. 576.]

[3]Mumford, op. cit., p. 10.

[4]Mumford, op. cit., p. 11.

Herd animals such as oxen, sheep, donkeys, and finally horses were first used during this period, allowing the available supply of food to be substantially increased and the first solid steps toward permanent settlement of a single site to be made. Animals such as the horse and the donkey could also serve, in addition to men, as beasts of burden and a source of pulling power. In all likelihood there were decreases in the very high mortality rates, and increases in population, at this same time.

Since the plow didn't yet exist—it was not invented until sometime in the fourth century B.C.—horticulturalists of this period used a form of "slash-and-burn" agriculture.[5] This meant cutting down what you could and burning off the rest before planting—an inefficient form of farming, but one with a long history. It was even used by the American pioneers who first crossed the Appalachian Mountains into the new lands of Kentucky and Ohio. The first horticulturalists in ancient times soon discovered that slash-and-burn farming quickly depleted the soil, and so they were forced to migrate—thus probably spreading their knowledge by means of cultural diffusion.

## AGRICULTURAL SETTLEMENTS

Eventually some men gained enough knowledge of the relationship between the seasons and the cycle of growth to forsake constant nomadism in favor of permanent settlement in one location. The Neolithic period is characterized by this change from gathering food to producing it. There is fairly clear evidence that about 8,000 B.C. in the Middle East there was a transformation from a specialized food-collecting culture to a culture where grains were cultivated.

Nomadic hunting and gathering societies had never been able to produce or accumulate more wealth than they could carry with them. Now all that was to change. Men could plan for the future: with cultivation a surplus could be accumulated. The earliest indisputable permanent village farming community so far excavated, Jarmo, in the Kurdistan area of Iraq, was inhabited between 7,000 and 6,500 B.C. It has been calculated that approximately 150 people lived in Jarmo, and archeological evidence indicates a population density of twenty-seven people per square mile (this is about the same as the population density today in that area).[6] Soil erosion, deforestation, and 10,000 years of human habitation have offset the technological advantages enjoyed by the area's present inhabitants.

[5]E. Cecil Curwin and Gudmund Hart, *Plough and Pasture,* Collier Books, New York, 1961, p. 64.

[6]Robert Braidwood, "The Agricultural Revolution," *Scientific American,* reprint, September, 1960, p. 7.

The inhabitants of Jarmo had learned to domesticate dogs, goats, and possibly sheep.[7] The farmers living in Jarmo raised an early form of domesticated barley and wheat but still had to hunt and collect much of their food. Since the earliest farmers lacked plows to break the tight grassland sod, they worked the hillsides where grass was scarce and trees broke the earth. Village farming communities like Jarmo had stabilized by about 5,500 B.C. and over the next 1,500 years such settlements gradually spread from the flanks of hills into the alluvial plains of river valleys like that of the Tigris-Euphrates. A similar process took place in the great river valleys of the Nile, the Indus, and the Hwang Ho. The invention of agriculture was quite possibly an independent development in China and was certainly independent in the New World.[8] The civilizations of Middle America were physically isolated from those of the Middle East and Asia and thus had to invent independently, since they were unable to borrow.

Egypt was among the first to reap the benefits of a sedimentary agriculture. By the middle of the fourth millennium B.C. the economy of the Nile Valley in Egypt had shifted once and for all from a combination of farming and food gathering to a major reliance on agriculture.[9] In the great river valley two and sometimes three crops a year were possible because the annual floods brought rich silt to replace the soil which was exhausted. To the dependable crops of wheat and barley was added the cultivation of the date palm. This was a great improvement, for in Mesopotamia the palm provided more than simple food; from it were obtained wood, roofing, matting, wine, and fiber for rope.

## POPULATION, TECHNOLOGY, AND SOCIAL ORGANIZATION

The immediate result of this agricultural revolution was a spurt in population size, since a larger population could be maintained on a permanent basis. Stable yields meant that larger numbers of people could now be sustained in a relatively compact space. Agricultural villages could support up to twenty-five persons per square mile, which was a dramatic improvement over the maximum of three to ten persons per square mile found in hunting and gathering societies.[10]

The establishment of settled agricultural villages also led to technological advances. Agriculture in the river valleys needed at least small-scale irrigation systems, something not necessary in the highlands. Thus

[7]Ibid.
[8]Braidwood, op. cit., p. 3.
[9]Robert W. July, *A History of the African People*, Scribner's, New York, 1970, p. 14.
[10]Gerhard Lenski, *Human Society*, McGraw-Hill, New York, 1970, p. 164.

rudimentary social organization and specialization began to develop; the periodic flooding made it necessary for the village farmers to band together to create a system of irrigation canals and repair the damage done by the floods.

The use of rivers for transportation further encouraged the aggregation of population, for now it was relatively easy to gather food at a few centers. Thus in the valleys of the Nile, the Tigris-Euphrates, and the Indus there first developed a population surplus which in turn permitted the rise of the first cities. By the third century B.C. the Egyptian peasant from the fertile river flood plain could produce approximately three times the food he needed.[11] Whether this surplus created institutions such as the city or whether the institution of the city brought about the process of creating and storing a surplus is one of history's unanswerable questions. The truth probably is that the relationship was reciprocal. The result of the realtionship was the first cities.

## URBAN REVOLUTION

Gordon Childe lists ten features which, he says, define the "urban revolution." They are:

**1** Permanent settlement in dense aggregations
**2** Nonagriculturalists engaging in specialized functions
**3** Taxation and capital accumulation
**4** Monumental public buildings
**5** A ruling class
**6** The technique of writing
**7** The acquisition of predictive sciences—arithmetic, geometry, and astronomy
**8** Artistic expression
**9** Trade
**10** The replacement of kinship by residence as the basis for membership in the community[12]

Whether all ten are necessary is debatable. Writing, for example, did not develop in the civilizations of Middle America. However, the list is useful in helping us define what we have come to accept as the characteristics of a city. What is important for our purpose is that cities possessing these characteristics did emerge in Mesopotamia and elsewhere.

These first cities were quite small: by contemporary standards the largest were little more than villages or small towns. However, in their own day they must have been viewed with the same awe with which

[11]July, op. cit., p. 14.
[12]V. Gordon Childe, "The Urban Revolution," *Town Planning Review,* **21**:4–7, 1950.

nineteenth-century immigrants viewed New York, for these first cities were ten times the size of the Neolithic villages which had previously been the largest settlements. Babylon, with its hanging gardens, one of the wonders of the ancient world, embraced a physical area of only roughly 3.2 square miles.[13] The city of Ur, located at the confluence of the Tigris and Euphrates rivers, was the largest city in Mesopotamia. With all its canals, temples, and harbors it occupied only 220 acres.[14] Ur was estimated to have contained 24,000 persons; other towns ranged in size from 2,000 to 20,000 inhabitants.[15]

Hawley estimates that although these cities were large for their time they probably represented no more than 3 or 4 percent of all the people within the various localities.[16] Even Athens at its peak had only 612 acres within its walls, which is an area less than 1 square mile. Ancient Antioch was roughly half this size; Carthage at its peak was 712 acres. Of all the ancient cities, only imperial Rome exceeded an area of 5 square miles. Kingsley Davis estimates that even the biggest places before the Roman period could scarcely have exceeded 200,000 inhabitants, since from fifty to ninety farmers were required to support one person in a city.[17] In an agricultural world the size of cities was limited by how much surplus could be produced and what technology was available to transport it.

It should be noted that the stable location of the city was not an unmixed blessing. It was not simply for the sake of convenience that gardens and pasture lands were found within the city walls. Cities had to be equipped to withstand a siege, since the earliest of them were vulnerable not only to conquest by other peoples but also to periodic attacks by nomadic raiders. The city dwellers' precautions in constructing walls were not always sufficient, however, and many cities perished, never to rise again. The Bible, for instance, devotes considerable attention to the successes of the nomadic Israelites in taking and pillaging the cities of their more advanced enemies. The description of the fall of the Canaanite city of Jericho tells us that

> the People went out into the city, every man straight before him, and they took the city. And they utterly destroyed all that was in the city, both man and woman, young and old, and ox and sheep and ass, with the edge of the sword—and they burnt the city with fire and all that was therein (Joshua 2:20–24).

[13]Kingsley Davis, "The Origin and Growth of Urbanization in the World," *American Journal of Sociology,* **60:**430, March, 1955.

[14]V. Gordon Childe, *What Happened in History,* Penguin Books, London, 1946, p. 87.

[15]Childe, *What Happened in History,* p. 86.

[16]Amos H. Hawley, *Urban Society,* Ronald Press, New York, 1971, p. 22.

[17]Davis, op. cit., p. 430.

## EVOLUTION IN SOCIAL ORGANIZATION

Keep in mind that the size of an urban population was, during this period, no measure of its significance. The importance of these cities was not their size but the fact that they frequently not only tolerated but actively encouraged innovations in social organization. Even though small in number the urban elite was the principle carrier of the all-important cultural and intellectual values of a civilization. Needless to say, the city also held economic and political sway over the more numerous country dwellers. The philosopher-sociologist Ibn Khaldun, writing in the fourteenth century, pointed out that the concentration of economic power and the proceeds of taxation in the cities led to a profound difference between the economic pattern of the city and that of the country. The concentration of governmental and educational functions in the city also stimulated new demands which affected the patterns of production and supply. The preindustrial city was an urban island in the middle of a rural sea.[18]

The city's greater population density, along with its sedentary way of life, made possible the development of an urban culture emphasizing trade, manufacturing, and services. The earliest cities began to evolve a social organization immensely more complex than that found in the Neolithic village. The slight surplus of food permitted the emergence of a rudimentary division of labor. No longer did each man have to do everything for himself.

Archeological records indicate that the earliest public buildings were temples, suggesting that specialized priests were the first to be released from direct subsistence functions. That the priests also assumed the role of economic administrators is indicated by ration or wage lists found in places where temples were located.[19] In Egypt the temples were also used as granaries for the community surplus. This surplus could be used to carry a community through a period of famine. The technology of food storage was a major achievement of the city. The biblical story of Joseph, who was jealously sold by his brothers into slavery in Egypt, only to become advisor to the Pharaoh and predict seven good years of harvest followed by seven lean years of famine, points out the vulnerability of the nomadic Israelites to their physical environment, and the relative control of the more advanced Egyptians over their environment. Even if the nomadic Jews had received Joseph's warning, they would have been unable to profit from it. They lacked the transportation and storage

[18]For a summary article on the role of the city in nonindustrial cultures, see Burt F. Hoselitz, "The Role of Cities in the Economic Growth of Underdeveloped Countries," *Journal of Political Economy*, **61:** 195–208, 1953.

[19]Robert M. Adams, "The Origins of Cities," *Scientific American*, reprint, September, 1960, p. 7.

technology of the more urban Egyptians. Long-term planning—whether to avoid famines, build pyramids, or construct temples—was possible only where a surplus was assured and storage was available.

## KINGSHIP AND SOCIAL CLASS

For a long time the temples were the largest and most complex institutions that existed; kingship and dynastic political regimes developed later. Apparently warrior-leaders were originally selected by all other males and served only during times of external threat. Eventually those chosen as short-term leaders during periods of war came to be retained even during periods of peace. As H. G. Creel describes the process in China in the fifth century B.C.:

> Perhaps whole settlements sometimes found it was easier to set up as warriors, and let the people around them work for them, than to labor in the fields. The chiefs and their groups of warriors, no doubt, provided the farmers with "protection" whether they wanted it or not, and in return for that service they took a share of the peasant's crop.[20]

It is hardly necessary to add that the size of the warrior's share of the peasant's crop was fixed by the warrior, not the peasant. The growth of military establishments did contribute, though, to technological innovations—metallurgy for weapons, chariots for battle, and more efficient ships.

It was but a short step from a warrior class to kingship and the founding of dynasties with permanent hereditary royalty. The gradual shifting of the central focus from temple to palace was accompanied by the growth of social and economic stratification. Records of sales of land indicate that even among the agriculturists there were considerable inequalities in the ownership of productive land. As a result, social differences grew. Some few members of each new generation were born with marked hereditary social and economic advantages over the others. If they couldn't afford the luxuries of palace life, they nonetheless lived in considerable comfort. Archeologically, the emergence of social classes can be clearly seen in the increasing disparity in the richness of grave offerings.[21] The tombs of royalty are richly furnished with ornaments and weapons of gold and precious metals; those of others, with copper vessels; while the majority have only pottery vessels or nothing at all. The building of burial pyramids was an extreme case of enrichment of graves.

[20]H. G. Creel, *The Birth of China,* Reynal and Hitchcock, New York, 1937, p. 279.
[21]Adams, op. cit., p. 9.

## TECHNOLOGICAL EVOLUTION

Technology was spurred on by the existence of the palace. The military required armor, weapons, and chariots; and the court demanded ever more ornaments and other luxuries. A constant market was created for nonagricultural commodities, and the result was the establishment of a class of full-time artisans and craftsmen. The near-isolation of earlier periods was now replaced with trade over long distances, which brought not only new goods but also new ideas.

In contrast to hunting and gathering societies, where everyone did practically the same thing, the ancient civilizations in their full flower contained not only the king and the court but also professional armies, craftsmen, artists, and engineers capable of master designs such as the pyramids. This elaborate social stratification was based on the agricultural surplus produced by peasants, serfs, and slaves.

## SOCIAL REVOLUTION

The first city was far more than an enlarged village—it was a clear break with the past, a whole new social system. It was a social revolution involving the evolution of a whole new set of social institutions. Unlike the agricultural revolution that preceded it, this urban revolution was far more than a basic change in subsistence. It was "pre-eminently a social process, an expression more of change in man's interaction with his fellows than in his interaction with his environment."[22]

Once begun, the urban revolution created its own environment. Inventions that have made large settlements possible have been due to the city itself—for example, writing, accounting, bronze, the solar calendar, bureaucracy, and the beginning of science.[23] Ever since Mesopotamia, the city as a social institution has been shaping man's life.

## ATHENS

It is evident that environmental factors played a decisive role in early cities. In fact, the history of the city can be considered the story of man's attempts, through the use of technology and social organization, to lessen the impact of environmental factors. Athens, widely regarded as the apex of ancient urbanism, was more or less forced to look toward the sea. Not only was its thin and rocky soil of marginal fertility, but the mountainous hinterland made inland transportation and communication almost impos-

[22]Adams, op. cit., p. 3.
[23]Davis, op. cit., p. 430.

sible. Aside from the sacred ways to Delphi and Eleusis, the roads were mere paths, suitable only for pack animals or porters. It is estimated that the cost of transporting goods 10 miles from Athens was more than 40 percent of the value of the goods.[24]

But Greece was blessed with fine harbors. Consequently, Athens turned to the sea. A Greek ship could carry 7,000 pounds of grain 65 nautical miles a day, and do it at one-tenth the cost of land transportation. (Storms at sea and pirates, however, often made this an ideal rather than a reality.) There were also technological contributions to Greek prosperity: the use of the lodestone as a basic nautical compass and the development of more seaworthy ships.

### Social Invention

The greatest achievement of the Greeks was not in the area of technology but in that of social organization. The social invention of the *polis,* or "city-state," enabled families, phratries (groups of clans), and tribes to organize for mutual aid and protection as citizens of a common state. Because they acknowledged a common mythical ancestry among the gods, different families were able to come together in larger bodies. Gradually the principle of common worship was extended to the entire community. Citizenship within the state and the right to worship at civic shrines were two sides of the same coin.

A citizen was one who could trace his ancestry back to the god or gods responsible for the city and thus could participate in public religious worship. An Athenian citizen was one who had the right to worship at the temple of Athena, the protector of the city-state of Athens. The ancient city was a religious community, and citizenship was at its basis a religious status.[25] Socrates' questioning the existence of the gods was considered a grave offense because, by threatening established religion, he was undermining the very basis of citizenship in the city-state. As punishment for such a subversive act he was forced to take poison hemlock. Unfortunately, the Greeks never devised a system for extending citizenship to political units larger than the city-state. That was to be the great achievement of the Romans.

### Physical Design

Physically, the Greek cities were of fairly similar design—a fact which is not surprising, given the amount of social borrowing that took place

[24]Gustave Glotz, *Ancient Greece at Work,* Norton, New York, 1967, pp. 291–293.

[25]Fustel de Coulanges, *The Ancient City,* Doubleday, Garden City, New York, 1956 (first published 1865), p. 134.

The dominant Acropolis of Athens with the remains of the Parthenon, the temple built to Athena, the goddess of the city, in the fifth century B.C. (*Editorial Photocolor Archives, Inc.*)

among the various city-states and the fact that the cities were built with military defense in mind. The major city walls were built around a fortified hill called an *acropolis.* Major temples were also placed upon the acropolis. The nearby *agora* served both as a meeting place and, in time, as a market place. All major buildings were located within the city walls. Housing, except for the most privileged, was outside the walls, but huddled as close to their protective shelter as was possible. Hippodamus designed a grid street pattern for Piraeus, the port city of Athens, but Athens itself had no such ordered arrangement. Outside the temple area, streets were no more than dirty, narrow, winding lanes. Housing for the masses was squalid and cramped. Athens was the center of an empire, but little of her genius was given to the areas of urban design or municipal management.

### Population

Although Athens had considerable population problems—partially due to the scarcity of productive land, which resulted in heavy migration from rural areas to the cities—during its peak the city achieved a population of only between 120,000 and 180,000. The major limit on population growth was the limited technological base. The city was still dependent on the surplus of agricultural activities. Much of the land within Athens itself was given over to gardening. The great sociologist Max Weber put the Greek city-states in perspective when he wrote, "The full urbanite of antiquity was a semi-peasant."[26]

Expansion of Greek cities was also limited by preference and policy. The ancient Greek preferred fairly small cities. Both Plato and Aristotle firmly believed that good government was directly related to the size of the city. Plato specified that in the ideal city there should be exactly 5,040 citizens, since that number had fifty-nine divisors and would "furnish numbers for war and peace, and for all contracts and dealings, including taxes and divisions of the land."[27] When noncitizens, such as women, children, slaves, and foreigners, are added into the calculation, the total population of the city-state becomes about 60,000.

Aristotle was less specific about the ideal size of the city, although he recognized that increasing the number of inhabitants beyond a certain point changes the character of a city. In his view, the city-state had to be large enough to defend itself and to be economically self-sufficient but not so large as to prevent the citizens from knowing each other's character. As he stated it:

> A state then only begins to exist when it has attained a population sufficient for a good life in the political community: it may somewhat exceed this number, but as I was saying there must be a limit. What should be the limit will be easily ascertained by experience.—If the citizens of a state are to judge and distribute offices according to merit, then they must know each other's characters: where they do not possess this knowledge, both the election to offices and the decisions of lawsuits will go wrong—Clearly then the best limit of the population of a state is the largest number which suffices for the purposes of life and can be taken at a single view.[28]

City-states were also restrained from growing overly large by the Greek policy of creating colonies. This policy reinforced the social preference for small cities. Between 479 and 431 B.C., over 10,000 families migrated from established cities to newer Greek colonial settlements. Colonization both met the needs of empire and provided a safety valve for a chronic population problem. This diffusion of population led in turn

[26]Max Weber, *The City* (trans. D. Martendale and G. Neuwirth), Free Press, New York, 1958, p. 71.

[27]Plato, *The Laws,* Book V, 437 (trans. B. Jowett), 1926 ed.

[28]Aristotle, *Politics,* Book VII, iv 7–8, (trans. B. Jowett), 1932 ed.

An upper-class villa in the Roman coastal city of Pompeii, which was buried by the eruption of Mount Vesuvius in 79 A.D. (*Brogi-Scala.*)

to a diffusion of Greek culture and ideas of government far beyond the Peloponnesus.

## ROME

The city as a physical entity reached a high point under the Roman Caesars. Not until the nineteenth century was Europe again to see cities as large as those found within the Roman Empire. Rome itself may have contained 1 million inhabitants at its peak, although an analysis of density figures would make an estimate of half that number seem more reasonable; scholarly estimates vary from a low of 250,000 to a high of 1.6 million. These wide variations are a result of different interpretations of inadequate data. The number given in the Roman census, for example, jumped from 900,000 in 69 B.C. to over 4 million in 28 B.C. No one is quite sure what this increase indicates—perhaps an extension of citizenship, perhaps the counting of women and children, perhaps something else.[29]

[29]William Petersen, *Population*, Macmillan, New York, 1969, p. 369.

All figures on the size of cities before the nineteenth century should be taken as estimates rather than empirical census counts.

### Size and Number of Cities

Expertise in the areas of technology and social organization enabled the Romans to organize, administer, and govern an empire containing several cities of more than 200,000 inhabitants. The population of the Roman empire exceeded that of all but the largest twentieth-century superpowers. According to the historian Edward Gibbons, "We are informed that when the emperor Claudius [reigned 41–54 A.D.] exercised the office of censor, he took account of six million nine hundred and forty-five thousand Roman citizens, who with women and children, must have amounted to about twenty million souls." He concludes that there were "about twice as many provincials as there were citizens, of either sex and of every age; and that the slaves were at least equal in number to the free inhabitants of the Roman world. The total amount of this imperfect calculation would rise to about one hundred and twenty millions."[30] The total world population at this time was roughly 250 million.

Gibbon further states that ancient Italy was said to contain 1,197 cities—however defined—and Spain, according to Pliny, had 360 cities.[31] North Africa had hundreds of cities, and north of the Alps major cities rose from Vienna to Bordeaux. Even in far-off Britain there were major cities at York, Bath, and London. What made all this possible for hundreds of years was a technology of considerable sophistication and—most important—Roman social organization. Wherever the legions conquered, they also brought Roman law and Roman concepts of government.

### Planning

However, as was the case in Athens, Roman municipal planning was definitely limited in scope. Magnificent though it was, it did not extend beyond the center of the municipality. Once one branched off the main thoroughfare leading to the city gates, there was only a maze of narrow crooked lanes winding through the squalid tenements that housed the great bulk of the population. The masses crowded in the poor quarters were offered periodic "bread and circuses" to keep their minds off revolt. Magnificent public squares and public baths were built with public taxes for the more affluent Romans, not for the masses. As the city grew, the old city walls were torn down and rebuilt to include buildings that had been

[30]Edward Gibbon, *The Decline and Fall of the Roman Empire,* Dell, New York, 1879 (first published 1776), p. 53.

[31]Gibbon, op. cit., pp. 54–55.

The Pont du Gard, a Roman aqueduct still standing in France. Such aqueducts for centuries provided fresh mountain water for the cities of the Roman Empire. (*Editorial Photocolor Archives, Inc.*)

constructed on the outer fringe. In time even the Forum became crowded and congested, as the ruins still standing amply testify.

The city was supplied with fresh water through an extensive system of aqueducts. The most important of these, which brought water from the Sabine Hills, was completed in 144 B.C. Parts of aqueducts still stand—testament to the excellence of their engineering and the skill of their builders. Rome even had an elaborate sewer system—at least in the better residential areas. It is an unfortunate comment on progress to note that present-day Rome still dumps untreated sewage into the Tiber River.

In many ways provincial Roman cities such as Paris, Vienna, Cologne, Mainz, and London exhibited greater civic planning than Rome itself. These cities grew out of semipermanent military encampments and thus took the shape of the standard Roman camp. The encampments and later the cities were laid out on a rectangular grid pattern with a gate on each side. The center was reserved for the forum, the coliseum, and municipal buildings such as public baths. Markets were also generally found in the forum. The common origins of European provincial Roman cities meant that they were all remarkably similar in design.

### Decline

Rome was an exporter of ideas—such as Roman law, government, and engineering—which enabled it to control the hinterland. It was an importer of necessary goods and therefore depended on the hinterland not only for tribute and slaves but for its very life. The city of Rome could feed its population and also import vast quantities of goods other than food into the city because of an unrivaled road network and peaceful routes of sea trade. Commercial farming in Iberia and North Africa could provide foodstuffs for the city because the "Mare Nostrum," or Mediterranean, was truly a Roman lake. Once the decline and dissolution of the Empire began, Rome declined in size. When its African grain-producing areas were lost to the Vandals, and barbarians elsewhere pressed the Empire and disrupted vital transportation routes, the imperial order was finished. During the centuries known as the Dark Ages, Rome shrank until it was a mere village inhabiting what once had been a great city.

## EUROPEAN URBANIZATION BEFORE THE INDUSTRIAL CITY

The preceding pages discussed the development of the city through the Roman period. Here we place particular emphasis on the reemergence of European urban places after the decline of Rome and on how such cities laid the basis for the Western industrial city with which we are all so familiar.

The fall of the Roman Empire in the fifth century after Christ marked the effective end of cities in Western Europe for a period of over 600 years. This is not the place to detail why Rome fell—it is sufficient to note that under the impact of the barbarian invasions the empire disintegrated and commerce shrank to a bare minimum. Once-proud Roman provincial centers disappeared or declined to the point of insignificance. Rome itself shrank to a bare shell of some 20,000 inhabitants living in the ruins of past greatness. The throttling of Mediterranean trade by the advance of Islam in the seventh century, and the pillaging raids of the Norsemen in the ninth century, did further damage to what remained of commercial life.

### The Feudal System

The fall of Rome meant that each locality was isolated from every other and thus had to become self-sufficient in order to survive. Local lords offered peasants in the region protection from outside raiders in return for the virtual slavery—called "serfdom"—of the peasants. Removed from outside influences, local social structures congealed into hereditary hierarchies with the local lord at the top of the pyramid of social stratification and the serfs at the bottom.[32]

Importantly, the economic and political base of the feudal system, unlike that of the Roman period, was rural, not urban. Its center was not a city but the rural manor or castle from which the local peasantry could be controlled. The economy was a subsistence agriculture based solely on what was produced in the local area; transportation of goods from one area to another was virtually impossible. Lack of communication, the virtual absence of a commonly accepted currency, and the land-tenure system that bound serfs to the soil all contributed to a narrow inward-looking localism.

However, not all former provincial cities were totally abandoned; a few managed to survive with greatly reduced populations. These were generally under the secular control of the residing bishop. The Catholic Church had based its diocesan boundaries on those of the old Roman cities; and as the empire faded and then collapsed, the bishops came to exercise secular as well as religious power. By the ninth century "civitas" had come to be synonymous with these "Episcopal cities."[33]

According to Henri Pirenne, the "Episcopal cities" were cities in name only, for they more clearly resembled medieval fortresses than true cities. They had a maximum of 2,000 or 3,000 persons, and were frequently even smaller. But they were to play a crucial historical role as "stepping stones."[34] By the ninth century the cities—or towns—had lost most of their urban functions:

> The Carolingians used the ancient cities as places of habitation, as fortified settlements from which to dominate the surrounding countryside. The surviving physical apparatus of the old town, the walls, and buildings, served because it already existed, a convenient legacy of an earlier age."[35]

### Medieval Revival

Cities began to revive, very slowly, in the eleventh century. According to Pirenne, most of these new towns were not continuations of ancient cities but new social entities. Originally they were formed as a byproduct of the merchant caravans that stopped to trade outside the walls of the medieval

[32]Henri Pirenne, *Medieval Cities,* Princeton University Press, Princeton, N. J., 1939, particularly pp. 84–85.

[33]Max Weber, op. cit., p. 49.

[34]Pirenne, op. cit., p. 76.

[35]Howard Saalman, *Medieval Cities,* Braziller, New York, 1968, p. 15.

"Episcopal cities" such as Amiens, Tours, and Cologne. Under the influence of trade the old Roman cities took on a new life and became repopulated, while new towns were also being established. Mercantile groups formed around the military burgs, along seacoasts, on river banks, and at the confluences and junctions of the natural routes of trade and communication.[36]

Over time the seasonal fairs that were held outside the town gates came to take on a more or less permanent year-round character. Since at this time the merchants were not allowed inside the town walls, they settled in the outside shadow of the walls and in some cases built their own walls which attached to the town walls. These *faubourgs* or medieval suburbs came to be incorporated into the town proper, and by the thirteenth century merchants had an accepted and important role in the growing medieval towns.

Two external factors during the Middle Ages also greatly contributed to the growth of towns: the Crusades and the overall population growth. A great impetus for the revival of trade came from the medieval religious crusades. The Crusaders returned from the urban Byzantine empire with newly developed tastes for the consumer goods and luxuries of the East. Trading activities greatly accelerated, despite the pillaging which traders suffered from highwaymen and the endless feudal taxes and dues the traders were forced to pay to each local lord as they transported goods through his territory.

Still the social system was definitely more stable than that of the early Middle Ages, with their marauding raiders and internal warfare. The increasing stability led to a more constant food supply, which in turn resulted in lower death rates and improvement in the rate of natural increase of the population.

Technological innovations also contributed to population growth. The moldboard plow, which had been used in Roman times, was rediscovered. This heavier plow could turn the tight soils of northern Europe, and came to be commonly used during the tenth century. The substitution of three-field rotation for the old two-field system also brought substantial gains in agriculture. In practice it permitted three plantings a year rather than two, while at the same time raising the productivity of each planting by 16 percent. The effect was to double production and permit stable growth.

England, in the time of William the Conqueror, had a population of approximately 1.8 million. Three hundred years later the population had increased to roughly 2.7 million. Some of this increased population

[36]Pirenne, op. cit., p. 102.

**Table 2-1 Estimated Populations and Areas of Selected Medieval Cities**

| City | Date | Population | Land area, acres |
|---|---|---|---|
| Venice | 1363 | 77,700 | 810 |
| Paris | 1192 | 59,200 | 945 |
| Florence | 1381 | 54,747 | 268 |
| Milan | 1300 | 52,000 | 415 |
| Genoa | 1500 | 37,788 | 732 |
| Rome | 1198 | 35,000 | 3,450 |
| London | 1377 | 34,971 | 720 |
| Bologna | 1371 | 32,000 | 507 |
| Barcelona | 1359 | 27,056 | 650 |
| Naples | 1278 | 22,000 | 300 |
| Hamburg | 1250 | 22,000 | 510 |
| Brussels | 1496 | 19,058 | 650 |
| Sienna | 1385 | 16,700 | 412 |
| Antwerp | 1437 | 13,760 | 880 |
| Pisa | 1228 | 13,000 | 285 |
| Frankfort | 1410 | 9,844 | 320 |
| Liège | 1470 | 8,000 | 200 |
| Amsterdam | 1470 | 7,476 | 195 |
| Zurich | 1357 | 7,399 | 175 |
| Berlin | 1450 | 6,000 | 218 |
| Geneva | 1404 | 4,204 | 75 |
| Vienna | 1391 | 3,836 | 90 |
| Dresden | 1396 | 3,745 | 140 |
| Leipzig | 1474 | 2,076 | 105 |

*Source:* J. C. Russell, *Late Ancient and Medieval Population* The American Philosophical Society, Philadelphia, 1958, pp. 60–62.

migrated to the small but growing towns. Without such increases, the growth of towns would hardly have been possible.

It should be noted that while the feudal order was basically rural, certain elements of the medieval legal system indirectly encouraged the growth of towns. Feudal lords were forbidden by custom to sell their lands, but a lord badly in need of new funds could sell charters for new towns within his lands. Also, by encouraging the growth of older towns he could increase his annual rents. Towns were frequently able to purchase or bargain for various rights, such as the right to hold a regular market, the right to coin money and establish weights and measures, the right of citizens to be tried in their own courts, and—most important—the right to bear arms.[37] Over time cities became more or less autonomous and

[37]Mumford, op. cit., p. 263.

self-governing. City charters, in fact, bestowed the right of citizenship upon those living within the urban walls. As a result, medieval cities attracted the more skilled, the more ambitious, and probably the more intelligent of the rural population.

### Characteristics of Towns

Medieval cities were quite small by contemporary standards, having hardly more inhabitants than present-day towns or villages (Table 2-1). Even during the Renaissance, cities of considerable prominence often had only 10,000 to 30,000 inhabitants.[38] Only Paris, Florence, Venice, and Milan are thought to have possibly reached populations of 100,000.[39] These figures are of course scholarly estimates of past size, rather than counts taken at the time.

Thick walls enclosed the medieval city; watchtowers and external moats added to its military defense. The internal spatial arrangement of the medieval town reflected its primary function either as an "Episcopal city" functioning as an administrative center for church officials or as a military, and later a commercial, center. The main thoroughfares led directly from the outer gates to the source of protection and power—the cathedral or the feudal castle.[40] Outside the medieval bourgs, land was reserved for expansion, so that when the population increased the older fortifications could be torn down and new city walls built further out. The magnificent ring-like boulevards of Vienna and Paris are reminders of the medieval origins of these cities. When the walls were finally demolished in the middle of the nineteenth century, the resulting open space was used to construct the now famous boulevards.

Within the medieval bourgs could be found a new social class of artisans, weavers, innkeepers, money changers, and metalsmiths, known as the *bourgeoisie.* This new class of merchants was in many ways the antithesis of the feudal nobility. They were organized into guilds, and their way of life was characterized by trade and functionally specialized production, not by the ownership of land. The rise of the medieval bourgeoisie undermined the traditional system and prepared the way for further changes, for, as a German phrase put it, "*Stadtluft macht frei*" ("City air makes one free").[41]

What eventually developed was a distinct form, a full urban community. Such communities, as defined by the German sociologist Max

[38]Frederick Hiorns, *Town Building in History,* Harrap, London, 1956, p. 110.

[39]Henri Pirenne, *Economic and Social History of Medieval Europe,* Harcourt, New York, 1936, p. 173.

[40]Rose Hum Lee, *The City,* Lippincott, Chicago, 1955, p. 27.

[41]In its precise sense, the phrase refers to the medieval practice of recognizing the freedom of any serf who could manage to remain within the walls of the city for a year and a day.

Weber, were economically based on trading and commercial relations. They exhibited the following features: (1) a fortification; (2) a market, a court of its own, and at least partial autonomous law; (3) a related form of association; and (4) at least partial political autonomy and self-governance.[42] Weber argues convincingly that such a totally self-governing urban community could emerge only in the West, where cities had political autonomy and urban residents shared common patterns of associations and social statuses.

Medieval towns sometimes became organized around a particular craft or product, but the majority of the towns developed their greatest economic strength because of their performance of commercial and financial functions. Examples of cities that grew and prospered because of trade and banking are Venice, Milan, and Marseilles in the Mediterranean area, and Bremen, Hamburg, Cologne, and later Antwerp in the North.[43] In the later Middle Ages great financial families came to dominate many of these cities both economically and politically.

By the fourteenth century it was clear that the growth of town-based commerce was turning Europe away from the earlier manorial self-sufficiency toward an urban-centered, profit-oriented economy. The more ambitious cities were starting to flex their economic muscles. The Italian port cities grew wealthy on trade and began to expand their influence over the surrounding hinterland. Economic competition among the Italian city-states was augmented by warfare. Florence eliminated the competition of Pisa and Siena by conquering them by military force. The cities to the north were equally active in carving out a hinterland under their economic domination. Rouen was the economic center for thirty-five villages; Metz controlled 168; and Lübeck claimed 240 dependent villages within its territory.[44]

## Plague

Even the devastation of the plague could not reverse the long-term growth of cities, although it certainly wrought havoc to a degree that is difficult to exaggerate. In its first three years, from 1348 through 1350, the plague, or Black Death, wiped out at least a fourth of the population of Europe. One scholar of the plague simply says that "it undoubtedly was the worst disaster that has ever befallen mankind."[45] Before the year 1400, mortality due to the plague rose to more than a third of the

[42]Weber, op. cit., p. 81.

[43]Bert Hoselitz, "The Role of Cities in the Economic Growth of Underdeveloped Countries," *Journal of Political Economy*, **61**:195–208, 1953.

[44]John H. Mundy and Peter Reisenberg, *The Medieval Town*, Van Nostrand, New York, 1958, p. 35.

[45]William L. Langer, "The Black Death," in Scientific American's *Cities, Their Origin, Growth, and Human Impact*, W. H. Freeman, San Francisco, 1973, p. 106.

population of Europe. Over half the population of most cities was wiped out; few cities escaped with losses of less than a third. Florence went from 90,000 to 45,000 inhabitants; Siena from 42,000 to 15,000; and Hamburg lost almost two-thirds of its inhabitants.[46]

While the blow to the cities was severe, the effect of the plague on the rural manorial system was fatal. The rural social structure almost totally collapsed. Those peasants who were not killed by the plague fled to the towns, thus depriving the manors of their essential labor force. Serfs fleeing the plague often found that labor shortages had turned them into contract laborers or even town artisans.

The structure of basic social institutions such as the Catholic Church was also dramatically altered by the Black Death. Many of the senior clergy were killed off; at the same time, the Church grew immensely wealthy through bequests from those who had died and gifts from those who hoped by their offerings to prevent the wrath and vengeance of God, as the plague was almost universally considered to be. New priests were hastily trained, if at all. Their desertions of their parishes when plague threatened and their participation in the general loose living and immorality of the time contributed to the religious revolutions that swept Europe for the next two centuries and culminated in the Protestant Reformation.

Various plagues occurred in Europe until the late seventeenth century, but by the fifteenth century the cities were beginning to grow again. The plague had given the rural-based feudal system a blow from which it did not recover. From this point onward the history of Western civilization was again to be the history of cities and city inhabitants.

## CITIES AFTER THE MEDIEVAL ERA

By the sixteenth century numerous cities, and particularly the Italian city-states, had developed a wealthy patrician class which had the interest, resources, and time to devote to the development and beautification of their cities. Renaissance cities such as Florence embarked on major building programs. The revival of interest in the classical style, and in classical symmetry, perspective, and proportion, had a profound effect on the design of both public and private structures. The artistic talents even of artists such as Michelangelo and Leonardo da Vinci were used to beautify the cities; Leonardo also developed proposals for urban planning. Rather than simply building at random, the more prosperous city-states hired architects to make planned changes. The classical effect can be seen in the use of straight streets and regular squares, and particularly in the use of perspective. The early medieval city with its

[46]Langer, op. cit., pp. 106–107.

semirural nature had aptly symbolized that age. The sixteenth- and seventeenth-century Renaissance city symbolized the humanistic ideology of its age and proudly proclaimed its urban culture.

The sixteenth-century city gained ever greater economic and cultural domination over rural areas, but it also marked the beginning of the end of the city as a self-governing unit independent of the larger nation-state. During the later medieval period, kings and city dwellers had been natural allies, since both wished to subdue the power of the local nobility. In order to cast off the last fetters of feudal restraint, the city burghers supplied the king with men and—most importantly—money to fight his wars; the king in turn granted ever larger charter powers to the towns. Once the monarchs had subdued the rural lords, however, they turned their attention to the prosperous towns. Gradually the independent powers of the cities were reduced as they became part of nations in fact as well as in name. The structure of social organization in Europe was changing to the larger geographical unit, the nation-state. The loss of political independence, however, was compensated for by the economic advantages of being part of a nation-state rather than a collection of semi-independent feudal states and chartered cities. National government usually meant better and safer roads and therefore easier and cheaper transport of goods, and a larger potential market area. Tradesmen also had the advantages of reasonably unified laws, a common coinage, and standardized measures of weight and volume—all things which today we take for granted.

### Influences of Technology—Population Growth

The technological development of gunpowder and the cannon also contributed to changing the nature of the walled city. The traditional defenses of rampart, bastion, and moat were of little utility in stopping cannon fire. Cities that hoped to resist the armies of a king or of rival cities had to shift their attention from interior architecture and urban planning to the engineering of fortifications. Only elaborate defensive outworks could stop cannon fire, so the city unwittingly became the captive of its own horizontal defenses. While one can question Lewis Mumford's view that the decline of the city began with the end of the Middle Ages, it is certainly true that the city of the seventeenth century was changing—and probably for the worse.

Unable to grow outward, cities began to expand vertically and fill in open spaces within the city walls. The increased crowding which resulted had a bad effect on both the quality and the length of life. Filthy living conditions combined with minimal sanitation and an absence of any knowledge of public health practices resulted in the rapid spread of contagious diseases and consequently in high death rates. Until the latter part of the nineteenth century an old English cliche, "The city is the graveyard of countrymen," was all too true. As John Graunt's pioneer research in the seventeenth century on the London Bills of Mortality demonstrated, London actually recorded more deaths than births. Only heavy migration from the countryside allowed the city to grow in population, rather than to decline as would otherwise have been the case with such a high mortality rate. As late as 1790 the city of London had three deaths for every two births.[47]

Large-scale urban growth was closely tied to the growth of the population as a whole. Until about the middle of the seventeenth century, the population of the world had been growing at a very slow rate: 0.4 percent a year. As a result, by the beginning of the eighteenth century the world population was roughly 500 million, or double that at the time of Christ. Then momentous changes occurred that resulted in what we call the "demographic transition" or the "demographic revolution." Population growth suddenly spurted in the latter part of the eighteenth century, not through increases in the birth rate—it was already high—but through declines in the death rate. Population increases continued in the nineteenth and twentieth centuries. The term "demographic transition" refers to this transition from a time of high birth rates, matched by almost equally high death rates, through a period of declining death rates, to a period where birth rates also begin to decline, and eventually to a period where population stability is reestablished—this time through low birth rates matched by equally low death rates.

### Changes in Agriculture

Much of the decline in the death rates can be attributed to technological changes in agriculture that assured both a better and a more reliable food supply. Without such increases in food supply, cities could not grow very much. The growth of massive cities was effectively constrained until the nineteenth century by the inability of agriculture to produce enough surplus. As late as the beginning of the nineteenth century, the produce of nine farms was still required to support one urban family. (Today each American farmer supports approximately forty-five other persons.)

At the beginning of the eighteenth century, English agriculture, for example, still practiced three-crop rotation, with the land divided into four quarters, one of which was left fallow and thus unproductive each year. Pasture lands were held in common, as were the woods which provided hunting and firewood. Water rights were also held in common.

[47]Dorothy George, *London Life in the Eighteenth Century*, Harper Torchbooks, New York, 1964, p. 25.

Since most animals had to be slaughtered each fall, the herds didn't increase in number. Then, within the period of half a century, English agriculture was revolutionized. Jethro Tull published the results of thirty years of research on his estates, and the new ideas were quickly adopted by much of the landed aristocracy. Tull advocated planting certain crops on fallow land to restore nutrients to the earth, thus radically increasing the usable acreage. He also recommended deep plowing and a system for foddering animals through the winter.

At the same time it was being discovered that selective breeding of animals was far superior to letting nature take its course. Striking changes can be seen by comparing the weight of animals at the Smithfield Fair in 1710 and 1795; the average weight of oxen went from 370 pounds to 800 pounds, that of calves from 50 to 150 pounds, and that of sheep from 38 to 80 pounds.

Accompanying these agricultural improvements in England were the notorious Enclosure Acts, which took the village commons from joint ownership and gave them to the lord enjoying ancient title to the land. While disastrous for the local yeoman, the larger enclosures could be worked more efficiently by the lords who were using the new agricultural knowledge. The result was an increase in both the quality and the quantity of the food supply. While it is extremely hazardous to generalize about living conditions, there apparently was an improvement over earlier centuries. Death rates began to go down, and population rapidly expanded. Some of the peasants forced from the land who migrated to the larger towns and cities provided an available labor force when factories were established and expanded.

The abandonment of traditional subsistence agriculture and the orientation to a market economy meant that rationality was replacing tradition and contract was taking the place of custom. The calculation implicit in the land-enclosure acts destroyed small peasant landholders, but made it possible for London and other cities to be assured of foodstuffs and thus to grow as manufacturing and commercial centers.

## Other Technological Improvements

The movement of agricultural surpluses was greatly facilitated by the construction of new toll roads, which were built in great number after 1745. The building of canals also greatly stimulated urban development. By 1800 the city of London was the largest in the world, with a population of 900,000. This was roughly 11 percent of the total British population. Without the technological breakthroughs in agriculture and transportation this type of urban concentration would have been impossible.

Roughly at the same time that agricultural improvements were both increasing yields and releasing men from rural bondage, inventions were being made that would allow for the growth of whole new industries. Eighteenth-century inventions in the manufacture of cloth, such as the flying shuttle and the spinning jenny, were capped in 1767 by Watt's invention of a usable steam engine. The cotton industry boomed, and it was soon followed by other industries. The machines, rather than eliminating the need for workers, rapidly increased the demand for an urban work force.

Without population growth and the release of men from the land, it is hard to see how the early industrial cities could have grown at all; for unhealthful living conditions in cities meant that they were not able to maintain, much less increase, their population without in-migration from rural areas.

Thus the second urban revolution was not the emergence of cities but rather the changes since the seventeenth century that for the first time made it possible for more than 5 percent—or at the outer limit 10 percent—of the population to live in urban places. This new urban revolution started in Europe. Rapid expansion of population and national economic expansion did not, however, translate into healthful living conditions in the bulging European towns that were turning into cities. Eighteenth-century London was a model of filth, crowding, and disease. The early stages of industrialism hardly did much to improve the situation. While rural mortality decreased, urban mortality was kept high by unbelievably poor sanitary conditions. The novels of Charles Dickens give an accurate portrayal of life in such cities. Cholera and other epidemics were common until the middle of the nineteenth century; and until the 1840s many of London's sewers emptied into the Thames just a

**Table 2-2 Percent of Total Population Living in Cities of 100,000 or More, by Major World Regions, 1800 to 1950**

| | Percent in cities of 100,000 or more | | | |
|---|---|---|---|---|
| **Region** | **1800** | **1850** | **1900** | **1950** |
| Asia (excluding U.S.S.R.) | 1.6 | 1.7 | 2.1 | 7.5 |
| Europe (including U.S.S.R.) | *2.9** | *4.9* | *11.9* | *19.9* |
| Africa | 0.3 | 0.2 | 1.1 | 5.2 |
| America | 0.4 | *3.0* | *12.8* | *22.6* |
| Oceania | — | — | *21.7* | *39.2* |
| World | 1.7 | 2.3 | 5.5 | 13.1 |

*The regional percentages above the world average at each date are italicized.

*Source:* Kingsley Davis and Hilda Hertz, unpublished manuscript, cited in Neil J. Smelser (ed.), *Sociology: An Introduction*, Wiley, New York, 1967, p. 118.

few feet above ducts used to take drinking water from the river. Only heavy rural in-migration could replace the losses in urban population.

## PREINDUSTRIAL AND INDUSTRIAL CITIES: A COMPARISON

A comparison of the social structures of preindustrial and industrial cities will help us understand how the cities we live in differ from preindustrial cities and from the cities of the developing nations of the "third world." The industrial and preindustrial cities described are "ideal types"—that is, they do not exist in reality, but are rather abstractions or constructs obtained by carrying certain characteristics of each type of city to their logical extremes. Such "ideal types" can never exist in reality, but they are most useful in accentuating characteristics for the purposes of comparative historical research.

In his much-quoted article "Urbanism as a Way of Life," Louis Wirth gives a number of characteristics that he suggests are common to cities, and in particular to industrial cities.[48] For Wirth, a city is a permanent settlement possessing the following characteristics: (1) size, (2) density, (3) heterogeneity. The city is the place where large numbers of persons are crowded together in a limited space—persons who have different skills, interests, and cultural backgrounds. The result is the independence, anonymity, and cultural heterogeneity of city dwellers.

Industrial cities are characterized by: (1) an extensive division of labor; (2) emphasis on innovation and achievement; (3) lack of primary ties to a localized neighborhood; (4) breakdown of primary groups, leading to social disorganization; (5) reliance on secondary forms of social control, such as the police; (6) interaction with others as players of specific roles rather than as total personalities; (7) destruction of close family life and a transfer of its functions to specialized agencies outside the home; (8) a diversity permitted in values and religious beliefs; (9) encouragement of social mobility and working one's way up; (10) universal rules applicable to all, such as the same legal system, standardized weights and measures, and common prices. In brief, urbanism as a way of life prizes rationality, secularism, diversity, innovation, and progress. It is change-oriented. According to Wirth, "The larger, the more densely populated, the more heterogeneous the community, the more accentuated the characteristics associated with urbanism will be."[49]

Gideon Sjoberg paints quite a different picture for preindustrial

[48]Louis Wirth, "Urbanism as a Way of Life," *American Journal of Sociology,* **44:**1–24, July, 1938.
[49]Wirth, op. cit., p. 9.

cities.[50] He suggests that a number of factors we associate with cities are probably only generic to industrial cities. Preindustrial cities serve primarily as governmental or religious centers and only secondarily as commercial hubs. Specialization of work is limited, and the production of goods depends on animate (human or animal) power. There is little division of labor; the craftsman participates in every phase of manufacture. Emphasis is on traditional ways of doing things; the guild system discourages innovation. Ascription rather than achievement is the norm; a worker is expected to do the job he was born into. A person lives and works in a particular quarter of the city and rarely moves beyond this area. Social control is the responsibility of the primary group rather than secondary groups; persons are known to one another and subject to strict kinship control. Formal police forces are unnecessary. Family influence is strong, with the traditional extended family accepted as the ideal. Within all classes, children, and especially sons, are valued. There is great similarity in values, and little diversity in religion is tolerated. Opportunity for social mobility is severely restricted by a caste system or rigid class system. There is little or no middle class, which is the backbone of the industrial city; one is either rich or poor. Finally, particularism rather than universalism is the norm. Different people pay different prices for the same goods and there is no universal system of weights and measures. Justice is based not on what you do but on who you are. In brief, the preindustrial city stresses ascription over achievement, and particularism over universalism. Class and kinship systems are relatively inflexible; education is the prerogative of the rich.

No real city, of course, exactly conforms to either the industrial model or the preindustrial model, although just a few decades ago a researcher could still find a feudal city, such as Timbuctoo, that was largely untouched by modern urban-industrial life.[51] Today it is impossible to find a city anywhere on the globe that has not been influenced by Western ideas and practices. Even Marrakesh now has a Holiday Inn. However, while Sjoberg somewhat overstates the case, he does make the important point that preindustrial and postindustrial cities differ in numerous respects.

In preindustrial cities increases in urban size, density, and perhaps even heterogeneity do not necessarily lead to decreases in the influence of the primary group, reliance on secondary institutions, or social disorganization. In large preindustrial cities the constructs of tradition do not necessarily diminish, nor do thoughts and actions automatically become

[50]Gideon Sjoberg, "The Preindustrial City," *American Journal of Sociology,* **60:**438–445, March, 1955.

[51]Horace Minor, *The Primitive City of Timbuctoo,* Doubleday (Anchor), New York, 1965.

rational and utilitarian. Increases in size, density, and heterogeneity do appear to diminish the power of informal social controls and lead to formal control mechanisms in the industrial city, but this is not necessarily true of the preindustrial city. The latter lacks what the great French sociologist Emile Durkheim called "moral density" or what we today call "social integration." By contemporary standards the preindustrial city is neither socially nor economically integrated. The walled quarters of the preindustrial city are largely independent units; their physical proximity to one another does not lead to social interaction. The city as a whole may possess heterogeneity, but actual social contacts rarely extend beyond one's own group.

### Contemporary Ethnic Enclaves

Social isolation and insularity similar to what has been described above are not unknown within the cultural and ethnic enclaves of contemporary American cities. Herbert Gans, for example, found that the Italians of Boston's West End formed a tight and homogeneous folk group having minimal contact with the remainder of the metropolitan area.[52] In this traditionally based subculture primary groups still retain a dominant social position. In spite of their cosmopolitan residence the people in this area of the city remain urban villagers. A similar pattern of cultural isolation is portrayed in Elliot Liebow's study of Negro street-corner men in Washington, D.C.[53] Likewise, the continuing vitality of territorially based Italian, Mexican, Puerto Rican, and Negro enclaves, each with its own standards of behavior, is visually illustrated by Gerald Suttles' recent study of inner-city Chicago.[54] (These subcultures will be discussed in Chapter 6.) Some contemporary suburbs are attempting to achieve this same type of social isolation by walling themselves off economically, politically, and socially from the central city.

[52]Herbert Gans, *The Urban Villagers*, Free Press, Glencoe, Ill., 1962.
[53]Elliot Liebow, *Tally's Corner*, Little, Brown, Boston, 1967.
[54]Gerald Suttles, *The Social Order of the Slum*, University of Chicago Press, Chicago, 1968.

Part Two

# The American City

Chapter 3

# The Growth of the American City

*Give me your tired, your poor, your huddled masses yearning to breathe free, the wretched refuse of your teeming shore—send these, the homeless, tempest-tost to me: I lift my lamp beside the golden door.*

Inscription at the base of the Statue of Liberty in New York Harbor

The first European colonists to arrive in North America found a continent without indigenous cities. Aboriginal cities did not exist in North America although the Indians of the Northwest Coast, with their reliable food supply from the sea, had established well-built settled villages with an elaborate social structure. By and large, the North American Indian population was nomadic or lived in small agricultural villages such as Cahokia in Illinois and Taos in the Southwest. At the time of Jamestown the indigenous population of the entire continent, by even the most generous estimates, numbered less than a million. Only south of the Rio Grande were there substantial population concentrations: in central Mexico and elsewhere in Mesoamerica there existed civilizations going back nearly 2,000 years.

The North American Indians lived in nature rather than building upon it. They viewed themselves as part of the ecology, as part of the physical world. They tried not to master nature, but to identify their niche and their relationship with the world around them. The Europeans came, on the contrary, not to adjust to the environment but to dominate and reshape it. The emphasis was on conquering nature. Unfortunately for the Indians, the colonists tended to view them as a part of the environment. The Indians were treated as just another environmental problem that had to be encountered and mastered before civilization could be introduced. The implication for the future was clear. There was no niche for the Indian in the town-oriented civilization of the colonists.

What has just been said is, of course, an overgeneralization, which glosses over variations between the diverse Indian cultures; but from our urban perspective the important point is that the concept of the city, and all the good and evil it represents, came to the New World from Europe with the first European colonists. This concept, with all the special technology, social organizations, and attitudes it entailed, was an importation from post-Renaissance Europe. This meant, among other things, that North American cities had no feudal period.[1]

The early colonists sorely missed their towns. William Bradford movingly describes the world of the Pilgrims of 1620:

> They had now no freinds to wellcome them nor inns to entertaine or refresh their weatherbeaten bodys, no houses or much less townes to repaire too, to seeke for succoure. . . . Besids, what could they see but a hidious and desolate wildernes, full of wild beasts and willd men? and what multituds ther might be of them they knew not.[2]

The plans of the various companies that settled the English colonies in North America envisioned the establishment of tight little villages and commercial centers. The first successful settlements at Jamestown and Plymouth colony were in fact small towns. What was needed in these small towns of the New World was not adventurers but skilled craftsmen. As John Smith wrote back to the English sponsors of the Jamestown colony,

> When you send againe I intreat you rather send but thirty Carpenters,

[1]Lewis Mumford would not agree with this statement. Mumford sees the New England villages and towns as being the last flickering of the medieval order. See, for example, Lewis Mumford, *Sticks and Stones*, Liveright, New York, 1924.

[2]*Bradford's History of Plymouth Plantation* (William T. Davis, ed.), Scribner's, New York, 1908, p. 96.

> husbandmen, gardeners, fisher men, blacksmiths, masons, and diggers up of trees, roots, well provided; then a tousand of such as we haus: for except we be able both to loge them, and feed them the most will consume with want of necessaries before they can be made good for anything.[3]

As a result of the settlement pattern, by 1690 almost 10 percent of the colonial population was urban, a far higher percentage than that found in England itself at the same time. With the subduing of the Indians and the opening up of the hinterland for cultivation, the percentage (not, of course, the actual number) of urban dwellers decreased between 1690 and 1790. The opening up of frontier hinterlands permitted greater population dispersal than had previously been possible. Not until 1830 was the urban percentage of the total population as high as it had been at the close of the seventeenth century.[4] Villages and larger towns had by this time a definite hierarchy consisting of the aristocracy, clerics, officials, entrepreneurs, tradesmen, artisans, laborers, and slaves.

Five communities spearheaded the urbanization of the seventeenth-century English colonies. The northernmost was Boston on New England's "stern and rockbound coast"; the southernmost was the newer and much smaller settlement of Charles Town in South Carolina.[5] Barely making an indentation in the 1,100 miles of wilderness separating these two were Newport, in the Providence Plantations of Rhode Island; New Amsterdam, which in 1664 became New York; and William Penn's Philadelphia on the Delaware River at the mouth of the Schuylkill. Environment played a heavy role in the early development of these first five cities. All five were seaports, either on the Atlantic or—as in the case of Philadelphia—with access to the sea. Later towns such as Baltimore had similar environmental advantages. As seaports they became commercial centers funneling trade between Europe and the colonies. In terms of social structure all were Protestant, and against the established church, except for the ruling class of Charleston and (partially) New York. As Bridenbaugh points out, the social structure of these towns was fashioned by a background of relatively common political institutions; and the economic and cultural roots, whether English or Dutch, lay for the most part in the rising middle class of the Old World.[6]

[3]John Smith, *The General Historie of Virginia, New England, and the Summer Isles,* University Microfilms, Ann Arbor, Mich., 1966 (first published in London, 1624), p. 72.

[4]Charles N. Glaab and A. Theodore Brown, *A History of Urban America,* Macmillan, New York, 1967, pp. 25–26.

[5]Constance McLaughlin Green, *The Rise of Urban America,* Harper, New York, 1965, p. 2.

[6]Carl Bridenbaugh, *Cities in the Wilderness,* Capricorn Books, New York, 1964.

## NEW ENGLAND

The story of early New England is the story of its towns, for New England from the very beginning was town-oriented. The Puritan religious dissenters who originally settled New England came heavily from the more populous centers of Old England. They numbered in their midst many tradesmen, mechanics, and artisans. In the New World these religious dissenters sought to create tight urban communal utopias rather than spreading themselves widely over the landscape. In Massachusetts, for example, there existed an organized social system of a nature unknown outside New England. The cordial union between the clergy, the bench, the bar, and respectable society formed a tight, self-reinforcing social elite.

Boston early outstripped its rivals in both population size and economic influence and kept its lead for a century in spite of Indian wars that twice threatened its existence. Boston numbered barely 300 residents in the 1630s. In 1742 it had a population of 16,000. The barrenness of Boston's hinterland inclined Bostonians to look to the sea, and the town grew to prosperity on trade and shipbuilding. Before Boston was a generation old it had "begun to extend its control into the back country, and to develop a metropolitan form of economy that was essentially modern."[7]

Newport, the second New England city down the coast, was founded in 1639 by victims of religious bigotry in Massachusetts. Newport's growth was steady but far from spectacular: in a hundred years the population grew from 96 to 6,200. However, although Newport remained small, its growing commerce and well-ordered community life gave it a significant place in emerging urban America. In Newport, as in Boston, education was encouraged; in addition, Newport had religious toleration.

## THE MIDDLE COLONIES

Manhattan was from the beginning the most cosmopolitan of the colonial cities, a fact reflected in the diversity of languages spoken there: Father Isaac Jacques recorded that as early as 1643 there were already "men of 18 different languages." Partially because of this mixture of national and religious backgrounds (Dutch Calvinists, Anglicans, Quakers, Baptists, Huguenots, Lutherans, Presbyterians, and after 1730 even a sprinkling of Jews), New York was by far the liveliest of towns, a position many people maintain it still holds. Interestingly enough, as of 1720 a third of New York's population was black—largely slaves and servants.[8] With the

[7]Carl Bridenbaugh, quoted in Glaab and Brown, op. cit., p. 15.
[8]Green, op. cit., p. 22.

abandonment of slavery in the North—largely for economic reasons—the proportion of blacks substantially declined. New York was already an American melting pot, although the stew would still be a bit lumpy three centuries later.

New York also had decisive environmental advantages that contributed heavily to her eventual emergence as "*the* American city." First, Manhattan had a magnificent deepwater natural harbor. Second, New York was blessed with a fertile soil. Third, the city had easy access to the interior hinterland by way of the Hudson River. The New England towns, by contrast, found their economic growth greatly hindered by the lack of an accessible, fertile hinterland.

Philadelphia, William Penn's "City of Brotherly Love," laid out in 1692, was the youngest of the colonial cities. This was in many ways an advantage, for by the time the city was organized the Indians had departed and the land was already being settled. A policy of religious toleration and an extremely rich and fertile hinterland allowed rapid growth. By the time Philadelphia was six years old it had 4,000 inhabitants; by 1720 the number had risen to 10,000.[9] At the time of the first United States Census in 1790, Philadelphia had 42,000 inhabitants. It may have been, after London, the largest English-speaking city in the world. Accounts of the day noted the regularity of the town's gridiron pattern with its central square, and most frequently the substantial nature of its buildings.

A City, and Towns were raised then,
    Wherein we might abide,
Planters also, and Husband-men,
    Had Land enough beside.
The best of Houses then was known,
    To be of Wood and Clay,
But now we build of Brick and Stone,
    Which is a better way.[10]

## THE SOUTH

The southernmost of the colonial cities was Charles Town (Charleston), founded in 1680 on a spit of land between the mouths of the Ashley and Cooper rivers. The town grew slowly; two decades after its founding it

[9]Green, op. cit., p. 27.

[10]Richard Frame, "A Short Description of Pennsylvania in 1692," in Albert Cook Myers (ed.), *Narratives of Early Pennsylvania, West New Jersey, and Delaware,* Scribner's, New York, 1912; reprinted in Ruth E. Sutter, *The Next Place You Come To,* Prentice-Hall, Englewood Cliffs, N.J. 1973, p. 90.

had only 1,100 inhabitants and had "not yet produced any Commodities fit for ye markett or Europe, but a few skins—and a little cedar."[11] For decades rice, indigo, and skins formed the basis of its commerce.

Charleston's social structure was unique among the major cities. The major difference was that by the 1740s over half of Charleston's inhabitants were slaves. The middle-class craftsmen and shopkeepers who were the backbone of the Northern cities were caught in Charleston between the aristocratic pretensions of the large landowners and the increasing skills of the trained slaves. The result was civic atrophy, the major local event being the opening of the horse-racing season. Charleston had few municipal services and could not claim even a single tax-supported school.

## URBAN INFLUENCE

Politically, economically, and socially these five towns dominated early colonial life. Because of their access to the sea they served as entreports exchanging the produce of the hinterland for the finished products of Europe. In addition to their commercial function they also served as the places where new ideas and forms of social organization could be developed.

Because the colonial cities had to meet uniquely urban problems, such as paving streets, removing garbage, and caring for the poor, collective efforts developed. In the words of one historian:

> In these problems of town living which affected the entire community lay one of the vast differences between town and country society, and out of the collective efforts to solve these urban problems arose a sense of community responsibility and power that was to further differentiate the two ways of life.[12]

Politically, the cities were dominant. With the exception of Virginia, where the landed aristocracy did not live in cities but nonetheless followed the latest London fashions and maintained a strong commerce with Europe, the cities set the political as well as the social tone. And the merchant classes were greatly dissatisfied with British policy. The Crown's tax measures had a bad effect on business. Boston was called "the metropolis of sedition"; and as Lord Howe, commander of the British forces, noted, "Almost all of the People of Parts and Spirit were in

[11]Green, op. cit., p. 21.
[12]Charles N. Glabb, *The American City,* Dorsey, Homewood, Ill., 1963, p. 3.

the Rebellion."[13] This was not surprising, since Britain's revenue policy had struck deep at urban prosperity. Business and commercial leaders were determined to resist the Crown rather than suffer financial reverses. This helps to explain the middle- and upper-class nature of much of the support for the American Revolution.

## THE NEW REPUBLIC

After the Revolutionary War the cities continued their growth, although the first United States Census, taken in 1790, revealed that only 5 percent of the new nation's 4 million people lived in places of 2,500 or more. Numerically America was overwhelmingly rural, but this demographic dominance was not reflected in the distribution of power or the composition of the leadership groups. The urban population had an influence on government, finance, and society as a whole far out of proportion to its size. The Federalist Party, which elected John Adams as the second President, was largely an urban-based party representing commercial and banking rather than agrarian interests.

Although three-quarters of the national population still lived within 50 miles of the Atlantic Ocean, there were already clear and widening differences between townpeople and rural dwellers. The farmer's orientation was toward the expanding Western frontier, while the townsmen were still oriented toward Europe. Because of their status as ocean ports, the American coastal cities frequently had more in common with the Old World, and certainly better communication with it, than with their own hinterlands.

The census of 1790 showed that the largest city in the young nation was Philadelphia, with 42,000 inhabitants (it was also the only city having both streetlights and sidewalks). New York was the second-largest city, with a population of 33,000. Ten years later Philadelphia had grown to 70,000, New York to 60,000, and Boston to 25,000.

Such rapid growth of the cities after the Revolutionary War was not only the result of foreign and rural immigration; an exceptionally high rate of natural replacement also played a large part. Precise data are lacking, but the birth rate is estimated to have been at least 55 per 1,000, or near the physiological upper limit. Each married woman in 1790 bore an average of almost eight children. One result of the high birth rate and the immigration from Europe of young adults was a national median age of only 16 years. (By comparison, the median age for the white population in 1970 was 29 years.) At the beginning of the nineteenth century the country was young demographically as well as nationally.

[13]Green, op. cit., p. 51.

**Table 3-1 Percent of Population Urban, United States, 1790–1970**

| | | | |
|---|---|---|---|
| 1790 | 5.1 | 1890 | 35.1 |
| 1800 | 6.1 | 1900 | 39.7 |
| 1810 | 7.3 | 1910 | 45.7 |
| 1820 | 7.2 | 1920 | 51.2 |
| 1830 | 8.8 | 1930 | 56.2 |
| 1840 | 10.8 | 1940 | 56.5 |
| 1850 | 15.3 | 1950 (old def.) | 59.0 |
| 1860 | 19.8 | 1950 (new def.) | 64.0 |
| 1870 | 25.7 | 1960 | 69.9 |
| 1880 | 28.2 | 1970 | 73.5 |

*Source:* U.S. Bureau of the Census.

As Table 3-1 indicates, the percentage of the population that is urban has grown every decade except 1810–1820. The decline in that decade was chiefly a result of the destruction of American commerce due to the Embargo Acts and the War of 1812. That war came close to destroying the coastal cities; and, partially as a result of isolation from English manufactures and products, the American cities began developing manufacturing interests. Even Thomas Jefferson, an ardent opponent of cities, was forced to concede: "He, therefore, who is now against domestic manufacture, must be for reducing us either to dependence on that foreign nation or to be clothed in skins and to live like wild beasts in dens and caverns. I am not one of them; experience has taught me that manufactures are now as necessary to our independence as to our comfort."[14]

## GREATEST EXPANSION

The period before the Civil War saw a rapid expansion of existing cities and the founding of many new ones. During the period from 1820 to 1860 cities grew at a more rapid rate than at any other time before or since in American history.[15] It is noteworthy that of the fifty largest cities in America, only seven were incorporated before 1816; thirty-nine were incorporated between 1816 and 1876; and only four have been incorporated since 1876. Most large American cities have their origins in the nineteenth century, a fact we are still coping with in terms of transportation networks and even physical plant. Most medium-size cities also were founded and incorporated during the nineteenth century.[16]

[14]P. L. Ford, *The Works of Thomas Jefferson,* Putman, New York, 1904, pp. 503–504.

[15]Glaab, op. cit., p. 65.

[16]Daniel J. Elazar, "Urban Problems and the Federal Government," *Political Science Quarterly,* **82:**505–525, December, 1967.

The influence of environmental factors on the growth of cities can be seen from the fact that of the nine cities which by 1860 had passed the 100,000 mark, eight were ports. The one exception really wasn't an exception: it was the then independent city of Brooklyn, which shared the benefits of the country's greatest harbor.[17] By the turn of the century, fifty cities had populations of over 100,000; the most notable of these new cities was the prairie metropolis of Chicago, which had bet heavily on the technology of the railroad. Chicago mushroomed from 4,100 at the time of its incorporation in 1833 to 1 million in 1890. Between 1850 and 1890 Chicago doubled its population every decade; in 1910 it passed 2 million. Nationally, in 100 years between 1790 and 1890 the total population grew sixteenfold, while the urban population grew 139-fold.

By the eve of the Civil War the first city of the nation was clearly New York. It had both a magnificent harbor and a large hinterland to sustain growth, and the relatively flat terrain westward from the Hudson River permitted the Erie Canal to be built. The completion of the canal in 1825 greatly stimulated New York City's trade and gave it an economic supremacy which has yet to be surpassed. Thus, the original environmental advantage stimulated a technological advance—the Erie Canal—which in turn led to population growth and social-organization changes in business and government. New York's quick acceptance of railroads as a technological breakthrough, and the possibilities thus presented, further solidified the city's dominant position. Not only was New York the most important American city; it also had become a major world metropolis by the time of the Civil War. New York grew from just over 60,000 in 1800 to over 1 million in 1860 (1,174,774, to be exact, including Brooklyn, which was then an independent municipality). Of the world's cities only London and Paris were larger. By 1860, in addition to serving as the nation's financial center, New York also handled a third of the country's exports and a full two-thirds of the imports. New York's increase in size was matched by the increasing heterogeneity of its inhabitants, with their different tastes, aspirations, and needs—all of which could be best satisfied only in the large city.

## IMPACT OF TECHNOLOGY

The booming cities of the West saw the most rapid development. Anthony Trollope, writing of midwestern cities, noted: "Men build on an enormous scale, three times, ten times as much as is wanted. . . . The speculator is very probably ruined, and then begins the work again, nothing daunted.

[17]Blake McKelveg, *The Urbanization of America, 1860–1915,* Rutgers University Press, New Brunswick, N. J., 1963, p. 4.

. . . He is greedy in order that he may speculate more wildly."[18] Cincinnati, the "Queen City of the West," for example, experienced a boom during the 1820s, and during that decade its population expanded rapidly as a result of the development and use of steamboats. In other cities the technology of the railroad played a similar role in spurring growth.

Only in the Deep South, where cotton was king, did the building of cities languish. In the plantation owners' view, cotton fields came before manufacturing and commerce. The dominance of agriculture can be seen in the development—or, more correctly, the lack of development—of Charleston. At the beginning of the nineteenth century Charleston was the fifth-largest American city; by 1860 it had slipped to twenty-sixth place.[19] While the South bitterly resented its dependence on Northern credit, Northern transportation, and Northern goods, it still could not give up its dependence on agriculture based on slavery. Even in urban Charleston over two-thirds of the population were Negro slaves.[20] It is significant that the first act of most Southern legislatures after declaring for the Confederacy was to repudiate all debts owed to Northern bankers and merchants.

## NEW PATTERNS

Before the Civil War the urban economy was still in a commercial rather than an industrial stage. Businessmen were primarily merchants who intermittently took on subsidiary functions such as manufacturing, banking, and speculating.[21] In 1850, 85 percent of the population was still classified as rural; 64 percent was engaged in agriculture.

At the same time changes in farming technology were converting the yeoman into an entrepreneur raising cash crops for market. Horse-drawn mechanical reapers, steel plows, and threshers heralded the shift from self-sufficient to commercial farming.

The Civil War accelerated the shift from a mercantile to an industrial economy. Aided by the new protective tariffs and the inflated profits, stimulated by the war, Northern industrialists began producing steel, coal, and woolen goods, most of which had previously been imported. The closing of the Mississippi was a boon to Chicago and the east-west railroads.

In the development of the West, towns were frequently in the

[18]Anthony Trollope, *North America,* Lippincott, Philadelphia, 1862.

[19]Nelson M. Blake, *A History of American Life and Thought,* McGraw-Hill, New York, 1963, p. 156.

[20]Frederick P. Bowes, *The Culture of Early Charleston,* University of North Carolina Press, Chapel Hill, 1942, p. 42.

[21]William Petersen, *Population,* Macmillan, New York, 1961, p. 28.

**Table 3-2 Number of Urban Places by Population Size: Selected Years, 1850–1970**

| Size of place | 1850 | 1900 | 1950 | 1960 | 1970 |
|---|---|---|---|---|---|
| Total—2,500 and over | 236 | 1,737 | 4,284 | 5,445 | 6,435 |
| 1,000,000 or more | – | 3 | 5 | 5 | 6 |
| 500,000 to 1,000,000 | 1 | 3 | 13 | 16 | 20 |
| 250,000 to 500,000 | – | 9 | 23 | 30 | 30 |
| 100,000 to 250,000 | 5 | 23 | 65 | 81 | 100 |
| 50,000 to 100,000 | 4 | 40 | 126 | 201 | 240 |
| 25,000 to 50,000 | 16 | 82 | 252 | 432 | 520 |
| 10,000 to 25,000 | 36 | 280 | 778 | 1,134 | 1,385 |
| 5,000 to 10,000 | 85 | 465 | 1,176 | 1,394 | 1,839 |
| 2,500 to 5,000 | 89 | 832 | 1,846 | 2,152 | 2,295 |

*Source:* U.S. Bureau of the Census, U.S. Census of Population, 1950, vol. II, and 1960, vol. I.; and 1970, vol. I, part A, table 5.

forefront. As Richard Wade aptly phrased it, "The towns were the spearhead of the frontier." This is particularly true west of the Mississippi, where the technological breakthrough of the railroad had reversed earlier patterns of settlement. Josiah Strong, writing in 1885, noted:

> In the Middle States the farms were the first taken, then the town sprang up to supply its wants, and at length the railway connected it with the world, but in the West the order is reversed—first the railroad, then the towns, then the farms. Settlement is, consequently, much more rapid, and the city stamps the country, instead of the country stamping the city. It is the cities and towns which will frame state constitutions, make laws, create public opinion, establish social usages, and fix standards of morals in the West.[22]

Strong may have exaggerated his case somewhat, but the railroad was crucial in the development of the West. During the second half of the nineteenth century, the railroads expanded from 9,000 to 193,000 miles—much of it built with federal loans and land grants.[23] The railroads literally opened the West.

During the last quarter of the nineteenth century, urbanism for the first time became a controlling factor in national life. This was a period of economic expansion for the nation. Industrialism was changing the nature of the economic system, rapidly changing America from a rural to an urban continent. The extent of this change can be seen in Table 3-2. As of

[22]Josiah Strong, *Our Country: Its Possible Future and Its Present Crisis*, Baker and Taylor, New York, 1885, p. 206.

[23]Petersen, op. cit., p. 34.

1880 over half the labor force was employed other than in agriculture; and by 1900, 40 percent of the nation's 76 million inhabitants were urban dwellers. Moreover, between 1880 and 1920, when the Bureau of the Census declared that over half the population was urban, most of the nation's largest cities (those with populations of 500,000 or more) had a sustained building boom. Much of what was built then still stands. The fact that New York, Chicago, Philadelphia, and St. Louis, to name only a few, are essentially cities of before the twentieth century and before the automobile is a problem we have to cope with today. Any attempt to deal with present-day transportation or pollution problems has to take into account the fact that these American cities were planned and built in the nineteenth century. We still live largely in cities designed for the age of steam and the horse-drawn streetcar.

## ENVIRONMENT AND POLLUTION

It is revealing, if depressing, to recognize that the problems of pollution and environmental destruction did not begin in the twentieth century. Until late in the nineteenth century most American cities, such as Baltimore and New Orleans, still relied on open trenches for sewage. The only municipal garbage collection provided by most cities until after the Civil War was that provided by scavenging hogs and dogs and other carrion-eaters. Colonial Charleston even passed an ordinance protecting vultures because they performed a public service by cleaning the carcasses of dead animals.[24] In 1666 a Boston municipal ordinance ordered the inhabitants to bury all filth, while "all garbidge, beasts entralls &c," were to be thrown from the drawbridge into Mill Creek.[25] Colonial Boston's system of burying what you can and throwing the rest into the nearest river is still used by many cities today.

A description of Pittsburgh dating from the late nineteenth century details its air pollution in these terms:

> Pittsburgh is a smoky, dismal city, at her best. At her worst, nothing darker, dingier or more dispiriting can be imagined. The city is in the heart of the soft coal region; and the smoke from her dwellings, stores, factories, foundries, and steamboats, uniting settles in a cloud over the narrow valley in which she is built, until the very sun looks coppery through the sooty haze. According to a circular of the Pittsburgh Board of Trade, about twenty per cent, or one-fifth of all the coal used in the factories and dwellings of the city escapes into the air in the form of smoke. . . . But her inhabitants do not seem to

[24]Glaab, op. cit., p. 115.
[25]Bridenbaugh, op. cit., p. 18.

> mind it; and the doctors hold that this smoke from the carbon sulphur, and iodine contained in it, is highly favorable to the lung and cutaneous diseases, and is the sure death of malaria and its attendant fevers.[26]

Public waterworks were luxuries found in few communities until well after the Civil War. Some medium-size cities such as Providence, Rochester, and Milwaukee relied entirely on private wells and water carriers. Sanitation fared little better. Boston, which had attained a level few communities could equal, had under 10,000 water closets for its 177,000 residents.[27] Until the twentieth century, facilities were all but nonexistent in the congested tenements of the slums.

## EVOLUTIONARY PATTERNS

The nineteenth-century city was a city of concentration and centralization accentuated by industrialization. Steam power totally altered the internal pattern of the cities. Before the steam era few cities exceeded 100,000 population.[28] The emergence of great cities had to await, with few exceptions, the coming of the Industrial Revolution. This was the age of steam, and since steam is most cheaply produced only in large quantities, and must be used close to where it is produced, a compact city was created. Thus, steam power encouraged the proximity of factory and power supply, and fostered the concentration of manufacturing processes. This in turn tended to concentrate managerial and wholesale distributing activities and, above all, population near the factory.

The centripetal effect of steam power meant that the factory and its power plant could not be far separated. In addition, the limited transportation technology meant that workers had to live near the factories; this in turn gave rise to row upon row of densely packed tenements. The distant separation of residence and place of work was a luxury only the very wealthy in their commuting suburbs could afford. As late as 1899 the average commuting distance in New York from home to place of work was roughly two blocks, or a quarter of a mile.

Downtown areas in cities of the late nineteenth century were also extremely crowded and compact. In the days before easy communication by telephone or transportation by automobile, it was necessary for offices to be close to one another so that information could be rapidly transmitted by messenger boys. Technological inventions such as the passenger

[26]Willard Glazier, *Peculiarities of American Cities,* Hubbard, Philadelphia, 1884, pp. 332–333.

[27]Blake McKelveg, op. cit., p. 13.

[28]National Resources Committee, *Our Cities: Their Role in the National Economy,* U. S. Printing Office, Washington, D. C., 1937, p. 30.

elevator in 1857 and the steel-girdered building later in the century enabled the core area to become even more densely inhabited by allowing offices and businesses to be stacked vertically upon one another. At the turn of the century, when Chicago contained 1,690,000 inhabitants, half of them lived within 3.2 miles of the city's center.[29]

A quick way of determining the boundaries of the early city is to note the location of cemeteries. Cemeteries were traditionally placed on the outskirts, so large cemeteries within present city boundaries effectively show earlier high-water marks of urban growth.

## ELECTRIC STREETCARS

Whereas the centralizing and concentrating forces of steam power molded the initial pattern of American urbanization, the coming of electricity and then the internal combustion engine had a dispersing effect. The effect of steam power was centripetal; that of electricity was centrifugal. The coming of the electric streetcar, first put into service in 1888 in Richmond, Virginia, changed the face of the city by making it possible for the ordinary wage earner to separate himself from his place of work.

The technological advance of the electric street railway expanded the potential space of the city. The electric car had twice the speed and over three times the capacity of the horse-drawn car.[30] The efficiency and low cost of the electric streetcar made it possible to commute as much as 12 miles to the central business district. The result was an outward expansion of the city, but in strips along the right of way of the streetcar line. Land lying between the "spokes" formed by the streetcar lines remained undeveloped. The cities thus came to have a rather pronounced star-shaped configuration, with the points of the star being the linear rail lines.[31] This is a shape cities would hold until the era of the automobile. Where street rail lines intersected, natural breaks in transit took place and secondary business and commercial districts began to develop. These regional shopping areas were the equivalent of the peripheral shopping centers of today. With the passage of time the city areas between the streetcar lines filled in, and by the 1920s most of our major cities had completed the bulk of their building. The Depression of the 1930s effectively stopped downtown building; many central business districts remained basically unchanged until building resumed again in the 1960s.

[29]Paul F. Cressey, "Population Succession in Chicago: 1898–1930," *American Journal of Sociology*, **44**:59, 1938.

[30]Amos W. Hawley, *Urban Society*, Ronald Press, New York, 1971, p. 92.

[31]Richard Hurd, *Principles of City Land Values*, The Record and Guide, New York, 1903.

Boss William Tweed, head of the Tammany Hall political machine built on the controlled votes of immigrants, looted the New York City treasury of some $60 million. He was convicted in 1872. (*Culver Pictures.*)

## MUNICIPAL GOVERNANCE

As Arthur Schlesinger put it, "This lusty urban growth created problems that taxed human resourcefulness to the utmost."[32] A particularly high price was paid in the area of municipal governance. Political institutions that were adequate under simplified rural conditions but inadequate to the task of governing a complicated system of ever-expanding public services and utilities presented an acute problem. Venality and urban politics became synonymous. As the perceptive observer Andrew White noted,

[32]Arthur M. Schlesinger, "The City in American History," *Mississipi Valley Historical Review*, **27**:43–66, June, 1940.

"With very few exceptions the city governments of the United States are the worst in Christendom . . . the most expensive, the most inefficient, and the most corrupt."[33] The noted British scholar James A. Bryce put it simply: "There is no denying that the government of cities is the one conspicuous failure of the United States."[34]

Boss Tweed of New York, who plundered the city of $60 million, was even more explicit: "The population is too helplessly split into races and factions to govern it under universal suffrage, except by bribery or patronage or corruption."[35]

On the other hand, although the political bosses emptied the public treasury, they also provided the poorer citizens with urban services, jobs, and help in solving minor problems with the police and other officials. The boss served as a mediator between the immigrant and the official bureaucracy. A study of twenty city bosses described them as warm and often sentimental men who had come from poor immigrant families. All were native urbanites and most were noted for their loyalty to their families.[36] The political machine provided a route for social mobility for bright and alert young immigrants. Police departments were also an avenue of upward mobility for first- and second-generation European immigrants. Without the humanitarian aid of the ward bosses the new immigrants would have had an even rougher time than they did. For the immigrants, boss rule was clearly functional.

## THE IMMIGRANTS

The dimensions of the immigrant flood are hard to overemphasize—perhaps some 30 million persons. From the 1840s onward, waves of immigrants landed in the major Northeastern ports. The first of the mass ethnic immigrations was that of the Irish, who were driven from Ireland in the late 1840s by the ravages of the potato blight. Later, Germans and Scandinavians poured into the Middle West, particularly after the development of steamships and the opening of the railroads to Chicago.

Immigration accelerated after the Civil War, spurred on by the need of the booming industrial cities for raw labor to provide the muscle for industrialization. This was a period of industrial and continental expansion. Between 1860 and 1870, 25 of the 38 states took official action to stimulate immigration, offering not only voting rights but also sometimes land and bonuses.

[33]James Bryce, *Forum*, vol. X, 1890, p. 25.

[34]James Bryce, *The American Commonwealth*, vol. 1, Macmillan, London, 1891, p. 608.

[35]Arthur M. Schlesinger, *Paths to the Present*, Macmillan, New York, 1949, p. 60.

[36]Harold Zink, *City Bosses in the United States*, Duke University Press, Durham, N. C., 1930, p. 350.

Tenements of the Lower East Side of New York as of 1922. Note the crowding and absence of open spaces other than the street. (*Culver Pictures.*)

Before 1880 the majority of the immigrants had come from the nations of northern and western Europe. With the exception of the Irish and a minority of the Germans, these immigrants were Protestant and melted without undue difficulty into the American melting pot. But about the 1880s there began a perceptible shift in the pattern of immigration. Now, the mass of immigrants were coming from southern and eastern Europe. To the older immigrant groups, who by now viewed themselves as pioneer settlers, the southern and eastern Europeans appeared distinctly inferior.

The traditions, customs, religion, and sheer numbers of these immigrants made fast assimilation impossible. Between 1901 and 1910 alone, over 9 million immigrants were counted by immigration officials. These newcomers came largely from peasant backgrounds. They were packed into teeming slums and delegated to the lowest-paying and most menial jobs. Native-born Protestant Americans suddenly became aware of the fact that 40 percent of the 1910 population was of foreign stock—that is, immigrants or the offspring of immigrants.[37] The percentage was considerably higher in the large Northern industrial cities, where over half the population was invariably of foreign stock.

## IMMIGRANTS AND CORRUPTION

To writers around the turn of the century, such as Josiah Strong, the sins of the city were frequently translated into the sins of the new immigrant groups pouring into the ghettoes of the central core. Slum housing, poor health conditions, and high crime rates were all blamed on the newcomers. Those on the city's periphery and in the emerging upper-class and upper-middle-class suburbs associated political corruption with the central city. Native-born Americans tended to view city problems as being the fault of the frequently Catholic, or even Jewish, immigrants who inhabited the central-city ghettoes.

Reformers of the period who focused on the problems of the city had a distinctly middle-class orientation. The Progressive Movement at the turn of the century, at least in its urban manifestation, was an attempt by the upper middle class to reform the inner city. This, of course, meant regaining political power. Businessmen organized in groups such as the National Municipal League. The writing of "muckrakers" like Lincoln Steffens, a Ralph Nader of his day in exposing municipal corruption, gave considerable publicity to the grosser excesses of municipal corruption, such as the deals with utility franchises. To destroy the power of the bosses and their immigrant supporters, reforms were pushed in city after city. By 1912 some 210 communities had adopted the commission form of government. Dayton in 1913 adopted the first city-manager system and during the following year 44 other cities followed suit. However, in the largest cities the political machines, while they lost a few battles, managed to weather the storm. The coming of World War I directed crusading energies into new channels, and the Roaring Twenties were not a decade noted for municipal reform. While there were exceptions, such as William Hoan, the socialist mayor of Milwaukee, the city after World War I was

[37]Donald J. Bogue, *The Population of the United States*, Free Press, Glencoe, Ill., 1969, p. 178.

more likely to have a colorful and corrupt mayor like Jimmy Walker in New York and Big Bill ("The Builder") Thompson in Chicago.

## IMAGES OF THE CITY

America has never been neutral regarding her great cities; they have been either exalted as the centers of vitality, enterprise, and excitement, or denounced as sinks of crime, pollution, and depravity. Our present ambivalence toward our cities is nothing new; even the founding fathers had great reservations about the moral worth of cities. The city was frequently equated by writers such as Thomas Jefferson with all the evils and corruption of the Old World, while an idealized picture of the yeoman farmer represented the virtue of the New World. Thomas Jefferson expressed the sentiments of many of his countrymen when he stated in 1787 in a letter to James Madison,

> I think our governments will remain virtuous as long as they are chiefly agricultural; and this will be as long as there shall be vacant land in any part of America. When they get piled upon one another in large cities, as in Europe, they will become corrupt as in Europe.[38]

In a famous letter to Benjamin Rush, written in 1800, Jefferson even saw some virtue in the yellow fever epidemics that periodically ravaged seaboard cities. Philadelphia, for example, lost over 4,000 persons, almost 10 percent of its population, in the epidemic of 1793. Jefferson wrote to Rush:

> When great evils happen I am in the habit of looking out for what good may arise from them as consolations to us, and Providence has in fact, so established the order of things, as that most evils are the means of producing some good. The yellow fever will discourage the growth of great cities in our nation, and I view great cities as pestilential to the morals, the health, and the liberties of man.[39]

Jefferson, of course, was not alone in his fear of large cities. Alexis de Tocqueville, certainly one of the most perceptive observers to visit our shores, wrote: "I look upon the size of certain American cities, and especially upon the nature of their population, as a real danger which threatens the security of the democratic republics of the New World."

[38]Quoted in Glaab, op. cit., p. 38.

[39]Andrew A. Lipscomb and Albert E. Bergh (eds.), *The Writings of Thomas Jefferson,* vol. X, The Thomas Jefferson Memorial Association, Washington, D.C., 1904, p. 173.

Writers as diverse as Emerson, Melville, Hawthorne, and Poe all had strong reservations regarding the city.[40]

Cowley's line "God the first garden made, and the first city Cain" expresses an attitude toward cities shared by many Americans. Thoreau, sitting in rural solitude watching a sunset, is an acceptable image. Thoreau, sitting on a front stoop in Boston watching the evening rush hour, creates an entirely different image.

Americans, even while pouring into the cities, have traditionally idealized the country. Even such a total urbanist as Benjamin Franklin felt compelled to state that agriculture was "the only honest way to acquire wealth . . . as a reward for innocent life and virtuous industry." Franklin himself, of course, never acquired wealth through farming; he was the American cosmopolitan *par excellence.*

The clearing of the wilderness by the pioneers, and the taming (eradication) of savage beasts and men, was considered a highly laudable enterprise. By contrast, the building of cities by the sweat and muscle of immigrants is ignored. It is as if we consider the history of the immigrants somewhat discreditable and thus best forgotten. The cowboy, not the factory hand, is the American hero. An extremely influential lecture by Frederick Jackson Turner at the turn of the century, "The Winning of the West," struck a responsive chord: it glorified the pioneer and the virtues of the West. Needless to say, such homage was not paid to tenement dwellers working under oppressive conditions, who were simply trying to raise decent families. Today, television perpetuates the same myth when it gives us drama after drama concerning life in the nineteenth-century American West, but nothing about the nineteenth-century American city dweller.

Criticism of the city contained some contradictory premises—although these were generally not noticed—while it was being castigated for not exhibiting rural or agrarian values, it was also being taken to task for failing to be truly urban and reach the highest ideals of an urban society. In short, the city was at the same time supposed to be both more rural and more urban.

Vigorous attacks on the city came from writers such as Josiah Strong, who condemned it as the source of the evils of rum, Romanism, and rebellion. Strong's book *Our Country* sold a phenomenal—for that date—175,000 copies. He effectively mirrored the fears of small-town Protestant America that urban technology and the growth of foreign immigrant groups were in the process of undermining the existing social order and introducing undesirable changes such as political machines,

[40]Morton White and Lucia White, *The Intellectual versus the City*, Harvard and M. I. T. Press, Cambridge, Mass., 1962.

slums, and low church attendance. Several excerpts give the general tone of his argument:

> The city has become a serious menace to our civilization. . . . It has a particular fascination for the immigrant. Our principal cities in 1880 contained 39.3 percent of our entire German population, and 45.8 percent of the Irish. Our ten larger cities at that time contained only nine percent of the entire population, but 23 percent of the foreign. . . .
>
> Because our cities are so largely foreign, Romanism finds in them its chief strength. For the same reason the saloon together with the intemperance and liquor power which it represents, is multiplied. . . .
>
> Socialism centers in the city, and the materials of its growth are multiplied with the growth of the city. Here is heaped the social dynamite; here roughs, gamblers, thieves, robbers, lawless and desperate men of all sorts congregate; men who are ready on any pretext to raise riots for the purpose of disruption and plunder; here gather the foreigners and wage-workers who are especially susceptible to socialistic arguments; here skepticism and irreligion abound; here unequality is the greatest and most obvious, and the contrast between opulence and penury the most striking; there the suffering is the sorest.[41]

This distrust and dislike of the city simmered during the latter part of the nineteenth century and finally crystallized around the issue of the free coinage of silver, with silver representing the agrarian West and gold the commercial and industrial East. William Jennings Bryan's campaign for the presidency in 1896 was a major attempt by the agricultural anti-urbanites to gain national political power. As Bryan put it in his famous "Cross of Gold" speech: "Burn down your cities and leave our farms, and your cities will spring up again as if by magic; but destroy our farms, and the grass will grow in the streets of every city in the country."[42] But by the end of the nineteenth century Bryan's day had passed, and although agricultural fundamentalism still had some strength, it was no longer a commanding ideology. The city, not the farm, represented the future.

The myth of the agrarian past nonetheless continued to outlive the reality. As Hofstadter has amusingly noted, one of President Calvin Coolidge's campaign photographs in 1924 showed him posing as a simple farmer haying in Vermont. However, the photograph said more than was intended, for the President's overalls are obviously fresh, his shoes are highly polished, and if one looks carefully one can see his expensive Pierce Arrow, with Secret Service men waiting to rush him back to the city once the picture-taking was completed.[43] Even today Senator Sam

[41]Strong, op. cit., chap. 11.
[42]Glaab and Brown, op. cit., p. 59.
[43]Richard Hofstadter, *The Age of Reform,* Knopf, New York, 1955, p. 31.

Ervin, one of the sharpest constitutional lawyers in the nation, affects country ways and refers to himself as a "simple country boy."

In reality, for half a century America has been a nation of urban dwellers, and with every census the percentage of urban dwellers climbs higher. Even the quarter of the population that does not live in urban places is clearly tied to an urban way of life. Dairy farmers and cattle raisers are today very much part of urbanism as a way of life. They understand quite clearly that their profits are tied more to the price-support system than to the weather or other natural factors. The enormous political contribution which the dairy farmers promised the White House in 1972 in return for raising the support price of milk emphasizes to what extent farmers have become city slickers.

*Small Town in Mass Society,* a community study of a town in upstate New York, documents the way even small-town America is totally enmeshed in an urban economic and social system, despite its pride in its independence of the city and cosmopolitan ways. The small town must even rely on the mass media to help reaffirm its own fading image of itself.[44]

Today our picture of how rural life is lived and the nature of the basic rural virtues is the creation of mass media based in and directed from cities. Television shows written in New York and produced in Hollywood try to create an image of small towns, filled with friendly folk, with "down home" wisdom, rather like a Norman Rockwell painting. Urban advertising also hits hard at the same bogus theme—commercials often depend heavily on nostalgia, with old cars, fields of wheat, the old farm house, and the front porch swing.

What all this reflects is a deep ambivalence regarding cities and city life. As a people, we chose to glorify rural life but to live in urban areas. North America is the most urbanized of the continents (excluding Australia), but our response to our major urban areas is still schizophrenic. We are an urban continent that treats our major cities as if we don't fully trust them and wish nothing more than that they would fade away and stop causing problems.

## THE MODERN ERA

The period from 1920 to the present is usually considered the modern period of American urbanization. The census of 1920 officially ended the rural era when it recorded that 50 percent of the population now resided in urban places. Henceforth, America would be a nation of cities. The 1920s

[44]Arthur J. Vidich and Joseph Bensman, *Small Town in Mass Society,* Doubleday Anchor, New York, 1960.

also were the high-water mark of American central cities. Expansion and development were the order of the day, and the central city was at its zenith. The railroad was the major interurban artery, and the electric street railway dominated urban transit. The full impact of the automobile, with its influence for dispersal and the creation of suburbs, had yet to be seriously felt. Densities of central cities have been declining since this period.

The 1920s and 1930s would see the beginning of large-scale dispersion of population, followed by industrial dispersion. The latter was encouraged by technological advances requiring more spacious sites, by the unavailability of city land, by lower costs of land in suburban areas, and, of course, by lower taxes in suburban areas. These topics will be treated in detail in the next four chapters.

Chapter 4

# The Developing Ecology of American Cities

*You can see how pleasantly our city is situated, but the water is polluted and the country is troubled with miscarriages.*

The people of Jericho to Elisha
Second Kings, 2:19

The renowned urban sociologist Louis Wirth suggests that urbanism as a way of life

> may be approached empirically from three interrelated perspectives: (1) as a physical structure comprising a population base, a technology, and an ecological order; (2) as a system of social organization involving a characteristic social structure, series of social institutions, and a typical pattern of social relationships; and (3) as a set of attitudes and ideas, and a constellation of personalities engaging in typical forms of collective behavior and subject to characteristic mechanisms of social control.[1]

[1]Louis Wirth, "Urbanism as a Way of Life," *American Journal of Sociology*, **44:**18–19, July, 1938.

In this chapter we shall be concerned with the first of these three perspectives: the ecology of the American urban area, its population and technology, and how these affect the second perspective—the city as a system of social organization.

"Ecology," in its broadest sense, is the study of the relationships among organisms within an environment. It is the study not of the creatures and objects themselves, but rather of the relationships among them. The sum total of these many relationships among organisms in a habitat is called a "biotic community," and the community together with its physical habitat forms an "ecosystem." Ecological reasoning, which owes much of its theoretical underpinnings to Charles Darwin's research on evolution, was first applied to the study of plants, in the latter part of the nineteenth century. Animal ecology emerged in the early twentieth century, and human ecology soon followed.

The term "human ecology" was first introduced by the sociologists Park and Burgess in 1921, and represented an attempt to systematically apply the basic theoretical scheme of plant and animal ecology to the study of human communities. Human ecology is concerned with the examination of the relationship between man and his environment and man within an environment. Its level of analysis is that of macrosociology, where the issue is the properties of populations rather than the properties of the individuals who make them up. Thus it is based on the study of groups rather than individuals—and this focus on the group or aggregate is basic to sociology, as opposed to disciplines such as psychology where the focus is on the individual.

Within sociology, human ecology has been the branch most concerned with the question of how people organize themselves socially to adapt to their habitat, and in particular to the habitat of cities and their environs.

However, until recently such a view of urban systems has not received widespread support. In fact, because of its emphasis on man's role in a physical environment, human ecology for years was considered by many sociologists to be only marginal to the discipline of sociology. Analogies to plant and animal life particularly disturbed the critics. The fact that early human ecology was heavily dependent on biology for both concepts and terminology was viewed as a damning fault by some sociologists. As one critic put it, "As the ecologists have admitted, practically all their basic hypotheses have been derived from natural science sources—and the influence of certain geographers and economists is apparent."[2] To such critics the multidiscipline base of human

[2]Warner E. Gettys, "Human Ecology and Social Theory," in George A. Theodorson (ed.), *Studies in Human Ecology*, Row Peterson, Evanston, Ill., 1961, p. 99.

ecology was weakness rather than a source of strength. Somehow, human ecology wasn't sociological enough. Not the ideas, but where they came from, was considered the more important factor. Fortunately such academic provincialism has few adherents today. Ecological analysis is now recognized as integral to sociology, for—as expressed by the sociologist Leo Schnore—"the central role given to organization—both as dependent or independent variable—places ecology clearly within the sphere of activities in which sociologists claim distinctive competence, i. e. analysis of social organization."[3]

## DEVELOPMENT OF HUMAN ECOLOGY

Classical human ecology first came into its own during the 1920s at the University of Chicago. Led by researchers such as Robert Park and Ernest Burgess, the so-called "Chicago School" of sociology produced a prodigious number of studies focused on the spatial-social environment of the city. The interest of the Chicago sociologists was not simply in mapping where groups and institutions were located, but rather in discovering how the sociological, psychological, and moral experiences of city life were reflected in spatial relationships. One member of the Chicago School said that human ecology "deals with the spatial aspects of symbiotic relationships of human beings and human institutions".[4]

Park felt that "most if not all cultural changes in society will be correlated with changes in its territorial organization, and every change in the territorial and occupational distribution of the population will effect changes in the existing culture."[5] This postulate of "an intimate congruity between the social order and physical space, between social and physical distance, and between social equality and residential proximity is the crucial hypothetical framework supporting urban ecological theories."[6]

Since its inception human ecology has split into various "schools." The sociocultural school has been the most critical of the classical urban ecology studies. Scholars of the sociocultural school tend to feel that early human ecology overemphasized economic factors while ignoring social-psychological variables. Milla Alihan, in his broadly based critique of ecological studies, attacked both the theory and the application of early human ecology.[7] Another critic, Walter Firey, demonstrated in his study

[3]Leo Schnore, "The Myth of Human Ecology," *Sociological Inquiry,* **31**:139, 1961.

[4]Roderick McKenzie, *The Metropolitan Community,* McGraw-Hill, New York and London, 1933, p. 314.

[5]Robert Park, *Human Communities,* Free Press, New York, 1952, p. 14.

[6]Ralph Thomlinson, *Urban Structure,* Random House, New York, 1969, p. 9.

[7]Milla A. Alihan, *Social Ecology,* Columbia University Press, New York, 1938.

of land use in central Boston that many acres of valuable land in the central business district had been allowed to remain in uneconomic use such as parks and cemeteries.[8] He suggests that "sentiment" and "symbolism" play an important part in determining spatial distributions, pointing out that the 48-acre Commons in the heart of downtown Boston had never been developed commercially and that Beacon Hill had largely remained an upper-class residential area in spite of its proximity to the central business district. Unfortunately, mass data such as census data fail to deal with such psychological variables. Another school of ecologists, the "neo-orthodox," see limitations in the early classical studies but also see much of value. While recognizing the importance of social-psychological variables, the members of the neo-orthodox school are more inclined toward the use of so-called "hard," or nonattitudinal, data. They most frequently use mass data such as censuses and favor interpretation on the macrosociological level. Sociologists such as Amos Hawley, Otis Dudley Duncan, and Leo Schnore are members of this school.

Recently, in a reversal of the socialcultural criticisms, William Michelson has effectively taken human ecology to task for giving too much attention to social variables and not enough to the effect of the physical environment on behavior.[9] According to Michelson, "space has been utilized as a *medium* in most human ecology rather than as a *variable* with a potential effect of its own."[10] The wheel has thus come close to full turn since the 1920s.

## DEFINITIONS

It is essential to define what we mean when we call a place "urban." Here we run into real difficulties, for no universally accepted definition exists. About thirty definitions of urban population are currently in use, none of them totally satisfactory.[11]

Urban places have been defined using cultural, economic, political, and demographic criteria.[12] Cultural criteria for defining an urban place are similar to those used to describe urbanism as a way of life. Using these criteria, a city is "a state of mind, a body of customs and

[8]Walter Firey, "Sentiment and Symbolism as Ecological Variables," *American Sociological Review*, **10:**140–148.

[9]William H. Michelson, *Man and His Urban Environment*, Addison-Wesley, Reading, Mass., 1970, pp. 3–32.

[10]Michelson, op. cit., p. 17.

[11]Milos Macura, "The Influence of the Definition of Urban Place on the Size of Urban Population," in Jack Gibbs (ed.), *Urban Research Methods*, Van Nostrand, New York, 1961, pp. 21–31.

[12]William Petersen, *Population*, Macmillan, New York, 1969, pp. 433–435.

traditions."[13] The city thus is the place, as sociologists put it, where relations are *Gesellschaft* ("society" or formal role relationships) rather than *Gemeinschaft* ("community" or primary relationships) and forms of social organization are organic rather than mechnical. In short, the city is large, culturally heterogeneous, and socially diverse. It is the antithesis of "folk society." The problem with the cultural definitions of an urban place is the impossibility of measurement; for example, if a city is a state of mind, who can ever say where the boundaries of the urban area lie?

Economic standards have also been used in defining what is urban. Using economic criteria, a country has sometimes been described as urban if less than half the occupied males are engaged in agriculture. Here "urban" and "nonagricultural" are taken to be synonymous. This distinction, of course, tells us nothing about the degree of urbanization or its pattern of spatial distribution within the country. A distinction has also been made between the town as the center for processing and service functions and the countryside as the area for producing raw materials.[14] However, it is becoming increasingly difficult to distinguish among areas by means of such criteria. How far out do the producing and service functions of a New York or a Los Angeles extend?

Politically, a national government may define its urban areas as such in terms of administrative functions. The difficulty is that there is no agreement internationally on what the political or administrative criteria shall be. In many countries small administrative centers are recognized as urban regardless of their population or economic significance. Kenya, for example, has a number of "urban" administrative centers with populations of well under 2,000, and the same is true of a number of other countries.

Finally, size of population is frequently used as a criterion in deciding what is urban and what is not. Demographically, a place is defined as being urban because a certain number of people live in it. Measurement and comparison of rural and urban populations within a country are relatively simple when demographic criteria are used, although the problem of making comparisons among nations still remains. Only 250 persons are necessary to qualify an area as urban in Denmark, while 10,000 are needed in Greece.

According to the definition adopted by the United States Bureau of the Census for the 1970 census, the urban population of the United States comprises all persons living in urbanized areas and all persons outside of

[13]Robert E. Park, "The City: Suggestions for the Investigation of Human Behavior in the Urban Environment," in Robert E. Park, E. W. Burgess, and Roderick D. McKenzie (eds.), *The City,* University of Chicago Press, Chicago, 1925.

[14]Amos H. Hawley, *Human Ecology: A Theory of Community Structure,* Ronald Press, New York, 1950, p. 245.

urbanized areas who live in places of 2,500 or more. For practical purposes the urban population of the United States therefore includes anyone in a place having 2,500 or more inhabitants. By this definition, three quarters of the United States population is urban.

The United Nations has attempted to bring some order out of the various national definitions by setting up its own classifications scheme, which it uses for publishing its international data. The definitions of the United Nations are as follows:

> A *big city* is a locality with 500,000 or more inhabitants.
> A *city* is a locality with 100,000 or more inhabitants.
> An *urban locality* is a locality with 20,000 or more inhabitants.
> A *rural locality* is a locality with less than 20,000 inhabitants.[15]

This is a reasonable classification scheme, for when data are available, they are likely to have such a basis. The major limitation of the United Nations definition is not logical but practical: most of the more urbanized countries, such as the United States, simply do not use them, preferring to keep their own national definitions.[16] To make a complicated situation as simple as possible, this book will use the definitions established by the United States when presenting data for the United States and the definitions established by the United Nations when presenting international data. The reader can thus assume that outside the United States "urban" refers to the population in places of 20,000 or more.

Another term used in a variety of ways is "community."[17] "Community," as used by ecologists, can be defined as a territorially localized population which is interdependent with regard to daily needs. Thus this usage implies a *territorial* unit, as opposed to other uses of the term, such as "community of scholars" or "religious community." Anthropologists dealing with localized semi-isolated populations generally find the concept of community more useful than sociologists doing research in contemporary urban areas, where the boundaries between distinct groups or patterns of activities become blurred. Today the term "community" has lost its descriptive preciseness and efficiency. It is applied arbitrarily to everything from one block in a neighborhood to the international "community."

[15]*Demographic Handbook for Africa*, United Nations Economic Commission for Africa, Addis Ababa, 1968, p. 38.

[16]A team working under Kingsley Davis during the 1950s defined "metropolitan areas" for 720 of the then 1,046 areas in the world having at least 100,000 persons in their metropolitan areas and at least 50,000 in the central city (International Urban Research, *The World's Metropolitan Areas*, University of California Press, Berkeley, 1959). This system will not be used in this text, since the United Nations system is far more widely accepted and provides more current data.

[17]Some 90 definitions of community are listed by G. A. Hillery, "Definitions of Community: Areas of Agreement," *Rural Sociology*, **20**:111–123, 1955.

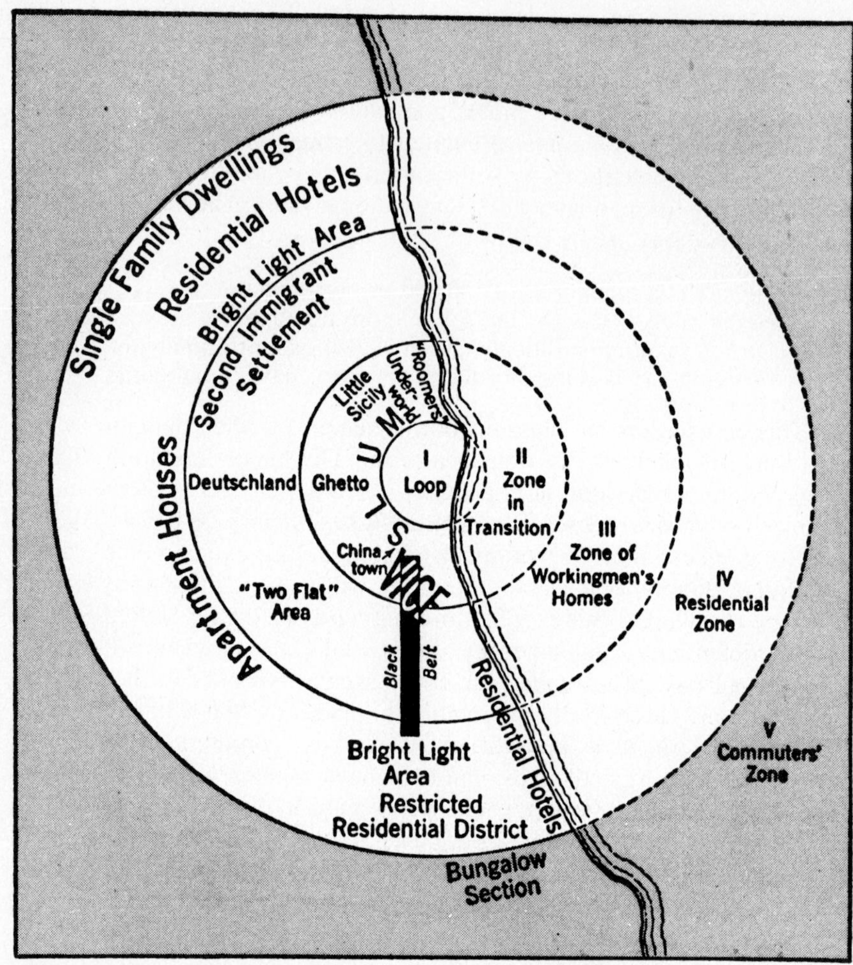


The classic representation of the zonal hypothesis. Note that zones are described in terms of housing and social characteristics. (*Robert E. Park, Ernest W. Burgess, and Robert D. McKenzie,* The City, *Chicago: University of Chicago Press, 1925, Chart II, "The Concentric Zone Principle of Urban Growth," p. 55.*)

## BURGESS'S GROWTH HYPOTHESIS

The most famous early product of the spatial-organizational concerns of the Chicago School was Burgess's concentric zonal hypothesis, first presented in 1924. This was an attempt to explain why cities grow the way they do.[18] Generations of sociology students have been exposed to the

[18]Ernest W. Burgess, "The Growth of the City: an Introduction to a Research Project," *Publications of the American Sociological Society,* **18:**85–97, 1924.

concentric zonal hypothesis—all too frequently in a bastardized form that makes it a static picture of city structure. This is unfortunate, for what Burgess was positing was the reorganization of spatial patterns that results from urban *growth,* in contrast to Gideon Sjoberg's picture of a static preindustrial city. Burgess was concerned with how industrial cities change over time. His hypothesis is a model, and only a model, of how cities develop spatially as a result of competition. In spite of criticisms, it still remains the principle theory of urban growth.

Burgess suggested that cities grow radially in a series of concentric zones or rings. Through a competitive struggle—expressed in ability to pay the cost of land and to tolerate nuisances such as noise and congestion—the most strategic or valuable land goes to the user who can afford to pay for it because of intensive use. Thus the ecologist would expect that the most convenient centrally located land, called the "central business district" and abbreviated CBD, would be occupied by intensive users, such as department stores, major business headquarters, and financial institutions. Near such dominant land users, one would also expect to find small establishments catering to their needs. Restaurants and coffee shops, quick printing firms, business supply houses, messenger services, and parking lots would be some of the related enterprises one would expect to find in the CBD. One would not expect to find used-car lots or industrial plants occupying the most costly central land.

The most familiar version of Burgess's theory divided the urban area into five zones. They are presented here essentially as they existed during the 1920s, so that they can serve as a baseline from which to examine patterns of change during the past fifty years.

Zone I was the central business district, the economic and (usually) the geographic center of the city. The heart of the zone was the retail shopping district, with its major department stores, theaters, hotels, banks, and central offices of economic, political, legal, and civic leaders. Consumption-oriented commercial activities tended to locate at the very core of the CBD, while the outer fringes, with lower rents, contained the wholesale business district: markets, warehouses, and storage buildings.[19]

[19]In Burgess's day at one edge of the CBD was located a sleazy but highly profitable area specializing in those activities and enterprises of a disreputable nature that needed accessibility, but could not for social reasons be located in the heart of the downtown area. Here were found cheap bars specializing in B girls hustling drinks, pornographic movie houses, strip joints, pinball arcades, and bookshops that sold magazines you couldn't buy in the suburbs. The clientele included conventioneers, soldiers and sailors on leave, and local drunks. Generally the only females in the area were those who were working there. Today these areas are dying, partially because of expressways and urban renewal and partially because they no longer perform an exclusive function. For example, it is no longer necessary to sit in a dirty movie house to see pornographic movies; they can be seen in major theatres in Times Square.

Until the period before World War I every major city in the United States also had a clearly marked "red-light district" just off the central business district that devoted itself to servicing needs that were not being met elsewhere. A turn-of-the-century social reform tract, *If Christ Came to Chicago,* provided a detailed map of every brothel, gambling place, and saloon in the downtown area of Chicago. The intent was to document the amount of vice, but the map also probably proved useful to many a visiting salesman

Here also were found the wholesale markets for fresh fruits and vegetables, the markets often looking as if they had been in disrepair for a century—as they sometimes had.

Today commercial and retail functions in CBDs are losing importance, while the function of providing office space is increasing. Specialized retailing of nonstandardized goods is still found in the CBD, but with the emergence of large convenient suburban shopping centers sales of general merchandise in central business districts have declined. Some larger stores have remained because of the prestige traditionally associated with the location, but even this is changing. Standardized goods can be sold just as well by regional shopping centers as by downtown stores, and there is less inconvenience in terms of traffic and parking problems.

On the other hand, as Chapter 5 will show, office space in the CBD is still in demand. Offices thrive on concentration, which permits the rapid exchange of information. The high-rise office building is well suited to provide the necessary concentration since "within itself, provided an adequate set of elevators, the skyscraper benefits from a facility of traffic which would not be possible if the working area were distributed on ground floor."[20]

At present American cities are pouring millions of dollars into CBDs with the hope of maintaining them the way they are or changing them back into what they once were. Not everyone agrees that this makes sense. As one national authority on planning said, "Many activities are downtown just because they are there, or in response to linkages which disappeared years ago. Many could be served better elsewhere."[21]

Zone II, the zone of transition, contained both older factory complexes, many from the last century, and an outer ring of deteriorating neighborhoods of tenements. The zone of transition was known as an area of high crime rates and social disorganization.

The zone of transition was where the immigrant received his first

---

and conventioneer. As a sidelight, it deserves mentioning that red-light districts were generally free of street crime. The owners and proprietors of the local brothels and gambling places were much opposed to having muggers steal money that their customers were going to spend in their establishments. Besides, crime gave the area a bad name and attracted attention to it which could result in public pressure on the police to make a raid or two.

The name "red-light district" comes from the red lights which prostitutes put in their front windows to indicate that they were open for business. Numerous European cities such as Amsterdam and Hamburg still have clearly defined red-light districts—lights and all. These areas become quite congested during the evening and the lunch hour. American red-light districts were shut down by local societies for the suppression of vice around the turn of the century. The result was that the displaced prostitutes set up business in apartments throughout the city, and the call girl replaced the brothel.

[20]Jean Gottman, "The Skyscraper Amid the Sprawl," in Jean Gottman and Robert Harper (eds.), *Metropolis on the Move,* Wiley, New York, 1967, p. 137.

[21]Edward Ullman, "Presidential Address, The Nature of Cities Reconsidered," *The Regional Science Association Papers and Proceedings,* **9**:21, 1962.

view of the city. It was the point of entry. Immigrants settled here in the cheap housing near the factories because they could not compete economically for more desirable residential locations. As they moved up in socioeconomic status, they moved out spatially and were in turn replaced by newer immigrants. Thus, a nonrandom spatial structure or pattern emerged, with groups of lower socioeconomic status most centrally located. In Burgess's day, land in the zone of transition was being held for speculation by landlords who provided only minimum maintenance in the expectation that the CBD would eventually expand into the area. It didn't happen that way, and half a century later many of the same slums remain—others having only recently been destroyed by urban renewal. Chapter 6, "Life-Styles: The City," discusses patterns of life in this zone in greater detail.

Zone III was the zone of workingmen's homes. This was the area settled by second-generation families, the children of the immigrants; it was the place where one moved when one could get out of the inner core. Physically it was (at least in Chicago, Burgess's model) a neighborhood of two-family houses rather than tenements, apartments, or single-family houses. Typically, the father of the family had a blue-collar job in the city. His children, however, planned to marry and move out of the old neighborhood, perhaps to live in suburbs of the Levittown type (see Chapter 7).

Zone IV was called the "zone of the better residences." The ring comprised the area beyond the neighborhood of the second-generation immigrants. This was the zone of the great middle class—small businessmen, professional people, salesmen, and those holding white-collar jobs. However, even in the 1920s this zone was in the process of changing from a community of single-family houses to one of apartment buildings and residential hotels (that is, there was an invasion of new land-use patterns).

The final zone, Zone V, was the commuter zone. In the early 1920s these were, thanks to the commuter railroads and the private automobile, the upper-middle-class and upper-class dormitory suburbs. Here were found the classic suburban life patterns—the husband leaving in the morning for the city and returning in the evening, the wife left to raise the children, maintain the house, and participate in civic affairs. Chapter 7, "Life-Styles: The Suburbs," deals further with this outer zone.

## THE PROCESS OF EVOLUTIONARY CHANGE

### Competition and Segregation

In discussing the growth of the city, Burgess and others used the ecological concepts of competition, segregation, invasion, succession, and natural areas. Burgess noted that factories, homes, and retail shops were not randomly distributed within the urban area. Rather, there was a process of sorting by economic and social factors that resulted in concentration of similar populations and land uses. Competition for space meant that persons, organizations, and institutions were distributed within urban space in a nonrandom fashion. The result is the ecological pattern of American cities.

Within the urban area, competition for land means that the most valuable property—usually centrally located—goes to those functions which can use space intensively and are willing to pay the costs. Costs include not only purchase price but also taxes and nuisance (congestion, noise, pollution, etc.) from other nearby land users. Centrally located land was thus in the past taken up by those economic units, such as department stores, that could effectively use space and required heavy pedestrian traffic. Consumption-oriented commercial activities still tend to be the most centrally located; production-oriented activities are in the next ring out; and residences are the least centralized. Residential uses tend to be pushed out of areas desired for commercial purposes, since residential users cannot pay the high cost of central location and do not want the pollution, noise, and congestion of trucks rumbling down the street and a factory next door.

The result is that land values are highest near the center of the city and tend to decrease as one moves toward the periphery. This means that if housing is to be centrally located it must use the land intensively. As a result, the two types of housing one finds in central areas are high-income, high-rise luxury apartments, and tenement and slum properties. High-rise apartments escape the pollution and noise of the city not by moving outward but by moving upward. A fifteenth-floor apartment not only is quiet and convenient but also has a beautiful view. Slums are likewise intensive users of space. Even when the rent per room is low (and often it is not), the rent *per acre* is high.

Consequently, there is a tendency toward an inverse relationship between the value of land and the economic status of those who occupy it. Inner-city slum land is more expensive than land in the suburbs. In inner areas higher land costs are compensated for by density of use. Through crowding, a slum lord can get a great number of rents from a relatively small piece of land. Since land in outer areas is less valuable, less intensive use, such as single-family houses on large lots, is economically feasible. Thus, as you move out from the center of the city toward the periphery, land values and rental per acre tend to grade downward, while the rental per housing unit grades upward.

### Invasion and Succession

The process of intrusion of a new usage into an area is called "invasion." The history of the American city is the story of the invasion of one land use by another. The end result when one group or function finally takes the place of another is called "succession."[22] None of the patterns of land use within a city are permanently fixed, although some zoning laws attempt to fix them. Patterns change when one land usage or function intrudes into the territory of another land usage. This process of invasion, as we have said, is part and parcel of the history of American cities. As cities have grown, areas that were once characterized by single-family houses have been converted to apartment, commercial, or industrial usage—this is succession. All too frequently such ecological processes are given overlays of values or morals. The city, if it is viable, is always in the process of changing. While changes should certainly be directed for the benefit of the community, we must remember that ecological patterns are dynamic rather than static. Cities that do not change become historical tourist attractions or stagnant backwaters.

Today the most spectacular instance of invasion and eventual succession is found in the racial changes taking place in the central city. Many whites fear the movement of blacks into a neighborhood because they believe it will threaten the stability of the area. By this they mean that their neighborhood will lose its middle-class character, the quality of the schools will decline, street violence will increase, and the area will generally deteriorate to the level of an inner-city slum. In spite of the evidence that blacks do not bring dilapidation and that the quality of a neighborhood is determined more by the age and condition of the housing and the incomes of the residents than by race, the belief that the coming of blacks means the end of a community still persists.

Partially this belief is due to the historical fact that blacks were a low-income group and could thus afford only the oldest and poorest housing. The category "black" and the category "lower class" are still viewed as being identical by many whites. Any blacks who move in are going to let the property deteriorate, let weeds overgrow the front yard, and perhaps even park a dilapidated car behind the house. College students, black and white, can laugh at this obvious caricature, but it is not funny to many whites who are fleeing the cities. They believe that the coming of blacks into the neighborhood will automatically bring other

[22]The term "function," as used by ecologists—not by most other sociologists—means recurrent patterns of activities which depend on other activities. "Structure," to the ecologist, is the orderly arrangements of the parts that make up the whole; the loci within which the functions or activities are performed.

Invasion of new housing patterns in the Roxbury area of Boston.
(*Michael Dobo/Editorial Photocolor Archives.*)

undesirable social changes, and they act as if their beliefs were true. This is an example of a self-fulfilling prophecy at work; one acts in such a way as to bring one's expectations to pass.

The process of economic succession, while less dramatic than racial changes, can be of equally great long-term importance. Examples are the moving out of industry, the transition within neighborhoods from single-family to multiple-family dwelling units, and the change from residential to commercial land use. Students will note that the last two of these invasion-succession patterns can commonly be found in residential areas abutting growing colleges and universities. Such changes are frequently viewed in moral terms—for example, as the decline of family neighborhoods. However, a city, if it is viable, is always in a process of change. Leo Schnore suggests that there may be an evolutionary pattern to the changes in urban land usages, and that Burgess's concentric zonal scheme as well as preindustrial land use patterns can be subsumed under a more general theory of residential land uses in urban areas.[23] However, such a theory has yet to be fully developed.

### Natural Areas

As a result of the process of selective competition, segregated areas emerged, whether automobile rows, racial ghettoes, apartment houses, high-income single-family neighborhoods, or warehouse districts. The Chicago sociologists called these areas "natural areas." They were natural in that they were the results of ecological processes rather than of planning or conscious creation by any government unit. When zoning laws were established, they generally recognized such natural areas so as to continue existing land-use patterns.

The existence of natural areas can be seen even in such basic data as age and sex distribution. Transient and skid row areas have a heavy excess of males of middle and old age. Women are few and children even rarer. Working-class districts have a more regular sex distribution, but the number of children is greater than in middle-class areas. Apartment areas have a majority of middle-aged adults and relatively few children. Areas with public housing projects are dominated by women and children, with few adult males. Areas with newer suburban housing tracts have large numbers of adults in their twenties and thirties and many children under ten. Older teen-agers are underrepresented, and adults over fifty years of age are virtually nonexistent.[24]

[23]Leo F. Schnore, *Class and Race in Cities and Suburbs*, Markham, Chicago, 1972, p. 21.

[24]For an older analysis of Chicago neighborhoods, see Charles Newcomb, "Graphic Presentation of Age and Sex Distribution of Population in the City," in Paul K. Hatt and Albert J. Reiss, Jr. (eds.), *Cities and Society*, Free Press, New York, 1957, pp. 382–392.

Skid Row "natural Areas" receive minimal medical and other services. (*Laima Turaley/Editorial Photocolor Archives.*)

## EVALUATION—CRITICISMS

In evaluating Burgess's theory we have to keep in mind that he was proposing a "model" or "ideal type" of what American cities would look like if other factors did not intervene—but of course other factors do intervene. Burgess's own statements make it clear that he recognized the effects of distorting factors. He said:

> If radial extension were the only factor affecting the growth of American cities, every city in this country would exhibit a perfect exemplification of these five urban zones. But since other factors affect urban development (including) situation, site, natural and artificial barriers, survival of an earlier use of a district, prevailing city plan and its system of transportation, many distortions and modifications of this pattern are actually found. Nevertheless, so universal and powerful is the force of expansion outward from the city's core that in every city these zones can be more or less clearly delimited.[25]

[25]Ernest W. Burgess, "Residential Segregation in American Cities," *Annals of the American Academy of Political and Social Science,* **140:**108, November, 1928.

In the decades following its formulation Burgess's hypothesis has come under severe criticism on both theoretical and empirical grounds. As Alihan pointed out, Burgess's zonal boundaries "do not serve as demarcations in respect to the ecological or social phenomena they circumscribe, but are arbitrary divisions."[26]

Burgess's zones are clearly not totally homogeneous units. Alternatives to Burgess's theory were not long developing. Homer Hoyt suggested a modification of the concentric-zone pattern which became known as the "sector theory."[27] Hoyt suggested that growth took place in sectors which extended radially from the center toward the periphery of the city. Residential areas thus extended rapidly along established lines of travel, where economic resistance was least. A pattern of land use was said to develop in which each use—industrial, commercial, high-income residential, or low-income residential—tended to push out from the city core in specific sectors or wedges that cut across concentric zones. Thus high-income housing could radiate from the core in one wedge, a racial ghetto in a second, industrial firms in a third, and working-class residences in a fourth. Hoyt's theory was based on the movement of high-rent districts in 142 American cities between 1900, 1915, and 1936. Since he did not attempt to locate social influences on phenomena within the metropolitan area, some sociologists seeking a compromise have used Hoyt's theory to explain residential movement and Burgess's theory to explain social-spatial phenomena.

A third theory of spatial growth rejected the idea of a unicentered city altogether and instead held that differing land uses had different centers. This "multiple-nuclei" theory was suggested by Chauncey Harris and Edward Ullman.[28] They argued that land-use patterns developed around what were originally independent nuclei. Four factors were said to account for the rise of the different nuclei:

**1** Certain activities require specialized facilities. Retailing, for example, requires a high degree of accessibility, while manufacturing needs ample land and railroad service.

**2** Like activities group together for mutual advantages, as in the case of the central business district.

**3** Some unlike activities are mutually detrimental or incompatible with one another. For example, it is unlikely that high-income or high-status residential areas will locate close to heavy industry.

**4** Some uses, such as storage and warehousing facilities, which

[26]Alihan, op. cit., p. 225.

[27]Homer Hoyt, "The Structure and Growth of Residential Neighborhoods in American Cities," U. S. Federal Housing Administration, U. S. Government Printing Office, Washington, D. C., 1939.

[28]Chauncy Harris and Edward Ullman, "The Nature of Cities," *Annals of the American Academy of Political and Social Science,* **242**:7–17, 1945.

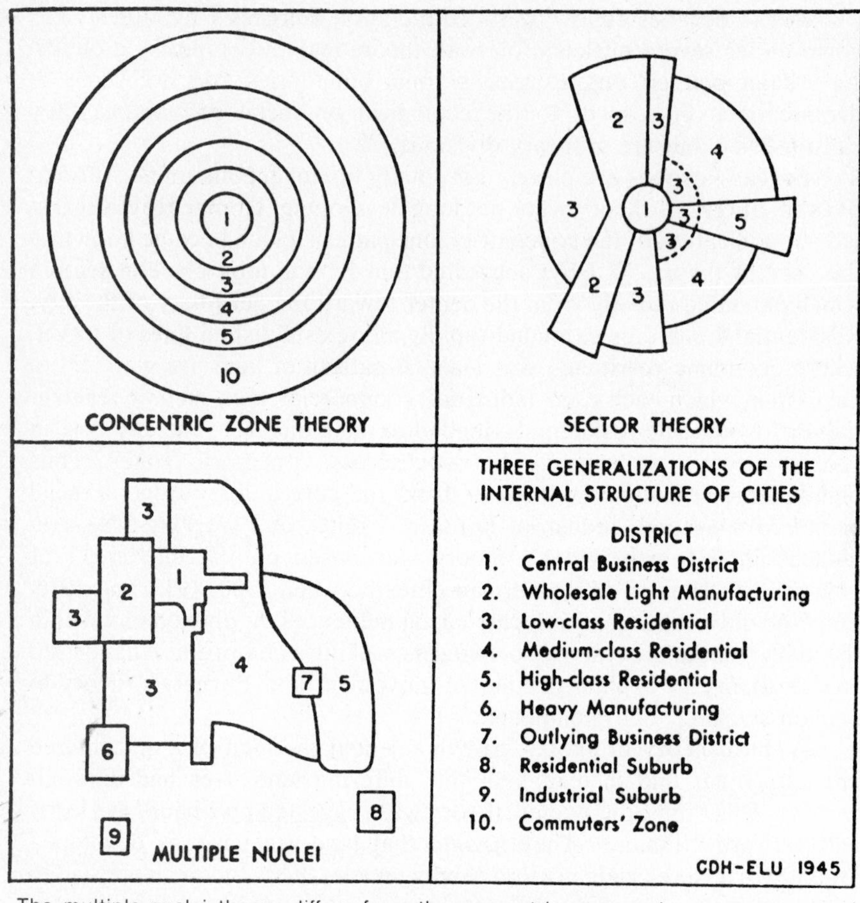


The multiple-nuclei theory differs from the concentric zone and sector theories in that it does not posit growth radiating from the city center. (*Chauncy Harris and Edward Ullman, "The Nature of Cities,"* Annals of the American Academy of Political and Social Sciences, *November 1945, vol. 242, p. 13.*)

have a relatively lower competitive capacity to purchase good locations, are able to afford only low-rental areas.[29]

Taking the extreme position that there can be no pattern of common spatial growth, Maurice Davie argued that "there is no universal pattern, not even an ideal type."[30] Davie suggested that rather than propping up

[29]Harris and Ullman, loc. cit.

[30]Maurice R. Davie, "The Pattern of Urban Growth," in George Murdock (ed.), *Studies in the Science of Society,* Yale University Press, New Haven, 1937, pp. 31–62.

inadequate hypotheses, sociologists should use their own powers of observation and analysis. He suggested that topographical features such as rivers, lakes, and hills interfere with or take precedence over social or geometrical patterns of growth. He maintained that level land attracts business; higher land and hills attract private residences; low land near water attracts industry; erratic street arrangement encourages central growth; and expressways expedite radial expansion. As Thomlinson points out, the difficulty with these statements is that they are a list of ad hoc descriptions, lacking any theory to bind them together into a compact system of generalizations.[31] Analysis without theory contributes little to knowledge, since it simply states what is. While such statements have a surface appeal, particularly when the shortcomings of other theories are considered, they provide no hypothesis to be tested and thus cannot be proven right or wrong.

We now know that Davie was mistaken in stating that no clear pattern exists. Research done by Schnore and others during the late 1960s shows that a rough version of Burgess's model does indeed hold at least for larger and older American cities. As Leo Schnore suggested, "An urban area might show a certain pattern of city-suburban status differences when it is relatively small and young but evolve toward another, predictable pattern of differences as it grows and ages."[32]

> More specifically, . . . (1) smaller and younger central cities in the United States tend to be occupied by the local elite, while their peripheral, suburban areas contain the lower strata; (2) with growth and the passage of time, the central city comes to be the main residential area for both the highest and lowest strata, at least temporarily, while the broad middle classes are overrepresented in the suburbs; and (3) a subsequent stage in this evolutionary process is achieved when the suburbs have become the semiprivate preserve of both the upper and middle strata, while the central city is largely given over to the lowest stratum. In a very rough fashion, of course, this last stage corresponds to the way in which the various social classes are arrayed in space according to the original Burgess (1924) zonal hypothesis.[33]

To date, empirical tests have both supported and failed to support the hypothesis.[34] Haggerty, for example, looked at changes in educational

[31]Thomlinson, op. cit., p. 151.

[32]Schnore, op. cit., p. 72.

[33]Schnore, op. cit., p. 72. Reprinted by permission of Rand McNally Publishing Company.

[34]Leo F. Schnore and Joy K. O. Jones, "The Evolution of City-Suburban Types in the Course of a Decade," *Urban Affairs Quarterly*, **4:**421–422, June, 1969; Joel Smith, "Another Look at Socioeconomic Status Distributions in Urbanized Areas," *Urban Affairs Quarterly*, **5:**423–453, June, 1970; Lee J. Haggerty, "Another Look at the Burgess Hypothesis: Time as an Important Variable," *American Journal of Sociology*, **76:**1084–1093, May, 1971.

levels from 1940 to 1960 in census tracts in eight large cities, using the statistical technique of Markov's analysis. He reported that there was a definite trend through time toward a direct association between an area's social status and its distance from the city center. This tendency toward higher status on the periphery held even in cities whose original or present pattern was for higher-status group to be more centrally located. Thus, whatever the original pattern, over time there appears to be a movement toward a concentric zonal system.[35]

The internal spatial structure of black city neighborhoods is also related to socioeconomic status. There is a fairly regular progression upward in socioeconomic status as one moves outward from the city center. Schnore's study of social-class segregation within the black communities of twenty-four large cities confirms that the higher social classes disproportionately occupy the more peripheral locations.[36] Marston, however, suggests that his research on variation by socioeconomic status in sixteen American cities shows that in addition to decentralization or distance from the city's center the age and prestige of the area being entered are of crucial importance. Simply put, groups of higher socioeconomic status move toward newer areas and areas of higher prestige, even if they are located close to the city center.[37]

In a longitudinal study of 198 metropolitan areas, James Pinkerton examined Schnore's model empirically and on the basis of his research suggested that the patterns that were true of larger metropolitan areas are, increasingly, being found in smaller areas as well. As Pinkerton puts it:

> I propose that a new stage is approaching in which the city-ring distribution of classes will no longer vary according to size and age of the metropolis: instead, all areas will house their lower status groups in the city.[38]

## CITIES ELSEWHERE

The concentric zonal pattern of urban growth as propounded by Burgess is far less useful in describing patterns of ecological growth outside North America. The theories discussed in this chapter assume that the city under discussion is a city of the industrial age. These theories also assume that there is growth through in-migration to the inner core area of the

[35]Haggerty, op. cit., pp. 1084–1093.

[36]Leo F. Schnore, *The Urban Scene,* Free Press, New York, 1965, Chapter 16.

[37]Wilfred G. Marston, "Socioeconomic Differentiation within Negro Areas of American Cities," *Social Factors,* **48:**165–176, December, 1969.

[38]James R. Pinkerton, "The Changing Class Composition of Cities and Suburbs," *Land Economics,* **49:**469, November, 1973.

cities, which produces a relationship between high socioeconomic status and distance from the center of the city.

As will be discussed in later chapters, this has not been the typical pattern of growth in nonindustrial cities elsewhere in the world. More common has been a pattern where upper-class and upper-middle-class groups occupy the city proper and poor in-migrants settle on the "suburban" periphery in squatter shantytowns. These *favelas, barriadas, gecekondulas,* or *bustees* can be found on the periphery of almost every major city in Latin America, Africa, and Asia.

Cultural differences also have to be taken into account. As one researcher stated:

> The literature of urban geography and urban sociology has a tendency to project as universals those characteristics of urbanism with which European and American students are most familiar. Thus, since a large proportion of all urban research has concerned itself with Chicago, there was until recently a tendency to ascribe to all cities characteristics which now appear to be specific to Chicago and other communities closely resembling it in history and economic function. . . .
>
> In the United States, almost all urban growth has been characterized by the rapid and uncontrolled expansion of the community and by unregulated competition for land. To a lesser degree this has been true also of modern Europe.[39]

There is also reason to question just how applicable Burgess's theory is to European cities. Certainly the major cities of Europe that were established before the Industrial Revolution have an internal distribution of social and economic classes that does not easily fit Burgess's model.[40] In the older cities the elites preempted the prestigious central locations and the poor were forced to live in more peripheral locations. Manufacturing and commerce, when located within the city, were restricted to specific areas. Thus the East End of London was, before the bombing of World War II, composed of small factories, workshops, and poor homes surrounding the dock area. On the other hand, the central and western districts of Westminster, Marylebone, and Kensington have continued to retain their upper-class airs for two centuries in spite of their central location.

With much of the central land already filled, heavy industry was confined to "suburban" areas where there was sufficient land for the growing factories. Thus Paris has a concentration of automobile and

[39]Theodore Caplow, "The Social Ecology of Guatemala City," *Social Forces,* **28:**132, 1949.

[40]Francis L. Hauser, "Ecological Patterns of European Cities," in Sylvia F. Fava (ed.), *Urbanism in World Perspective,* Crowell, New York, 1968, pp. 193–216.

aircraft factories to the south and east of the city, and the population of such suburban areas is heavily working class. The continuation of a preindustrial ecological pattern results in social-class distribution and political voting patterns that are quite different from those found in American cities. Suburban areas of Paris, the so-called "red ring," provide major political support for the Communist Party, while the inner-city middle class districts vote for the more conservative candidates exactly opposite to the American stereotype.

Gideon Sjoberg sees this pattern of indentification of high-status groups with central-city location as a persistence of a "feudal tradition" that is not present in American cities. In his view, "In many European cities, including those in the U.S.S.R., the persistence of the feudal tradition has inhibited suburbanization because high status has attached to residence in the central city."[41]

One can seriously question whether a preference for central-city locations, be it in Paris, London, or Moscow, is today "feudalistic" or part of a "feudal tradition." Manhattan doesn't have a feudal tradition, but it still has a pattern of the well-to-do locating in certain areas of the central city. Cosmopolites, whether in London or New York, prefer to live where they can easily get to work, easily get to good restaurants, easily get to the theater and other cultural activities, and easily get a drink or a sandwich at 2:00 in the morning. It can be argued that, particularly in Europe, upper-status urban populations live in the city because they feel it is an exciting and attractive place to live.

## ECOLOGICAL METHODOLOGY

Ecologists, by and large, collect their data in the same manner as other sociologists. What does distinguish them is their preference for operating on the group level rather than the individual level. Ecologists, concerned as they are with the behavior of groups, rely heavily on mass data and are most comfortable with so-called "hard data." Probably the most-used source of data is the United States Census, which provides a wealth of information on the social and economic characteristics of groups, their housing patterns, and their business activities. In the United States the decennial census is supplemented by the monthly Current Population Survey of 50,000 households across the nation, which yields far more detailed information. The Current Population Survey provides up-to-date information on social and economic questions—detailed information no single researcher or group of researchers could afford to gather. The use of computers now enables researchers to obtain previously unavailable

[41]Gideon Sjoberg, "Cities in Developing and in Industrial Societies: A Cross-cultural Analysis," in Philip M. Hauser and Leo F. Schnore, *The Study of Urbanization*, Wiley, New York, 1965, p. 230.

information on the characteristics of neighborhoods or groups within urban areas while still protecting the anonymity of the respondents.

The human ecologist's interest is in the characteristics and behavior of groups rather than the attitudes, motivations, and personalities of the individual members of groups. As a result, ecologists use quantitative rather than qualitative data. Their use of nonsocial variables such as distance, transportation, and physical environment means that ecologists sometimes have more in common with economists than sociologists doing behavioral studies in the social psychology of small groups.

For example, in a study of occupational stratification and residential location, the Duncans empirically demonstrated the relationship between what one does and where one lives. Spatial distances between occupational groups are closely related to their social distances, whether measured in terms of the conventional indicators of socioeconomic status (income, education, occupation) or in terms of differences in occupational origins. In accordance with accepted ecological theory, they found that the occupational groups most segregated physically were those at the very bottom and very top of the occupational scale. Likewise, residence in low-rent areas and residence near the center of the city were inversely related to socioeconomic status. However, near the middle of the socioeconomic scale, where blue-collar and white-collar clerical occupations meet, the pattern is less clear. Although white-collar clerical workers on the average have considerably lower income than blue-collar

**Table 4-1 Indexes of Dissimilarity in Residential Distribution among Major Occupational Groups, for Employed Males in the Chicago Metropolitan District, 1950**

| Major occupational group | Major occupational group | | | | | | | |
|---|---|---|---|---|---|---|---|---|
| | Professional | Managers, etc. | Sales workers | Clerical workers | Craftsmen and foremen | Operatives | Service workers | Laborers |
| Professional | — | 13 | 15 | 28 | 35 | 44 | 41 | 54 |
| Managers, etc. | | — | 13 | 28 | 33 | 41 | 40 | 52 |
| Sales workers | | | — | 27 | 35 | 42 | 38 | 54 |
| Clerical workers | | | | — | 16 | 21 | 24 | 38 |
| Craftsmen and foremen | | | | | — | 17 | 35 | 35 |
| Operatives | | | | | | — | 26 | 25 |
| Service workers | | | | | | | — | 28 |
| Laborers | | | | | | | | — |

*Source:* Otis D. Duncan and Beverly Duncan, "Residential Distribution and Occupational Stratification," *American Journal of Sociology,* **60:**498, March, 1955, table 3.

craftsmen and foremen, they have a pattern of residential distribution more in common with other white-collar groups. It appears that social status, or prestige, is more important to clerical groups, although their relatively lower income level *vis à vis* other white-collar groups does set up cross-pressures, as is indicated by a high rent-to-income ratio for clerical workers.[42]

## SOCIAL-AREA ANALYSIS

Social-area analysis is a technique for analyzing subpopulations or urban subcommunities under the assumption that persons living in one type of social area differ in attitudes and behavior from persons in other types of social areas. It seeks to classify urban phenomena systematically. The originators of this system, Eshref Shevky and Wendell Bell, differentiate the structure of urban subareas according to three variables: social rank, urbanization, and segregation.[43] These variables were chosen because they were believed to measure crucial factors distinguishing types of urban populations. The "social rank" index is derived from census-tract measures of occupation and education; "urbanization," sometimes called "familism," is derived from measures of the ratio of children to women, the proportion of working women, and the percentage of single-family dwellings; "segregation" is derived from the measurement of spatial isolation of ethnic groups.

The objective is to classify small sections of the city on the basis of their social attributes. Thus the areas are not determined by spacial criteria but rather are established on the basis of the social characteristics of the residents, although the basic unit for analysis still remains the spacially defined census tract of roughly 4,000 persons. The technique is designed to get finer detail and a more accurate map of social space by giving social values to the various census tracts, and to create a picture of the city's pattern from the social areas. It differs from the more conventional ecological position, which first hypothesizes a given spacial-social pattern and then examines the data to discover the degree of fit. The nature of the clustering of variables and the relationships among them are taken as measuring "societal scale," or the degree of the division of labor and social intergration. Proponents of the technique argue that it has proved itself valuable in directing attention to social rather than

[42]Otis Dudley Duncan and Beverly Duncan, "Residential Distribution and Occupational Stratification," *American Journal of Sociology*, **60**:493–503, March, 1955.

[43]Eshref Shevky and Wendell Bell, *Social Area Analysis*, Stanford University Press, Palo Alto, Calif., 1955.

spacial concerns, more adequately delineating subcommunities within the urban area, and facilitating comparative and longitudinal study of cities. Certainly social-area analysis stimulated needed urban research.

Social-area analysis has not had an uncritical reception. It has been strongly criticized by ecologists as lacking both theoretical rationale and empirical utility.[44] A major criticism is that the abstract variables of social rank, urbanization, and segregation are said to be an arbitrary grouping of several census measures into another type of index where the index gives less detail than the component parts of which it was created.[45] Duncan argues that the discussion of theoretical reasons for choosing particular index variables does not lead to a unique selection of variables or even to a useful criterion for selection, and that there is no clear theoretical relationship between the basic conceptual concepts and the variables used in the index.[46]

Bell and Greer in turn suggest that critics of social-area analysis have applied unreasonable standards, been uncautious in making conclusions unsupported by data, and reach different evaluations because of basic differences in intellectual approach.[47]

Thus it can be seen that social-area analysis has both strong supporters and vocal opponents. Its eventual position in urban research is still uncertain.

[44]Otis Dudley Duncan, Review of *Social Area Analysis, American Journal of Sociology*, **61**:84–85, July, 1955; and Amos Hawley and Otis Dudley Duncan, "Social Area Analysis: A Critical Appraisal," *Land Economics*, **33**:337–345, November, 1957.

[45]Maurice Van Arsdol Jr., Santo F. Camilleri, and Calvin F. Schmid, "The Generality of Urban Social Area Indexes," *American Sociological Review*, **23**:277–284, 1958.

[46]Duncan, op. cit., pp. 84–85.

[47]Wendell Bell and Scott Greer, "Social Area Analysis and Its Critiques," *Pacific Sociological Review*, **5**:3–9, 1962.

Chapter 5

# The Metropolitan Region

*He also built Upper-Beth-horon and Lower-Beth-horon as fortified cities with walls and barred gates, and Baalath as well as all his store-cities, and all the towns where he quartered his chariots and horses; and he carried out all his cherished plans for building in Jerusalem, in the Lebanon, and throughout his whole dominion.*

Solomon's SMSA
Second Chronicles, 8:6

The last fifty years have witnessed a massive "population implosion," or ingathering of the American population into urban concentrations. This centripetal movement has both depopulated rural counties and magnified urban problems thus amplifying the effects of the better-known population explosion. However, within metropolitan areas the movement has been in the opposite direction—that is, from the center toward the periphery. Flying from Washington to Boston along the densely populated East Coast, one becomes acutely conscious of how much of urban growth is concentrated on the periphery of urban areas while outlying areas look uninhabited. In fact, owing to the abandonment of smaller outlying farms there is probably more unused and unsettled acreage than there was fifty years ago.

Until the early years of the twentieth century the forces promoting concentration were stronger than those favoring decentralization. Today the pattern has changed: the edges of metropolitan areas are increasingly being converted from less intensive land uses, such as agriculture, to more intensive uses, such as housing and manufacturing. Less intensive land uses such as grain production and cattle grazing are pushed outward; near the city even agriculture is intensive—truck farms, greenhouses, chicken farms, etc. The fertility of the soil is less important than the nearness of the city: consider, for example, the intensive use of relatively poor farmland near New England cities.

The problem in America is not that we are about to run out of raw land, because that clearly is not the case. Figures compiled by the Bureau of the Census indicate that three-quarters of the population is concentrated on a mere 1½ percent of the nation's land area.[1] Moreover, out of a total 3,536,855 square miles in the country, the amount of urban land in use totals 54,103 square miles or a land area roughly equal to the state of Florida. The overall United States population density is only 51 persons per square mile, compared with 970 persons per square mile in the Netherlands, which is densely settled and heavily urbanized. Obviously, the United States is not suffering from an overall land shortage. The problem is that we do not have open land in the right places—that is, near the cities, where it is needed. Open land in Alaska is hardly usable by city dwellers in Baltimore, Philadelphia, or New York. It is significant that, despite its high population density, the Netherlands has large cities which give far more of a feeling of openness and easy access to the countryside than comparable American cities do. The Dutch are also creating communities on new land (polders). As we will see in Chapters 11 and 12, planning makes the difference. The United States is beginning to plan, but only in a piecemeal way. While the Dutch are actively working to save open space near their cities, the Americans are allowing open spaces near urban centers to disappear. In 1972 alone, new urban growth and new highways consumed 430,000 rural acres in the United States.[2]

[1] *United States Department of Commerce News,* Social and Economic Statistics Administration, U.S. Government Printing Office, Washington, D.C., April 21, 1972, p. 1.

[2] Gladwin Hill, "The Environmental Revolution Enters a Crucial Phase," *National Wildlife,* April–May, 1973, p. 28.

## THE SITUATION IN THE 1970s

The census of 1970 showed that 149.3 million persons, or 73.5 percent of the population of the United States, were then living in urban areas. Ten years earlier the urban population had been 69.9 percent. In 1970 about four-fifths of the urban population—118.4 million people—lived in urbanized areas, i.e., places of 50,000 or more plus their suburban areas. About half of the nation's population lives in only eight of the fifty states—California, Illinois, Michigan, New Jersey, New York, Ohio, Pennsylvania, and Texas. The overall picture of urban change is as follows:

> During the decade of the 1960's the West replaced the Northeast as the most urban region, the first time in the history of the nation that the Northeast has not been the most urban region. The West's proportion of population was 82.9 percent while in the Northeast the proportion was 80.2 percent. The South, long the most rural region of the country, is now becoming urbanized at the fastest rate. In 1970, 64.4 percent of the South's people were urban, up from 58.5 percent in 1960. In the North Central region the proportion of urbanites was 71.6 percent. . . .
>
> California is the most urban state in the nation, 91 percent of its population resides in cities or towns. New Jersey with 90, Rhode Island, Massachusetts, Illinois, Florida, Utah, Nevada, and Hawaii all are more than 80 percent urban. The least urban state is Vermont with only 32 percent of its population in urban areas. West Virginia with 38 percent urban is next with South Dakota, North Dakota, and Mississippi each with 56 percent urban tied for third place.[3]

The percentage of the population living in the nation's fifty largest cities decreased 2 percent between 1960 and 1970. Twenty-two of these cities lost population during the decade. While the overall urban area is expanding at a rapid rate, the large central cities no longer dominate the total metropolitan area the way they did as recently as two or three decades ago.

## THE AUTOMOBILE AND URBAN SPATIAL EVOLUTION

What really changed the spatial pattern of twentieth-century American cities was the technological breakthrough of the automobile. The automobile provided mobility to the average urban dweller and allowed and even encouraged rapid settlement of previously inaccessible areas on the

[3] *Small-Area Data Notes*, vol. 6, Department of Commerce Bureau of the Census, U. S. Government Printing Office, Washington, D.C., March, 1971, pp. 6–7.

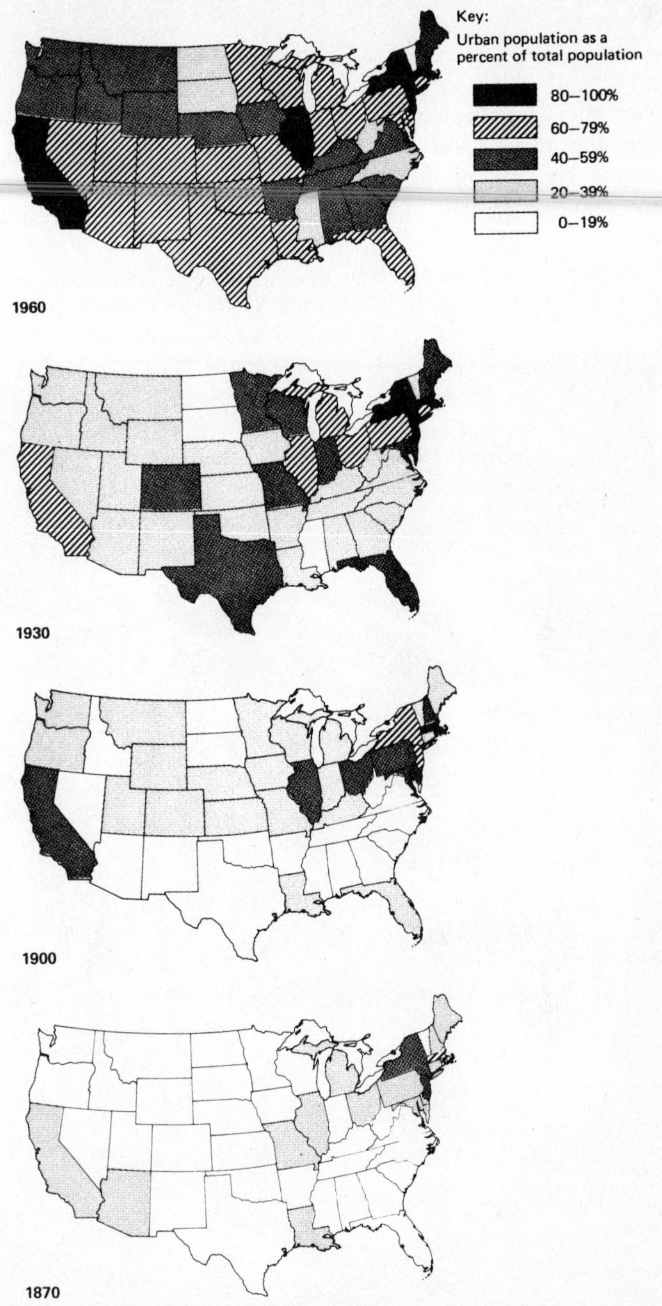


In a period of 100 years, the United States has changed from an overwhelmingly rural to an overwhelmingly urban nation. (John R. Borchert, *The Growth of Urbanization by State,* 1870–1960, "The Urbanization of the Upper Midwest: 1930–1960," Upper Midwest Economic Study, February 1963, Urban Report No. 2, p. 2.)

periphery of the central city. Automobiles, during the early decades of this century, soon changed from a rich man's toy to a middle-class necessity. Automobile registration in the United States increased from $2^1/_2$ million in 1915, to 9 million in 1920 and 26 million in 1930. A study

Los Angeles, a city built with the assumption of automobile ownership, moves traffic by means of the ever-present freeways. *(J. E. Eyeman/Black Star.)*

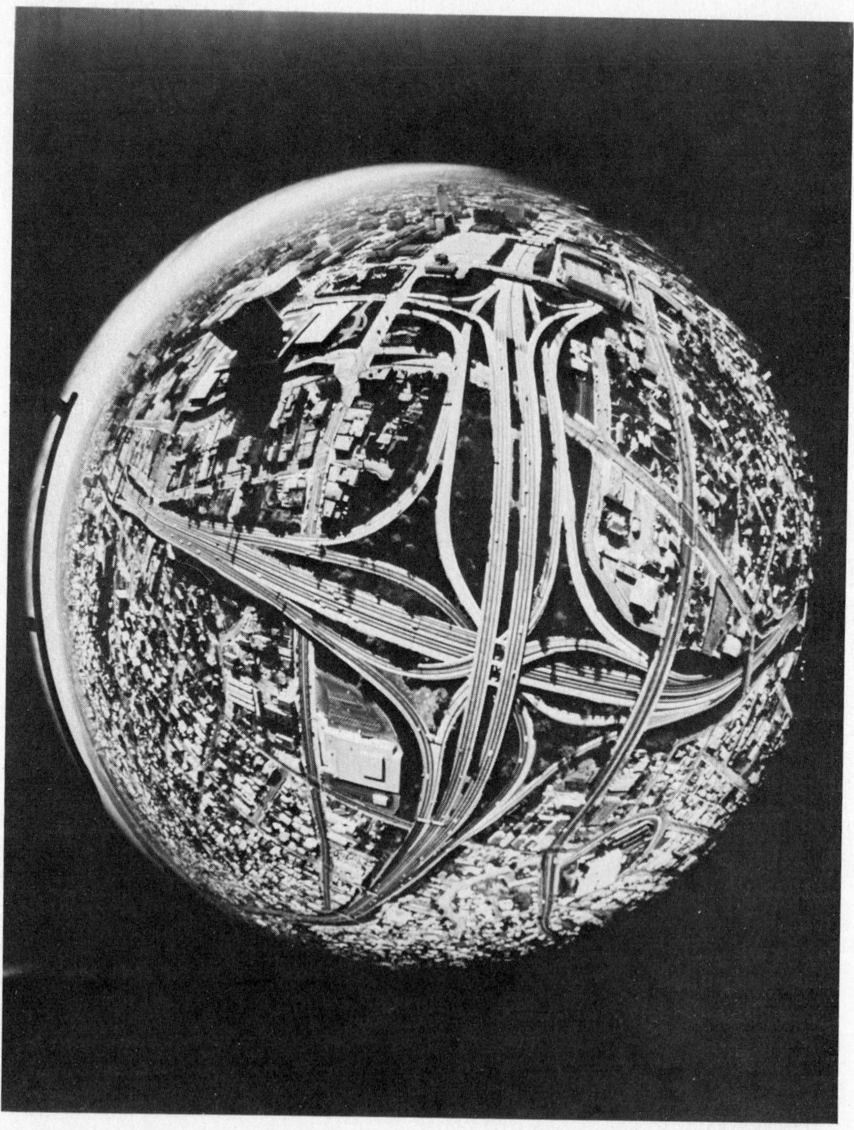

made in Chicago indicated that in 1920 the average distance from home to workplace was 1.5 miles.[4] By 1960 the distance had increased to 4.7 miles.[5] Just at the time that Burgess was expounding his theory of growth from the center through intermediate zones, the automobile and the truck were partially outdating his work.

For instance, trucks were incomparably more flexible than the railroads for short hauls. Trucks were free of fixed routes and fixed schedules, needed no elaborate terminal facilities on expensive inner-city land, and could make door-to-door pickups and deliveries. For all but the longest hauls, the speed of motor trucks was also superior. However, during the 1920s and 1930s the major advantage of motor transport was its lower cost per mile within the first 250 miles of the city.[6] Not only were equipment and maintenance costs far lower, but in truck cartage the cost was lowest for the shortest distances. In train transport, on the other hand, the lowest cost per mile was for the longest trips. The motor truck, then, was by far the superior competitor for the short haul—an advantage that was considerably increased by the public building of new roads, particularly the interstate expressway system.

In the American city of fifty years ago, industry was concentrated in an inner belt located between the CBD and the better residential areas. Many of the factory buildings of this era are still standing—frequently with a "Floor for Rent" sign tacked over the main entrance. As the firm occupying one of these buildings prospered, the original space became more and more crowded. But expansion was both difficult and expensive. Internally, assembly lines or other factory operations had to be fitted into the existing building, and even moving goods from floor to floor became a serious problem. At the same time, external expansion was limited by the cost, both in land and in taxes, of growing horizontally. Surrounding land was already occupied, which meant that whatever was already on the land had to be bought and torn down before the factory could expand. Transportation also became an increasing problem. Trucks had to move down busy city streets before lining up to wait to get into inadequate loading docks. Parking space for workers' cars developed into another major problem.

The move of manufacturing and industry out of the central city was greatly accelerated by the building of interstate superhighways. The building of the interstate expressway system in the 1950s and 1960s gave industry genuine alternatives to central-city locations. Suburban land was cheap, and suburban taxes were low. Most important, the plant could be

[4]Beverly Duncan, "Factors in Work-Residence Separation: Wages and Salary Workers, 1951," *American Sociological Review,* **21**:48–56, 1956.

[5]Amos H. Hawley, *Urban Society,* Ronald Press, New York, 1971, p. 191.

[6]National Resources Committee, *Technological Trends and National Policy,* U. S. Government Printing Office, Washington, D.C., 1937.

designed from the inside out. The assembly line, for example, could be laid out all on one level and then walls simply built around the work space. The size and shape of the building could be determined by the needs of the factory rather than by the size and shape of a lot or an existing plant. Suburban plants were also closer to the homes of executives who lived in the suburbs, and this was another factor encouraging the move of management to the suburbs.

Increasingly, industry has leapfrogged over intermediate city residential areas and moved directly from the inner city to suburban industrial parks. When a firm was serving only local markets, a central-city location, with its ease of access to all parts of a city, made sense. Such a location was even reasonable if the major transport between cities was done by rail. Today, however, firms with national markets usually seek a location on or near an interstate expressway, which is far more valuable than one which gives rapid access to all parts of any single city.

The location of factories in suburbs in turn encouraged workers to move to new suburban tract-type housing developments that were sprouting in the cornfields near the factories. Before long, shopping centers followed; and more and more mixed industrial-residential suburbs were born.

## METROPOLITAN REGION

A result of the technological revolutions in transportation and communication (telephones) was that the metropolitan region, rather than the central city, became the economic unit. Mere spatial distance was no longer the crucial factor; the time needed to get from one point to another within the region became more important. An area with a radius of roughly 25 miles could be within an hour's travel time of the central city, a fact which meant that the possible interactions were multiplied.

As a result of the development of an urban region, smaller previously independent retailing communities either declined in importance or began to perform specialized functions for the larger metropolitan area. Such previously independent communities are called "satellite cities" to distinguish them from suburbs which physically surround the central city. The larger metropolitan unit was seen as organizing the hinterland, mediating exchanges between regions, and, at least before World War II, providing the requisite financial facilities for its own commercial and industrial functions.

Research done by Amos Hawley shows that if a "constant criterion" is used—that is, if changes in the definitions of "metropolitan area" are taken into account—metropolitan areas gained population at a rate far in

**Table 5-1 Growth of Metropolitan and Nonmetropolitan Population**

| Decade | Conterminous United States, total | Constant criterion | | Constant area | |
|---|---|---|---|---|---|
| | | Metro-politan | Nonmetro-politan | Metro-politan | Nonmetro-politan |
| | | Numerical increase, millions | | | |
| 1900–10 | 16.0 | 10.6 | 5.4 | 7.5 | 8.5 |
| 1910–20 | 13.7 | 11.5 | 2.2 | 8.5 | 5.2 |
| 1920–30 | 17.1 | 16.0 | 1.1 | 12.4 | 4.7 |
| 1930–40 | 8.9 | 5.9 | 3.0 | 5.0 | 3.9 |
| 1940–50 | 19.0 | 17.6 | 1.4 | 14.4 | 4.6 |
| 1950–60 | 27.8 | 27.5 | .2 | 21.6 | 6.2 |
| 1960–70 | 20.8 | 22.5 | −1.7 | 15.1 | 5.7 |
| | | Percentage of increase | | | |
| 1900–10 | 21 | 44 | 10 | 31 | 16 |
| 1910–20 | 15 | 33 | 4 | 25 | 9 |
| 1920–30 | 16 | 35 | 2 | 27 | 8 |
| 1930–40 | 7 | 10 | 5 | 8 | 6 |
| 1940–50 | 14 | 26 | 2 | 21 | 7 |
| 1950–60 | 18 | 32 | 0 | 25 | 10 |
| 1960–70 | 12 | 20 | −3 | 13 | 9 |
| | | Percentage distribution of increase | | | |
| 1900–10 | 100 | 66 | 34 | 47 | 53 |
| 1910–20 | 100 | 84 | 16 | 62 | 38 |
| 1920–30 | 100 | 94 | 6 | 72 | 28 |
| 1930–40 | 100 | 66 | 34 | 56 | 44 |
| 1940–50 | 100 | 92 | 8 | 76 | 24 |
| 1950–60 | 100 | 99 | 1 | 78 | 22 |
| 1960–70 | 100 | 108 | −8 | 73 | 27 |

*Source:* Amos H. Hawley, Beverly Duncan and David Goldberg, "Some Observations of Changes in Metropolitan Population in the United States," *Demography,* 1:149, 1964, table 2; and Amos H. Hawley, *Urban Society,* Ronald Press, New York, 1971, p. 154.

excess of nonmetropolitan areas during the period from 1900 to 1970.[7] If this criterion is used, all population growth in the United States, except for Alaska and Hawaii, occurred in metropolitan areas (see Table 5-1). A second measure of growth, the actual increase in the number of people within the area defined as "metropolitan" at the beginning of the decade (listed under the heading "Constant Area" in Table 5-1), shows a somewhat more conservative picture. According to Hawley:

> It may be seen that the amount of increase in metropolitan areas did not exceed that in nonmetropolitan areas until 1910–20; thereafter the rate of growth was more than twice as great in the former in all decades but one, the depression decade of 1930–40. In the last thirty years of the seven-decade

[7]Hawley, op. cit., pp. 153–154.

period, metropolitan areas absorbed three quarters or more of all population increase in continental United States. The decline in the metropolitan growth rate in the 1960–70 decade, assuming the 1970 preliminary figures are indicative, was due very likely to a further enlargement of the area over which metropolitan growth is spread. Such a trend has been gathering momentum since early in the century.[8]

The metropolitan region, or particularly that part of it delimited by daily contact, is sometimes defined in terms of the county-based "Standard Metropolitan Statistical Area" (defined on page 97) and sometimes by other criteria. Some indexes for indicating areas of daily interaction are areas of newspaper circulation, delivery areas of department stores, traffic surveys showing commuting distances, areas of local telephone calls, the proportion of an area's total labor force working in the central city, and the distribution of checking accounts at banks.

Beyond this area of potential daily interaction is a larger metropolitan region which is economically integrated with the central metropolis. Indicators of metropolitan influence include areas of wholesale trade, the volume of long-distance calls to various central cities, the center at which farmers sell truckload lots of produce, and where high school graduates migrate for work. Another socially significant criterion might be which professional football team people root for and watch on television. Generally, population density decreases with distance from the central metropolis, and wholesaling and banking for the entire area tend to be highly concentrated in the metropolis. The metropolis also serves as an administrative center for the major regional corporations and associations.[9]

## DEFINITIONS OF "METROPOLITAN AREA"

The Bureau of the Census uses two concepts to define larger metropolitan areas. The term "Urbanized Area" refers to the actual urban population of an area, regardless of local city, suburban, or county boundary lines. An Urbanized Area is made up of at least one city (or a pair of contiguous twin cities) of 50,000 or more, plus the surrounding densely settled territory, whether incorporated or unincorporated.[10] By convention, the suburban area outside the central city but within the Urbanized Area is known as the "suburban fringe."

[8]Hawley, op cit., p. 154. (Based on Amos H. Hawley, Beverly Duncan, and David Goldberg, "Some Observations of Changes in Metropolitan Population in the U. S.," *Demography,* **1**:148–155, 1964.)

[9]Theodore R. Anderson, "Comparative Urban Structure," *International Encyclopedia of the Social Sciences,* Crowell Collier and Macmillan, New York, 1968, p. 470.

[10]U. S. Bureau of the Census, Census of Population: 1970, *General Social and Economic Characteristics,* Final Report PC(1)-CI, U. S. Government Printing Office, Washington, D.C., 1972, App-3.

The major advantage of the Urbanized Area is that it accurately delimits urban growth regardless of political boundaries such as county and state lines. This is also the major weakness of the concept, for since the Urbanized Area has no permanently fixed boundaries, but rather changes from census to census, doing longitudinal research becomes very difficult. The Urbanized Area of Houston, for example, covered different land areas in 1950, 1960, and 1970. The 1970 census listed 248 Urbanized Areas.

The second concept used to define metropolitan units, the "Standard Metropolitan Statistical Area" (SMSA), is based not on population density but rather on the territory which is economically integrated with the central city. The SMSA is defined as one or more contiguous nonagricultural counties containing at least one city (or pair of cities) with at least 50,000 inhabitants, and having an essentially metropolitan character based on the social and economic integration of the counties with the central city.[11] In general, then, the SMSA includes the county in which the central city is located plus any adjacent counties that are metropolitan in character and socially and economically integrated with the county containing the central city. There were 243 areas designated SMSAs at the time of the 1970 census. Of the fifty states, only Vermont, Wyoming, and Alaska do not have a single SMSA. In addition, both in 1960 and 1970 there were two "super-SMSAs" known as "Standard Consolidated Areas" (SCAs). These are the New York–Northeastern New Jersey SCA and the Chicago–Northwestern Indiana SCA.[12]

There are three advantages to the SMSAs: (1) County boundaries do not usually change from decade to decade. (2) Much census and other information is aggregated on the basis of the county unit, so that data can be compared. (3) The county, more than any other legal subdivision, realistically contains the territory which is integrated with the central city. Thus the SMSA is most useful when the county or counties which it comprises are overwhelmingly urban in social and economic orientation. However, an SMSA usually includes some rural land and some small towns which are not suburbs of the central city. The 1970 census indicated there were some 16 million rural persons in SMSAs. Obviously, such people should not be considered suburban. Thus using entire counties can, at times, exaggerate the extent of metropolitan influence. The most extreme example of this problem is probably San Bernardino County, California: it stretches all the way to the Nevada and Arizona state lines and includes some of the most desolate desert lands in the

[11]U. S. Bureau of the Census, op. cit., App-4.

[12]In January, 1970, two new SCAs were created for the Los Angeles and San Francisco areas; but in October, 1971, this recognition was withdrawn. There are still only two SCAs. *Small-Area Data Notes*, vol. 6, Department of Commerce Bureau of the Census, Washington, D.C., October, 1971, p. 4.

entire country, but nonetheless these sparsely settled lands are part of the SMSA.

Whether the Urbanized Area or the SMSA is the superior unit depends upon the way the metropolitan unit is to be used. The Urbanized Area most effectively measures residential patterns and the actual extent of urban population growth. It is closest to what Europeans call a "conurbation" (unplanned urban sprawl). The outer boundaries of the urbanized area are not artificially or arbitrarily set, as they are with the SMSA.

On the other hand, the SMSA is a better measure of the broader territory which is socially and economically integrated with the central city. Both, however, are attempts to realistically measure different aspects of the social aggregate known as the "metropolitan area" without being confined by the out-of-date political boundaries of the legally defined city and other minor administrative borders of incorporated or unincorporated places.

## DECENTRALIZATION

As was stated in the first paragraph of this chapter, the ecological process of current American urbanization can be described as "implosion" to metropolitan areas and then increasing decentralization within the metropolitan areas. This redistribution began in the larger and older metropolitan areas and then became general for cities of all sizes—except the very newest—after 1920. During the 1920s the outlying areas increased at a rate 50 percent higher than the central city. By the 1950s the growth for outlying areas rates averaged five or more times the rate for the city.[13] As one journalist has put it:

> Business is moving out for a variety of reasons. The explanation immediately after World War II was the attraction of cheap land in the suburbs, permitting single-story factories that were convenient for truck loading. In recent years, the motive is more push than pull. Executives complain about the abominable phone service in many cities, horrendous commuting conditions, rapidly rising crime. Even bomb threats are mentioned, when GT&E actually had a bomb go off in the building, the bosses lost no time in making the final decision to get the hell out. Then there are problems with the work force. Many young women seem to be avoiding the big cities, while young execs no longer consider a move to the New York office a promotion; indeed, they demand differential pay to cover the increased cost of living. There is also the desire to get away from it all, which was one of the big reasons why

[13]Hawley, op. cit., p. 161.

> Xerox moved its top men from Rochester to pastoral Connecticut: the company president felt that they would get a better perspective of the whole company from the new, more isolated locale. But the biggest appeal of the suburbs, of course, is that much of the population, housing and development is there, or headed there.[14]

However, this decentralization has been specific rather than general as regards industrial movement rather than population movement. Decentralization of business and industry to fringe locations has been selective. Operations that require large plants and large amounts of ground space per worker, have a high "nuisance factor" (that is, create noise, pollution, odor, and waste), and need little contact with local buyers tend to be increasingly drawn toward the periphery. Automobile plants, chemical firms, steel mills, and petroleum refineries require large areas of fringe land for their newer operations. Generally, production and distribution have decentralized; and as markets have decentralized, wholesaling has also decentralized, since it needs space as well as access to markets. The use of trucks rather than railroads for transportation also argues for the more flexible outer locations. Rapid transportation provides a form of storage on route.

On the other hand, finance, management, and control have shown far less inclination to decentralize. New York City, for example, lost 42,000 manufacturing jobs between 1947 and 1955; but jobs in corporate offices, finance, insurance, and real estate increased by 28,000.[15] Management, finance, government, and law still remain at the center of the city because they do not require great amounts of space per worker and need access to one another.

Businesses also do not automatically move to the suburbs. In many cases a downtown location makes far more sense. Their services are oriented not to individuals but to other organizations. In the center, communications are easy and informal—business may be conducted over lunch, for example—and there are many services and economies available outside the firm itself. Outside specialists are readily accessible to cover areas such as advertising, legal services, accounting, tax information, and mailing. Firms located on the periphery must provide all sorts of services often not required of those in the center, such as parking lots, cafeterias, and medical services. Top management may also remain in the city so that it does not become isolated from the informal information networks regarding competitors, government policy, and buying patterns that are

[14]R. Cassidy, "Moving to the Suburbs," *New Republic,* **166:**21, January 22, 1972. Reprinted by permission of *The New Republic,* © 1972 Harrison-Blaine of New Jersey, Inc.

[15]Raymond Vernon, "Production and Distribution in the Large Metropolis," *The Annals of American Academy of Political and Social Science,* **314:**25, 1957.

always found when a number of firms in the same sort of business are located in the same spatial area.

Retail trade outlets follow a predictable pattern of distribution. Convenience goods, such as food, and other items which have a high degree of standardization, a low price, a low margin of profit, and rapid turnover tend to be located throughout the entire metropolitan area. Shopping goods which are purchased less frequently, are less standardized (style being a factor), and have higher prices and a higher margin of profit, are usually found clustered. Central shopping districts or peripheral shopping centers provide ideal locations, since they allow customers to "comparison shop." An ideal location for a furniture store is next to similar stores. Automobile dealers also find it is best to be located near their competitors. Luxury goods such as furs and works of art which are rarely purchased and have very high prices are still found downtown or near high-income areas. Since the rate of turnover of such goods is very low and emphasis is on their rarity or uniqueness rather than their standardization, a store site which has easy access from all upper-income areas is desirable. Downtown executive offices also employ people who are a potential market for luxury goods.

There is no question that the central business district has been losing ground as the dominant shopping center. For retail sales of personal and household goods, the outlying shopping malls have gained business as the downtown areas have lost it. In 1972, shopping centers accounted for 44 percent of all sales in personal and household items.[16] Shopping malls have sometimes almost become cities unto themselves. San Jose has an enclosed air-conditioned center which includes 130 stores, 27 restaurants, and 9,000 parking spaces. Houston's "Galeria," which is modeled after a century-old gallery in Milan, Italy, has three levels which in addition to the usual department stores, restaurants, and shops also includes an athletic club with ten air-conditioned tennis courts and a jogging track. (Many college athletic departments would gladly exchange their facilities for those of this shopping mall.) It is connected to two high-rise office buildings and a 404-room hotel. Shopping plazas, with their fountains, film festivals, and wine-tasting contests, have come a long way from the mercantile stores of the last century. The shopping mall is replacing Main Street as the core of the community. Increasingly, the malls serve social as well as commercial functions. Columbia, Maryland, has a mall with a "crisis counseling center" and an Interfaith Center where Protestants, Catholics, and Jews share religious facilities.

Meanwhile, the central business district continues to be the center

[16]"How Shopping Malls Are Changing Life in United States," *U. S. News and World Report*, **74**:43–46, June 18, 1973.

**Table 5-2 Central Business District Retail Sales as Percentage of Metropolitan Retail Sales (by Type of Goods, Selected Metropolitan Areas, 1948 to 1967)**

| Metropolitan area | Convenience goods | | | | | Shopping goods | | | | |
|---|---|---|---|---|---|---|---|---|---|---|
| | 1967 | 1963 | 1958 | 1954 | 1948 | 1967 | 1963 | 1958 | 1954 | 1948 |
| New York | 10.0 | 10.9 | 11.5 | 12.1 | NA | 26.6 | 27.9 | 33.9 | 38.3 | NA |
| Chicago | 3.9 | 4.1 | 4.7 | 5.0 | NA | 15.9 | 18.9 | 23.3 | 28.2 | NA |
| Los Angeles | 1.4 | 1.6 | 2.2 | 2.8 | NA | 6.0 | 7.9 | 11.3 | 15.2 | NA |
| Detroit | 1.9 | 2.6 | 2.9 | 4.2 | 5.8 | 11.7 | 16.1 | 23.0 | 29.9 | 43.8 |
| Philadelphia | 4.8 | 5.5 | 6.0 | 6.6 | 9.0 | 19.1 | 25.5 | 34.6 | 40.3 | 50.6 |
| Baltimore | 3.2 | 3.3 | 4.6 | 6.3 | NA | 18.3 | 21.2 | 33.7 | 42.7 | NA |
| Boston | 4.0 | 5.2 | 5.4 | 6.2 | NA | 21.7 | 27.8 | 34.0 | 42.0 | NA |
| Cleveland | 4.2 | 4.7 | 6.0 | 6.8 | 9.4 | 21.3 | 28.1 | 41.1 | 50.3 | 61.2 |
| Cincinnati | 4.4 | 5.2 | 7.7 | 7.9 | 10.2 | 26.2 | 37.4 | 51.4 | 59.2 | 63.8 |
| San Francisco | 6.3 | 7.7 | 8.2 | 8.6 | NA | 20.0 | 24.1 | 28.9 | 31.4 | NA |
| Milwaukee | 3.3 | 3.6 | 3.7 | 4.5 | NA | 18.7 | 23.9 | 30.1 | 39.6 | NA |
| Minneapolis | 4.6 | 5.2 | 7.3 | 8.6 | NA | 20.6 | 29.8 | 40.1 | 47.0 | NA |
| Dayton | 3.8 | 4.6 | 6.5 | 9.6 | NA | 32.4 | 47.0 | 62.4 | 66.5 | NA |
| Rochester | 4.3 | 6.0 | 9.9 | 12.0 | 15.0 | 35.2 | 45.2 | 65.1 | 75.1 | 79.1 |
| Kansas City | 3.6 | 4.2 | 4.8 | 6.8 | 9.4 | 16.8 | 23.0 | 34.7 | 45.1 | 54.9 |
| Atlanta | 5.6 | 6.7 | 8.3 | 10.2 | NA | 26.1 | 37.5 | 56.8 | 59.7 | NA |
| Birmingham | 7.8 | 9.7 | 12.1 | 14.0 | 18.3 | 38.1 | 50.2 | 62.4 | 70.7 | 72.2 |
| Seattle | 4.5 | 5.5 | 7.6 | 10.3 | NA | 27.2 | 37.5 | 44.5 | 52.4 | NA |
| Denver | 4.3 | 5.4 | 8.0 | 10.2 | NA | 19.2 | 25.5 | 40.4 | 50.5 | NA |
| Austin | 6.3 | 8.0 | 12.1 | 15.1 | 26.1 | 28.0 | 36.8 | 73.9 | 76.9 | 88.1 |

NA means "not available."

*Source:* 1958 Census of Business, *Central Business District Statistics*, Summary Report BC 58-CBD 98, U.S. Census Bureau, Washington, D.C., 1961; *Major Retail Centers*, Summary Report BC 63-MRC-1, Washington, D.C., 1965; *Major Retail Centers in Standard Metropolitan Statistical Areas*, United States Summary BC 67-MRC-1, Washington, D.C., 1967. From Amos H. Hawley *Urban Society: An Ecological Approach*, Ronald Press, New York, 1971, p. 172.

for administrative offices. As long as the downtown area remains, or grows, as a major employment center, it will also be a solid location for retail sales, particularly of the more expensive and fashionable goods. But in general the central business district is changing its preeminent function from shopping to office activity, especially administrative offices.

## MEGALOPOLIS

In the more highly industrialized sections of the world a new and larger supermetropolitan unit, called a "megalopolis," has emerged. The term "megalopolis" refers to the overlapping and interpenetration of previously separate metropolitan areas so that a continuous urbanized land area is created. Where once there was a metropolitan area made up of small towns and cities, there is now emerging a larger area where metropolitan centers are the basic units.

These exploding areas are sometimes referred to as "conurbations," particularly in Britain, where Sir Patrick Geddes coined the term; but in America the term "megalopolis" is more frequently heard. The name *Megalopolis* originally applied to a Greek colonial city that had the ambition, never realized, of becoming the largest and most powerful of the Greek city-states. Today, as a result of the writings of the geographer Jean Gottman, megalopolis has come to mean the overspill of urban areas into one another, as on the Northeastern coast of the United States. According to Gottman's colorful description:

> An almost continuous system of deeply interwoven urban and suburban areas, with a total population of about 37 million people in 1960, has been erected along the Northeastern Atlantic seaboard. It straddles state boundaries, stretches across wide estuaries and bays, and encompasses many regional differences. . . . It is, *on the average,* the richest, best educated, best housed, and best serviced group of similar size (i.e., 25-to-40-million-people range) in the world. . . . It is true that many of its sections have seen pretty rural landscapes replaced by ugly industrial agglomerations or drab and monstrous residential developments; it is true that in many parts of Megalopolis the air is not clean any more, the noise is disturbing day and night, the water is not as pure as one would wish, and transportation at times becomes a nightmare.[17]

The megalopolis along the East Coast of the United States, from the northern suburbs of New York in Connecticut, or even from Boston, to the suburbs of Washington, D.C., now includes a population of over 45 million. This strip city, which is sometimes called "BosWash," includes land covering ten states, the District of Columbia, and hundreds of local governments—land which is predominantly urban. It has an overall population density of more than 2,000 per mile and a median income level more than $1,000 higher than that of the rest of the country.[18] In 1970 New Jersey, much of which is within commuting distance of New York City, displaced Rhode Island as the state with the highest population density—953 people per square mile.

Is the density of this area too high? Certainly some of the commuters in the corridor think so; still, they are not leaving this crowded sector for

[17]Jean Gottman, *Megalopolis: The Urbanized Northeastern Seaboard of the United States.* © 1961 by The Twentieth Century Fund, New York. First published November, 1961. First M.I.T. Press Paperback Edition, February, 1964.

[18]Ansley J. Coale, "Population and Economic Development," in Philip M. Hauser (ed.), *The Population Dilemma,* Prentice-Hall, Englewood Cliffs, N. J., 1969, p. 73.

less densely settled areas of the country. Many of those who complain the loudest would not think of leaving themselves; what they have in mind is other people leaving. Additional megalopolises can be seen forming: from Chicago to Cleveland, or perhaps even Pittsburgh, and on the West Coast from San Francisco to San Diego. As the metropolitan growth of these newer areas increases, the overwhelming dominance of BosWash has declined from over 50 percent of the nation's total metropolitan population to less than 30 percent (although its size has not declined). The remaining years of this century should see these new megalopolises take on a more definite shape and form.

It is still an open question whether true supercommunities are emerging in the megalopolises or whether they are merely configurations of metropolises that share a common geographic area. On the basis of a selected analysis of thirty-one metropolises within the area Gottman described, Robert Weller concludes:

> There is but limited evidence of increasing economic interdependence among the metropolitan areas of Megalopolis. If anything their labor forces have become more homogeneous. One must therefore question the validity of concepts like Megalopolis as representing a new community form and ecological unit and consider them as clusters of large, contiguous cities until some evidence is made available to support the Megalopolis concept.[19]

The whole question of whether the megalopolis is indeed a new form remains open to further research and debate. It is, however, significant that weather reports in Washington, D.C., commonly also give the weather in the "commuter cities," which include not only New York and Boston (as expected) but increasingly frequently also Chicago. Numerous air shuttles tie all these cities together: a commuter between New York and Chicago, for example, is able to catch a flight in either direction almost every half hour from dawn to dusk. It is one of the peculiarities of modern life that the air shuttles from city to city offer better, more frequent, and even faster transportation than that available between some parts of a single metropolitan area.

## THE FUNCTION SPECIALIZATION OF CITIES

Even casual observation confirms the idea that the placement of cities over the landscape is anything but random. Large cities are overwhelmingly located on major bodies of water or on major navigable rivers.

[19]Robert H. Weller, "An Empirical Examination of Metropolitan Structure," *Demography*, **4**:743, 1967.

Historically, two other environmental considerations—suitability for defense and the fertility of the surrounding hinterland—also greatly influenced the location of cities. Only during the last century or so has it been possible for factors pertaining to technology and social organization to outweigh environmental considerations. Cities such as the Brazilian capital, Brasilia, located 600 miles inland from the coast in an area without roads, were impossible before modern transportation. During the initial stages of its growth Brasilia could be reached only by air, and in recognition of the role played by technology in its founding, the city was planned to resemble the shape of an airplane.

## ECONOMIC-ACTIVITIES DIVISION

The location of cities is related to the various economic functions they perform. Numerous activities, such as the distribution of food, are common to all cities; these are called "service activities." There are other activities which are concentrated in only some cities. The size of a particular city is related to its occupational-industrial composition. Very large cities tend to be quite diversified in terms of their economic activities.[20]

### A Seven-Category Division

The most widely used classification of the economic function of cities is that developed by the geographer Chauncy Harris.[21] Several revisions have been made over the years. Basically, each of the nation's cities of over 10,000 persons is placed in one of seven categories according to its dominant function. The major categories are "manufacturing," "diversified-manufacturing," "industrial," "retailing," "diversified-retailing," "dormitory," and "specialized."[22]

Over 40 percent of the SMSA fall into the "manufacturing" class. This includes most of the large midwestern cities, such as Chicago, Cleveland, Detroit, Milwaukee, and St. Louis. Larger cities elsewhere tend to be more diversified; over half the nation's cities with populations of over 500,000 are listed as "diversified-manufacturing."[23] Boston, New York, Dallas, and Los Angeles are in this category. The pattern is for

[20]Otis D. Duncan et al., *Metropolis and Region,* Johns Hopkins Press, Baltimore, 1960.

[21]Chauncy Harris, "A Functional Classification of Cities in the United States," *Geographical Review,* **33**:86–99, January, 1943.

[22]Richard L. Forstall, "Economic Classification of Places over 10,000," *Municipal Year Book: 1967,* International City Managers Association, Chicago, 1967.

[23]John C. Bollens and Henry J. Schmandt, *The Metropolis,* Harper and Row, New York, 1970, p. 74.

manufacturing and diversified-manufacturing cities to be most concentrated in the Northeast and the Midwest.

"Industrial" cities, contrary to what one might think, are found among the smaller urban places, and their number has been decreasing over the years. There are now only 74 places (such as Dubuque, Iowa) which are classified as "industrial." "Diversified-retailing" cities are most common in the South. There are only four such cities with over 500,000 inhabitants: New Orleans, Phoenix, San Antonio, and San Francisco. "Retailing" cities are most common in the South and the West, principally in less industrialized areas, where they serve as trading centers for agricultural hinterlands. Aberdeen, South Dakota, is an example. The "dormitory" towns are found as suburbs surrounding every great city. "Specialized-function" cities—such as university towns—provide specific services, as their name suggests. The only really large city in this category is Washington, D.C.[24]

### A Three-Category Division

Another, even simpler, system divides cities into three categories: those serving as central places, those serving as transportation nodes where there is a break-in-bulk (that is, where goods must be transferred from one carrier to another, as when wheat is loaded from freight cars onto ships), and those serving specialized functions. The geographers Harris and Ullman have given this description:

> **1** Cities as central places performing comprehensive services for a surrounding area. Such cities tend to be evenly spaced throughout productive territory. For the moment this may be considered the "norm" subject to variation primarily in response to the ensuing factors.
>
> **2** Transport cities performing break-of-bulk and allied services along transport routes, supported by areas which may be remote and distant but close in connection because of the city's strategic location on transport channels. Such cities tend to be arranged in linear patterns along rail lines or at coasts.
>
> **3** Specialized-function cities performing one service such as mining, manufacturing, or recreation for large areas, including the general tributary areas of hosts of other cities. Since the principal localizing factor is often a particular resource such as coal, water power, or a beach, such cities may occur singly or in clusters.[25]

[24]For the question of the function of cities, see: Robert C. Atchley, "A Size-Function Typology of Cities," *Demography,* **4**:721–733, 1967; Otis D. Duncan et al., *Metropolis and Region,* Johns Hopkins Press, Baltimore, 1960; Jeffrey K. Hadden and Edgar F. Borgatta, *American Cities,* Rand McNally, New York, 1965; Albert J. Reiss, Jr., "Functional Specialization of Cities," in Paul K. Hatt and Albert J. Reiss, Jr. (eds.), *Cities and Society,* Free Press, New York, 1957, pp. 555–575.

[25]Chauncey D. Harris and Edward L. Ullman, "The Nature of Cities," *The Annals,* **242**:8, November, 1945.

The first of the above categories, central-place theory, was developed largely in Europe by scholars such as von Thünen, Losch, and Christaller in order to explain the fairly regular pattern of cities in nineteenth-century Europe. The trouble is that although the model, which posits the city as providing trade and services for a tributary hinterland, roughly fits agricultural nonindustrial areas, and even parts of the American Midwest it does not really predict the location of industrial cities. And because it assumes a relatively flat terrain, it cannot deal with the often important influence of typography on urban location.

Cities in the second category, transportation centers, are likely to be located at deepwater ports or where a break-in-bulk occurs (e.g., Salt Lake City). The focusing of transportation routes alone does not produce a city, but if a break in transit occurs, the point of focus becomes a natural place to process goods.[26] The first five major American cities were all deepwater ports, and even Chicago, in the interior, has direct access to the sea and to Europe through the Great Lakes and the St. Lawrence Seaway.

Finally, cities in the third category arise because they serve as concentration points for specific purposes. The discovery of coal created Scranton and Wilkes-Barre; and the history of Western mining towns such as Virginia City is well known. Las Vegas and Miami Beach specialize in tourist services; Rochester, Minnesota, with its Mayo Clinic, provides health services. The specialized function of the city frequently has a direct effect on the socioeconomic status of the population. Madison, Wisconsin, with its university, insurance, and governmental functions has a vastly different social composition from a city such as Gary, Indiana, which is built upon the economy of the steel mills.

## THE ECOLOGICAL COMPLEX

One of the more stimulating recent developments in human ecology is the attempt by Otis Dudley Duncan to extend the conceptual scheme of the ecosystem to social-ecological research.[27] An "ecosystem" can be defined as a natural unit in which there is an interaction of an environmental and a biotic system: that is, a community together with its habitat. At the upper extreme, the whole earth is a world ecosystem. Earlier chapters in this book have been implicitly organized by means of the ecosystem

[26] C. H. Colley, "The Theory of Transportation," *Publications of the American Economics Association,* **9:**1–148, May, 1894.

[27] Otis Dudley Duncan, "From Social System to Ecosystem," *Sociological Inquiry,* **31:**140–149, 1961.

Miami Beach, Florida, is a prime example of a specialized-function city. *(Don Rutledge/Black Star.)*

approach of the interactions of environment, population, technology, and social organization.[28]

Urban ecologists study urban growth patterns in terms of changes in the system using a set of categories known as the "ecological complex." In basic terms the ecological complex identifies the relationship between four concepts or classes of variables: population, social organization, environment and technology. The ecological complex thus reminds us of the interrelated properties of life in urban settings and how each class of variables is related to and has implications for the others. In sociological research, organization is commonly viewed as the "dependent variable" to be influenced by the other three "independent variables"; but a more sophisticated view of organization is to see it as reciprocally related to the other elements of the ecological complex.[29] In Duncan's words: "These categories: population, organization, environment, and technology (P.O.E.T.), provide a somewhat arbitrary simplified way of identifying systems of relationships in a preliminary description of ecosystem process."[30]

A major advantage of the ecological complex as a conceptual scheme is its simplicity, since economy of explanation is a basic scientific goal. The categories themselves are somewhat arbitrary, so the boundary between them is not always precise—particularly the boundary between technology and social organization.

Thus, if our interest is in social organization as the dependent variable—the thing to be explained—our focus is on how population, technology, and environment operate singly and jointly in the modification of urban social organization. Duncan, for example, using the example of smog in Los Angeles, suggests that as transportation technology changed, the environment, organization, and population of the city also changed. In Los Angeles a favorable natural environment led to large-scale increases in population, which resulted in organizational problems (civic and governmental) and technological changes (freeways and factories). These in turn led to environmental changes (smog), which resulted in organizational changes (new pollution laws), which in turn resulted in technological changes (antipollution devices on automobiles).

This example illustrates how sociologists can use the conceptual scheme of the ecological complex to clarify significant sets of variables when studying urban growth patterns.[31]

[28]See Lee R. Dice, *Man's Nature and Nature's Man: The Ecology of Human Communities*, University of Michigan Press, Ann Arbor, 1955, pp. 2–3.

[29]Otis Dudley Duncan and Leo Schnore, "Cultural, Behavioral, and Ecological Perspectives in the Study of Social Organizations," *American Journal of Sociology*, **65:**136, September, 1959.

[30]Duncan, "From Social System to Ecosystem," p. 145.

[31]For further discussion and use of the ecological complex see J. John Palen and Karl Flaming, *Urban America*, Holt, Rinehart and Winston, New York, 1972.

## A NOTE ON ECOLOGICAL CORRELATION

Sometime in his academic career the student is likely to hear the terms "ecological correlations" and "ecological fallacy" tossed around. Here, in nonstatistical language, is what these terms mean.

A "correlation" is the amount of statistical relationship between two variables. Such a correlation between groups—as opposed to correlations at the psychological level, between individuals—is known as an "ecological correlation." It is so named because the aggregates being correlated are most often defined in terms of where they are located. This is quite legitimate and useful.

Politicians have long understood the importance of ecological correlations. Congressmen are well aware that districts with certain demographic characteristics (age, income, occupation, education, religion, ethnic membership) are likely to vote in certain predictable ways. The successful politician isn't as much concerned with how these characteristics combine in various individuals as he is in the demographic characteristics of the *district*. Insurance companies have the same type of interest in the characteristics of groups rather than individuals. Insurance rates are based on membership in certain groups classified by age, sex, marital status, and occupation.

The problem is that people occasionally misinterpret ecological correlations, thinking they say something about individuals. This misinterpretation is known as the "ecological fallacy." It happens when one makes correlations between characteristics of groups and then goes on to suggest that they say something about the association among these variables for a given individual. W. S. Robinson, for example, points out that using data from the census of 1930 one gets a high correlation ($r = .773$) between the percentage of Negroes in each state of the United States and percentage of illiterates in the same state.[32] To some this might suggest a high correlation between being black and being illiterate. However, when one uses the same source of data and identifies individuals separately, there is only a very low correlation ($r = .203$) between race and illiteracy. The high *ecological* correlation thus says very little about *individuals*. In this particular case, the high ecological correlation reflects the fact that the Southern states with the highest proportion of Negroes also had the highest proportion of illiterate whites.

To sum up, ecological correlations are useful when the concern is with groups or aggregates; individual correlations are useful when the concern is with the individual. Neither can do the job designed for the other.

[32]W. S. Robinson, "Ecological Correlations and the Behavior of Individuals," *American Sociological Review*, **15**:351–357, June, 1950.

Chapter 6

# Life-Styles: The City

*The din of the Market increases upon me; and that, with frequent interruptions, has made me say some things twice over.*

Benjamin Franklin

Cities differ from towns and rural areas not only in their size and patterns of economic activities, but also in their tone, texture, and pace. Heterogeneity, variety, and change are assumed, as is a potpourri of different occupations, social classes, cultural backgrounds, and interests.

In New York, Chicago, or a score of other cities, one can walk in a few blocks from luxurious high-rises to decaying tenements; around the corner from fashionable shops are cheap novelty and souvenir stores; changes are frequent and sometimes brutal.

> The city has more wealth than the country, more skill, more erudition within its bounds, more initiative, more philanthropy, more science, more divorces,

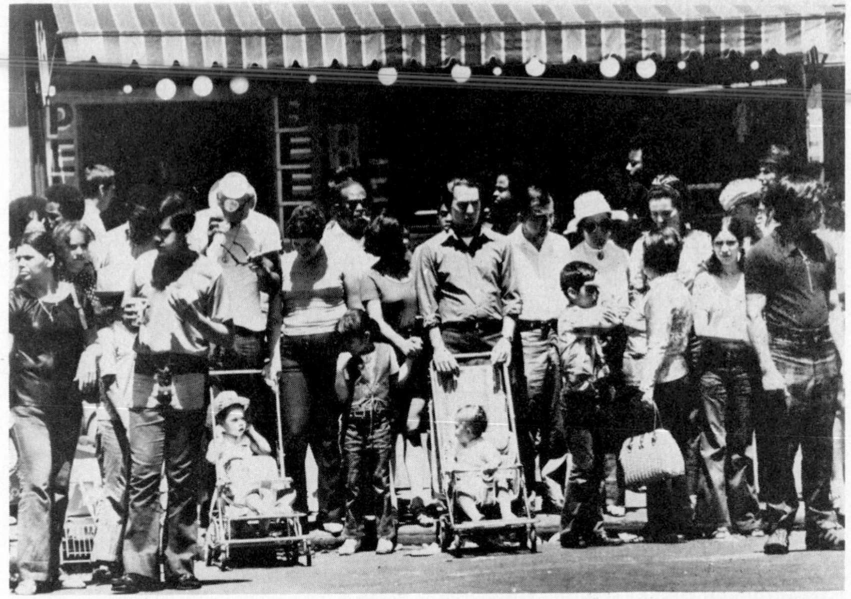

Growing up in a city, one takes ethnic and racial diversity for granted. *(Above: Charles Gatewood; below: Mary Doody.)*

> more aliens, more births and deaths, more accidents, more rich, more poor, more wise men and more fools.[1]

The city dweller, however, rarely thinks about such things; he or she accepts the infinite variety as part of the normal order of the universe. The contrasts of the city are taken for granted.

Innovation or change, particularly in the economic and technological spheres, is not only tolerated in the city; it is actively rewarded. As the sociologist Louis Wirth wrote in his classic article "Urbanism as a Way of Life":

> The city has been the melting-pot of races, peoples, and cultures, and a most favorable breeding-ground of new biological and cultural hybrids. It has not only tolerated but rewarded individual differences. It has brought together people from the ends of the earth *because* they are different and thus useful to one another, rather than because they are homogeneous and like-minded.[2]

The city creates a distinct way of life, called "urbanism," which is reflected in how people dress and speak, what they believe about the social world, what they consider worth achieving, what they do for a living, where they live, whom they associate with, and why they interact with other people.

Wirth suggested that urbanization and its components—size, density, and heterogeneity—are the independent variables which determine urbanism, that is, urban life-styles. Moreover, the relationship is linear; the larger, denser, and more heterogeneous the city, the more prevalent urbanism as a way of life. As Wirth stated it:

> The central problem of the sociologist of the city is to discover the forms of social action and organization that typically emerge in relatively, permanent, compact settlements of large numbers of heterogeneous individuals. . . .
>
> Thus the larger, the more densely populated and the more heterogeneous a community, the more accentuated the characteristics associated with urbanism will be.[3]

## CITY VERSUS COUNTRY

A comparison between city and country, whether explicit or implicit, was very much a part of urban studies and writings before World War II. The terms used to define the dichotomy sometimes differed, but the underly-

[1]William B. Munro, "City," *Encyclopedia of the Social Sciences*, Macmillan, New York, 1930, p. 474.

[2]Louis Wirth, "Urbanism as a Way of Life," *American Journal of Sociology*, **44**:10, July, 1938.

[3]Wirth, op. cit., p. 9.

ing content remained remarkably similar; the country represented simplicity, the city complexity. Rural areas were typified by stable rules, roles, and relationships, while the city was characterized by innovation, change, and disorganization. The city was the center of variety, heterogeneity, and social novelty, while the countryside or small town represented tradition, social continuity, and cultural conformity. The stereotype also included a view of city people as possessing greater sophistication but less real warmth and feeling. The idea of the "superficiality" and "impersonality" of city life as compared with the life of "real folks" in rural areas, who care about their neighbors, is still encountered today; it may even be seen in urban television commercials.

## THEORETICAL SCHEMES

### European Theory

In their attempts to explain emerging forms of social organization, descriptive studies of the 1920s and 1930s were at least implicitly responding to the various ideas that had been propounded by European social theorists as explanations of the momentous social changes which seemed to accompany urbanization. These changes were frequently presented in terms of logical constructs which sociologists refer to as "ideal-types." Among the most noteworthy of these dichotomies, in terms of its impact upon later urban research, was Ferdinand Tönnies' elaborate description of the shift from *Gemeinschaft*—a community where ties were based upon kinship—to *Gesellschaft*—a society based on common economic, political, and other interests. Equally important was the division formulated by the German social theorist Max Weber between "traditional society" and "rational society" and Emile Durkheim's distinction between societies based on "mechanical solidarity" and those based on "organic solidarity." Durkheim's distinction, which is the difference between societies based on shared sentiments and tasks and those based on the integrating of complementary but different economic and social functions, has probably had the greatest impact on urban theory.[4] Even Marx and Engels discussed the dichotomy between the urban and the rural.

> The greatest division of material and mental labour is the separation of town and country. The antagonism between town and country begins with the transition from barbarism to civilization, from tribe to State, from locality to

[4]For a discussion of this and related points, see Paul Wheatley, "The Concept of Urbanism," in Peter Ucko, Ruth Tringham, and G. W. Dimbleby (eds.), *Man Settlement and Urbanism*, Schenkman, Cambridge, Mass., 1972, pp. 602–637.

> nation, and runs through the whole history of civilization to present day (the Anti-Corn Law League).
>
> The existence of the town implies, at the same time, the necessity of administration, police, taxes, etc., in short, of the municipality, and thus of politics in general. Here first became the division of the population into two great classes, which is directly based on the division of labour and on the instruments of production.[5]

Commonly such comparisons had an implicit time frame, in which rural areas represented the past—sometimes in a glorified form ("the good old days")—and the city represented the future, with its technology and division of labor. But there is nothing particularly modern in this dichotomy. The names "pagan" and "heathen" originally referred to rural people, while the adjective "urbane" and the noun "citizen" are derived from Latin and Greek terms for "city."

The common thread running throughout all the formulations is that the city produces a characteristic mode of life natural and unique to all urban places. "Weber, Simmel, and Spengler all assumed the characteristics of city culture—the large impersonal bureaucracies, the rule of rational exchange and rational law, the lack of warm personal contact between city men—to be qualities that pertain to the city *as a whole.*"[6]

### American Application

The so-called "Chicago School" of sociology developed out of a particularly active group of scholars assembled at the University of Chicago and concerned with change induced by urbanization. Some of their writings on such diverse phenomena as juvenile delinquency, organized vice, ethnic community ghettos, and the nature of the city's ecological growth have become sociological classics. Writings of the 1920s such as *The Ghetto* (Wirth), *The Gold Coast and the Slum* (Zorbaugh), and *The Polish Peasant in Europe and America* (Thomas and Znaneicki) are descriptive gems giving insights into this unique period in the urbanization of the United States.[7]

One of the better-known formulations of the dichotomy between urban and rural places and the characteristics common to each was that of the anthropologist Robert Redfield, based upon his study between what

[5]From Karl Marx and Friedrich Engels, *The German Ideology*, R. Pascal (ed.), International Publishers Company, New York, 1947, pp. 68–69.

[6]Richard Sennett, *Classic Essays on the Culture of Cities*, Appleton, New York, 1969, p. 12.

[7]Louis Wirth, *The Ghetto*, University of Chicago Press, Chicago, 1928; Harvey W. Zorbaugh, *The Gold Coast and the Slum*, University of Chicago Press, Chicago, 1929; William I. Thomas and Florian Znaniecki, *The Polish Peasant in Europe and America*, 5 vols., University of Chicago Press, Chicago, 1918–1920.

he called "folk" and "urban" societies in Latin America. Redfield never did define "urban life," saying simply that it was the opposite of folk or peasant society. He characterized peasant society thus:

> . . . small, isolated, non-literate, and homogeneous, with a strong sense of group solidarity. The ways of living are conventionalized into that coherent system which we call "a culture." Behavior is traditional, spontaneous, uncritical, and personal; there is no legislation, or habit of experiment and reflection for intellectual ends. Kinship, its relationships and institutions, are the type categories of experience and the familial group is the unit of action. The sacred prevails over the secular; the economy is one of status rather than market.[8]

A few years later (1954) Redfield and Milton Singer developed a more sophisticated typology of urban forms that distinguished between cities whose economic institutions were subordinate to religious and traditional norms and those where change and the economic marketplace played major roles. In cities of the first type, the moral order was defined by a literate hierarchy that was guided by tradition. The city was said to play an "orthogenetic" role, in that its function was to pass on the customs and beliefs of the past. The function of the orthogenetic city was administrative and political-religious, with an emphasis on refining and embellishing existing modes of life. Cities of the second type played a "heterogenetic" role, which emphasized rationality, technical criteria, and the economic demands of the marketplace; tradition and custom were subordinate. Redfield and Singer said that change and conflict which were central to the heterogenetic role led to painful discontinuities between past and future and to anomie and alienation among the population.[9]

### The Limitations of Logical Constructs

The problem with such logical constructs is that they are of only limited utility in empirical research. The opposed categories are so all-encompassing that they tend to result in considerable oversimplification. A related problem is that we often forget that ideal types are created by abstracting certain elements and deliberately heightening their significance, while other elements or factors are ignored. Unfortunately the constructs are sometimes treated not as theoretical formulations but as if they actually exist.

Real life is more complex than such simple constructs, as research on

[8]Robert Redfield, "The Folk Society," *American Journal of Sociology*, **52**:53–73, 1947.

[9]Robert Redfield and Milton Singer, "The Cultural Role of Cities," *Economic Development and Cultural Change*, **3**:53–77, 1954.

developing countries amply testifies. It is quite possible for a city dweller to base his economic decisions on modern economic theory and principles while at the same time controlling his family life according to established traditional principles. Real people rarely fall into neat all-or-nothing categories. Nor can urbanism be territorially limited to a certain geographic area. As Louis Wirth stated, "As long as we identify urbanism with the physical entity of the city, viewing it merely as rigidly delimited in space, and proceed as if urban attributes abruptly ceased to be manifested beyond an arbitrary line, we are not likely to arrive at any adequate conception of urbanism as a mode of life."[10]

## STIMULATION, SOPHISTICATION, AND OVERLOAD

Until recently it was assumed by most sociologists—as well as by observers going back to de Tocqueville—that in the complex goal-oriented city simpler customs and beliefs would be swept away. On the positive side, this would mean a more rational society; on the negative side, it was prophesied that calculated sophistication would replace close and meaningful relationships. Frequently the effects of the city were expressed in social-psychological terms, as in a famous article by Georg Simmel, "Metropolis and Mental Life," where he suggests that the pace of city life and the overwhelming number of stimuli in the city result in a state of mental overstimulation and excitement.

Simmel said that there is a constant nervous stimulation produced by shifting internal and external situations and that the city dweller has difficulty in maintaining an integrated personality in a social situation where the reference points are constantly changing: as a result, he seeks to protect himself by anonymity and sophistication. Calculating expediency takes the place of affective feelings and personal relationships. One is forced to become blasé in the urban environment in order to protect her or his psyche from overstimulation.

> If so many inner reactions were responses to the continuous external contacts with innumerable people as are those in the small town, where one knows almost everybody one meets and where one has a positive relation to almost everyone, one would be completely atomized internally and come to an unimaginable psychic state.[11]

Contemporary reformulations of Simmel's belief that the city pro-

[10]Wirth, "Urbanism as a Way of Life," p. 4.

[11]Georg Simmel, *The Sociology of Georg Simmel,* trans. Kurt H. Wolff, Free Press, Glencoe, Ill., 1950, p. 415.

duces "nervous stimulation" among its inhabitants, and of Wirth's views on the socially disorganizing and disruptive effects of urbanism as a way of life, can be found in Alvin Toffler's popular book *Future Shock*[12] and in the use of the concept of "psychic overload."[13] The term "overload" comes from systems analysis, where an overload is said to occur when a system cannot process inputs, because they are coming too fast or because there are too many of them. Under such circumstances, adaptations occur.

### Coping

Among urban dwellers there are several possible responses to overload. First, less time can be given to each input. The brusqueness of city dwellers is part of the common culture. Second, inputs of low priority can be disregarded. The urbanite "doesn't see" others walking in a crowd or the drunk sitting on the curb. Third, the burden of responsibility in a transaction can be shifted to the other person. The bus driver is no longer expected to provide change; this is the responsibility of the rider. Fourth, reception can be blocked off before the system is entered. The telephone number is unlisted and the door is always locked; an unfriendly scowl can effectively prevent others from approaching. Fifth, the intensity of inputs can be reduced by means of filtering devices that keep all inputs at a relatively low level. Sixth, special institutions such as welfare departments can be created to handle specific problems, so that individuals can ignore them. All these mechanisms of noninvolvement help to prevent constant psychic overload; they also explain the supposed coldness and detachment of city dwellers.

This supposed detachment can also be seen as the city dweller's acceptance of new standards of noninvolvement. People do not implicate themselves in each other's affairs and do not interfere in each other's lives: these tenets are so well defined as a part of urban life that people are reluctant to violate them. City dwellers do not have colder personalities than ruralites. In fact, the coolness and even overt hostility of small-towners to "outsiders" who act, dress, or think differently has long been a theme of American drama, from Sinclair Lewis's *Main Street* through the movie *Easy Rider.* In both city and country, people respond with warmth and familiarity to those they know and are more guarded with others.

Certainly urban densities offer an unparalleled number of contacts with others. It has been calculated that in Nassau County, a suburb of New York City, a person can meet 11,000 others within a ten-minute

[12]Random House, New York, 1970.
[13]Stanley Milgram, "The Experience of Living in Cities," *Science,* **167:**1461–1468, March 13, 1970.

radius of his office by foot or car. In Newark he can meet 20,000 persons within this radius, and within midtown Manhattan he can meet 220,000. In such places it is also quite possible that a person would not know a single one of these thousands of others. On the other hand, it is quite unlikely that someone in a small town could walk downtown for ten minutes without running into several persons he or she knew. The potentialities of urban interaction quite frequently remain unfulfilled. Nor do most urban dwellers seek to realize these potentialities. As Anthony Downs has expressed it:

> It is true that some people want themselves and their children to be immersed in a wide variety of viewpoints, values, and types of people, rather than a relatively homogeneous group. This desire is particularly strong among the intellectuals who dominate the urban planning profession. They are also the strongest supporters of big-city life and the most vitriolic critics of suburbia. Yet I believe their viewpoint—though dominant in recent public discussions of urban problems—is actually shared by only a tiny minority of Americans of any racial group. Almost everyone favors at least some exposure to a wide variety of viewpoints. But experience in our own society and most others shows that the overwhelming majority of middle-class families choose residential locations and schools precisely in order to provide the kind of value-reinforcing experience described above. This is why most Jews live in predominantly Jewish neighborhoods, even in suburbs; why Catholic parents continue to support separate school systems; and partly why so few middle-class Negro families have been willing to risk moving to all-white suburbs even where there is almost no threat of any harassment.[14]

It should be noted that while it might be reasonable to argue that most upper-middle and middle class families chose "people like us" as neighbors, it is not reasonable to imply that the poor and minorities have similar choices regarding residence in ghettos.

### Role Playing

In practice most of us do not find that urban life involves overwhelming stimulation. We have learned to function in the urban environment by placing our experiences in a limited set of categories which require relatively preset responses. Thus we respond to the bus driver not as a total individual but in his limited role as a driver of a bus. If we have any conversation with him—which is doubtful, since regulations forbid it—it will probably be restricted to the bad weather or the bad traffic. We don't

[14]Anthony Downs, "Alternative Futures for the American Ghetto," in John Walton and Donald E. Carns (eds.), *Cities in Change: Studies on the Urban Condition,* copyright © 1973 by Allyn and Bacon, Boston, pp. 668, 669.

expect the bus driver to discuss his family problems—cab drivers may, but never bus drivers. The overwhelming number of our daily contacts with others are carried on with both players clearly understanding the roles they are playing and the rules governing the situation. Whether in a small town or in a large city, the daily pattern of life for most of us is highly predictable. Only when other persons behave in an unpredictable manner do we become flustered. The television show "Candid Camera" has made a small fortune demonstrating what happens when other people do not behave in a predictable manner. Because such situations are so rare, we frequently are at a loss as to what to do in them—with predictably funny results for the viewer. Of course, if someone constantly does unpredictable things, we have a way of categorizing that as well—we say he is crazy and lock him up.

### Tolerance

City people are relatively tolerant of different or deviant behavior. This is not because they are some special type of superliberals but because life in the city encourages the development of a "live and let live" attitude. Hard hats, Jesus freaks, homosexuals, and straights all must make accommodations and compromises in order to maintain a reasonable degree of peace, stability, and safety.

Howard Becker and Irving Horowitz refer to this casual and relatively unconcerned approach to social deviance which is not physically threatening to others as "the culture of civility."[15] They suggest that San Francisco as a city best typifies the cosmopolitanism that doesn't want its Italians, Russians, or Chinese to become standard Americans but prefers differences to be retained—ethnically, religiously, and particularly in the culinary arts. San Francisco, they suggest, emphasizes sophisticated livability which thrives on a mosaic of life-styles.

Becker and Horowitz speculate that there are a number of reasons why a culture of civility has arisen in San Francisco. First, San Francisco has always been a major seaport and has long tolerated the vices that cater to the sailors' needs. Its history is one of redefining conventional social controls. Secondly, the working class, usually the least tolerant segment of the population, is more libertarian and politically sophisticated than is true elsewhere. Finally, San Francisco is oriented toward single people, and as a consequence people worry less about what deviance will do to children. White middle-class families, the usual guardians of public morality, are less dominant than elsewhere.

This picture of San Francisco may be rather overdrawn and stereo-

[15]Howard S. Becker and Irving Louis Horowitz, "The Culture of Civility: San Francisco," *Trans-Action*, April, 1970, pp. 12–19.

typed, but Becker and Horowitz do note that toleration and accommodation have their limit—the point where the majority of the population feels that things have gotten "out of hand." San Francisco cracked down hard on the Haight-Ashbury scene after an influx of out-of-towners began and violence and hard drugs became commonplace. Toleration is given only to those dissenters or deviants who in effect are willing to compromise to be "reasonable." For urban dwellers, the price of civility is not getting everything you want.

## SOCIAL DISORGANIZATION

Given the momentous changes taking place in the growing, immigrant-crowded, industrializing cities of the first part of this century it is not surprising that writers on the city tended to emphasize the negative rather than the positive aspects of urban change. The alienation, atomization, and social isolation of the city were stressed in studies dealing with juvenile delinquency, suicide, mental illness, and divorce, and a whole subfield was developed in sociology under the value-loaded title "social disorganization."

Wirth summed up the prevalent view of the influence of the city on the lives of its inhabitants when he said:

> The distinctive features of the urban mode of life have often been described sociologically as consisting of the substitution of secondary for primary contacts, the weakening of bonds of kinship, and the declining social significance of the family, the disappearance of the neighborhood, and the undermining of the traditional basis of social solidarity.[16]

The effect of urban patterns on institutions such as the family can be severe. As Neil Smelser has put it:

> One consequence of the removal of economic activities from the family-community setting is that the family itself loses some of its previous functions and becomes a more specialized agency. As the family ceases to be an economic unit of production, one or more members leave the household to seek employment in the labor market. The family's activities become more concentrated on emotional gratification and socialization. . . .
>
> The social implications of these changes in family life are enormous. The most fundamental of these implications—imposed mainly by the demands for mobility of the family—is the individuation and isolation of the nuclear family. If the family has to move about through the labor market, it cannot

[16]Wirth, "Urbanism as a Way of Life," pp. 20, 21.

Isolation in the city can be particularly severe for the aged. *(Charles Gatewood.)*

> afford to carry all of its relatives with it, or even to maintain close, diffuse ties with extended kin. Thus the ties with collateral kinsmen begin to erode; few generations live in the same household; newly married couples set up new households, and leave the elders behind.[17]

City life was thought to be so tension-filled and disruptive that until the baby boom after World War II it was universally accepted that cities grew only because of in-migration. It was agreed that cities did not create families that reproduce themselves, because the very nature of urban life was opposed to family life and the rearing of children. Writing in the late 1930s, the prestigious National Resource Committee foresaw a marked decline in urban growth rates, for "if the larger cities are to grow or even to maintain themselves their population must be recruited in the future to an increasing extent from other communities." Further, since foreign immigration had been curtailed and rural birth rates were also down, it was thought likely that "we must ultimately face the prospect of declining population not only in the city but in the Nation as well, or we must attempt to reverse the trend toward urbanization."[18]

Today conventional wisdom still holds that cities, and particularly the inner areas of cities, are sliding downhill, with increasing rates of crime, delinquency, desertion, drugs, and immorality. On every side one reads or hears of the "crisis of the cities," usually with a great deal of information documenting the catastrophe at hand. As Scott Greer, a critic of this view, puts it, "A very common image of cities in the United States is that of disorder, regression, decadence—in short, disorganization."[19]

## REEVALUATION

We now know that the sociologists of Wirth's day (the 1930s), in their fascination with the socially disorganizing aspects of urban life, largely overlooked the role of the city as a social integrator and underestimated the strength of traditional ways of life. William F. Whyte's excellent study of street life in an Italian slum of Boston just before World War II was one of the very few to stress the sociocultural continuity and the vitality of traditional culture.[20] More than forty years later, we are still predicting the imminent disappearance of these same traditional life-styles. The ethnic affiliations that were supposed to have vanished long ago, and are continually being pronounced dead, seem somehow to be constantly

[17]Neil J. Smelser, *Sociology: An Introduction,* Wiley, New York, 1967, pp. 720–721.

[18]National Resources Committee, "The Process of Urbanization: Underlying Forces and Emerging Trends," in Paul K. Hatt and Albert J. Reiss, Jr., *Cities and Society,* Free Press, New York, pp. 68–69.

[19]Scott Greer, *The Urbane View,* Oxford University Press, New York, 1972, p. 322.

[20]William F. Whyte, *Street Corner Society,* University of Chicago Press, Chicago, 1943.

coming back to life. If anything, ethnic identification is currently undergoing a revival, with many Americans showing an active interest in their ethnic heritage.[21]

Herbert Gans criticizes Wirth's perspective on a number of grounds. He suggests that Wirth's "urbanite" is a depersonalized and atomized member of a mass society, a representative of urban-industrial society rather than of the city itself.[22] It is very hazardous to generalize from core areas of the inner city to the city as a whole. Residents of the outer city, Gans suggests, have a life-style resembling that of suburbanites far more than it resembles the behavior patterns of inner-city residents. These outer-city neighborhoods, and even most inner-city populations, consist "mainly of relatively homogeneous groups, with social and cultural moorings that shield [them] fairly effectively from the suggested consequences of number, density, and heterogeneity."[23]

## THE URBAN POPULATION MIX: ONE VIEW

Since inner-city populations show such strong contrasts, to understand them we need to group them into a number of subcultures. Gans uses the following classifications:

1. The "cosmopolites"
2. The unmarried or childless
3. The "ethnic villagers"
4. The "deprived"
5. The "trapped" and downwardly mobile.[24]

The cosmopolites are those who chose to remain in the city in order to be near the unique cultural benefits the city has to offer. They include artistically inclined persons such as writers and artists, as well as intellectuals and professionals who are attracted to the center of the city. Generally they are single, and if married they are usually childless.

The second group is the unmarried or childless. For many of these, residence in the city is a reflection of the stage they are at in the life cycle. Frequently the apartment areas in which young unmarried people settle is one that has an active night life, with singles bars and other places of

[21]Andrew M. Greeley, *Why Can't They Be Like Us?: America's White Ethnic Groups*, Dutton, New York, 1971.

[22]Herbert J. Gans, "Urbanism and Suburbanism as Ways of Life: A Re-evaluation of Definitions," in J. John Palen and Karl H. Flaming (eds.), *Urban America*, Holt, Rinehart and Winston, New York, 1972, pp. 184–200.

[23]Gans, op. cit., p. 186.

[24]Ibid.

entertainment. Once married and with the arrival of the first or second child, they may move to a single-family home in the suburbs.

Larger cities have old, sometimes deteriorating ethnic areas that are sometimes mislabeled "slums," although they are stable neighborhoods. Ethnic villagers, the third group, although they live in the city, try to isolate themselves from what they consider to be the harmful effects of urban life, preferring to live in their own tight-knit ethnic neighborhoods. They desperately resist the encroachment of other ethnic or racial groups. Such primarily working-class neighborhoods place heavy emphasis on kinship and primary-group relationships and resent the secondary formal control mechanisms of the larger city. Some of these Italian, Puerto Rican, or Eastern European enclaves are no larger than a census tract, but some are quite extensive. Chicago and Detroit both claim the largest Polish population outside Warsaw; Cleveland's Hungarian population is said to be second only to that of Budapest.

The cosmopolites, singles, and ethnic villagers are in the central city largely by choice. The fourth group, the deprived population, are there largely because they have no choice. The very poor, those with unstable or broken families, and many blacks are in the central city simply because there is no other alternative. Most will stay there, generally living in deteriorating housing in blighted neighborhoods or in public housing. A few of the deprived will use the slum as a stopover where they will save money for the move to a better outer-city or suburban location.

The final group—the trapped and downwardly mobile—overlaps the fourth group. It consists of those who cannot afford to move when a neighborhood changes and those who can no longer compete economically for good housing. Aged persons living on fixed incomes fall into this fifth category, as do many families lacking an adult male breadwinner.

Of the five groups only the last two, which can be combined, demonstrate the type of social disorganization and alienation that has been associated with city life. This is not to say that the city—and particularly the inner city—does not have more than its share of poverty, crime, and social disorganization. It does; but many of the assertions about how people live in cities and suburbs are directly related to specific subpopulations, social classes, and points in the life cycle. There is no clear-cut city life-style. As we have said, those who live in the outer residential neighborhoods of cities have life-styles more similar to those in the suburbs than to those in the core of the city. Outer-city areas of most cities differ little from the abutting older suburbs. Differences in housing between outer city and abutting suburbs are small, with both areas characterized by owner-occupied single-family houses. Both areas tend to be socially homogeneous and to attract middle-class child-rearing families. Gross comparisons of the entire city with the suburbs must be refined in order to provide meaningful comparisons. A change of street signs may be the only outward sign that one has passed from an outer-city community to a suburban community.

Chapter 9 will deal in detail with urban minorities. The remainder of this chapter will discuss the unmarried, the ethnic villagers (particular attention will be given to these), and the deprived and trapped.

### Singles

Of Gans's five groups, the singles received the least attention until the mass media, which had discovered "sex in the suburbs" during the 1960s, turned their attention back toward the city and the "swinging singles" in the 1970s. The singles scene is supposedly composed of endless numbers of would-be Joe Namaths and "fly me" stewardesses who nightly crowd the city's singles bars looking for one-night stands without any emotional commitments or hangups.

The realities of single life in the city are more humdrum. Each year

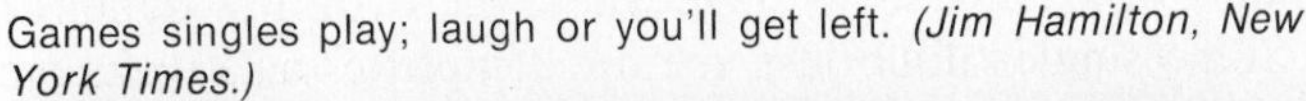

Games singles play; laugh or you'll get left. *(Jim Hamilton, New York Times.)*

colleges turn out large numbers of more or less similar young graduates who are more or less committed to a career. The marriage market removes some, who settle in apartment areas or move directly to the suburbs. Others follow the available job opportunities to the city. Singles in cities are trying to cope with the everyday problems of making friends, getting some satisfaction from their jobs, finding a decent place to live, and at the same time finding social partners and eventually a mate. They are far from being social or economic radicals. They are trying to achieve essentially middle-class happiness and essentially middle-class material goals without being able to rely on many of the usual institutional supports for their activities.

Large "singles only" apartment complexes emerged first in southern California and then elsewhere to meet the housing and social needs of this group. In most places, buildings supposedly for young singles contain a good proportion of residents who are neither single nor under twenty-five. But life in the complexes still has an almost self-conscious quality something like that of a college dormitory. Observers have commented on the desire to remain at the adolescent stage where there are few duties or responsibilities. Some singles doubtless see the complexes as a welcome escape from the encounters and perhaps failures to be faced outside.

Joyce Starr and Donald Carns conducted some seventy semistructured face-to-face interviews with singles in their early twenties or mid-twenties who had opted to come to Chicago to work.[25] Most single people do not live in singles complexes, and the Chicago data indicate that housing and neighborhood are not significant in establishing meaningful social interaction, either friendships or dating relationships. Neighbors do not get to know one another; the idea of "turf" or territory, while it is crucial to the understanding of some urban minorities, "is not a useful concept in understanding the life styles of this large and growing urban subpopulation."[26] Housing environment, or place of residence, is not significant in shaping the social contacts of singles.

Singles bars, according to some reports, serve as substitutes for a community. Here liberated men and women establish the highly transitory relationships that are said to characterize the singles world. Available data, however, indicate that this idea is considerably exaggerated. Interest in, and attendance at, singles bars evidently decreases with the time spent in the city. According to the Chicago study: "By the sixth month or so it is a fairly unusual woman who continues to frequent these places and establish her social contacts in this way. Certainly by the time she is approaching the upper age point in this sample, twenty-five, the

[25]Joyce R. Starr and Donald E. Carns, "Singles and the City: Notes on Urban Adaptation," in John Walton and Donald E. Carns (eds.), *Cities in Change,* Allyn and Bacon, Boston, 1973, pp. 280–292.

[26]Starr and Carns, op. cit., p. 291.

typical female has little use for this scene."[27] Men sometimes continue this activity longer, in order to pick up high-school-educated secretaries who hope that casual sexual relationships may become more permanent relationships. Few singles can take for long the forced conviviality and the strained and artificial social patterns of the single bars, commonly referred to as "meat markets." Those who consistently frequent them are viewed as "plastic" and one-dimensional.

Most singles have few community roots. They do not belong to organizations and view membership in organizations as a poor way of meeting possible mates, since many of the organization's members are likely to be married. Where most people do meet others, make friends, and meet potential mates is on the job. One's work takes up most of the day; it is the place where one is most likely to meet others of similar background and interests in a setting that facilitates easy familiarity. Of course one may not meet others of the same age and marital status on the job; but if one does, the odds are that friendship will develop. The workplace provides the most frequent institutional setting for meeting friends and possible mates.

### Ethnic Villagers

Among the various inner-city residents, the working-class ethnic populations probably lead the most highly organized lives. Far from being characterized by depersonalization, isolation, and social disorganization, working-class neighborhoods, particularly when they are dominated by a single ethnic group, often embody the family-oriented provincialism of a tight, homogeneous small town.

Before World War II most sociologists considered the traditional cultures of the ethnic immigrants to be in conflict with modernizing forces, and the survival of the old ways to be the last stages of a "cultural lag." Even the basic institution of the family was said to be on its last legs—which is somewhat analagous to the situation today. It was assumed that in the hustle and bustle of the large, complex, goal-oriented city, the simpler folkways would be swept away. They haven't been.

**Territoriality** Studies of inner-city working-class areas indicate that space as a social variable has a special meaning in working-class areas as compared with middle-class areas. Working-class neighborhoods have a much stronger sense of spatial identity, of being tied to a specific place. Daily routines, interpersonal relationships, and the whole web of social life are closely related to a certain limited space. The type of spatial mobility from community to community that is accepted as an inevitable

[27]Starr and Carns, op. cit., p. 288.

part of life by achievement-oriented middle-class families is not part of the life-style of ethnic neighborhoods. Here, long-term residence in the area is the accepted norm, and moving from the community is neither expected nor desired. A family's social life is closely tied to a territorially bounded network of relatives, friends, and neighbors, with the result that any forced dislocation from the neighborhood—such as by urban renewal—can be highly disruptive and disturbing to the whole fabric of a family's social world. Psychologically, this has been shown to result in severe grief and loss of a sense of identity.[28]

Studies of inner-city working-class areas often find that the residents, although living near the center of a large metropolis, still manage to remain physically, socially, and psychologically isolated from the rest of the urban area.[29] While they are clearly urbanites, the residents of such areas are not cosmopolites but rather urban provincials. The city outside the neighborhood is viewed as a foreign land—and a potentially hostile one—into which one ventures only when necessary. This is particularly true of the women who do not have jobs that necessitate their going outside the immediate community. Even in cosmopolitan New York there are people living in Brooklyn who have never been to Manhattan, and have no real desire ever to go there.

Ecologically settled ethnic areas are usually characterized by *ordered segmentation.* That is, each ethnic group carefully and specifically defines its territory. Boundaries between different ethnic groups, while invisible to the outsider, are well known and respected by the local residents. Gerald Suttles in his study of the Addams area of Chicago points out that the Italian, Mexican, Puerto Rican, and Negro groups living in the area have their own provincial enclaves and conduct their daily lives within these known borders.[30] Within these territorial units, one is safe and comfortable. Outsiders are made to feel unwelcome unless they are there as guests. The use of community facilities such as churches and parks is exclusively for one group. The movement of one ethnic or racial group into what is known as the social area of another is likely to lead to violence or the threat of violence. This occurred in the inner-city Addams area of Chicago when an enlarging black population began intruding into an area of a public park that had long been accepted as Italian territory. Within larger cities, public facilities such as parks, swimming pools, and even beaches are not really regarded as open to the general public.

[28]Marc Fried, "Grieving for a Lost Home," in Leonard J. Duhl (ed.), *The Urban Condition,* Basic Books, New York, 1963, chap. 12.

[29]For an examination of how urban workers view their own lives and achievements, see Richard Sennett and Jonathan Cobb, *The Hidden Injuries of Class,* Vintage Books, New York, 1973.

[30]Gerald D. Suttles, *The Social Order of the Slum,* University of Chicago Press, Chicago, 1968.

Rather, particular facilities are by informal general agreement allocated to various ethnic and racial groups, depending on the size, aggressiveness, and influence of the various groups.

Awareness and concern over territory are not limited to public or semipublic facilities. Business establishments, particularly bars, but even grocery stores, are viewed by local inhabitants as being the exclusive property of a single minority group. In the words of Suttles:

> When someone from outside the area or from another ethnic group enters, the proprietor and regular customers view them with great suspicion and, in some cases, use *ad hoc* measures to insure their safety. Sometimes they will simply wait for the intruder to get his bearings and leave. If that fails the proprietor may eventually get around to asking what he wants. In the meantime, everyone in the store stops and stares. The treatment of regular customers, of course, is exactly the opposite. Commercial relations with these people are intimate and all economic transactions are buried in the guise of friendship and sentiment. In large part this is the reason they cannot tolerate the presence of strangers from another ethnic group. Among themselves the customers set aside their public face and disclose much of their private life to one another.[31]

Private information is too intimate to be revealed to potentially hostile strangers. In establishments such as small snack shops that may be near the boundary line between different ethnic groups, the problem of privacy may be solved by taking turns. One teenage group will not enter while another is inside. Rather, they will wait until the other ethnic group leaves.

**Community and Space** High population densities and rows of buildings directly abutting on one another do not permit the same degree of personal or family privacy possible in less crowded sections of the metropolitan area. Neighbors generally know a good deal about one another's lives, activities, and problems. Watching the social life from the front window, or in the summer from the front stoop, is a popular spare-time activity.

There is evidence to suggest that being alone is neither expected nor particularly welcome by most residents of ethnic areas. Close involvement in the lives of others is accepted and desired. Contact with others is viewed positively, as a sign of belonging, rather than negatively, as a sign of crowding—as it might be viewed by upper-middle-class suburbanites. Inner-city youngsters from such areas are more comfortable being with

[31]Suttles, op. cit., pp. 48–49.

Surviving remnants of the outdoor Maxwell Street Market adjacent to the Addams area of Chicago. *(Mary Doody.)*

others than being alone. Gans reports how social workers in the West End of Boston were forced to abandon an experimental summer program that gave the innner-city boys a chance to spend a vacation exploring nature at Cape Cod. The boys became very unhappy when removed from the activity and contacts of the city. They could not understand why anyone would want to visit, much less live, in such a lonely spot. The boys were accustomed to, and thrived on, crowded and noisy street life. They wanted to be where the action was and were emotionally unprepared for wide vistas and open unused space.

The difference between the perceptions of middle-class and working-class populations can also be seen in how the two groups orient themselves to a common spatial feature, such as streets. For working-class and lower-class urban groups, much daily activity takes place in the streets; streets are seen as living space, a place to congregate and gather with others in the neighborhood. Streets serve a vital social function. Middle-class groups, on the other hand, are far less likely to see the streets as performing a social function. In their view streets are corridors to be used to travel from place to place; and they think that people should be kept off the streets, lest they interfere with rapid movement.[32]

**Density** High population density definitely has an effect on the social organization of urban life, but for some communities the effect is strongly positive—not the negative effect that most of the literature of professional urban planning depicts. Upper-middle-class writers on urban problems have much too glibly applied their own preferences for space and separation from one's neighbors to evaluations of the "problem" of what they define as slums (i.e., areas unlike their own).

Much more research remains to be done on the importance of density to different types of populations. Unfortunately, at present we probably know as much about the behavior of rats under conditions of crowding as we do about that of city dwellers. John Calhoun's now famous article, "Population Density and Social Pathology," indicates that in experiments with Norway rats pathological conditions develop under conditions of crowding even when there is an abundance of food and freedom from disease and predators. In his experiment, a behavioral sink developed in which infant mortality increased and homosexuality and even cannibalism became widespread. When the experiment was terminated, the rat population was well on the way to extinction.[33]

Unfortunately, the results of this excellent study of Norway rats are sometimes taken as saying something about the effect of population density on humans. One writer goes so far as to suggest this:

> The implications of animal and human studies are clear-cut. Just as the offspring of frustrated mother rats, part of whose pregnancy was spent trapped in problem boxes with no exits, carried an emotional disturbance throughout their own lives, so too many children of frustrated human mothers, trapped by urban slums, show behavioral manifestations of emotional disturbance.[34]

This is a misleading and dangerously simplistic analogy. For humans the relationship between density and social behavior is far from clear-cut.[35] What is clear is that different urban populations respond differently to

[32]Marc Fried and Peggy Gleicher, "Some Sources of Residential Satisfaction in an Urban Slum," *Journal of the American Institute of Planners,* **27:**305–315, 1961.

[33]John B. Calhoun, "Population Density and Social Pathology," *Scientific American,* **206:**139–148, February, 1960.

[34]Shirley Foster Hartley, *Population Quantity vs. Quality,* Prentice-Hall, Englewood Cliffs, N. J., 1972, p. 76.

[35]See for example, Omer R. Galle, Walter R. Gove, and J. Miller McPherson, "Population Density and Pathology: What are the Relations for Man?" *Science,* April 7, 1972, pp. 23–30.

density. The evidence indicates that, far from always viewing high density as an evil, some ethnic working-class subgroups consider it a positive social value. This is pointed out by Jane Jacobs in her writings on what really makes a city livable.[36]

Residents of established inner-city areas frequently view high density as a preventer rather than a cause of social disorganization and alienation. While not cosmopolites, they are true urbanites in that they thrive on the crowding, contact, and pace of the city. Often they see the lower densities of the suburbs in a distinctly negative light. Women living in the West End of Boston, for example, thought of suburbs as cold and dreary places where one could not easily and spontaneously meet friends on a daily basis. How do you easily run into people when homes are set back from the sidewalks and people have to *drive* to get to each other's homes? Suburbs are perceived as having better-quality housing but as being too quiet and lonely.

**Moral Order** Provincialism is the keynote of the moral order of ethnic enclaves. Studies done in Boston, Chicago, and London all stress that some areas which outsiders view as slums because of their deteriorating housing are far from being socially disorganized.[37] All three areas have a highly structured form of social organization, but it is a social organization which differs in significant respects from that of middle-class people. Moral behavior is expected, but the local definition of "moral" may not correspond with that of the larger society. The larger society, for instance, might frown on gambling, while the local racketeer who runs policy wheels might be considered a supporter of the local church and a pillar of the community. Ethnic neighborhoods use a practical rather than an idealized set of guidelines for conduct. Personal, informal sanctions are more important than official regulations enforced by outside authorities such as the police. In the community a person's reputation in the neighborhood (he is honest and can be trusted) governs his social relations more than "outside" views by the society at large (he is a mob figure and has a police record).

**Peer Groups** The primary integrative mechanism of stable inner-city ethnic neighborhoods is the peer group. As Gans says, "The peer group society continues long past adolescence, and, indeed, dominates the life of the West Ender [Boston] from birth to death."[38] Most of the

[36]Jane Jacobs, *The Death and Life of Great American Cities,* Random House, New York, 1961.

[37]William F. Whyte, *Street Corner Society,* University of Chicago Press, Chicago, 1943; Gerald Suttles, *The Social Order of the Slum,* University of Chicago Press, Chicago, 1968; Michael Young and Peter Willmott, *Family and Kinship in East London,* rev. ed., Penguin Books, Baltimore, 1962.

[38]Herbert J. Gans, *The Urban Villagers,* Free Press, Glencoe, Ill., 1962, p. 37.

social relationships a resident of one of these areas has are with peers: people of the same age, sex, and stage of the life cycle. It goes without saying that these peer groups occupy fixed physical as well as social space within the community. The peer group, be it a gang of adolescent boys or a clique of married friends and relatives of the same sex, provides a vital buffer between the individual and the larger society.

The peer group is the basic building block of the local social system. Gans has described the relationship of the peer-group society to the larger world as follows:

> . . . The life of the West Ender takes place within three interrelated sectors: the primary group, the secondary group, and the outgroup. The primary group refers to that combination of family and peer relationships which I shall call the *peer group society.* The secondary group refers to the small array of Italian institutions, voluntary organizations, and other social bodies which function to support the workings of the peer group society. This I shall call the *community.* . . . The outgroup, which I shall describe as the *outside world,* covers a variety of non-Italian institutions in the West End, in Boston, and in America that impinge on his life—often unhappily to the West Ender's way of thinking.[39]

The peer group sets standards for behavior and acts as a filter through which one can obtain information. It provides psychological support in that it serves as a sounding board against which one can bounce his ideas and receive confirmation of his values. It reduces anonymity and tells the individual that he belongs. Frequently this in-group membership is signified by a distinctive way of dressing and locally distinctive speech patterns.[40] The values held by the peer group are not those of the more achievement-oriented middle class. Whyte's classic treatment of a peer-group society, *Street Corner Society,*[41] deals extensively with the conflict in values between the locally oriented "corner boys" and those neighborhood adolescents who were success- and object-oriented, the so-called "college boys." Peer groups of "corner boys" discouraged striving and emphasized personal relationships. If someone got a job and made some money (this was during the late Depression), he was expected to share his good fortune with his friends. Being a good guy was socially rewarded, while putting on airs of social striving was negatively sanctioned. On the other hand, the college boys were oriented toward the achievement values of the outside world, saved rather than shared their money, and constantly sought to "better them-

[39]Gans, *The Urban Villagers,* pp. 36–37.
[40]Suttles, op. cit., chap. 4.
[41]Whyte, op. cit.

Clothes styles are uniforms that signify to others who you are and where you fit in the system. *(Charles Gatewood.)*

selves." The more recent studies of Boston's West End and the Addams area indicate that little has changed over the years: the priority of personal relationships over goal-oriented relationships remains. The absence of material wealth and luxurious consumer goods is rationalized:

these goods are associated with the outside world and a cold, impersonal, friendless way of life. The desire for outside material attractions is more than compensated for by the satisfaction of a personal peer-group life.

The close, warm feeling that some inner-city residents have for their community and their neighbors was well expressed by a mother of six children, separated from her husband, who lives in a neighborhood on the Near West side of Chicago:

> I got everybody on this block that would do something for me. If one of my children were sick, I wouldn't feel any compunction of waking up the man across the street to take me to the hospital. He expects this. He would expect me to do this for him.
>
> One night I took my daughter to the hospital at eleven o'clock at night. Next morning, at least eight people, on my way to work asked me how my daughter was. When I got home it was worse than that. It took me an hour to get home. Because everybody wanted to know about Christine. Did the doctors do anything? Did I need anything? I get a cheery hello from everybody. Old ladies, when I get dressed to go out or to go to work: "Oh, how nice you look." Old and young blend together here. In the summertime, everybody's outside. There's no fear here. I have friends who live in the suburbs, they wouldn't dare be out in the dark.
>
> I know friends of ours, who've moved away from here, who bitterly lament their predicament now. They've got beautiful homes—I guess the city planners would say they've done better for themselves. Their plumbing works, their electricity is good, their environment is better . . . supposedly. If you're a type of person who considers a mink stole and a fountain in your living room and big bay windows, front lawn beautifully kept, all these things mean something to you, well . . . to me, we're more concerned about people.[42]

**Family Norms** Family life in settled ethnic working-class areas is generally adult-oriented. Children are frequently not planned; they come naturally and fairly often and are expected, once they are out of infancy, to accommodate and adjust themselves to a world run by adults. The child is not the center of the family as in many middle- and upper-middle-class families, where everything is adjusted so as to not conflict with the child's needs, schedule, and general "development." The role of the children is to stay out of the way and behave, at least around the home, like miniature adults. When girls reach eight or nine they are expected to start helping their mothers around the home, frequently by caring for younger siblings. Boys are given a great deal more freedom to roam the streets. Children soon pick up the notion that the home is the preserve of the mother. The

[42]Studs Terkel, *Division Street: America,* Pantheon Books, a division of Random House, (Avon ed.), New York, 1967, p. 198.

father is expected to spend much of his leisure time elsewhere, frequently in the corner tavern, which serves as the poor man's social club. Group sports activities such as bowling, in which a person can easily socialize with friends of the same age and sex, are also popular.

Husband and wife are not expected to be as close or to communicate as extensively as in the middle-class family model. The husband has his role, the wife hers. A wife who asked her husband to do the housework would be ostracized by other married women. Bott's description of this phenomenon among English families applies equally well to American cities:

> Husband and wife have a clear differentiation of tasks and a considerable number of separate interests and activities. They have a clearly defined division of labor into male tasks and female tasks. They expect to have different leisure pursuits, and the husband has his friends . . . the wife hers.[43]

One difference between American and English studies is that in the United States interaction is primarily with relatives of the same generation. In the East End of London, the interaction may focus on the family matriarch, "Mum." Mum is the one who settles family quarrels, lends money and looks after the grandchildren. It is at her house that the family gathers, and if a married daughter does not live in the same building she will be within a short distance.[44] Family ties in the United States are more likely to be horizontal as well as vertical, with greater importance given to cousins and other relatives of the same age.

Sociability for married adults does not revolve around occupation or involve a search for new or different friends. The basis for gathering with others is kinship or long-standing friendship and association. Brothers, sisters, cousins, and local friends get together on a more or less regularized basis one or more times a week. Parties in the middle-class sense—gatherings for which specific invitations are issued and at which you expect to meet some people you do not know—are not part of the local life style. As one West Ender put it: "I don't want to meet any new people. I get out quite a bit all over Boston to see my brothers and sisters, and when they come over, we have others in, like neighbors. You can't do that in the suburbs."[45] Usually the same people come the same days of the week. There are no formal invitations; these are used only for major family events such as a christening, graduation, or wedding. In all cases

[43]Elizabeth Bott, *Family and Social Network*, Tavistock Publications, London, 1957, p. 53.
[44]Young and Willmott, op. cit.
[45]Gans, *The Urban Villagers*, p. 75.

the conversation is sex-segregated, with the men usually in one room and the women in another.

**Housing** Housing has a different meaning in established ethnic working-class neighborhoods than it does in middle-class groups. For the middle class, how one decorates one's home is viewed as an extension of one's personality. The home is a reflection of one's tastes and style of life. The working-class home, on the other hand, is not viewed as a status symbol. Those visiting one's apartment are local relatives or close friends who evaluate a host on his friendliness, and perhaps on his wife's cooking, but not on the quality of his housing. All tend to live in similar circumstances. Homes are old but quite comfortable. Rents are usually well below the average for the city.

Since the buildings are old, outsiders sometimes mistake the area for a slum. Exteriors of buildings are not always in the best repair. However, inside the apartments everything is clean and in good repair. To have more than one's neighbors is perceived as trying to be "better than you are," "snooty" or "stuck up." Social closeness among neighbors is encouraged by the tendency of local landlords to rent apartments to their married children, relatives, and friends. The goal is a "respectable enough" neighborhood where neighbors are of the same general ethnic, religious, and economic background. For the upwardly mobile groups hopeful of moving into the middle-class, the home frequently is a symbol of one's "respectability." Cleanliness and order are emphasized, and the furniture is carefully protected by plastic seat covers and the carpeting by plastic runners. The covers come off only for ceremonial occasions and major holidays, and heaven help the family member who actually sits on an uncovered chair before company comes.

**Imagery and Vulnerability** Blue-collar ethnic neighborhoods, although physically a central part of the city, manage to maintain a psychological distance between themselves and other areas. Their negative images of major urban institutions are remarkably similar to those of small-town dwellers, who also feel powerless in face of the large urban institutions and organizations that control much of their lives. The urban provincials may be city dwellers, but they think of the city as something removed from themselves and their neighborhood. Their area is perceived as being different from the big city outside.

Thus the neighborhood is considered friendly, but the city is cold and hostile. People in the neighborhood believe in God and support the churches, while other city dwellers are atheists or secularists who want to drive all mention of God out of the schools. The people in the neighborhood are good, solid Americans, while other urbanites are, if not radicals, at least soft on communism and more likely to have supported the Viet Cong than "our boys" during the war in Vietnam. The wife of a high school teacher expressed her feelings as follows:

> There's something wrong, that's what I say; and it all started with this civil rights business, the demonstrations, and then the college radicals and on and on. It used to be that you could go to church and pray for your family and country. Now they're worried about colored people and you even get the feeling they care more about the enemy, the people killing our boys in Vietnam, than our own soldiers. And the schools—I mean, take them over, that's what. They don't like what's being taught, and they don't like the teachers, and a day doesn't go by that they don't have something bad to say, or a new threat for us to hear. My husband says he'd quit tomorrow if he didn't have so much seniority, and he could get another job. It's pretty bad for you these days if you're just a law-abiding, loyal American and you believe in your country, and in people being happy with their own kind, and doing their best to keep us first in the world.[46]

The peer-group orientation of working-class urban neighborhoods leaves them vulnerable to change induced from the outside. The emphasis within the community on personal relations makes residents ill-equipped to participate in large-scale formal organizations or community-wide activities. One learns from the peer group how to get along with others, but not how to deal effectively with an outside bureaucracy.

This means that the community as a whole is rarely able to respond effectively as a unit to threats to its existence, such as urban renewal or an urban expressway that cuts it apart. A traditional distrust of politicians and a lack of knowledge as to how to lobby on the level of city government further handicap the working-class neighborhood. Suburban upper-middle-class groups are by training and inclination well equipped to organize *ad hoc* committees for any purpose under the sun. Working-class people are used to working within an environment of limited size, oriented toward persons more than organizations. Except in cases where a powerful community-wide ethnic church exists, there is no large-scale organization that has the power both to organize and to speak for the neighborhood in its dealings with the larger city. A peer-group society based on ethnicity, age-grading, dominance of a single sex, and limited territoriality is at a considerable disadvantage when it necessarily comes into contact and confrontation with large-scale, complex bureaucratic middle-class society.

[46]Robert Coles and Jon Erikson, *The Middle Americans*, Little, Brown and Company in association with The Atlantic Monthly Press, Boston, 1971, p. 11.

Urban provincials do not turn to outside bureaucratic structures in time of trouble. They distrust the city hall bureaucracy and that of the courts. They don't understand the system and feel that whatever happens they are going to lose. They are right, and their lack of knowledge of how to fight the system the way someone like Ralph Nader does make it all the easier for city hall and other outside interests to have their way.

### Unstable Slums

**Socioeconomic Factors** Established low-income areas populated by working-class blacks or whites can be thought of as "stable slums." The type of slum inhabited by the very poor is considerably different. Here we use the term "unstable slum," with all it connotes—crime, violence, poverty, alcoholism, drugs, and disorganization. For the 15 to 20 percent of the overall population who are on the bottom in terms of social status (unskilled manual workers, people with unstable and erratic work histories, and people on welfare) the slum has the character more of an urban jungle than an urban village. Unstable slums house the rejects of society—the very poor, the old, and the unadjusted. This group, below the manual blue-collar workers, is not simply poorer, although that is also the case: it is in many ways cut off from the social system that includes both the rich and the manual workers. Unstable slums are the slums of despair, for their residents are for all practical purposes excluded from the economic and social life of the larger society. Working-class parents can sacrifice to raise the level of their children, but for those at the very bottom there is little realistic hope of moving from the slum to something better.

Those on the bottom, sometimes called the "disreputable poor" by the larger society, are those who have been left behind by that society—people who are downwardly mobile, frequently because of drugs, alcoholism, or mental problems, and newer in-migrants to the city who have come without marketable skills or knowledge of urban ways and who thus frequently find themselves victimized by other, more experienced and cleverer, slum dwellers. Additionally, some old people and handicapped people drift into unstable slums because they are not wanted elsewhere and are powerless to prevent their downward slide.

**Psychology of the Slum** What all the so-called "disreputable poor" have in common is that they are essentially outside the urban society that includes all other populations within the city. Economically such populations, because of their lack of marketable skills and their educational, emotional, and mental liabilities, are virtually excluded from modern industrial life.[47] Life in unstable slums is an often unsuccessful attempt to minimize the negative aspects of daily life rather than maximizing its potentially positive aspects.

Everywhere one turns in the lower-class community, one is beset by a bewildering variety of difficulties. Slum dwellers are never able to find enough money to have a style of life which both they and society would define as reasonable. Slum dwellers are also surrounded by others who are out to exploit them whenever possible. They are considered fair game by everyone from landlords to hustlers.

For those locked into lower-class status, it is unrealistic to have long-range goals. Success is measured in terms of developing strategies for day-to-day survival, not in terms of long-range goals. Protection from hostile others has to take first priority. Lower-class individuals try, with only slight success, to isolate themselves from the violence of their world.

Housing for the poor living in unstable slums is not a matter of self-realization or self-expression; it is a matter of providing a place of security safe from the physical and emotional dangers of the outside. The urban poor, particularly those stored in public housing projects, have to be constantly on guard against violence against themselves and their possessions. Assaults, robberies, and muggings are a constant danger in stairwells, corridors, laundry rooms, and even apartments. In addition to physical violence, symbolic violence on the part of building supervisors, social workers, and others who perform caretaker services for the lower classes is also endemic in slums and public housing. Lower-class persons protect themselves from such symbolic violence and shaming by avoidance, sullenness, and feigned stupidity when contact cannot be avoided.[48] Certainly the image of lower-class life as presented on television to the slum dweller's children is one that demeans the slum dweller and emphasizes his isolation from the larger society.

To the extent that the world is seen as consisting of dangerous others, the very act of making friends involves risks for the lower-class person. A friend could turn out to be an enemy and might report one to the housing authorities or cause other problems. Lower-class persons are constantly being exploited and thus it is not surprising that they view the world as threatening. In the words of Lee Rainwater, "To lower class people the major causes stem from the nature of their own peers. Thus a great deal of blaming goes on and reinforces the process of isolation, suspiciousness, and touchiness both blaming and shaming."[49] Such patterns of

[47]David Matza, "The Disreputable Poor," in Neil J. Smelser and Seymour M. Lipset (eds.), *Social Structure and Mobility in Economic Development,* Aldine, Chicago, 1966, pp. 310–339.

[48]Lee Rainwater, "Fear and the House-as-Haven in the Lower Class," in J. John Palen and Karl H. Flaming, *Urban America,* Holt, Rinehart, and Winston, New York, 1972, pp. 311–321.

[49]Rainwater, op. cit., p. 319.

distrust and recrimination make it difficult to establish any type of organization for cooperation to solve problems.

**Prognosis** For the deprived and trapped poor, life is not getting better. As of 1950 the poorest fifth of the nation's population received 4.5 percent of the total national income; twenty years and an infinite number of poverty programs later, the poorest fifth received only 5.5 percent of total national income.[50] For the very poor, life is sometimes getting worse in absolute as well as relative terms.

A special census of the inner city of Cleveland, including Hough, where a riot took place in 1966, indicated that there was extreme polarization among blacks. The study indicated that there was an increasing gap between the "haves" and the "have-nots," with a particularly striking difference among the black population. Blacks on the whole have begun to cash in on the American dream, and this is particularly true of younger educated men. However, one effect of this upward mobility is that core neighborhoods are losing their successful residents, so that their percentage of families headed by women and by the aged is increasing—and these two groups have the most limited economic potential. In Cleveland, the area dubbed the "crisis ghetto" had two-thirds of the city's poor female-headed households. While incomes of blacks and whites elsewhere in the city went up between 1960 and 1965, those in the crisis ghetto declined absolutely as well as relatively. Unemployment was higher, income lower, and a larger percentage of the population poor.[51]

By 1965 the Hough area had been virtually depopulated of stable middle-income black households. The fact that four out of ten families were able to move out of the crisis ghetto between 1960 and 1965 increased the relative disadvantage of those who were unable to escape. With those having economic strength or potential fleeing the unstable slums, the isolation of those who are left behind locked into their poverty increases. Decreases in discrimination *heightened* the isolation between the very poor and other strata of blacks. Poverty and economic instability lock these welfare poor at the bottom into the crisis ghetto as effectively as discrimination once did. The ability of the better trained, educated, and motivated to move out heightens the separation and isolation of those who are left behind. Certainly the feeling of being ignored and bypassed while all around others rise can lead to explosions of frustration—or, worse, despair—not only for oneself but also for one's children. The

[50]"Consumer Income," *Current Population Reports*, Bureau of the Census, series P–60, no. 80, October, 1971, p. 28.

[51]Walter Williams, "Cleveland's Crisis Ghetto," *Trans-Action*, September, 1967, pp. 33–42.

bondage of the crisis ghetto is made doubly oppressive by the relative prosperity of those outside its boundaries.

Recent (1973) government data indicating an increase from 7.4 million to 7.7 million in the number of blacks living in poverty indicate that the problem is far from solved. Most blacks made notable improvements in their economic status during the past decade, with the result that unstable slums are becoming the permanent residences of an underclass that is economically and socially isolated from the bulk of black as well as white society. The major problem for the future may not be the emergence of two Americas, one white and one black, but the emergence of two Americas, one economically viable, and one a permanent poverty class. It is not unreasonable to foresee certain areas of cities, or even entire cities, serving essentially as ghetto reservations for the deprived underclass. A few once-viable cities such as Newark already exhibit major characteristics of urban reservations for the welfare poor.[52]

## CRIME

Among the most serious problems facing urban residents in general, and inner-city residents in particular, is the danger of crime. A Gallup poll taken in 1973 indicated that among residents of the nation's largest cities (500,000 and up) 22 percent named crime as their city's worst problem. The next highest on the list of problems were transportation and traffic (11 percent) and the crime-related problem of drugs (10 percent). In 1949, only 4 percent cited crime as their city's worst problem.[53] The problem of crime is also overlayed by racial fears.

### Differences within Cities

Within cities the highest crime rates today, as in the past, have been in the inner-city neighborhoods surrounding the downtown business district. As was noted earlier, this is the area that served as a point of entry for European immigrants at the turn of the century and for blacks after World War II. In most large cities these areas of "first immigrant settlement" are now ghettoes housing black, Mexican, or Puerto Rican newcomers.

Inner-core areas have historically had high crime rates. Table 6-1 compares the crime rates in five districts of Chicago. Of the five districts, one is a high-income white neighborhood on the periphery of the city; two others are predominantly white, one with mainly lower-income white families and one with a mixture of high- and low-income whites; the remaining two are black districts near the city's core, low-income areas

[52]Joseph M. Conforti, "Newark: Ghetto or City," *Society*, **9**:20–32, September–October, 1972.
[53]*The Milwaukee Journal*, January 16, 1973.

**Table 6-1 Incidence of Index Crimes and Assignments of Patrolmen per 100,000 Residents in Five Chicago Police Districts, 1965**

| Number | High-income white district | Low-middle-income white district | Mixed high- and low-income white district | Very-low-income Negro district 1 | Very-low-income Negro district 2 |
|---|---|---|---|---|---|
| Index crimes against persons | 80 | 440 | 338 | 1,615 | 2,820 |
| Index crimes against property | 1,038 | 1,750 | 2,080 | 2,508 | 2,630 |
| Patrolmen assigned | 93 | 133 | 115 | 243 | 291 |

*Source: Report of the National Advisory Commission on Civil Disorders.*

with numerous public housing projects. The table indicates that one of the poor black districts had over 35 times as many serious crimes against persons per 100,000 population as did the upper-income white area—in spite of the fact that the black area had over three times as many patrolmen assigned per 100,000 population. The presence of many policemen does not prevent a high crime rate in an area of social disorganization. Variations in the rate of crimes against property are smaller, but still substantial; the highest crime rate was 2 $^{1}/_{2}$ times greater than that in the higher-income neighborhood.

High as these figures are, they are a considerable understatement of the actual situation. Studies conducted by the President's Crime Commission in Washington, D.C., Boston, and Chicago showed that three to six times as many crimes against persons and homes were actually committed as were reported to the police. Police figures greatly underreport the actual amount of crime. The best data on the amount of underreported crime are provided by a sampling by the Bureau of the Census of 200,000 persons in eight cities—Atlanta, Baltimore, Cleveland, Dallas, Denver, Newark, Portland, and St. Louis—as a project of the Justice Department's Law Enforcement Assistance Administration. The findings show that police statistics on the average recorded only half the serious crimes that had actually occurred. While almost all stolen cars were reported, there had been 2.1 actual rapes, 2.3 robberies, and 2.7 burglaries for each of these crimes that was reported.[54]

[54] "Eight Cities Show a Crime Disparity," *New York Times,* January 27, 1974, p. 34.

### Racial Variations

The common opinion among criminologists has long been that blacks are proportionally much more likely than whites to be victims of crimes. However, the elaborate study by the Bureau of the Census seriously questions this assumption. Contrary to expectations, the white and black residents of the eight cities told questioners from the Bureau of the Census that they had suffered from a roughly similar overall rate of crime. In fact, in three cities—Atlanta, Dallas, and St. Louis—whites reported more criminal attacks in relation to population than blacks did.[55]

Although blacks are only one-ninth of the population, more blacks than whites were arrested for crimes of violence in 1970—105,000 arrests versus 96,000. This means that official figures show a rate for violent crimes among blacks ten times that for whites, with the result that middle-class whites often see crime in terms of black against white. In fact, however, blacks are even more fearful of crime than are whites. The Gallup poll indicates that as regards walking in their neighborhoods at night, and even being in their own homes at night, blacks feel less secure than whites. Among those polled, one-third of the people living in the central cities had been mugged or robbed or had suffered a loss of property during 1972.

A special tabulation by the President's Crime Commission indicates that over 85 percent of the crimes against persons committed by blacks also involve blacks as victims. Blacks have a much greater chance of being murdered than whites. In 1970, 7,490 blacks were murdered as compared with 5,999 whites. How much of crime by blacks reflects discriminatory patterns of arrests and how much is due to genuine racial variation are matters of considerable dispute.

### Drugs

Much of crime, other than rape, is related to hard drugs. The consensus among both policemen and urban researchers is that somewhere between one-fourth and one-half of all crimes against property committed in the nation's largest cities are at least partially drug related.[56] An addict must steal to feed his habit. The estimate is that robbery losses account for $3 billion a year in New York City and $400 million a year in Washington, D.C.[57] The cost of protection against crime must be added to this, as must

[55]Ibid.

[56]James Markham, "What's All This Talk of Heroin Maintenance?" *New York Times Magazine,* **6**:6–12, July 2, 1972.

[57]John Robertson and Norman Zinberg, *Drugs and the Public,* Simon and Schuster, New York, 1972, p. 205.

the social cost of crime. Attempts at jailing addicts and cutting the supply of heroin have been largely ineffective.

Methadone maintenance as a treatment has reached only a small minority of addicts, and some methadone has found its way into black markets. However, while a cure for addiction is still in the future, there is controversial evidence that New York's methadone-maintenance program is working for those fortunate enough to be on it; of nearly 9,000 voluntary applicants treated, four out of five have stayed on the program.[58] It is estimated that 50,000 addicts would volunteer for methadone-maintenance programs in New York City alone if the necessary facilities could be provided. However, there is a danger in expecting technological solutions to deep-rooted social problems. Methadone-maintenance doesn't cure poverty and racism. Therapy to reorient the heroin addict to a normal noncriminal life is badly needed. Meanwhile, many urban dwellers in the largest cities live in fear because of the tremendous amount of crime related to hard drugs.

The result is a "fortress mentality" that affects every aspect of urban life. Even behind locked doors, people feel insecure. Cab drivers don't carry change or even enter some areas; buses and gas stations demand exact change only; policemen patrol junior high schools; and streets are deserted at night. In some city areas, residents carry on their lives in a state of virtual siege. Along with fear has gone a demand for tougher law-and-order campaigns against criminals; but in spite of everything, from special community programs to federal funds for law-enforcement training, crime rates continue to climb. The presidential election of 1972 produced the strange sight of Republicans attempting to take credit for the fact that the rate of crime had climbed less under Nixon than it did under Johnson. No one claimed that things were not getting worse—just that they weren't getting worse quite as fast as before.

### Differences between Cities and Suburbs

The crime rate of the large cities is still considerably higher than that of the suburbs, although the gap is closing. The National Advisory Commission on Civil Disorders points out that within cities the crime rates are highest in the inner-city black ghettoes. The most commonly used index of crimes is the number of serious crimes in relation to population (homicide, forcible rape, aggravated assault, robbery, burglary, grand larceny, and automobile theft). For 1966 the national rate was 1,754 such crimes for every 100,000 population. Cities with populations of over 250,000 had a rate of 3,153, and cities of over 1 million had a rate of

[58]Francis Clines, "Methadone Care Cutting Arrests," *New York Times*, September 3, 1972, p. 3.

3,630—which was more than double the national average. The rate in suburbs was 1,300, or just over one-third the rate in the largest cities.[59]

Smaller population and lower density, however, offer no immunization against crimes against property and persons. Annual figures on crime indicate that the rapid rise in crime of the last decade is leveling off in the cities but that crime in the suburbs is now on the increase, particularly in those suburbs abutting the central city. Crime has inevitably followed the middle class into its suburban residential areas. While the rate of major crimes went up 117 percent in the cities from 1960 to 1969, the rate in suburbs increased 181 percent. One-fifth of all suburbanites interviewed by the Gallup poll had been robbed or mugged or had suffered a loss of property in 1972. Some suburbs are beginning to develop the same siege mentality found in the larger cities.

[59] *Report of the National Advisory Commission on Civil Disorders,* Government Printing Office, Washington, D.C., 1968, p. 133.

Chapter 7

# Life-Styles: The Suburbs

*Come forth into the light of things; let Nature be your teacher.*
Wordsworth

With all the debate about the nature of urbanization and the future of metropolitan areas, one factor appears reasonably certain: suburbs are going to continue to grow. While New York, Chicago, and Philadelphia have been losing population for two decades, their outlying suburbs have mushroomed in size and numbers. Suburbs actually have been growing faster than central cities since the 1920s, but the lack of new construction during the 1930s and 1940s for a time masked the extent of potential suburban growth. However, since World War II suburbanization has been a major population trend.

The data on population document the recency and magnitude of the exodus to the suburbs. In 1920 only 17 percent of all Americans were suburbanites (18 million persons). The percentage was only 19 percent by 1930 and only 20 percent by 1940. The percentage increased to 24 in 1950, and then shot up to 33 percent in 1960 and 37 percent in 1970. Today population growth in metropolitan areas is all but synonymous with suburban growth. According to the Bureau of the Census: "Within metropolitan areas virtually all, if not all, the population growth between 1960 and 1969 occurred in suburban rings."[1] Census data for 1970 show that during the preceding decade the suburban population increased a spectacular 28 percent. One effect of this suburban sprawl has been to reduce the urban population density from 6,580 people per square mile in 1920 to 3,376 in 1970. The density of New York's Manhattan Island went from 103,822 to 67,808 during the same years.

The census also documented a major transition in American life, for as of 1970 the suburban area of Standard Metropolitan Statistical Areas (SMSAs) exceeded central cities in overall population. In 1970 these suburban areas had a population of 76 million persons, whereas central cities had 64 million. The population outside the SMSAs was slightly lower: 63 million. Thus, for the first time in the nation's history a greater percentage of its population resides in suburbs (37 percent) than in cities (32 percent) or in nonmetropolitan areas (31 percent).[2] Roughly two-thirds of the present suburban population previously lived in central cities.

Demographically, the United States is now more a nation of suburbanites than one of city dwellers. Ironically, the late President Lyndon B. Johnson was coining his often-repeated phrase about the United States being "a nation of cities" just at the time, in the technical sense, it was ceasing to be true.

## ORIGIN OF SUBURBS

### The Nineteenth Century

American suburbanization as we know it began in the latter part of the nineteenth century. The first suburbs were generally upper-class villages of substantial country homes. Over time some of these rural residences became converted to year-round occupancy. Almost invariably, these first suburbs were conveniently located along a railroad line and housed commuters. In some cases small rural towns also came to have as year-round residents affluent commuters who could afford to combine an urban occupation with a rural residence. In the absence of a reliable

[1]U.S. Bureau of the Census, "Trends in Social and Economic Conditions in Metropolitan and Nonmetropolitan Areas," *Current Population Reports,* series P–23, no. 33, U.S. Government Printing Office, Washington, D.C., 1970.

[2]Conrad Taeuber, "Population Trends in the 1960's," *Science,* **176:**774, May 19, 1972. If the Urbanized Area rather than the Standard Metropolitan Statistical Area is the base unit, the city still has an advantage over the suburbs. Using the Urbanized Area, the national population broke down as follows in 1970: central cities, 31.5 percent; urban fringe, 26.8 percent; other urban places, 15.2 percent; rural, 26.5 percent.

Suburban elegance, 1907. *(Culver Pictures.)*

transportation technology, one could venture no farther from the railway station than one could conveniently walk, or at least have one's coachman drive. As a promotional pamphlet of the 1870s put it:

> The controversy which is sometimes brought, as to which offers the greater advantage, the country or the city, finds a happy answer in the suburban idea which says, both—the combination of the two—the city brought to the country. The city has its advantages and conveniences, the country has its charm and health; the union of the two (a modern result of the railway), gives to man all he could ask in this respect.[3]

[3]Quoted by Scott Greer in "The Urbanization of the Suburbs," in Louis H. Masotti and Jeffrey K. Hadden (eds.), *The Urbanization of the Suburbs*, Sage Publications, Beverly Hills, 1973, p. 155.

The invention of the street railway in the late nineteenth century similarly permitted middle- and upper-middle-class population growth along the streetcar lines. Sam Warner has interestingly detailed the growth of Dorchester, Roxbury, and West Roxbury as streetcar suburbs of Boston.[4]

Before the twentieth century, areas on the periphery of central cities often fought to get into the central city rather than stay out of it. Suburbs sought to be annexed by the city in order to benefit from its superior fire protection, schools, and roads, gain access to its water supply, and pay its lower taxes. However, by the turn of the century the pattern had generally reversed: suburbs increasingly actively sought "home rule" and opposed annexation. In the twenty-five metropolitan districts defined by the census of 1910, the pattern for the future was emerging. A full quarter of the metropolitan population already lived outside the core city.

### The 1920s

The second big change in suburbs took place in the 1920s and was in large part due to the influence of the automobile. Car registrations, which had been 2½ million in 1915, took a jump to 9 million in 1920, and then skyrocketed to 26½ million in 1930. The car was no longer a rich man's plaything. Henry Ford's assembly lines were doing more than producing cars; they were bringing a revolution that was changing the face of the land. The automobile meant that previously inaccessible land was open for suburban development. No longer was it necessary to be located along a railroad line; the commuter who was willing to pay the costs in money and time could drive his own car to work and live where he pleased.

The out-migration from the city was restricted to those who could afford the high costs of commuting from the residential suburbs. High-income residential suburbs that were constructed at this time established an image of suburbs as places of substantial single-family houses surrounded by lawns free of crab grass, populated mainly by white Anglo-Saxon Protestants of upper-middle income and educational levels. Voting Republican was frequently included in this image.

These suburbs of before World War II had the advantage of appealing to the long-standing antiurbanism of Americans—suburbs were supposedly closer to nature and thus better places to live, while at the same time close enough to the city to have all the advantages of the urban life that the suburbanite really didn't want to abandon. Many suburban houses built during this period reflect the romanticism of their owners. Styles were wildly eclectic; houses half-timbered in the grand English Tudor style were built next to pillared Georgian colonial houses and

[4]Sam B. Warner, Jr., *Streetcar Suburbs*, Harvard University and M.I.T. Presses, Cambridge, Mass., 1962.

Spanish-Moorish villas. To their owners, these homes were far more than mere housing; they represented the romantic idealization of an earlier nonurban era. The home was a man's castle, where he could live, if not as a lord, at least as a latter-day country gentlemen—and all without being isolated from the advantages of twentieth-century city life.

### The 1950s to the Present

The third major change in suburbia was the housing boom which followed World War II. After the war, the exodus from the city included not only the rich and well-to-do but also large numbers of middle-class families and even blue-collar families. New housing construction, FHA and GI Bill loans, suburban employment opportunities, and discontent with city life all accelerated suburbanization. The pent-up demand for housing that had been frustrated first by the Depression and then by World War II really gained momentum during the 1950s—a momentum that carried

Suburban developments of the post-World War II era were characterized by a numbing standardization of design. *(United Press International.)*

through the 1960s into the 1970s. Since city housing was full and cities contained little vacant land for new housing, the expansion in the housing market had to come in the suburbs. Farmers' fields were rapidly converted to mass single-family housing developments. Tract developments of the Levittown type opened up suburban living to middle- and lower-middle-class families at a price they could afford, particularly with the aid of FHA and VA loans. The esthetic vapidness of these tracts of "little boxes" has been justly condemned. On the other hand, it should be kept in mind that the city neighborhoods from which many middle- and lower-middle-class people migrated were far from being architectural gems. Suburbs have no monopoly on drabness and look-alike uniformity.

The titles of many suburban subdevelopments built after World War II—Rolling Meadows, Apple Orchard Valley, Oak Forest Estates—are really epitaphs for what has been destroyed by the housing developments that carry on the names. This author once lived for two years in a suburban apartment complex of several hundred units named Seven Oaks Farm. The farm had been plowed under by the housing project and there were only three oaks, mere saplings hardly three feet tall. Country names are used to suggest an openness and rural nature which—if they ever existed—are certain to vanish as soon as the subdivision is built. But, of course, suburban developments called Congested Acres Estates or Flood Plains Hollow, while perhaps more accurately named, wouldn't have the same sales appeal.

## EMPLOYMENT PATTERNS

Historically suburbs have been considered "sub" because they were not economically self-supporting but rather appendages of the central city serving as dormitories. Suburban residents had to commute to the central city in order to earn their livelihood. The suburb as a dormitory area which one leaves in the morning to commute to the city and returns to at the end of the work day was changed after World War II, with the diversification of industry and services. Census figures reveal that in the 15 largest metropolitan areas a full 72 percent of workers who live in the suburbs also work in suburban areas. This means that only 28 percent still commute from the suburbs to the central city. Even in the New York area, the legendary citadel of the commuter, only 22 percent of the suburban workers actually commute into New York City. Our image of the suburbs has not caught up with reality.

Between 1958 and 1967 rates of growth for employment in central cities in wholesale and retail trade were 10.5 percent and 7.7 percent, respectively, while the comparable rates in suburbs were 90.2 percent and 60.6 percent. Significantly, an examination of the fifteen largest metropolitan areas shows that as of 1970, the central cities had only 52 percent of the total jobs in metropolitan areas. Only ten years earlier the central cities had two-thirds of the jobs in the metropolitan areas. As of 1970, in nine of the fifteen largest SMSAs, the suburbs exceeded the city as the principal location of jobs. Even in Washington, D.C., with its heavy concentration of government employment, over 55 percent of all jobs are now in the suburbs. As a result of suburban employment opportunities, reverse commuting is becoming more common—e.g., from New York City to New Jersey or even Connecticut.

Moreover, the overwhelming majority of new jobs that are being developed are coming into existence in suburban locations. New industries and services and the modern plants and offices of older industries are most likely to be located outside the central city. Even more ominous for central cities is the fact that the cities are experiencing a decline in the absolute number of jobs. Of the fifteen largest cities, only the two in Texas—where annexation is facilitated by state laws—had more jobs in 1970 than they did in 1960. The most extreme drop was in riot-scarred Detroit, where employment in the central city dropped 23 percent. Most other cities barely held their own. Aging buildings, outdated plants, high taxes, changing needs of consumers, and the city's reputation for riot and crime all argue against expansion of employment in the central city.

This was not what had been predicted by most business leaders, public officials, and even scholars during the 1920s and 1930s. They saw that American cities had grown during the early twentieth century in wealth, numbers, and power, and saw no reason that the concentrating trend of the previous hundred years should change. The skyscraper, as a symbol of urban dominance, had as clearly planted its image on the American city as the spires of the cathedral had expressed the spirit of the medieval European city. The city was at its zenith, and downtown businessmen expressed confidence that the only direction in which the city could go was up, toward a bigger and bigger future. Now the downtown areas are desperately trying to hold their own and prevent vacancy rates from climbing higher. The momentum has passed to the suburbs, and much of the change is related to the technology of the automobile, which made the population concentration of the city unnecessary.

The decentralization of business and industry not only resulted in the previously noted increases in suburban jobs but also encouraged suburbanization of the work force. Industrial parks, now a suburban hallmark, are frequently surrounded by working-class or blue-collar suburbs which house their work forces. Certainly businessmen and professional persons live in suburbs, but so do increasing numbers of other people.

The image of suburbs as areas exclusively of single-family houses will also have to undergo some revision if current trends continue. As a result of higher building costs and a demand for apartments, particularly among young singles and the elderly, suburbs are increasingly building high-rise apartments and other apartment housing. Higher costs of land and construction are making more and more new multiunits necessary. Suburbs passed a milestone of sorts in 1972 when, for the first time, more multiunits than private houses were started. Once one's family has grown up and left home, it is no longer necessary to move back to the city if one is seeking smaller housing or rental housing. Suburban rental apartments and condominiums have become increasingly commonplace. Suburbs are no longer only for families with children.

## DEMOGRAPHIC CHARACTERISTICS OF SUBURBS

The distinction between city and suburb is, of course, basically legal rather than sociological. While local municipal boundaries are significant in many ways—including financing, taxing, and provision of public services and schools—other social, organizational, ecological, and demographic criteria could be used, such as population density, the proportion of single-family dwellings, and distance from the center of the city. However, none of these alternative schemes have gained anywhere near the acceptance of the traditional city-suburb division. The city line is significant in that it is commonly viewed as a social, economic, and racial boundary. Demographically, suburbs are still more frequently the home of married couples and their children. Although, as has been mentioned, condominiums for the elderly and apartment complexes for singles are increasingly being built in the suburbs, there are still proportionally fewer unattached adults and couples without children in the suburbs than in the cities. In 1970, of all females fourteen years old and older 63.8 percent in the urban fringe of urbanized areas were married, but only 56.1 percent in central cities were married. Young single adults and the elderly are underrepresented in the suburbs, while children below the age of thirteen and adults between the ages of twenty-five and forty-four are overrepresented.

No longer are suburbs dominated by upper- and upper-middle income groups. However, although blue-collar workers and others of similar income levels have been suburbanizing in large numbers, the suburbs have not totally lost their selectivity: levels of socioeconomic status in the suburbs are, on the average, higher than those of the central cities. The most recent census indicated that in 1969 median family income in the suburbs was about $11,000, while the median in the central

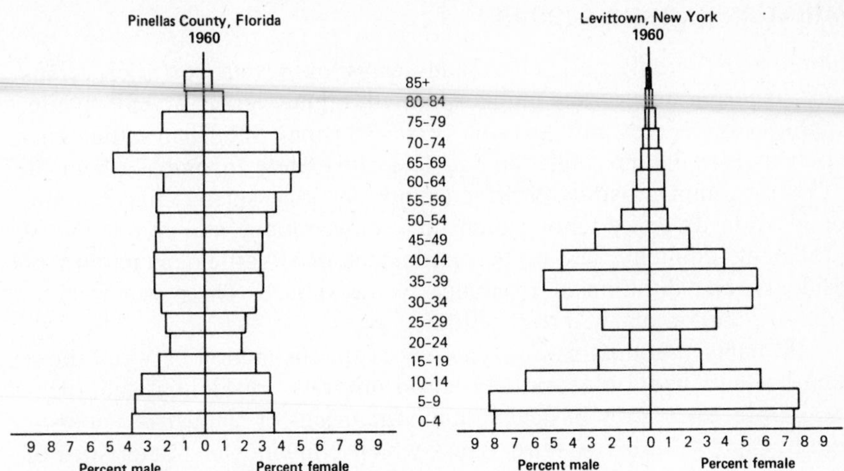


The population age differences between the retirement area of St. Petersburg, Florida (Penellas County), and suburban Levittown are dramatic. St. Petersburg has almost 30 percent of its population over sixty-five, while the figure in Levittown is only 3 percent. *(U.S. Bureau of the Census, U.S. Census of Population, General Population Characteristics, 1960.)*

city was about $9,000. Educationally, 62 percent of adults in the suburbs had completed high school, as compared with 51 percent in the cities.[5] A larger proportion of suburban residents are in white-collar occupations, particularly business and the professions. Finally, suburbs remain overwhelmingly white (95 percent), while the central cities are more and more nonwhite.

This thumbnail sketch does not, of course, apply to all suburban communities. The most recent census counted some 76 million suburbanites, and they are far from being a totally homogeneous population or living in identical suburban communities. In fact, 11 million suburbanites live in places of over 50,000 inhabitants, and if these suburban "cities" were not located in the shadow of even larger SMSAs they themselves would be listed as central cities with their own SMSAs. But while there are all types of suburbs and suburbanites, it is nonetheless true that suburbanites *as a whole* have higher socioeconomic status than city dwellers.[6]

[5]U.S. Bureau of the Census, Census of Population: 1970, *General Social and Economic Characteristics*, Final Report, PC[1]-C-1, Washington, D.C., 1972, p. 405.

[6]Leo F. Schnore, "The Socio-Economic Status of Cities and Suburbs," *American Sociological Review*, **28**:76–85, February, 1963.

## VARIATIONS AMONG SUBURBS

Suburbs can be differentiated in many ways: old versus new, rich versus poor, incorporated versus unincorporated, ethnic versus WASP (white, Anglo-Saxon, Protestant), growing versus stagnant. Suburban settlements are so diverse that no single typology can adequately encompass them all.

For example, a study of fifteen suburban areas surrounding Toronto found wide diversity among them in socioeconomic status, density of settlement, ethnicity, age of the settlement, past settlement pattern of residents, and duration of residence in the suburb. There was far less structure than in planned tract settlements.[7]

Probably the most useful typology is the distinction between those suburbs that function essentially as dormitories—residential suburbs—and those that are basically manufacturing or industrial areas—employment suburbs. A third type—which combines characteristics of the other two—can also be delineated. Leo Schnore has empirically demonstrated the differences among these types of suburbs in terms of their social and economic characteristics.[8] Schnore used one sample of seventy-four suburbs surrounding New York City and a second sample of 300 suburbs found within the nation's twenty-five largest Urbanized Areas. He discovered that there were systematic differences in age and ethnic composition, fertility and dependency, socioeconomic status, population growth, and housing characteristics in residential, mixed, and employing suburbs. Employing suburbs contain higher proportions of both foreign-born inhabitants and nonwhites than residential suburbs, with the mixed suburbs in the middle.

The percentage of nonwhites in residential suburbs was only 2.4, notably smaller than in the other types of suburbs. Interestingly, the highest fertility ratios and the highest proportion of married couples with children under six years of age are found in the mixed type of suburbs; in the two other types, these figures are lower. Socioeconomic status was highest in the residential suburb, as were the percentage having completed high school, the percentage employed in white-collar occupations, and the median income level. In 1960, a gap in excess of $1,350 separated the median incomes of the residential and employing suburbs. The intermediate type of suburb was in the middle. Residential suburbs were also likely to outstrip the growth of industrial suburbs. Three out of ten of the employing suburbs actually lost population during the decade before the census of 1960.

[7]S. D. Clark, *The Suburban Society*, University of Toronto Press, Toronto, 1966.

[8]Leo F. Schnore, "The Social and Economic Characteristics of American Suburbs," *Sociological Quarterly*, **4**:122–134, 1963.

Suburbs also differ systematically with regard to housing characteristics. Residential suburbs have the highest proportion of new housing, the highest percentage of owner-occupied units, and the highest percentage of single-family units; the employment suburbs were lowest on these measures.

Suburban growth is not as chaotic as it might seem. Research such as Schnore's indicates that while suburbs may vary in many respects, there is a predictable pattern to the variation. There are persistent systematic differences which contribute to predicting the evolutionary development of suburban areas.

## PERSISTENCE OF CHARACTERISTICS

Within the evolving metropolitan area, not all sectors change at the same speed; and while suburbs taken as a whole are no longer homogeneous, individual communities are often quite homogeneous. Research done by Reynolds Farley indicates that there is considerable persistence over time in the suburbs.[9] Farley's research on 137 suburbs of twenty-four central cities suggests that although we tend to see the suburbs as experiencing a rapid rate of change, there is considerable consistency at least among older established suburbs. The socioeconomic status of individual suburbs in 1960 was generally the same as it had been twenty or forty years earlier. In fact, a sound prediction of the educational level of a suburb can be made if one knows the school-attendance rate of the high-school-age population of forty years earlier. Individual suburbs thus have changed far less than the central cities. For example, Wilmette, north of Chicago, and Chevy Chase, just outside Washington, occupy positions of social status remarkably similar to the positions they occupied in 1920. Farley suggests that suburban persistency may result because a suburb originally establishes a distinct composition, so that the persons who tend to move to it have socioeconomic characteristics similar to those already living there. Different suburbs have different political systems, different economic bases, different demographic characteristics, and different social environments. Although the entire suburban area is remarkably diverse, individual suburbs tend to be homogeneous in characteristics and do retain these characteristics over time. While the persistence of social and economic characteristics over, say, forty years is commonplace in European cities, the same has not been true on this side of the Atlantic. Most of us would be hard-pressed to name central-city neighborhoods that have retained their characteristics for as long as forty years.

[9]Reynolds Farley, "Suburban Persistence," *American Sociological Review*, **29**:38–47, 1964.

Older established suburbs, such as Wilmette on Chicago's North Shore, have changed remarkably little over the decades. They still represent a comfortable upper-middle-class style of life. *(Mary Doody.)*

## "CAUSES" OF SUBURBANIZATION

On the social-psychological level, the appeal of suburbs continues to increase while the appeal of city life decreases. A Gallup poll taken in 1972 indicated that only 13 percent of the 1,464 interviewed said they would prefer living in a city to a suburb, small town, or farm. As recently as 1966, 22 percent had said they preferred city to nonurban residence. Even among city dwellers themselves (those living in cities of half a million or more), only 20 percent said they preferred city living; in 1966, nearly twice that proportion (36 percent) had said they would prefer living in a city. While the declining appeal of cities was recorded among both whites and blacks and the young and the elderly, and in all regions of the nation, the preference for nonurban life was greatest among blue-collar families, persons living in the East, and those in their thirties and forties. According to Hawley and Zimmer:

> Over half of the reasons given for moving from central cities to suburbs have

> had to do with a quest for privacy, cleanliness, safety, and greater space in house and yard. For these amenities families are willing to sacrifice accessibility and to assume higher residence costs.[10]

(See "Children and Familism," page 167, for data on people who leave the city to seek a better environment for their children.)

The suburban boom, however, has been fueled by more than a simple desire to escape from the cities. There are a number of reasons why young couples, and others, move to the suburbs.

First, and most important, in the eastern and northern sections of the country all or almost all the land within the legal boundaries of the city was already developed by the 1950s. This meant that additional growth of the urban area would, by definition, *have* to be suburban growth. The Depression years of the 1930s saw little building, and during the 1940s there was a war on, so by the 1950s there was a tremendous pent-up demand for new metropolitan housing, and the available open land was, by definition, suburban.

Second, economics has played a major role. Young families moved to suburbs not just for "togetherness" or safety, but because houses in suburban subdevelopments were frequently cheaper than housing in the city. More importantly, FHA and VA mortgages with low down payments could be obtained easily on new suburban homes; to buy older homes in the city required larger down payments. To new families just becoming economically established, this was a major consideration. The FHA program will be discussed in some detail in Chapter 10, "Urban Renewal and Related Housing Issues."

Third, taxes in the suburbs were considerably lower than those in the central city—although recently suburban taxes have been increasing, as residents put in "extras" which the builders have not included, such as sewers, sidewalks, street lighting, and, of course, schools. Still, during the 1950s and 1960s the initial costs of housing in the newer "package" suburbs were frequently lower and easier to finance than housing in the central city.

Fourth, the "baby boom" after World War II directly encouraged movement out of the city. The housing in cities was simply not adequate to absorb large numbers of additional children. New city housing had not been built since before the war, existing housing was badly overcrowded, and landlords were not inclined to be tolerant of young children. Young couples with children were, to a degree, forced toward the suburbs, since they were not welcome as renters in city apartments and could not afford

[10]Amos H. Hawley and Basil Zimmer, *The Metropolitan Community: Its People and Government*, Sage Publications, Beverly Hills, 1970, pp. 31–33.

to purchase city houses. The suburban "baby boom" children (born between 1947 and 1959, the "baby boom" years) have now come of age, and they in turn are having children of their own and looking for suburban housing for their families. Once the second child is on the way or being thought about, couples start serious house-hunting, and the houses and areas they like are generally in the suburbs. Even if birth rates continue to remain at the present low levels, the number of children born will still be considerable. Women in the most prolific childbearing years, twenty to twenty-nine, numbered 13.6 million in 1967 and 18.3 million in 1975, an increase of 35 percent.[11] Between 1950 and 1974 the population of the United States grew from 150 million to 210 million, and the metropolitan area's share of the additional 70 million people was added to the urban fringe rather than to the central city.

Finally, data indicate people have an overwhelming preference for single-family houses on their own lots, and these are easiest to find in the suburbs. More distantly located single-family houses are rated high above more centrally located high-rise luxurious apartments or even town houses. This preference is clearest among couples with children, but it is also true of other groups. Most Americans do not have the same housing goals as professional planners and urbanists; most people prefer suburban sprawl to other alternatives.[12]

Among other things, this means that people are getting pretty much what they want in housing design. Look-alike suburban tract developments succeed while urban developments seek tenants because even when alternatives are open most people prefer suburban locations. The fact that most professional urbanologists and architects deplore the "little boxes all in a row" has had little impact on the mass of the population who continue the exodus from the city.

## THE MYTH OF SUBURBIA

Over the years suburbs have become more than mere places of residence. They have become examples of a way of life. The caricature described below has been called by some sociologists "the myth of suburbia," the myth being the belief that there is, in fact, a uniquely suburban way of life.[13]

[11]Philip M. Hauser, *The Population Dilemma*, Prentice-Hall, Englewood Cliffs, N. J., 1969, p. 91.

[12]William Michelson, "Most People Don't Want What Architects Want," *Trans-Action*, July–August, 1968, pp. 37–43.

[13]Bennett M. Berger, "The Myth of Suburbia," *Journal of Social Issues*, **17**:38–49, 1971; Herbert J. Gans, "Urbanism and Suburbanism as Ways of Life: A Re-Evaluation of Definitions," in Arnold Rose (ed.), *Human Behavior*, Houghton Mifflin, Boston, 1962.

Suburbia has become endowed with a long list of physical and even psychological attributes: ranch-style houses, neat lawns, station wagons and car pools, up-tight parents, and togetherness. It is the place where one supposedly finds

> . . . a home of one's own, a small piece of real estate on which to practice yeoman's skills, good schools, plenty of land for recreation, clean and traffic free neighborhoods, a small town atmosphere, Christmas lights, a Fourth of July parade, a homogeneous community without social tensions . . . [14]

Accordingly to this view, people living in suburbs are, or become, somehow different from those who remain in the city. They are supposedly middle- and upper-class, nonethnic whites who have fled the central city. Stereotypes of suburbia are frequently less than complimentary. The suburban way of life is one of wide lawns and narrow minds where family life is child-oriented rather than adult-oriented. Critics have described the suburban family as surrendering all individuality and creativity. The social anthropologist Margaret Mead characterized suburban life as consisting of "a living room or recreation room which often resembles a giant playpen into which the parents have somewhat reluctantly climbed."

In terms of life-style, suburbanites, particularly those in the newer suburbs, are said to be gregarious. Numerous cocktail parties are interspersed with extensive informal visiting or neighboring. Togetherness is a way of life. Organizationally, suburbanites are said to be hyperactive joiners, with hobby groups, bridge clubs, neighborhood associations, and church-related social activities taking several nights a week. On top of this, there are a proliferation of women's groups, scout troops, and kaffeeklatsches. Husbands are said to spend their weekends cutting grass, watching football games, picking up the kids, going to parties, going to church, and watching more football games.

While the "myth of suburbia" is something of a straw man, it is unfortunately true that suburbs have not received enough study. For all the talk, the study of suburbs has not been a popular topic during the last decade. During the 1960s, "urban research" came to mean the study of inner-city poverty or minority groups. The vacuum left by the absence of hard research on suburban life-styles was filled with a plethora of popular books and articles dealing with suburban conformity, adultery, alcoholism, divorce, and plain boredom. Even the best of the popular writing on

[14]Robert Lineberry and Ira Sharkansky, *Urban Politics and Public Policy*, Harper and Row, New York, 1971, p. 34.

suburban life (e.g., *Bullet Park, The Organization Man, The Man in the Grey Flannel Suit*) painted a highly selective, if not downright inaccurate, picture.

Suburbanites, particularly in the new tract suburbs, are expected to be young (twenty-five to thirty-five), to be well educated (at least some college), to have white-collar jobs (junior or middle management, salesmen, young lawyers, teachers, government workers), and to be upwardly mobile. Because of these characteristics and because they work for large organizations, suburbanites are expected to be geographically as well as socially mobile. Within the hierarchy of an organization, a move up frequently means a move to a new metropolitan area. Here, the suburbanite and his family find a new suburb, quite similar to the one they left, into which they can easily blend.

Much of the above is based on William H. Whyte's extremely influential study, *The Organization Man.*[15] Unfortunately, many of Whyte's imitators were not as careful as he had been, and Sunday newspaper supplements were soon full of articles either praising or condemning the new suburban way of life. Very few stopped to ask whether the picture of suburbia fit the reality all that well.

Three problems with the early suburban studies can be cited. First, the problem with most of the postwar suburban studies was not that they were inaccurate but that they were selective of one type of suburb. Attention was focused on the large tract developments for young families, while little attention was given to industrial suburbs, working-class suburbs, or even older established suburbs. The end result was that the image of suburbia was loaded by emphasizing middle-class tract suburbs with their culture of backyard barbecues, picture windows, and station wagons. Generalizing from these studies, which presented a loaded sample, to all suburbanites is not scientifically valid, but it was nonetheless done by many writers of the period. Some of the studies are also an example of the ecological fallacy discussed in Chapter 5—generalizing from characteristics of an area to characteristics of individuals. Second, it is possible that some of the communities chosen for study were selected precisely because they were in some respects atypical and thus presumably more interesting. Third, many of the observations were based on a single look at a suburb immediately after the first wave of settlement. It is highly likely that another look five or ten years later, after the community had "matured," would show changes in the pace of life.[16]

[15]Doubleday (Anchor), Garden City, New York, 1956.

[16]On this point, see S. D. Clark, op. cit.

## WORKING-CLASS SUBURBS

In predominantly working-class suburbs the supposed suburban "involvement syndrome" may not occur at all. Bennett Berger looked at the working-class suburb of Milpitas, California, which was inhabited by many automobile workers who had moved to the suburban community when the Ford Motor Company closed its plant in Richmond, California, and moved its operations a few miles north of San Jose. Two and a half years after the move, 70 percent did not belong to a single club, organization, or association other than their union. Visiting was rare unless relatives lived nearby. There had been none of the supposed suburban "return to religion"; half went to church rarely or not at all. Nor had the move to the suburbs affected their political affiliations; they still voted 81 percent Democratic. Finally, they had no expectations or illusions regarding their social mobility; they had no great hopes of getting ahead in their jobs. They overwhelmingly viewed the suburb not as a transitional stop on the career ladder, but rather as a permanent place of settlement. The move from the city to the suburb did not affect the life-style of these workers. Although it definitely improved the quality of their homes, it did not change their behavior patterns.[17] Crossing into suburbia didn't change Democrats into Republicans or nonjoiners into joiners. No magical transformation in social customs took place. Working-class norms, attitudes, and behavior persisted with little modification.

Differences between blue-collar urbanites and blue-collar suburbanites were explored further by Albert Cohen and Harold Hodges, Jr., in their study of approximately 2,600 male family heads living in the San Francisco Bay area. They found no significant differences between urban and suburban blue-collar workers in areas such as self-concept, concern over status, familial loyalty, and sex norms.[18] Furthermore, there do not appear to be any changes in involvement with unions, according to a study of forty-six urban and suburban dwellers in New Jersey done by William Spinrad. There were some differences, but these were not great or systematic.[19]

The shift from city to suburb usually means a change in type of housing (from an apartment or older house to a ranch-type or split-level house), but not necessarily a change in style of life. The working-class

[17]Bennett M. Berger, *Working Class Suburbs*, University of California Press, Berkeley, 1960.

[18]Albert K. Cohen and Harold M. Hodges, Jr., "Characteristics of the Lower Blue-Collar Class," *Social Problems*, **10**:307, Spring, 1963.

[19]William Spinrad, "Blue-Collar Workers as City and Suburban Residents—Effect of Union Membership," in A. Shostak and W. Gomberg (eds.), *Blue-Collar World*, Prentice-Hall, Englewood Cliffs, N.J., 1964, pp. 215–224.

suburb does not generally represent an alteration of the blue-collar life-style, but rather a transposition of existing patterns into the new setting.

## LEVITTOWN

Probably the most thorough case study of a suburban community is Herbert Gans's study of the social organization of Levittown, New Jersey, during the first two years of its existence.[20] The various Levittowns were prototypes of the postwar "package suburbs" that can now be found near all of the country's larger cities. Levitt and Sons, Inc., originally built for a lower-middle-class market, but over the years the size of their houses and their prices have increased considerably.

Gans's findings were based upon interviews with two sets of Levittowners and his own observations, made while he lived in Levittown for two years. Gans suggests that the sociability found within the community is a direct result of the compatibility or homogeneity of the backgrounds of the residents. Homogeneity was most evident in terms of age and income. But diversity in regional backgrounds, membership in ethnic groups, and religious beliefs provided variety for the community. Even the similarity in income did not indicate as much homogeneity as the statistics indicated; for one family might be headed by a skilled worker at the peak of his earning power, another by a white-collar worker with some hope of advancement, and a third by a young executive or professional just at the start of his career. Active sociability emerged only when neighboring residents shared common tastes and values, were similar with regard to race and class, and shared similar beliefs regarding child-raising practices.[21] Family togetherness was seen by the residents as a positive attribute of the community. Parents and children all felt that they spent more time together as a family. Even the husbands' commuting did not have the often-alleged negative effect on family activities. Most Levittowners did not really mind commuting unless it involved a trip of over forty minutes.

Although the popular literature is rather heavy with criticism of suburban anomie (normlessness) and malaise, boredom was not a serious problem in Levittown. Depression and loneliness appeared if anything to be less common than in the city. Almost all the emotional difficulties were concentrated among working-class women who were for the first time cut off from their parents, and wives with husbands whose jobs kept them on the road and away from the family.

[20]Herbert Gans, *The Levittowners*, Pantheon Books, New York, 1967.
[21]Gans, op. cit.

Surprisingly, only 14 percent of those who had formerly lived in the nearby city of Philadelphia said that they found the community to be dull. Most residents thought there were a great number of things to do. Those most likely to find the community lacking were upper-middle-class people who had tried Levittown's organizational life and found it wanting.

Adolescents also had a hard time. The community was particularly deadly for teen-agers owing to the lack of recreational facilities and even of places to go. It was designed for families with young children, not adolescents. Thus, bedrooms were small and they lacked the privacy or soundproofing necessary to allow a teen-ager to have his friends visit. Shopping centers were designed for adults who owned cars and discouraged adolescents who hung around and made only marginal purchases. Even the high school discouraged its students from using its facilities after school hours because of the school administrator's fear of increasing maintenance costs.

Overall, Gans's description of Levittown is of a community that was not overly exciting but that generally met the needs of its residents. The worst thing that can be said about the community is that for anyone with cosmopolitan tastes, it is rather dull. But then Levittowns weren't built for cosmopolites.

### A Comparison: Levittown and Pullman

It is interesting to compare Levittown with the planned worker's community of Pullman, which was built just outside of Chicago three-quarters of a century earlier. Both received considerable national and worldwide publicity, although neither was quite what it was thought to be. Both initially also received favorable publicity. But Pullman eventually erupted in the Great Pullman Strike of 1894, and Levittown by the 1960s had become synonymous with everything that was supposed to be wrong with suburbia.

Both Levittown and Pullman tried in their own ways to affect the behavior of their residents. Levitt carefully screened buyers to keep out undesired class and racial groups; Pullman attempted to select workers and renters for their reliability and freedom from the taint of union ideas. Neither community was totally successful in this; in both cases working-class families also resisted pressures for moral uplift. Nor were attempts to legislate morality particularly successful, although Pullman tried it by decree and Levittown by the ballot. Both towns were "dry": alcoholic beverages were not allowed to be sold within community boundaries. As a result, both communities remained "clean" by forcing their residents to go elsewhere for their good times. Legislation in both cases changed only appearance, not values.

Pullman was never as good or Levittown as bad as it was portrayed by journalists; each was surrounded by a myth: Pullman by the myth that it encouraged working-class virtue and ensured a reliable work force, Levittown by the myth that it engendered ticky-tacky dullness and mindless conformity.[22]

## A "STATUS SUBURB": CRESTWOOD HEIGHTS

A picture of a different type of culture, a status-conscious suburb of social climbers, is presented in *Crestwood Heights,* which is a study of an upper-middle-class suburban area of Toronto.[23] Crestwood Heights comes close to the stereotype—such as was shown in the movie *The Graduate*—of the established affluent suburb with its cocktail parties and well-manicured lawns. However, being successful economically doesn't lead to a relaxed life-style, for the picture of Crestwood Heights is one of compulsive behavior. Even the children are constantly indoctrinated with anxiety over status by their competitive parents. The authors emphasize the great insecurity and striving of the community's adults and the transference of their goals of social mobility to their children. Constant stress on status and a heavy reliance on outside health experts to provide guidance on child rearing were viewed as indications of the parents' insecurity. Even the home became a status symbol rather than a place to relax—as much a showcase of goods as a place to live.

Whether Crestwood Heights is typical of well-to-do suburban areas is open to question. In fact, technically the area is not a suburb at all but rather an outer area of Toronto. Further, the population of the community is predominantly Jewish—which is definitely not the case in most suburban areas. It is an open question to what extent the findings of the study reflect behavior patterns typical of an ethnic group rather than a social class. Crestwood Heights may be a better profile of an upper-middle-class Jewish community than of typical suburban life-styles.

## EXURBANITES

Beyond the built-up suburbs surrounding the very largest cities there is a special class of suburbanites who have become known as "exurbanites." These are the people who have achieved success in their professions—frequently the communications industry or writing—and have moved

[22]For descriptions of the two communities, see Stanley Buder, *Pullman,* Oxford University Press, New York, 1967; and Gans, op. cit.

[23]John Seeley, R. Alexander Sim, and Elizabeth Loosley, *Crestwood Heights,* Basic Books, New York, 1956.

farther out to get away from the rat race.[24] Their work may allow them to use their own offices at home several days a week and avoid daily commuting. Thus, if their base is New York, they can live as far out as Fairfield, Bucks, and Winchester counties.

Unfortunately, the best-known study of exurbia, *The Exurbanites,* is a caricature of hyperactive, upwardly mobile, creative people all living in their trilevel houses. The picture is of people desperately trying to find meaning in their lives, people who find that moving out of the city doesn't reduce the anxiety of working in extremely competitive industries where the standards for judging performance are highly subjective and fickle. Since living in the country is a strain on the budget, there is also often the pressure of having to live up to a standard of living that one can't afford. Living in exurbia can also put considerable pressures on wives, who find themselves locked into a schedule of maintaining a house and providing a station-wagon shuttle service for children and commuting husbands while they remain isolated from the city.

This general outline has, of course, served as the framework for dozens of novels, television dramas, and movies. Unfortunately, it is sometimes taken to be a scientifically valid reflection of reality, rather than inventive fiction. Although solid research is scarce, there does not appear to be evidence that exurbanites are significantly different from suburbanites. In fact, exurbs have a way of turning into suburbs as more and more people with the same background move into the same area—all seeking to get away from it all.

## CHILDREN AND FAMILISM

The idea that suburbanites have excessively large families when compared with urbanites is one of those myths that refuse to die. The number of children in the suburbs is frequently commented upon, with the implicit assumption that fertility rates of suburbanites are substantially higher than those of otherwise similar urban dwellers. In fact fertility rates of suburban dwellers are only marginally higher than those of city dwellers as a whole, and lower than those of inner-core residents. The highest fertility levels are found in rural areas.[25] Newer suburban developments appear to have higher fertility simply because the communities are made up of young couples, and young couples in their twenties and thirties tend to have children. Some observers of the suburban scene noted the

[24] A. C. Spectorsky, *The Exurbanites*, Berkley, New York, 1958.

[25] Ben J. Wattenberg and Richard Scammon, "The Suburban Boom," in John Kramer (ed.), *North American Suburbs*, Glendessary Press, Berkeley, 1972, p. 80.

obvious number of children and jumped to the hasty conclusion that fertility per couple was higher in the suburbs.

Suburban patterns of life are usually associated with the value of "familism" and, in particular, with an emphasis upon the activities of the nuclear family as the basic unit of interaction with friends and neighbors. The suburban model is one of mother, father, children—and possibly the family dog—jointly engaging in the same activities. Whether it is a Sunday afternoon drive, a PTA bazaar, or a Little League game, the presence of the nuclear family of parents and children is the norm. If a family member is absent, the absence has to be explained.

The choice of suburban single-family housing over other alternatives is frequently explained by the fact that the suburbs are seen as a good place to raise children. William H. Whyte, in his study of Park Forest, suggests that this was one of the major reasons that families originally moved into the suburb from Chicago.[26] A decade later Gans stressed that the same was true for those who moved to the New Jersey Levittown he studied.[27] Another study, this one of the Levittown outside New York City, indicated that the search for a better place to raise children was the chief reason for moving to the suburbs. Two-thirds of those who had previously lived in New York City gave this as their primary reason.[28]

As the earlier discussion of the economics of suburban housing indicated this reason may not, in fact, be the most important, but it is generally accepted that single-family housing with adjacent open spaces is a good place to raise children, while urban housing, particularly high-rise apartments, is not. As a woman living in a high-rise in Chicago put it: "A mother can't look out for her kids if they are fifteen floors down in the playground." Even in high-income high-rises, unless the family is wealthy enough to have a nurse or the mother spends a great deal of time taking the children in and out, it is all but impossible to supervise children's outdoor play. Corridors, elevators, and stairwells also pose problems of safety, particularly in public housing. Even a child's basic needs, such as having to come inside to go to the bathroom, can become a logistical problem if the home is on the eighth floor. Nor do high-rises as a rule invest their valuable outside space in play areas for children. Similarly, providing meeting and game rooms for older children and teen-agers means taking that space away from some income-producing use. Needless to say, this is rarely done.

Thin walls and active children also contribute to unhappy relation-

[26]William H. Whyte, *The Organization Man*, Doubleday (Anchor), Garden City, N. Y., 1956.

[27]Gans, op. cit.

[28]Harold Wattel, "Levittown: A Suburban Community," in William Dobriner (ed.), *The Suburban Community*, G. P. Putnam's Sons, New York, 1958, p. 290.

ships with neighbors and create constant pressure to be quiet and to restrain exuberance. Thus, it is not surprising that the single-family house where space is provided for play and the mother can watch the children from her kitchen window is the overwhelming choice of most people with children.

It has been suggested that persons choosing to live in a suburban setting have deliberately chosen a life-style that emphasizes "familism" and deemphasizes alternative life-styles such as "careerism" and "consumership."[29] If such is the case, it would mean that suburbanites put family values above achievement in their careers and the accumulation of consumer goods. David Riseman, for instance, thinks that suburbanism is a form of escapism whereby men devote their time to family roles when they could be—and should be—participating in the public affairs of the city. He believes the suburban emphasis on lawn and Little League rob the city of men with the skills and the natural ability to act as leaders in addressing city problems.[30] Riseman's emphasis on the role of *men* as achievers, by the way, was obviously written when less attention was given to the equality of women.

On the other hand, research done by Scott Greer on the metropolitan St. Louis area suggests that suburbs do foster greater political participation:

> In general, it seemed that the familistic neighborhoods, with their dense networks of neighboring and voluntary organizations, did produce more involvement and informed political action. However, the size of the municipality made a difference: the kind of people who were local political actors in the suburbs were much less likely to be so in the City of St. Louis. So, organizational type of neighborhood and political unit had independent effects. In general, the type of sub-area (urbanism-familism) predicted the proportion of local actors, but their *political* activity was affected by the organization of the polity.[31]

### Caveat

None of this is to suggest in any way that inner-city residents do not value children or family contacts. They obviously do have close family ties, but the way family relationships are expressed sometimes differ in suburbs and inner cities. In the tight ethnic communities of the West End of

[29] Wendell Bell, "The City, the Suburb, and a Theory of Social Choice," in Scott Greer, Dennis L. McElrath, David W. Minar, and Peter Orleans (eds.), *The New Urbanization*, St. Martin's Press, New York, 1968, pp. 132–168.

[30] David Riseman, "The Suburban Sadness," in Dobriner, op. cit., pp. 375–408.

[31] Scott Greer, *The Urbane View*, Oxford University Press, New York, 1972, p. 97.

Boston or the Addams area of Chicago, family relationships were all-important, but they clearly involved segregation by age and sex. Adult males congregated with other males, wives talked to other wives, and children interacted with other children. Adults certainly were not expected to involve themselves in the activities of their children. Suburban norms, on the other hand, are more likely to encourage such involvement.

## MENTAL HEALTH AND THE CULTURE OF SUBURBS

Suburban literature of the period since World War II has frequently stressed the shallowness, anxiety, and sheer desperation of suburban life. For example, in Maurice R. Stein's article "Suburbia: Dream or Nightmare" we see a grim picture of suburban life: the man is forced to spend his energy and time away from the home, engaged in a constant ulcer-ridden struggle for advancement that fills him with anxiety and neuroses. His wife fares little better; she is caught up in a compulsive and demanding routine that leaves her both bored and depressed.[32] Even the value of "togetherness" is seen, in William H. Whyte's study of Park Forest, as being only a shallow compensation for the absence of true meaningful involvement and solid roots.

Since there is an even longer tradition of literature on the anomic and alienating life within the city proper, one is left with the baffling impression that life in the city is detrimental to one's mental health, while the suburb is a sea of neurosis and anxiety. Either way you can't win. Fortunately, the truth is that while anomie in the city and togetherness in the suburbs can be problems, they are too frequently presented as stereotypes which have only marginal resemblance to the communities in which most of us actually spend our lives.

Suburban areas also frequently are attacked as cultural vacuums. Suggestive, but not conclusive, evidence does indicate that cultural interests rank somewhat lower among the values of suburbanites than among the values of those who prefer an urban environment. Likewise, a study of a national sample of graduating college seniors found that, while there is no evidence that those raised in the city differ in intellectual attitudes from those raised in suburbs, the students who found access to cultural activities less important were more likely to show a preference for suburban living.[33] Also, data gathered by the Survey Research Center of the University of Michigan and based on families in all the metropolitan areas in the United States (except in New York City, which was

[32]Maurice R. Stein, *Eclipse of Community*, Harper and Row, New York, 1960.

[33]Joseph Zelan, "Does Suburbia Make a Difference: An Exercise in Secondary Analysis," in Sylvia Fleis Fava, (ed.), *Urbanism in World Perspective*, Thomas Crowell, New York, 1968, p. 408.

judged atypical) indicate that those living in single-family homes were more likely to enjoy family and home-centered activities such as gardening and cooking out in the yard.[34]

There is no evidence, however, that suburbanites as individuals make less use of city museums, art galleries, theaters, and concerts than city residents. In many cities suburbanites provide the major support for cultural activities. Thanks to expressways, suburbanites can reach downtown facilities and events such as concerts and plays in little more time than a city resident living in one of the outer neighborhoods. Suburbs also frequently have their own community playhouses, theater groups, and festivals, which, if not up to downtown professional standards, at least indicate interest in the arts.

Some suburbs are indeed cultural wastelands; but so again are many city neighborhoods. Manhattan may be the center of the nation's theater, ballet, and opera, but very little of it seems to have rubbed off on the Bronx or Queens. Many suburbanites do not make use of the central city's cultural facilities, but there is no evidence to suggest that they supported or attended cultural activities even when they were city residents. It remains to be proven that suburbanites differ from city dwellers of similar socioeconomic status in their interest in, and support of, cultural activities.

## RACIAL CHANGE

A common characteristic of suburbs is their whiteness. Of the nation's population, 11 percent is black; but 21 percent of the population of central cities is black, while the figure for the suburbs is under 5 percent. Over the tumultuous decade between 1960 and 1970 the black suburban population increased 34 percent—or at a slightly higher rate than that of whites—but the change was not as impressive as might at first be thought, since there had been relatively few suburban blacks at the beginning of the decade. Census figures for 1970 show that suburbs are 4.7 percent black, which is only a marginal change over the 4.2 percent recorded in 1960. Blacks have been moving to the suburbs; but while their numbers have been increasing, the white flood to suburban locations has also continued. While over 800,000 blacks became new suburbanites during the decade of the 1960s, over 15 million whites poured into the suburbs during this same period. So long as the white exodus to the suburbs continues, suburban areas are going to remain predominantly white, regardless of how many blacks also move in.

[34]William H. Michelson, "Potential Candidates for the Designer's Paradise," *Social Forces*, **46**:190–196, 1967.

During the 1960s black ghettoes began to spill out of cities into inner suburbs, but today blacks are still overwhelmingly found in central-city locations. According to Harold Rose, "Large scale ghettoization of suburban populations during the sixties was essentially confined to New York, Newark, Miami, Chicago, St. Louis, and Washington, with the rate of growth in the Washington metropolitan area far outstripping the rest."[35]

Among blacks, the total population increase between 1960 and 1970 was 3.8 million, and a full 3.2 million of this took place in central cities. For whites, just the opposite was the case; of a total increase of 18.8 million, a full 15.5 million was in suburban areas.[36]

Comparisons of some cities with their suburbs tell the story vividly. Washington, D.C., is over 71 percent black, while its suburbs are under 8 percent black. In Cleveland, the city is 38 percent black; the suburbs are 3.4 percent black. The city of Boston is 16 percent black; its suburbs are 1.1 percent black. Milwaukee is even more segregated: only three-tenths of 1 percent of the suburban area is black, while the central city is 15 percent black.

The above figures should not be taken to mean that cities are in any meaningful sense less segregated than suburbs. Having a higher percentage of blacks living in a city does not mean that blacks and whites live in the same neighborhoods. Most city neighborhoods are racially segregated. Integrated areas in the city are frequently merely those that are in transition from all-white to all-black. Statistically, cities *taken as wholes* are less segregated than suburbs; but the more socially meaningful comparisons, those done neighborhood by neighborhood or block by block, show high segregation indices for central cities.[37]

## BLACK SUBURBANIZATION

Blacks, nonetheless, are suburbanizing. In every region of the country, except the South, blacks increased as a proportion of the SMSA ring population, although increases were small. In the South the black population in the suburban rings declined from 12.6 to 10.3 percent.[38]

Today the absence of blacks in suburbs is a reflection of racial attitudes more than economics. As of 1970 one-third of black urban families had incomes of $10,000 or over, so it is clear that blacks are not

[35]Harold M. Rose, *The Black Ghetto*, McGraw-Hill, New York, 1971, p. 21.

[36]Bureau of the Census, "The Social and Economic Status of Negroes in the United States, 1970," *Special Studies*, series P–23, no. 38, U.S. Government Printing Office, Washington, D.C., 1971, p. 12.

[37]Karl E. Taeuber and Alma F. Taeuber, *Negroes in Cities*, Aldine Press, Chicago, 1965.

[38]William W. Pendleton, "Blacks in Suburbs," in Massotti and Hadden, op. cit., p. 173.

**Table 7-1 Population Distribution and Change, Inside and Outside Metropolitan Areas: 1950, 1960, and 1970**

| | Population (in millions) | | | | | |
|---|---|---|---|---|---|---|
| | Negro | | | White | | |
| Area | 1950* | 1960 | 1970 | 1950* | 1960 | 1970 |
| United States | 15.0 | 18.9 | 22.7 | 135.1 | 158.8 | 177.6 |
| Metropolitan areas | 8.8 | 12.8 | 16.8 | 85.1 | 106.4 | 121.3 |
| Central cities | 6.6 | 9.9 | 13.1 | 46.8 | 50.1 | 49.5 |
| Outside central cities | 2.2 | 2.8 | 3.7 | 38.3 | 56.3 | 71.8 |
| Outside metropolitan areas | 6.2 | 6.1 | 5.8 | 50.0 | 52.5 | 56.4 |

| | Change, 1960–1970 | | | |
|---|---|---|---|---|
| | Negro | | White | |
| | Number change (in millions) | Percent change | Number change (in millions) | Percent change |
| United States | 3.8 | 20 | 18.8 | 12 |
| Metropolitan areas | 4.1 | 32 | 14.9 | 14 |
| Central cities | 3.2 | 33 | .6 | −1 |
| Outside central cities | .8 | 29 | 15.5 | 28 |
| Outside metropolitan areas | −.3 | −4 | 3.9 | 7 |

*1950 data for metropolitan areas are not strictly comparable to the 1970 definition of SMSAs.
*Source:* U.S. Bureau of the Census, "The Social and Economic Status of Negroes in the United States, 1970," *Current Population Reports,* ser. P-23, no. 38, U.S. Government Printing Office, Washington, D.C., p. 12.

suburbanizing at the rate one would expect on the basis of economics alone. Some degree of this segregation of more affluent blacks is doubtless by choice; much of it is not. Extensive research by Karl E. Taeuber on the relationship between economic factors and racial patterns of American housing led to a discovery that the effects of income alone were minimal. He says that "poverty has little to do directly with Negro residential segregation—that if income were the only factor at work in determining where white and Negro families live, there would be very little racial residential segregation."[39] Whatever the cause, the result is that, overwhelmingly, suburbs are *de facto* racially segregated areas.

Overall, suburbanizing blacks are generally younger (in their late

[39]Karl E. Taeuber, "The Effect of Income Redistribution on Racial Residential Segregation," *Urban Affairs Quarterly,* **4**:10, September, 1968.

twenties and early thirties) and have higher levels of income, education, and occupation than blacks remaining in the city. In other words, they resemble other suburbanites. Half the upper-middle-class families leaving Washington, D.C., for the suburbs are black. Blacks moving into particular suburbs can generally be said to have the same social and economic characteristics as other residents of the community. Middle-class blacks move into middle-income suburbs and rich blacks into upper-income suburbs.

Suburbanization of blacks should not automatically be equated with racial integration. In some metropolitan areas black suburbanization represents not integration but rather the natural growth of the ghetto until it overflows city boundaries. Black suburbanization in this case is not integration but more of the same, although in the suburbs the housing is better. These black "gilded ghettoes" are becoming a common feature of larger American cities. A ghetto that expands into another town is still a ghetto; only the name of the town is different. Additionally, many suburban blacks live either in industrial suburbs or relatively small segregated ghettoes within older suburbs (e.g., Mount Vernon, New York). "Black only" suburbs are also found surrounding many of the largest cities.

Older suburban areas directly abutting the central city are the best candidates for absorbing the overflow from city ghettoes. Many of these communities are essentially urban in character and have been for many years. Communities such as Yonkers have densities approaching those of the central city, while an older racially changing suburb such as Oak Park in Chicago already is composed heavily of multiple dwellings.

## SUBURBAN POOR

The myth of suburbia has so permeated our unconscious thinking that we automatically associate poverty with city slums or marginal rural areas. Yet the New York metropolitan area alone has 800,000 poor.[40] Suburban poor are unseen poor, and thus their needs remain largely unmet. After all, the feeling goes, if they can afford to live in the suburbs, why should they get sympathy? "Suburban" equals "middle-class" in the thinking of most people. Core areas of central cities are expected to have poverty; suburbs are not. For example, it would be difficult to imagine Congress considering, much less passing, any bill to alleviate poverty in the suburbs.

[40]This is based on figures from the Federal Office of Economic Opportunity; see Ralph Blumenthal, "800,000 Suburban Poor Suffer Amid Environment of Affluence," in Charles M. Haar (ed.), *The End of Innocence,* Scott, Foresman, Glenview, Ill., 1972, pp. 73–77.

An extreme example of how little "suburban" a suburb can be is Kinloch, outside of St. Louis. Kinloch is the second largest black suburb in the nation, but it can be aptly described as a poverty area. It is a desperately poor community surrounded by affluent white suburbs. Kinloch's single-family homes are in various stages of deterioration; its streets are largely unpaved; and at the same time it has the highest rate of school taxes in the county, the lowest tax base, and the worst schools.[41]

Kinloch survives as a community simply because no other area is willing to absorb it and its problems. Meanwhile everything is done to isolate the black suburb from its wealthier neighbors. Roads from the next community, Ferguson, actually stop one foot before Kinloch's borders, and while a full-scale wall like that in Berlin has not been constructed around the community, the northern community of Berkeley has built a chain-link fence all along Kinloch's border.

## FUTURE

It doesn't take a crystal ball to foresee that suburbanization will continue, and that most suburban subdevelopments will continue to be white and basically middle-income, for some time. Radical changes in the housing industry, or a massive commitment by Congress to a national housing program, could change this; but the odds are strongly against any such occurrence. The current housing market is such that new unsubsidized suburban housing is not available outside the South to about half of the families making less than the median national income ($12,000 in 1973). Rising costs of material and labor, plus inflation, are making the situation worse every year. Increasing gasoline prices also increase the cost of suburbanization. Substantial lower class suburbanization will have to await both subsidization of housing costs and changes in restrictive zoning practices, neither of which appears particularly likely at this point in time.

[41]John Kramer, "The Other Mayor Lee" in John Kramer (ed.), *North American Suburbs*, Glendessary Press, Berkeley, 1972, pp. 185–200.

Chapter 8

# Urban Stratification and Power

*The rich man in his castle,*
*The poor man at his gate,*
*God made them, high or lowly,*
*And order'd their estate.*

From a Church of England hymn,
*"All Things Bright and Beautiful"*

Social stratification is not a uniquely urban phenomenon, but it is so important that any treatment of the city and city life-styles that did not include it would be incomplete. Certainly in the city there has always been an association between one's address and one's social status. Certain addresses—Park Avenue in New York, Beacon Hill in Boston, the Gold Coast in Chicago, and Nob Hill in San Francisco—have traditionally signified not only spatial location but also an upper-class life-style. Similarly, Cleveland's Shaker Heights and Washington's Chevy Chase have come to be almost stereotypically identified with the professional upper middle class. At the other end of the spectrum, areas such as the

Bowery in New York and Back of the Yards in Chicago have a more proletarian image. The point is that there is often a clear relationship between urban space and social class.

Burgess, it will be recalled, suggested that social status of the various urban populations is directly correlated with their distance from the center of the city; the lowest-status ethnic immigrants are found in the zone immediately surrounding the central business district, while people having the highest income, education, and occupational levels are located in the suburbs.[1]

This hypothesized relationship between spatial location and social class level was for several decades accepted as fact. More recently, sociologists have been systematically examining the patterns of status distributions in American cities and suburbs. A study by Schnore (1963) based on a comparison of central cities and their suburbs looked at 200 urbanized areas and compared levels of socioeconomic status using median family income, percent completing high school, and percent in white-collar occupations as variables. He found that the older and larger urbanized areas exhibited the expected pattern: the suburbs had higher socioeconomic status than the central cities. However, this became less true as city size and age decreased. In the smallest Urbanized Areas the status of city residents tended to be higher than that of suburbanites. Statistically, the age and size of the urban area were the best predictors of its status pattern.[2]

Further research by Palen and Schnore into status differences between cities and suburbs added two other variables: race of the population and region of the country. Comparisons were made for 180 Urbanized Areas for whites and 131 areas for nonwhites. For the white population, it was found that regardless of the region of the country, the larger and older the city, the more likely that its suburbs possessed higher levels of income, education, and occupation. For nonwhites, on the other hand, the pattern of higher status in suburbs was found only in the North and West. In the South, the persistence of traditional patterns—poor blacks living on the city's periphery—meant that there was no consistent pattern of higher-status blacks' being located either in the city or in the suburbs.[3]

Additional research has used census-tract data to study in detail status patterns of black ghettoes in twenty-four large cities. These studies

[1]Ernest W. Burgess, "The Growth of the City: An Introduction to a Research Project," *Publications of the American Sociological Society*, **18**:85–97, 1924.

[2]Leo F. Schnore, "The Socioeconomic Status of Cities and Suburbs," *American Sociological Review*, **28**:76–85, February, 1963.

[3]J. John Palen and Leo F. Schnore, "Color Composition and City-Suburban Status Differences," *Land Economics*, **41**:87–91, February, 1965.

showed that Burgess's hypothesis that levels of socioeconomic status increase with distance from the center of cities clearly held true in the North; but in the South four out of five cities displayed a different pattern: socioeconomic status of blacks rose as one moved from the center of the city and then declined.[4] Further research has tended to support this general picture.[5]

## DIMENSIONS OF CLASS

We like to think of ourselves as a relatively classless society, or at least as one with mobility—anyone, if he works hard enough and gets a few breaks, can make it to the top. In our actions, however, we recognize clear differences between groups of persons. Social inequality exists in America as it does in all complex human societies. We have a class system—that is, an ordering of social positions and the roles (social expectations) associated with each one. The inequalities are not random; they are systematic and organized into patterns that are generally recognized by society.

Within the urban area, we rank others in categories on a scale of superiority–inferiority. While there are no universal criteria for evaluation, the standards for grouping persons into social classes in the United States usually include these factors: income, education, type of occupation, race, family background, and general life-style.[6] Some sociologists also distinguish between *class* position and *status* position. "Class position" is the power, particularly economic, which one controls in the marketplace. "Status position" refers to the more intangible prestige or honor that is attached to a position. The impoverished aristocrat, a classic and much overworked fictional character, is a clear example of one having a higher status position than class position. A Mafia leader in Chicago would, conversely, have high power but low status. However, in sociological usage the distinction between class and status frequently becomes blurred, and the terms are often used interchangeably.

According to traditional urban theory, the city is noted for placing less emphasis on class and more on achievement. Ascribed social-class characteristics are those that are *not* the result of our own learning, efforts, or endeavors. Whether race, sex, ethnic background, or physical appearance, we inherit them automatically. Even a theoretically changeable characteristic, such as religion, is, at least for the first twenty years or

[4]Leo F. Schnore, *The Urban Scene*, Free Press, New York, 1965, chap. 16.

[5]Joel Smith, "Another Look at Socioeconomic Status Distributions in Urbanized Areas," *Urban Affairs Quarterly*, **5**:423–453, June, 1970.

[6]See, for example, W. Lloyd Warner, *The Social Life of a Modern Community*, volume I of Yankee City Series, Yale University Press, New Haven, 1941.

so of a person's life, an ascribed characteristic. Children do not choose a religion but rather assume that of their parents. Likewise, their social-class level is set not by their own efforts or merits but rather by the position occupied by their father.

Achieved status, on the contrary, theoretically reflects what someone *does* rather than simply who he *is*. An adult's level of income, his education, his type of occupation, the neighborhood where he lives, his home—these reflect what he has done. The line between ascription and achievement is not as clear in practice as in theory.[7]

Even in a society, such as the United States, that tends to emphasize achievement, there is a remarkable recapitulation of occupational level: that is, the son's level reflects the father's. As Natalie Rogoff said in her now classic study of mobility patterns across generations: "One of the recurrent findings in . . . research on occupational mobility is that sons are more likely to enter their father's occupation than to enter any other single occupation."[8]

The influence of ascribed social-class characteristics is particularly noticeable at the extremes of the social pyramid. Urban groups as dissimilar as the upper-class Boston "Brahmins" and the Vice Lords of Chicago both live in worlds where rigid social codes determine what they eat (oatmeal or "soul food"), how they dress (the Bostonian's clothing is conservatively dull; the Vice Lord's is modish and highly stylized), and how they view outsiders (both are hostile to other groups).[9]

It could be argued that to the extent that central cities are losing their middle classes, the lives of remaining city residents are becoming more dominated by ascriptive rather than achieved characteristics. Still, stratification systems in cities are less rigid than those in the countryside and provide more chances for both upward and downward mobility. The tremendous changes taking place in the nation's urban centers, and particularly the impact of science and technology, have convinced many sociological observers that traditional ascribed characteristics and patterns of living are certain to be supplanted in the long run by the universal norms of urban society. Where minority-group customs or life-styles still persisted, they would be viewed as "cultural lags" inevitably to be replaced by the achievement-oriented standards of the city, where spatial

[7]Certain achieved characteristics, such as a college education, are all but assumed for white upper-middle-class children. Their parents and teachers operate on the assumption that such children will "of course" go to college, and such children are automatically assumed by the school system to be college material unless clear and consistent evidence says otherwise. On the other hand, black ghetto children are "ascribed" both low educational motivation and abilities and are often provided with a type and level of schooling that helps to ensure that the prophecy of academic inferiority will come true.

[8]Natalie Rogoff, *Recent Trends in Occupational Mobility*, Free Press, Glencoe, Ill., 1953.

[9]See Cleveland Amory, *The Proper Bostonians*, E.P. Dutton, New York, 1947; and R. Lincoln Keiser, *The Vice Lords: Warriors of the Streets*, Holt, Rinehart and Winston, New York, 1969.

mobility is both possible and expected. Even a sympathetic account of traditional life, William Whyte's study of life in what was then the Italian slum of the North End of Boston, suggests that the life-style of the "street corner boys" reflects the past while that of the "college boys" reflects the pattern of the future.[10] However, as the section on ethnic neighborhoods and norms in Chapter 6 indicates, traditional life-styles are still very much alive some thirty years after Whyte's study of street-corner life.

## MEASURING SOCIAL CLASS

There are a number of ways to measure social class. Perhaps the most common is to use objective measures: income, education, and occupation. Income and education are easy to rank—college is obviously higher than high school—but occupation presents greater problems. One solution is to use the classification of the Bureau of the Census, which places occupations under the following headings:

1. Professional, technical, and kindred workers
2. Managers, officials, and proprietors, except farm
3. Clerical and kindred workers
4. Sales workers
5. Craftsmen, foremen, and kindred workers
6. Operatives and kindred workers
7. Private household workers
8. Service workers, except private household workers
9. Laborers, except farm and mine workers
10. Farmers and farm managers
11. Farm laborers and farm foremen

For urban research, categories 1 through 4 are frequently combined to create the category "white-collar"; categories 5 through 9 are combined to create the category "blue-collar." Another measure of occupational prestige are the studies by the National Opinion Research Center, which rank the relative prestige of some ninety occupations on a five-point scale by taking a national sample. An abbreviated example of the scale is provided in Table 8-1. A comparison of the rankings in 1947 and 1963 showed virtually no change. The correlation between the two samples was .99, or virtually perfect—a rare occurrence in social science.[11] While occupation cannot be matched directly with class, it continues to be used

[10]William Foote Whyte, *Street Corner Society*, University of Chicago Press, Chicago, 1943.

[11]Robert W. Hodge, Paul Siegel, and Peter H. Rossi, "Occupational Prestige in the United States: 1925–1963," *American Journal of Sociology*, **70**:297, November, 1964.

**Table 8-1 Occupational Prestige Scale—1963**

| Occupation | Prestige score | Rank |
|---|---|---|
| U.S. Supreme Court Justice | 94 | 1.0 |
| Physician | 93 | 2.0 |
| Scientist | 92 | 3.5 |
| Cabinet member in the federal government | 90 | 8.0 |
| Lawyer | 89 | 11.0 |
| Psychologist | 87 | 17.5 |
| Mayor of a large city | 87 | 17.5 |
| Civil engineer | 86 | 21.5 |
| Banker | 85 | 24.5 |
| Sociologist | 83 | 26.0 |
| Owner of a factory that employs about 100 people | 80 | 31.5 |
| Musician in a symphony orchestra | 78 | 34.5 |
| Official of an international labor union | 77 | 37.0 |
| County agricultural agent | 76 | 39.0 |
| Farm owner and operator | 74 | 44.0 |
| Newspaper columnist | 73 | 46.0 |
| Radio announcer | 70 | 49.5 |
| Insurance agent | 69 | 51.5 |
| A local official of a labor union | 67 | 54.5 |
| Traveling salesman for a wholesale concern | 66 | 57.0 |
| Playground director | 63 | 62.5 |
| Owner-operator of a lunch stand | 63 | 62.5 |
| Truck driver | 59 | 67.0 |
| Clerk in store | 56 | 70.0 |
| Restaurant cook | 55 | 72.5 |
| Dockworker | 50 | 77.5 |
| Coal miner | 50 | 77.5 |
| Farmhand | 48 | 83.0 |
| Clothes presser in a laundry | 45 | 85.0 |
| Garbage collector | 39 | 88.0 |

*Source:* Modified from Robert W. Hodge, Paul M. Siegel, and Peter H. Rossi, "Occupational Prestige in the United States, 1925-63," *American Journal of Sociology*, 70: 290-92, November, 1964, table 1.

as an indicator of class because it provides the best available approximate index in complex urban societies. Comparisons with other countries also show a high degree of similarity, with agreement being greatest among Western countries such as Great Britain, New Zealand, Germany, and the United States.

Another method of determining social class is to have families assign other families to social-class levels according to their reputation in the community. This is the method Hollingshead used in his study of Morris, Illinois, *Elmtown's Youth*.[12] Since this method is based upon respondents' personal knowledge of others, it is inappropriate for urban research, except where the unit of study is a relatively small homogeneous neighborhood.

A combination of objective and subjective methods was used in perhaps the most famous of all studies of social stratification, Warner's study of Yankee City.[13] Yankee City—actually Newburyport, Massachusetts—was studied from top to bottom by a team of researchers under Warner's direction during the mid-1930s. While the methodology is not always clear, families were apparently weighted for status on the basis of four seven-point scales: occupational level, source of income (inherited, profits, salary, wages, relief), type of residence, and area of the community. Income level was given a weight of four, source of income and housing each a weight of three, and area a weight of two. Such elaborate procedures are hardly possible in more modest studies, particularly where social class is not the major focus of the study. As a result, the objective categories as defined by the Bureau of the Census are the measure most frequently found in the professional literature.

Warner, on the basis of his data, divided the American population into six classes, a system that has come to be the standard. According to Warner, each class has its own behaviors, values, and style of life. They can be briefly sketched as follows:

**1** *Upper upper class.* This group includes the families of old wealth who have had their money for several generations. The men sit on boards of directors. Emphasis is put upon reverence for the past and gracious living. Members of this elite class have enough security to allow a person to be an individualist or even a bit of a character. The emphasis is on being a well-rounded person. Community service is often a characteristic of the second generation and later generations. Religious affiliation is almost always to traditional Protestant denominations such as Episcopalian and Presbyterian.

**2** *Lower upper class.* This group is generally even richer than the upper upper class, but it consists of new rich, and families are not as socially prominent. While the new rich may never achieve full acceptance by the upper upper class, their children, if they go to the right schools and achieve the proper polish, will be socially accepted. Acceptance into the

[12]A. B. Hollingshead, *Elmtown's Youth,* Wiley, New York, 1949.
[13]W. Lloyd Warner (ed.), *Yankee City,* Yale University Press, New Haven, Conn., 1963.

upper upper group is dependent as much on knowing how to spend money properly as on knowing how to make it.

3 *Upper middle class.* The key word for the upper middle class is "career." While the upper groups are generalists, the upper middle class consists of specialists. These are successful business and professional people who live in large homes in the better suburbs. Education, particularly for the professional men, is extremely important, and graduate education is common. These are the people who run community organizations, but they do not make top decisions. Family life-style, not lineage, is important.

4 *Lower middle class.* This group includes small businessmen, government bureaucrats on the middle levels, most teachers, and the more successful blue-collar workers, such as electricians, plumbers, and foremen. Respectability is of paramount importance to this class. Most are high school graduates with perhaps some further training. Homes are in the less affluent suburbs or perhaps in the city.

5 *Working class.* In the past this group was sometimes referred to as the "upper lower class." Those in this class have factory jobs or other semiskilled jobs and work for wages rather than salary. They make adequate incomes, but there is little hope of substantial social or economic advancement. Union contracts frequently determine the pace of economic advancement. Homes are clean but not fancy. Foreign background is common. Roman Catholicism is overrepresented.

6 *Lower class.* This group consists of people with irregular work histories and the poorest-paying jobs. It includes those on welfare and others with poor reputations. Education is rarely much beyond the legal minimum, with completion of grade school often the highest level. Housing is rented, not owned, and is frequently located in slum neighborhoods.

In the Midwest and West, categories 1 and 2 are frequently combined, since there is not usually an established class of old families as in parts of the East and the South. Family history is generally more important in smaller cities, where local inhabitants know each other's family history and react appropriately. In bigger cities families are more anonymous, and money alone makes more of a difference. A detailed evaluation of the stratification system of urbanized areas is clearly handicapped, since most of the research has been done on smaller communities. It is a reasonable assumption that the class system is far less complex in small towns than in major metropolitan centers.

Class even affects such vital factors as how long one lives, who one marries, and even at what age one gets married. (The lower classes have a lower life expectancy; marriage is still heavily within one's class; and lower-class persons marry younger than their upper class counterparts.)

There is also a substantial amount of evidence indicating an inverse relationship between class and a number of psychiatric conditions. However, the relationship between class and mental illness is extremely complex; we certainly cannot say that as one goes up the class scale, mental health improves.[14]

While it would be absurd to suggest that all members of a class hold similar attitudes or have an identical style of life, it is nonetheless true that social class has a more pervasive effect than Americans, with their lip service to equality, always recognize. We take it for granted that the upper class makes more money than the middle and lower classes, and perhaps we even recognize that they obtain better medical care and live longer. However, the upper class has a pronounced advantage in other areas as well. As an example, the upper class has more marital stability—23 percent of low-income white males in the age group 25–34 have had one or more broken marriages, as compared with 10 percent for the middle-income group, and only 6 percent for the upper-income group.[15] Even being overweight is correlated with social class—52 percent of low-income women have problems with obesity, compared with 43 percent of middle-income women and only 9 percent of high-income women.[16] Although it is not always apparent, social class makes an impact on all aspects of our lives.

## STATUS CONSISTENCY

Particularly within urban areas, it is possible for an individual to be high on status measures such as income and residence, while being low on other measures such as occupation and ethnic background. Urban upper-class blacks with a superior education have had, particularly in the past, status inconsistency of this sort. George Washington Carver was once forced to ride in a service elevator to get to a banquet at which he was the principal speaker. More recently, urban blue-collar workers in certain building trades have enjoyed a very high income as against low educational background and occupational rank. Such status inconsistency is said to be a source of stress for individuals and leads to such dissimilar reactions as supporting political parties advocating change, and higher incidences of psychosomatic illness.[17]

[14]A. B. Hollingshead and Fredrich Redlich, *Social Class and Mental Illness*, Wiley, New York, 1958.

[15]Richard J. Udry, "Marital Instability by Race and Income Based on 1960 Census Data," *American Journal of Sociology*, **72**:673, 1966.

[16]Robert Burnight and Parker Marden, "Social Correlates of Weight in an Aging Population," *Milbank Memorial Fund Quarterly*, **45**:75–92, 1967.

[17]Gerhard E. Lenski, "Status Inconsistency and the Vote: A Four Nation Test," *American Sociological Review*, **32**:298, April, 1967; and Elton Jackson, "Status Consistency and Symptoms of Stress," *American Sociological Review*, **27**:469–480, August, 1962.

Empirical study of status consistency is usually associated with the research of Gerhard Lenski, who, working with a probability sample in the Detroit area, interviewed 749 persons to test the hypothesis that "individuals characterized by a low degree of status crystallization differ significantly in their political attitudes and behavior from individuals characterized by a high degree of status crystallization, when status differences in the vertical dimension are controlled."[18] (Lenski uses the term "status crystallization" rather than "status consistency" to refer to a situation in which all statuses are equally high or equally low.)

It has already been mentioned that one reaction to status inconsistency is political support for liberal and radical rather than conservative political policies. An example might be the support of affluent, well-educated urban Jews for the Democratic Party. Another reaction to status inconsistency is the tendency to blame others for one's problems and to strike out at those who appear threatening. For example, lower-middle-class groups living in ethnic enclaves sometimes seek to block the aspirations and expectations of those below them in order to protect what position they have. "Let them do it the way we did," is the cry. If the class division is also a racial division—and this is frequently the case—the hostility is all the greater. To those groups not yet secure in their own grip on a decent income and quality of life, an aggressive and demanding group immediately below them is a threat to their own position. Paradoxically, those who have experienced poverty and discrimination themselves are frequently hardest on those lower down.

As a blue-collar worker expressed it:

> The blacks have had a hard time. I don't deny that a minute. But they're always complaining and wrecking things and goofing off. Not all, but a lot of them. The way I see it, they've gotten a lot in the last years. They've moved into the cities, like into my neighborhood, and taken them over. They've moved up into all the top jobs. They're in the offices and the plants. They've done a hell of a lot better than I have—or my family—or people like me. Everybody's getting ahead but us.[19]

It was not accidental that Martin Luther King said that he felt the greatest hatred toward blacks was not in the South but in the lower-middle-class white ethnic neighborhoods of Chicago.

Status inconsistency should, however, be kept in proper perspective. Urban life, because it emphasizes and rewards change and innovation, has built into it a certain degree of status tension, and most urban dwellers

[18]Gerhard E. Lenski, "Status Crystallization: A Non-Vertical Dimension of Social Status," *American Sociological Review*, **19**:405–406, August, 1954.

[19]Patricia Cayo Sexton and Brendan Sexton, *Blue Collars and Hard Hats*, Vintage Books, a Division of Random House, Inc., New York, 1971, p. 54.

expect this as a part of urban life. Many persons prefer this inconsistency and the potential mobility it suggests to the more static social structure of smaller and older communities.

## MOBILITY

### Myths and Reality

The mythology of social mobility in nineteenth-century and early twentieth-century America emphasized the rags-to-riches urban careers of unlettered men of low origins, such as Andrew Carnegie and Henry Ford. On the other hand, the actual data paint a somewhat less spectacular picture. There are very few examples of members of the industrial elite who rose from boyhood poverty by their own efforts. What consistently is shown by the various studies done on the entrepreneurs at the very top of the social and economic order is that the best way to become rich is to be born to rich parents.[20] For example, William Miller studied the careers of just under 200 of the leaders of early-twentieth-century corporations. He concluded that among these powerful financiers, corporation officials, and railroad and utility executives one could find hardly any who started as poor immigrants. In fact, 95 percent of his sample came from native upper-class or at least middle-class families.[21]

The findings of Frances Gregory and Irene Neu are substantially similar. They carefully studied the careers of the business leaders in railroads, steel, and textiles in seventy-seven large firms as of the 1870s. The sample included the president, vice-president, and general manager of the seventeen largest railroads, the general managers of thirty steel mills, and the treasurers and agents of thirty very large textile mills. Gregory and Neu found that the typical industrial leader in their sample was an American-born Protestant of upper-class origin. Moreover, he was most likely to have been raised in an urban environment and to have been well educated for the times. Examining the occupations of 194 men, they found that only sixteen of them (8 percent) were the sons of workers. They therefore concluded that there was little evidence to support the belief that the top-level businessman of the late 1800s had worked his way from rags to riches.[22]

On the other hand, Herbert Gutman found that in the case of urban

[20]See Seymour M. Lipset and Reinhard Bendix, *Social Mobility in Industrial Society*, University of California Press, Berkeley, 1959.

[21]William Miller, "American Historians and the Business Elite," in William Miller (ed.), *Men in Business, Essays on the Historical Role of the Entrepreneur*, Harper and Row, New York, 1962, pp. 309–328.

[22]Frances W. Gregory and Irene D. Neu, "The American Industrial Elite in the 1870s, Their Social Origins," in Miller, op. cit., pp. 193–211.

Paterson, New Jersey, during the years 1830 to 1880, the rags-to-riches promise was not mere myth. All the thirty-odd entrepreneurs he studied had started as apprentices and later went on to open shops of their own.[23] Unfortunately, the data are not sufficient to let us generalize from these findings. Available data do suggest, however, that mobility was probably most likely in industries that required only limited initial outlays of capital. Mobility was probably also most likely in the newer, rapidly expanding cities.

When one moves away from examining elite groups such as railroad presidents and factory owners and looks at the social mobility of lower-status urban groups, the data are far more scanty. Lloyd Warner in his famous studies of Yankee City emphasized the mobility that had been possible for working men during the nineteenth century and contrasted it with the more limited mobility he observed in his study of Yankee City in the twentieth century. Warner suggested that between the nineteenth century and the twentieth there had been a hardening of the social structure and a decline in social mobility. This he attributed to the change, brought by industrialization, from craft work to mass assembly-line production.[24]

Stephen Thernstrom's research on the class system of nineteenth-century Newburyport indicates that social mobility in Newburyport during the nineteenth century was actually far less than Warner had assumed.[25] Thernstrom looked at the career patterns of nearly 300 day laborers in Newburyport between 1850 and 1880. He found a good deal of geographical mobility out of the town, but the most common form of social mobility was advancement within rather than out of the working class. There was no rags-to-riches mobility: "In the substantial sample of workers and their sons studied for the 1850–1880 period not a single instance of mobility into the ranks of management or even into a foremanship position was discovered."[26]

However, on the basis of later and more extensive research, Thernstrom suggests that the minimal mobility of Newburyport was an exception to the general pattern in nineteenth-century urban America.[27] Newburyport, it is evident, had notably lower upward mobility than other communities; Thernstrom attributed this to the city's relative economic

[23]Herbert G. Gutman, "The Reality of the Rags-to-Riches Myth," in Stephen Thernstrom and Richard Sennett (eds.), *Nineteenth-Century Cities,* Yale University Press, New Haven, 1969, pp. 98–124.

[24]Warner, op. cit.

[25]Stephen Thernstrom, "Yankee City Revisited: The Perils of Historical Naivete," *American Sociological Review,* **30:**236–242, April, 1965.

[26]Ibid.

[27]Stephen Thernstrom, *The Other Bostonians: Poverty and Progress in the American Metropolis, 1880–1970,* Harvard University Press, Cambridge, Mass., 1973, p. 247.

stagnation in the late nineteenth century and the preponderance of Irish of low mobility in the sample.[28]

Research does not support the view that the coming of industrialization made class lines more rigid. Thernstrom's study of social mobility in Boston indicates that as traditional skilled callings became obsolete, there was an enormous expansion of other skilled trades, and that many craftsmen moved rapidly into these positions.[29]

### Intergenerational Mobility

Data on intergenerational mobility for the past century suggest several things. First, there were clear and definite rigidities in the occupational structure which gave strong preference to those of higher social class. Sons of professional men and substantial businessmen were four times as likely as children from low-status white-collar families to attain upper-status white-collar levels. When compared with the sons of skilled workers they were six and a half times as likely to reach upper levels, and twelve times as likely as sons of unskilled or semiskilled laborers.[30] Second, while few men from laboring households achieved positions of power and high income, there was a substantial amount of short-distance upward mobility of laborers into skilled and minor white-collar posts. In Boston, for example, "an average of 4 in 10 of the sons in families on the lowest rung of the occupational ladder found their way into middle-class jobs of some kind, and a significant proportion of the remainder—roughly 1 in 6—entered a skilled trade.[31]

Similarly, Natalie Rogoff's data on urban occupational mobility across generations in Indianapolis indicated that the sons of displaced artisans were likely to move into other skilled trades or white-collar occupations rather than down the ladder.[32]

In another study by Thernstrom the career mobility of native-born whites was compared with that of foreign-born immigrants during the last half of the nineteenth century. Consideration of movement between manual and nonmanual callings revealed that regardless of their fathers' occupational level, men of foreign birth—and even those of native birth but foreign parentage—were handicapped vis-à-vis old-stock Americans of similar class origins.[33] Thernstrom also discovered that there were

[28]Ibid.

[29]Stephen Thernstrom, "Urbanization, Migration, and Social Mobility in Late Nineteenth-Century America," in Alan Trachenberg, Peter Neill, and Peter C. Bunnell (eds.), *The City: American Experience,* Oxford University Press, New York 1971, pp. 99–111.

[30]Thernstrom, *The Other Bostonians,* op. cit., p. 257.

[31]Loc. cit., p. 245.

[32]Natalie Rogoff, *Recent Trends in Occupational Mobility*. Free Press, Glencoe, Ill., 1953.

[33]Stephen Thernstrom, "Immigrants and WASPS: Ethnic Differences in Occupational Mobility in Boston, 1890–1940," in Stephen Thernstrom and Richard Sennett (eds.), *Nineteenth-Century Cities,* Yale University Press, New Haven, 1969, p. 148.

important differences in the experiences of newcomers of various national backgrounds. Some groups, such as the British and the Eastern European Jews, were dramatically successful, while others, such as the Irish and Italians, were slower in entering the American middle-class mainstream.[34] The tradition-oriented social systems and religion of the Irish and Italians in the past set them apart from the "official" Protestant work ethic of the nation. It is instructive to note that while over 80 percent of all Catholics are urban—compared with roughly 60 percent of all Protestants—Catholics are still much underrepresented in fields such as banking, financing, and corporate control. It is in the realm of political control that the Catholic ethnic groups have been most successful.

### Current Mobility

Today there are four principal causes of movement from one class to another:

1 Individual or career mobility. This is the type of mobility most familiar to the average individual. It occurs when some people slip down or move up and thereby make room for others to move up.

2 Technological mobility. Over the past century there has been a constant upgrading of the occupational distribution, which has been outdating unskilled and manual jobs at the bottom of the occupational structure and replacing them with higher-level technical and administrative positions. The space industry, for example, was virtually nonexistent twenty years ago, and much the same can be said about automatic data processing.

3 Reproductive mobility. At least in the past, the upper classes had smaller families than those at lower levels, and this made room at the top. The old cliché about marrying the boss's daughter implies that the boss does not have sons to inherit the business.

4 Immigration mobility. Before the 1920s, when immigration was legally restricted, hundreds of thousands of immigrants yearly came to the United States, and the vast majority started at the bottom as semiskilled or unskilled workers. By taking blue-collar manual jobs, they pushed earlier ethnic groups up a rung. A not uncommon pattern at the turn of the century was for the boss to be Anglo-Saxon, the foreman Irish, and the workers from Southern or Eastern Europe. A generation earlier, the Irish had been the workers. Today black in-migrants from the South occupy the bottom rungs, while the Eastern Europeans are now the foremen or skilled workmen.

Examining changes between 1920 and 1950, Kahl estimated that two-thirds of the work force was intergenerationally mobile: that is, sons

[34]Ibid.

were in different occupations from their fathers. Of the changes, he attributed 43 percent to individual mobility in both directions, the same percentage to technological mobility, 13 percent to reproductive mobility, and 1 percent to immigration mobility.[35] However, because of the methodological problems involved in this type of research, these figures should be taken as good educated assumptions rather than fact. While upward mobility is far from being as universal as the Chamber of Commerce might suggest, there still has been enough upward mobility to sustain the myth that any person can achieve success if only he will work hard enough.

However, one does not become wealthy from working for wages or salary. Birth, property, and investments are the route to becoming a millionaire. As the British sociologist T. B. Bottomore put it, "Indeed, it would be a more accurate description of the class system to say that it operates, largely through the inheritance of property to ensure that each individual maintains a certain social position, determined by his birth and irrespective of his particular abilities."[36] Data on corporate wealth indicate that about 1 percent of the adult American population owns about 80 percent of all publicly held corporation stock.[37] Furthermore, if the question is one of total wealth—that is, home and business ownership, bank deposits, insurance policies, and real estate, in addition to corporate wealth—it turns out that less than 1 percent of the population accounts for a full third of the nation's wealth.[38]

### Factors Affecting Mobility

Much mobility comes from changes in social structure rather than from individual efforts and achievement. Some mobility may reflect only changes in definitions or boundaries, rather than changes in the actual circumstances of individuals. For example, in 1973 the Nixon administration, embarrassed by federal figures on poverty which showed that a greater percentage of the population was falling into the poverty classification than had been true during the previous administration, sought to combat this situation by changing the classification system.

The most elaborate and complete study of current social mobility is that by Blau and Duncan, which was based upon a representative sample of the United States population of labor age. Some of Blau and Duncan's

[35]Joseph Kahl, *The American Class Structure,* Holt, Rinehart, and Winston, New York, 1957, particularly chap. 9, pp. 251–298.

[36]T. B. Bottomore, *Classes in Modern Society,* Vintage Books, New York, 1968, p. 11.

[37]Robert Campman, *The Share of Top Wealth-Holders in National Wealth,* Princeton University Press, Princeton, N. J., 1962, p. 8.

[38]Ferdinand Lundberg, *The Rich and the Super Rich,* Bantom Books, New York, 1969, p. 25.

findings and generalizations, based upon a substantial body of data, are as follows:

**1** In terms of movement among occupational groups, there are three broad occupational classes in the United States: white-collar workers, including managerial and professional workers; blue-collar workers; and farm workers.

**2** A small fourth class is made up of self-employed professionals such as doctors, lawyers, dentists, and other free professionals. Mobility into this group is very difficult, and occupational inheritance from father to son is the highest of any group.

**3** Social-class boundaries are more of a barrier to downward than to upward mobility. For example, white-collar workers or their offspring only rarely move down into blue-collar positions.

**4** Social mobility appears to be increasing, with most mobility being for relatively limited social distances. The evidence is not clear, but it is possible that downward mobility is more common than it was in the past.

**5** Physical geographical migration (spatial mobility) and social mobility are related. Those who move spatially are more successful than those who do not, and those who are downwardly mobile are likely to be geographically immobile.

**6** The most successful migrants are those from one urban area to another urban area. Farm migrants are usually the least successful, doing worse than nonmigrants. Those migrating from the South, whether black of white, are less successful in terms of social mobility.

**7** Blacks with equal educational and family background are less socially mobile than comparable whites. Occupationally, blacks suffer from restricted occupational mobility.

**8** Immigrant whites do not suffer any handicap to occupational mobility. Their occupational levels, although lower than those of the total native population, are nonetheless equal to the occupational levels of natives with similar education and family background.[39]

The study also found that only four factors account for 50 percent of a person's chances for mobility: education, first job held, occupation of father, and education of father. Note that these factors all reflect one's background at least as much as one's abilities, and two of them refer to the father's characteristics rather than the child's. Individual achievement and mobility are possible for many, but they are most likely if one has the good fortune to be born to an economically successful father.

The size of the community in which a person spends his childhood and adolescence is also of importance in determining the probable

[39]Peter M. Blau and Otis Dudley Duncan, *The American Occupational Structure*, Wiley, New York, 1967.

**Table 8-2 Percentage Planning to Go to College, by Place of Residence and Intelligence—for Male and Female High School Seniors in Wisconsin**

| Sex and place of residence | Intelligence | | | |
|---|---|---|---|---|
| | Low | Middle | High | Total |
| Males | | | | |
| Farm | 7.7 | 22.4 | 43.8 | 22.0 |
| Village (under 2,500) | 14.3 | 31.5 | 55.1 | 31.8 |
| Small city (2,500–25,000) | 13.0 | 32.3 | 66.1 | 38.4 |
| Medium city (25,000–100,000) | 18.3 | 39.8 | 65.2 | 41.7 |
| Large city (100,000 and more) | 22.9 | 47.0 | 69.4 | 50.7 |
| Females | | | | |
| Farm | 11.1 | 19.8 | 35.8 | 21.1 |
| Village (under 2,500) | 11.1 | 25.9 | 38.5 | 23.9 |
| Small city (2,500–25,000) | 13.2 | 26.3 | 50.8 | 29.5 |
| Medium city (25,000–100,000) | 12.1 | 30.3 | 52.5 | 32.8 |
| Large city (100,000 and more) | 13.4 | 32.8 | 57.4 | 35.7 |

*Source:* William H. Sewell, "Community Residence and College Plans," *American Sociological Review,* **29**:31, February 1964, table 4.

mobility of the children of manual workers.[40] This is apparently because the larger cities offer a youngster far greater exposure, through both education and general experience, to a wide range of possible occupations. Those from smaller communities are less likely to be aware of all the occupational alternatives. But size of community does not appear to influence the mobility of middle-class children whose fathers are in white-collar positions. This is probably because the middle-class child learns about alternatives and picks up his aspirations within the family.

William H. Sewell, in his research on the effect of place of residence, intelligence, and social class on educational and occupational aspirations, found that the size of the community did indeed have a profound effect on aspirations to go to college. Seven out of ten city boys of high intelligence, but only four out of ten farm boys of high intelligence, planned to go on to college. (See Table 8-2.)

Sewell describes his findings this way:

> The results of the statistical analysis show that there are sizable differences

[40]Seymour Martin Lipset and Reinhard Bendix, *Social Mobility in Industrial Society,* University of California Press, Berkeley, 1959.

in the college plans of rural and urban youth which are not artifacts of the sex, intelligence, and socioeconomic (class) composition of the sample. Many factors would probably help to account for this finding. At the most general level, the opportunity structure provided by the more rural communities is clearly very limited both in its educational and occupational dimensions. . . . Greater access to higher education in urban areas, however, is not the only education factor that encourages the higher aspirations of urban youth. Urban schools generally provide a more academically stimulating climate than rural schools because of their better trained faculties, superior facilities, and more varied and challenging curricula.

Equally obvious is the fact that urban communities offer a much wider and more varied range of occupational opportunities than do rural communities. Many of these occupations require a minimum of college training for entry. While rural high school seniors are probably not completely unaware of either the rewards or the entrance requirements of many of the high-prestige professional, managerial, and technical positions available in urban communities, they are certainly less likely to have had first-hand exposure to most of them.[41]

### Mobility of Women

There are few data on the intergenerational mobility of women, partially because the research was done by men and partially because women have a lower participation in the labor force (42 percent, as opposed to 80 percent for men, as of 1970) and because women of marriage and childbearing age move into and out of the labor force. As a result of this mobility, and of discrimination, women frequently are relegated to the less interesting and poorer-paying jobs—jobs that may not reflect their actual social status. Further, although caring for a home is of significant economic as well as social value, research on occupations rarely takes it into account in any regular, structured fashion.

Consequently, the mobility of a woman has usually been determined by comparing the occupational status occupied by her father with that occupied by her husband. The daughter of a garbage man who marries a lawyer is described as being upwardly mobile; the daughter of a lawyer who marries a garbage man is downwardly mobile. This kind of vertical mobility, based upon marriage, tells us a great deal; but it is not the same thing as comparing the occupation of the father with that of the son. Moreover, the explicit and implicit assumptions that have long been made regarding the social position of women are increasingly being chal-

[41]William H. Sewell, "Community of Residence and College Plans," *American Sociological Review*, **29**:35, February, 1964.

lenged.[42] As more and more women develop long-term career patterns, research on intergenerational mobility among women should become more common.

### International Differences

The most commonly held position is that the overall pattern of social mobility is much the same in Western industrialized countries.[43] However, some sociologists disagree, believing that Americans are more mobile than those in other industrial nations. A comparative study of national samples in the United States, Australia, and Italy indicated that when mobility from father to son was examined, the United States had the greatest upward mobility of manual workers: 36 percent of the sons were mobile, Australia had 31 percent mobile, and Italy had only 20 percent mobile.[44] This would indicate that social mobility is somewhat more common in the United States than in other industrialized countries. However, these findings are far from definitive.

## COMMUNITY DECISION MAKING

The questions of who has power in metropolitan areas and how this power is exercised are of major interest to both sociologists and political scientists. Do the formal governmental mechanisms really indicate how community decisions are made, or are there more important informal mechanisms? During recent decades the field has experienced vigorous growth and considerable controversy on how urban decision making is accomplished. Although the concern has sometimes been with the attributes of the individuals wielding power, a social-psychological approach, the main issue is the structure of decision-making processes.

### Pluralists and Elitists

Two general schools of thought have emerged—one more closely associated with sociology and the other with political science. The first school, made up heavily of sociologists, has suggested that power is concentrated in an elite. Those who support this view argue that community power structures are frequently pyramidal, and that businessmen or economic elites most commonly dominate the top positions, with

[42]See Joan Acker, "Women and Social Stratification: A Case of Intellectual Sexism," in Joan Huber (ed.), *Changing Women in a Changing Society,* University of Chicago Press, Chicago, 1973, pp. 174–183.

[43]Seymour M. Lipset and Hans Zetterberg, "Social Mobility in Industrial Societies," in Seymour Lipset and Reinhard Bendix, op. cit., pp. 60–64.

[44]Leonard Broom and F. Lancaster Jones, "Father-to-Son Mobility: Australia in Comparative Perspective," *American Journal of Sociology,* **74:**333–342, January 1969.

Atlanta's powerful businessmen have changed the city's skyline, but not the poverty of those at the bottom of the social system. *(United Press International.)*

elected political officials having secondary importance as decision makers. The second school of thought, usually associated with political science, suggests that power is widely distributed and that community power structures, to the degree that they exist at all, are highly pluralistic, with political officials playing a leading role and exerting considerable influence.

Those holding that power is widely distributed—"pluralists"—have disputed the methodology of those they call "elitists," charging that their methodology biases their results in the direction of finding economic elites dominating the community.[45] The pluralists' methodology has in turn been subject to criticism, and pluralists have been said to be biased toward finding that elected political officials dominate community power systems.

[45]Nelson W. Polsby, "How to Study Community Power: The Pluralist Alternative," *Journal of Politics*, **22**:474–484, August, 1960.

Empirical study of community decision-making processes is a relatively recent development in the social sciences. Until roughly twenty years ago, writing on the subject was either theoretical or descriptive (e.g., how a mayor had passed a particular bill) rather than analytical. The term "community power structure" came into popular use as the result of the systematic study of a "Regional City" (Atlanta, Georgia) by Floyd Hunter in the 1950s. Hunter's basic thesis was that in Atlanta the important community decisions were made by a group of about forty men who constituted a "power elite." This pyramidal power structure was dominated by an economic elite (mostly businessmen) who set policy. Under this group there was a larger group of several hundred who had some influence but basically carried out the wishes of those at the top. Elected and appointed governmental officials were in this secondary group, not at the top.

Hunter's method of research was to ask a panel of knowledgeable judges to rank individuals "who in your opinion are the most influential . . . from the point of view of ability to rank others."[46] Forty persons influential in the areas of civic affairs, business, government, and social status were selected, of whom 27 were interviewed and asked to rank the influence of those on the list and add other names when appropriate. This has come to be known as the "reputational" method. Hunter found that when the respondents were asked to name the ten on the list who were top "leaders that nearly everyone would accept," the same names continually reappeared. Of these ten key people, only one (the mayor) was not a business executive. Not only were elected political leaders relatively unimportant, but Hunter found that the top influential individuals made the major policy decisions within their own crowd and only then exposed them to public discussion through associations, newspapers, and the like.

Hunter's portrait of how community decisions were made by economically dominant people immediately came under attack from political scientists who felt that his overall picture was inadequate on both methodological and ideological grounds. Critics of Hunter's results noted that the reputation for power and the exercise of power are different things, and that the reputational technique appeared to measure opinions about power rather than power itself. The technique was said to identify, not those who had power and exercised it, but rather those who merely had the potential for such power. The technique was also criticized for starting with the assumption that there is a power structure and asking how individuals fit into it, rather than asking if any sort of power structure exists.

[46]Floyd Hunter, *Community Power Structure,* University of North Carolina Press, Chapel Hill, 1953, p. 258.

Strong arguments were made that what was needed was a study of actual issues and how and by whom they were resolved. However, even more than the methodology, the underlying assumptions of an elitist model of power deeply upset those who held that community decision making was pluralistic and that the mayors and political officials were indeed important.[47]

Pluralists, as those opposed to the theory that economic dominants controlled urban decision making came to be called, held that American communities were composed not of a single elite but rather of a series of competing elites. On any given issue *ad hoc* coalitions form, so that a group may win on one issue and lose on others.

Coalitions are constantly in flux, with the composition of the group varying with the issue at hand. Moreover, men who are powerful may decide not to take any action at all and thus not affect the decision in any way. Pluralists tend to work by analyzing who participated in resolving particular issues; thus, their method is called the "positional" or "decision-making" approach.

The best-known of the studies by the pluralists is Robert Dahl's extensive research on how decisions were made in New Haven, Connecticut, in three areas: urban development, public school officials and policy, and nominations for mayor of New Haven. Dahl defined his elite on the basis of their leadership positions (e.g., president or vice-president of a large corporation) or their personal assessed wealth. Two-hundred and thirty-eight economic notables were defined in this fashion. Additionally, a separate group of social notables were defined on the basis of their having been invited to the New Haven Assemblies (231 families).

The finding of the New Haven study was that there was very little overlap between the various types of notables. Only 24 economic notables were also identified as social notables. More important, neither the economic nor the social notables participated in significant numbers in the three areas of issues noted above. Dahl found that there was virtually no participation by notables in the public schools or the mayoral nomination. They participated somewhat more in urban renewal, but even here only one out of five notables was involved. Dahl concluded that there was little support for the belief in the economic elites that dominate all community issues.[48] He emphasized that there were many special-interest groups which combined on various issues to form temporary power groupings, but there was no vertically controlled power elite.

[47]See Robert A. Dahl, "A Critique of the Ruling Elite Model," *American Political Science Review*, **52**:463–469, June, 1958; Nelson W. Polsby, "The Sociology of Community Power: A Reassessment," *Social Forces*, **37**:232–236, March, 1959; and Thomas J. Anton, "Power, Pluralism, and Local Politics," *Administrative Science Quarterly*, **7**:425–457, March, 1963.

[48]Robert A. Dahl, *Who Governs?*, Yale University Press, New Haven, 1961.

But Dahl's study also had some substantial methodological weaknesses. Two of the three issues, the school board and the mayoral nominations, were hardly crucial for Dahl's economic notables. Since most of the economic notables lived in the suburbs and none of their children attended New Haven city schools, their lack of concern with this issue is hardly surprising. Unfortunately, unless one can commit time and resources to a long-term longitudinal study it is difficult to choose key issues, since there are few objective indices. Even an analysis of the space that the local newspaper gives to various issues may be misleading, because publishers are generally part of the elite. It is thus likely that if an elite does exist the only issues that would surface in the newspapers would be those upon which the elite itself had some disagreement. Real community issues such as poverty and segregation might not, according to this view, be publicly discussed, while questions such as where a new highway should be built might receive great attention.

In the particular case of Dahl's study, he has identified not economic influentials but rather a pool of those who have the potential to become powerful if they so choose. Thus whether participation by one out of five in the issue of urban renewal is a high or low rate of participation is largely a matter of professional judgment. Also weakening Dahl's case is the fact that New Haven is highly atypical in the area of urban renewal. Its mayor pushed urban renewal over all opposition to the point where New Haven has received more funds per citizen than any other city in the nation. Statistically, New Haven is eight standard deviations above the mean, which raises serious question as to whether it is a typical city.[49]

### Comparative Findings

It is obvious that Atlanta and New Haven differ in variables such as size, age of the physical city, presence of ethnic groups, economic base, class composition, and race. Comparisons that ignore these urban differences are likely to be misleading. Today there is general agreement that what is needed is much greater comparative application of *both* methods to the same issues in order to understand the patterns of community decision making. One way patterns can be discerned with the presently available data is to do studies of the studies—that is, to use the present available studies as a sample and examine them comparatively. This was done by John Walton in his comparative analysis of the results of thirty-nine studies dealing with sixty-one communities. His conclusions were as follows:

[49]Michael Aiken and Paul E. Mott. *The Structure of Community Power*, Random House, New York, 1970, p. 198.

> 1. The reputational method tends to identify pyramidal power structures more frequently than the decisional approach. . . . 2. Studies focusing on public issues tend to find factional and coalitional structure, while a focus on private issues results in a pyramidal description. . . . 3. Political scientists tend to find factional and coalitional structures more frequently than sociologists who find both types equally often. . . . 4. Discipline and method are linked in a developmental sequence with the type of power structure obtained. . . . 5. A small number of community leaders is associated with a more concentrated power structure. . . . 6. Studies generally find a high proportion of businessmen and a lower proportion of public officials in the leadership group. Relatively speaking the number of leaders is quite small. . . . 7. Population growth is moderately associated with less concentrated power structure. . . . 8. A large proportion of absentee ownership is highly associated with less concentrated power structures. . . . 9. Competitive party politics is highly associated with less concentrated power structures. . . . 10. Community power structures are changing in the direction of a greater dispersion of power.[50]

Controlling for bias due to methodology, factors such as the size of population, the economic base, the type of city, its population composition, and the type of government were not related to the findings.[51] In an additional attempt to identify some of the structural attributes of communities that are associated with their community power structures, Aiken examined a sample of fifty-seven communities that have been the subject of community decision-making studies. He reported:

> A large number of community characteristics—location in the north, a high degree of absentee ownership, non-reform political structures, heterogeneous population, lower socioeconomic status of the population—are found to be consistently, although not strongly, related to dispersion of community power.[52]

While Walton and Aiken do not agree on all points—Aiken sees regional location as being of greater importance, for example—studies of the available research literature indicate that proponents of both pluralism and elitism should devote more attention to research that controls their biases rather than to interdisciplinary polemics. The development of more adequate conceptual schemes to specify the meaning of terms such as "elitism," "pluralism," and "power" is necessary, as is more longitudinal research on stability and change in power relationships.

[50]John Walton, "A Systematic Survey of Community Power Research," in Aiken and Mott, op. cit., p. 452.

[51]Aiken and Mott, op. cit., p. 453.

[52]Aiken and Mott, op. cit., p. 407.

Studies of community power structure have grown from a virtually nonexistent subfield in the early 1950s, through a period of violent methodological and philosophical debate in the 1960s, to the point where they have a potential for productivity and synthesis.

## MIDDLETOWN

One of the most interesting studies of power and stratification in a community was done long before the current debate over methodology and its effects on findings. This was the remarkably productive Middletown studies by Helen and Robert Lynd.[53] In their first book, the Lynds studied the effects of industrialization on a small city which would "be as representative as possible of American life" and at the same time "compact and homogeneous enough to be manageable."[54] Middletown (Muncie, Indiana) remarkably reflected the white, Protestant "middle America" of the 1920s, and there is a significant correspondence between the sociological study of Middletown and the socially aware novels of the period, such as Sinclair Lewis's *Babbitt.*

The later book, *Middletown in Transition,* explored the effects of the Depression on the community and on the attitudes of its people. The most specific change was the overwhelming dominance in 1935 of every aspect of the community's life by the X family (the Ball family) who owned a plant that manufactured glass jars for household canning and thus continued to profit during the Depression while other factories were closing. The Depression brought into bold relief the economic dominance of this family and their control over the political and social as well as economic life of the city. As it was put in 1935 by one local citizen:

> If I'm out of work I go to the X plant; if I need money I go to the X bank, and if they don't like me I don't get it; my children go to the X college: when I get sick I go to the X hospital; I buy a building lot or house in an X subdivision; my wife goes downtown to buy clothes at the X department store; if my dog strays away he is put in the X pound; I buy X milk; I drink X beer, vote for X political parties, and get help from X charities; my boy goes to the X Y.M.C.A. and my girl to their Y.W.C.A.; I listen to the word of God in X-subsidized churches; if I'm a Mason I go to the X Masonic Temple; I read the news from the X morning newspaper; and, if I am rich enough, I travel via the X airport.[55]

As others had gone under in the Depression, the X family had

[53]Robert Lynd and Helen Lynd, *Middletown,* Harcourt, Brace, New York, 1929; and Robert Lynd and Helen Lynd, *Middletown in Transition,* Harcourt, Brace, New York, 1937.

[54]Lynd and Lynd, *Middletown,* p. 7.

[55]Lynd and Lynd, *Middletown in Transition,* p. 74.

expanded their influence to the point where in addition to having their own glass factory they also controlled the only bank, the only department store, the newspaper, the school board, the college, and a wealthy subdivision, and they had co-opted all the prominent lawyers and other sources of potential opposition in the city.

The picture of the community power structure was thus Marxian: a small number of economic dominants controlled all major economic, political, social, and religious organizations. However, this pattern of consolidation of power ended with the Depression, for two major reasons. First, the Depression itself was a unique, temporary situation; as business began to revive, other economic influentials reasserted themselves. General Motors, for example, reopened its Muncie plant, which was under absentee ownership and control. Second, the older members of the X family, who had devoted their interests to Muncie, were passing from the scene, and their Eastern-educated children had far less concern with local affairs. Their interests were statewide, or larger. Moreover, generalizing from Muncie to larger cities is difficult, for there is no evidence that Muncie is typical of larger cities.

Although the Depression changed or brought into focus the economic dominance of the community by a small self-serving elite, it had small effect on the attitudes of the community. Economic crisis did not lead to Marxian revolt or even to much heightening of class-consciousness. The old ideology and its slogans continued to be mouthed, although they were less applicable than ever. "Middletown, capitalism, and progress" was still the official ideology—and it was shared by many workers. Unionism came to Muncie, but because of changes outside the community rather than because of local militancy. "Getting ahead" was still the goal and central value, in spite of the loss of the means to do so. The desire for security was modifying the old system, but only gradually. The economic collapse of the system did not result in a radical divorce from its basic goals, values, and ideology.

Unfortunately, the Middletown study was not replicated elsewhere, and it was a score of years before Hunter's research on Atlanta rekindled interest in empirical examinations of community power structures.

## BLACKS AND POWERLESSNESS

What is empirically known about the position of blacks in urban power structures? Studies of ghetto violence, most notably the Report of the National Advisory Commission of Civil Disorders,[56] have documented

[56] *Report of the National Advisory Commission on Civil Disorders*, Government Printing Office, Washington, D.C., 1968.

the exclusion of blacks from the opportunity structure: there is high unemployment among black ghetto youth, housing is inadequate, and educational opportunities are scanty for low-income black ghetto residents. Studies of riots have focused attention on the exclusion of blacks from entry-level jobs, but less notice has been given to the extent to which blacks are excluded from positions of power in major institutional sectors. Community power studies also have provided relatively little information on participation by blacks in community decision making.

In a study of the powerlessness of blacks in Chicago it was found that Negroes occupied only 285 of the 19,997 top policy-making positions in the Chicago area—2.6 percent.[57] Black representation in Chicago was greatest in the elected public sector, welfare and religious voluntary organizations, and industrial unions. In the words of the Chicago study:

> The sectors and individual groups in the Chicago area with the highest Negro representation were those with Negro constituency-elective offices, supervisory boards, labor unions, and religious and welfare organizations. [58]

Blacks were virtually unrepresented in the policy-making positions of private institutions such as business corporations, banks, insurance companies, universities, and professional organizations.

A replication and extension of this research examined the degree to which blacks were found in key policy-making positions in the Milwaukee, Wisconsin, metropolitan area. At the time of the study the city of Milwaukee had a population of about 750,000, of which 90,000 (12 percent) were black. The county was 9 percent black. In this study a total of 4,930 policy-making positions in the sectors of business, public government, education, and voluntary organizations were identified and the number of blacks holding such policy-making positions were identified.[59] A total of 1,867 policy-making positions in the private sector were surveyed. Business and industrial concerns, law firms, banks, stock brokerage firms, insurance companies, and hospitals were included. Forty-four business and industrial concerns based in Milwaukee with a thousand or more employees or annual sales of over twelve million dollars, and firms based outside Milwaukee which employed at least 700 persons; sixteen banks with announced assets of at least $10 million; seven major insurance companies; twenty-six law firms with six or more

[57] H. M. Baron et al., "Black Powerlessness in Chicago," *Trans-Action*, November, 1968, p. 28.

[58] Baron et al., op. cit., p. 29.

[59] Karl H. Flaming, J. John Palen, et al., "Black Powerlessness in Policy-Making Positions," *Sociological Quarterly*, **13**:126–133, Winter, 1972.

partners or with at least two public-owned corporations as clients; and twenty-four private hospitals qualified for the study.

Only *one* black occupied any of the 1,867 key positions in the business sector. The all-but-total absence of Negroes in these critical positions is a major handicap to black entrepreneurship.

Blacks fared somewhat better in the sector of public government. There, twenty blacks held 42 of the 856 policy-making positions (4.9 percent) in the city and county. The picture was similar in the academic sector: of a total of 553 policy-making positions, blacks held 21, or 3.8 percent.

The highest degree of representation of Negroes was found in the voluntary sector. Blacks were highly visible in programs and organizations primarily concerned with minority groups and problems of poverty. Of the 472 policy-making posts in the voluntary service organizations, 125 (26.5 percent) were held by blacks. However, the majority of these voluntary organizations, such as the Urban League and the Social Development Commission (the latter funded by the O. E. O.), had only limited influence in the community. Blacks were most visible in organizations dealing directly with minority-group problems. On the other hand, it is noteworthy that in civic associations (Association of Commerce, Bar Association, Board of Realtors) as opposed to service organizations, only two of the 121 posts were held by blacks. Finally, within organized labor, there were no blacks in the 26 policy-making posts and only two blacks were found in the 36 regional decision-making positions surveyed.

**Table 8-3 Percentage of Blacks in Policy-Making Positions in the Private Sector**

| Selected areas | Number of positions | Number of blacks | Percent of blacks |
|---|---|---|---|
| Business and industrial concerns | 622 | 0 | 0.0 |
| Law firms | 399 | 0 | 0.0 |
| Banks | 413 | 0 | 0.0 |
| Stock brokerage | 68 | 0 | 0.0 |
| Insurance firms | 145 | 0 | 0.0 |
| Hospitals | 220 | 1 | 0.5 |
| Total | 1,867 | 1 | 0.05 |

*Source:* Karl H. Flaming, J. John Palen, et. al., "Black Powerlessness in Policy-Making Positions," *Sociological Quarterly,* **13**:131, winter, 1972, table 1.

In reality, Milwaukee blacks are even more poorly represented than the above data indicate. There are two major reasons for this. First, according to black decision makers, blacks who are appointed to decision-making positions are those who are best known to, and have the widest acceptance in, the white community. More militant blacks, while they may be known, tend to be distrusted. Second, those few blacks who are known and acceptable to white decision makers tend to be appointed to a much larger number of positions than their white counterparts. Thus, a small number of blacks tend to be repeatedly used and reused as representatives of the black community. For example, 605 whites held 814 policy-making positions in the public government sector, while at the same time only 20 blacks held 42 positions in the same sector. The same pattern of duplication was found in the other sectors where a significant number of blacks were present. Given the level of specialization and professionalism required in our society, this duplication further weakens the actual participation of blacks in decision making.

On the basis of their findings, the researchers formulated these hypotheses:

> **1** Blacks have a greater probability of occupying high appointive positions than high elective positions or civil service positions.
>
> **2** The probability of a black being appointed to a position having a potential for power is directly related to the similarity of his political and economic philosophy to that of whites already occupying positions of power.
>
> **3** Significant black participation in the making of decisions is inversely related to the amount of resources involved.
>
> **4** Black representation is inversely related to the relative prestige of the formal position held.[60]

## WOMEN AND POWER

In examining the research of recent decades on community power, it is difficult to find more than a cursory mention of the status, prestige, or even presence of women in power structures. This is because in sociological research, as elsewhere, women have been largely "nonpersons." This situation is changing radically, but one result of past inattention is a virtual lack of solid data on participation by women other than the obvious counts of women in Congress and the Senate, as state governors, as local mayors, etc.

One exception is a study done by Babchuk and others of the role

[60]Flaming, Palen, et al., op. cit., p. 133.

Congresswoman Bella Abzug speaking out. *(Diane Henry/Editorial Photocolor Archives.)*

played by women in the voluntary civic associations of a large Northeastern city. They found that while women participated extensively on the Council of Social Agencies and Community Chest boards—522 of the 1,937 memberships were held by women—there were substantial differences between participation by men and by women.[61]

Agencies were classified according to their function and according to whether they were "instrumental," "instrumental-expressive," or "expressive." Instrumental agencies as a group provided a service or produced a good—for example, a Council of Social Agencies or a hospital. Expressive agencies provided a framework in which actions were immediately gratifying—for example, a settlement house. Instrumental-expressive agencies included both instrumental and expressive activities consciously exercised. It was hypothesized that agencies with instrumental functions would have the greatest status, the largest budgets, and correspondingly the fewest women. It was expected that women

[61]Nicholas Babchuk, Ruth Morsey, and C. Wayne Gordon, "Men and Women in Community Agencies: A Note on Power and Prestige," in Nona Glazer-Malbin and Helen Youngelson Waehrer (eds.), *Women in a Man-Made World,* Rand McNally, Chicago, 1972, pp. 248–253.

would be more likely to be members of boards with expressive functions and smaller budgets.

The findings were as predicted. The authors of the study concluded that the more vital, high-status boards were overwhelmigly dominated by men. The researchers found:

> Of the 222 board members of the agencies ranked as most vital, 198 or 89 percent, were men. Only 147 of the 240 members, or 61 percent, of the boards of agencies ranked as least vital were men. Thus, while men tend to dominate the boards of both types, they are most likely to be represented on boards of agencies ranked as most vital. . . .
>
> Of the 25 members of the most vital boards only one was a woman.[62]

It is reasonable to assume that research currently in progress will indicate that the numbers and percentage of women in positions of community power is increasing and will continue to do so as women achieve economic as well as legal and social equality with men.

[62]Babchuk et al., op. cit., p. 25.

Chapter 9

# Minorities: Black, Brown, Red, and Yellow

*We hold these truths to be self evident; that all men are created equal; that they are endowed by their creator with certain unalienable rights; that among these are life, liberty, and the pursuit of happiness.*

Declaration of Independence

Minority groups are defined by sociologists as those who lack power and are systematically discriminated against by other groups. Minority groups almost always have fewer numbers than the majority population, but size itself is not the criterion. Patterns of prejudice and discrimination, not size, make a minority. Minorities have unequal access to services, goods, opportunities, and power.

This chapter will concentrate on four urban minorities: blacks, Mexican Americans, Indians, and Japanese Americans. These four minorities indicate the differences among urban minorities and the difficulty of applying similar labels and solutions to all, as if they had all come from the same mold. The four groups differ not only in size but also in degree of assimilation and economic and social mobility. The city may or may not be a true "melting pot," but it is definitely a stew with considerable variety.

## THE MELTING POT

It is a cliché to state that America is a nation of immigrants, but it is sometimes forgotten that the American in-migration was the largest mass migration in the history of the world. Precise data are lacking, but it is possible that some 45 million immigrants have arrived in the United States since 1820. From the earliest days of the nation there has been agitation to restrict the immigration of certain groups, and there is still debate regarding the effectiveness of the melting pot in blending the diverse groups that make up America. Glazer and Moynihan in *Beyond the Melting Pot,* a study of the enduring importance of ethnicity in New York City, state, "The point about the melting pot . . . is that it did not happen. At least not in New York and, mutatis mutandis, in those parts of America which resemble New York."[1] On the other hand, the urban sociologist Scott Greer maintains that the melting pot was effective and that the result is a common American culture.

The immigrants were not always welcomed with open arms. On the West Coast the minorities most feared and despised were the Chinese and Japanese. On the East Coast there was no equivalent of the Oriental Exclusion Acts, but immigrants from the poorer European countries were far from universally welcomed. Some of the most virulent early criticism of the whole concept of the melting pot was provided by social reformers and physical scientists at the turn of the century. Discovering genetics, they jumped to the conclusion that not only hair color, size, and bone structure were genetically transferable, but also crime, poverty, illiteracy, and all social behavior. Blood would tell—and what they believed it told was that Anglo-Saxon America was genetically committing suicide by allowing in unrestricted numbers of genetically inferior races such as Poles, Italians, Slavs, and other Eastern and Southern Europeans. The introduction to the 1921 edition of an anti-immigrant classic called *The Passing of the Great Race* put it graphically:

> To admit the unchangeable differentiation of race in its modern scientific meaning is to admit inevitably the existence of superiority in one race and of inferiority in another. . . .

[1]Nathan Glazer and Daniel Patrick Moynihan, *Beyond the Melting Pot,* The M.I.T. Press, Cambridge, Mass., 1963, p. v.

Steerage immigrants had to undergo physical examinations at Ellis Island. There was no such requirement for first-class passengers. (*Culver Pictures.*)

> The resurgence of inferior races and classes throughout not merely Europe but the world, is evident in every dispatch from Egypt, Ireland, Poland, Rumania, India, and Mexico. It is called nationalism, patriotism, freedom and other high-sounding names, but it is everywhere the phenomenon of the long-suppressed, conquered servile classes rising against the master race.[2]

In the United States the effect of the genetic argument was seen in the immigration laws of 1924, which remained in force with minor

[2]Madison Grant, *The Passing of the Great Race,* Charles Scribner's Sons, New York, 1921, pp. xxviii, and xxxi.

amendment until 1968. These laws were based on the assumption that the genetic strength of the nation was contingent upon restricting or outlawing genetically inferior races and peoples. Thus, "inferior" Southern and Eastern Europeans were reduced from 45 percent of all immigrants under the already restrictive law of 1921 to 12 percent under the law of 1924. Northern and Western Europeans were welcome—particularly if they were Protestant—but others were not wanted. About 85 percent of the quota went to Northwest Europe, and roughly half the total quota went to three countries: England, Germany, and Ireland. Poles, Slavs, Greeks, Italians, and other Eastern and Southern Europeans were given only minor quotas. It is more than a little ironic that a generation after being labeled "inferior" by the immigration laws of the United States, some of these same white ethnic groups have been among the most hostile to newer urban groups such as blacks.

The days of mass migration are past, but we still have a substantial foreign-born population, and that population is overwhelmingly urban. As of 1970 there were still 9.6 million foreign-born whites in the United States, 91 percent of whom resided in urban places. Cities such as Boston, New York, Chicago, Detroit, Milwaukee, San Francisco, and Los Angeles still have substantial ethnic colonies. "Little Italys," "Greektowns," and "New Polands" remind us of the heterogeneity of the metropolis. While European enclaves may be decreasing in size and importance, the ethnic and racial ghettoes of blacks, Mexican Americans, and Indians are expanding. Ecologically these are often the same spatial areas that earlier in the century were occupied by other in-migrant groups.

In recent years the term "ghetto" has come to have more and more of a racial reference.

> Historically, the word "ghetto" meant an area in which a certain identifiable group was compelled to live. The word retains this meaning of geographic constraint, but now refers to two different kinds of constraining forces. In its *racial* sense, a ghetto is an area to which members of an ethnic minority, particularly Negroes, are residentially restricted by social, economic, and physical pressures from the rest of society. In this meaning, a ghetto can contain wealthy and middle-income residents as well as poor ones. In its *economic* sense, a ghetto is an area in which poor people are compelled to live because they cannot afford better accommodations. In this meaning, a ghetto contains mainly poor people, regardless of race or color.[3]

In order to minimize confusion, the word "ghetto" will be used in this book in its racial rather than its economic sense.

[3]Anthony Downs, "Alternative Futures for the American Ghetto," *Daedalus*, **97**(4):1331–1378, Fall, 1968. Reprinted by permission of *Daedalus*, Journal of the American Academy of Arts and Sciences, Boston, Massachusetts. Fall 1968, *The Conscience of the City*.

## BLACK AMERICANS

The 23 million black Americans constitute America's largest continuing minority group—11 percent of the national population in 1970. This is a minority group larger than the total population of Canada. At the time of the first census in 1790, blacks made up 19 percent of the total population. In spite of a high rate of natural increase, the proportion of blacks in the population declined during the nineteenth century because of heavy European immigration. European immigration was greatly restricted by the immigration laws of the 1920s, and, since 1930, blacks have been increasing as a proportion of the population. (See Table 9-1.) The black population continues to have a birth rate significantly higher than that of the white population. Estimates are that the black population will number between 30 and 34 million a decade from now (1984–1985). Every indication is that the overwhelming bulk of this increase will take place in metropolitan areas, and particularly in central cities.

### Population Changes

Historically, the black population was an overwhelmingly rural and Southern group until this century. Despite the Civil War and the extensive political and social upheavals of Reconstruction, there was but slight change in this pattern. As recently as 1910, nine out of ten blacks still lived in the South and 73 percent of blacks were rural.

Significant migration of blacks out of the South began with World War I. When the war cut off the tide of European immigrant labor and flooded industries with war orders, a new source of labor had to be found.

**Table 9-1 Negro Population in the United States, by Numbers and Percent, 1790 to 1970.**

| Year | Number | Percent of total population |
|---|---|---|
| 1790 | 757,000 | 19.3 |
| 1800 | 1,002,000 | 18.9 |
| 1850 | 3,639,000 | 15.7 |
| 1900 | 8,834,000 | 11.6 |
| 1930 | 11,891,000 | 9.7 |
| 1940 | 12,866,000 | 9.8 |
| 1950 | 15,042,000 | 10.0 |
| 1960 | 18,860,000 | 10.6 |
| 1970 | 22,672,570 | 11.2 |

*Source:* U.S. Bureau of the Census: Fifteenth Census Reports, *Population,* vol. II; Sixteenth Census Reports, *Population,* vol. 11, part I; *U.S. Census of Population: 1950,* vol. II, part 1; *U.S. Census of Population: 1950,* vol. 1; U.S. Bureau of the Census, *Current Population Reports,* series P-25, nos. 367, 416, 441, and 460.

Soon labor recruiters were scouring the South, encouraging Negroes to migrate North to "the promised land." In some cases, one-way railroad tickets were even provided. The pull of Northern industrial jobs combined with the boll weevil's destruction of cotton and the mechanization of agriculture to encourage migration. Cotton production was shifting out of the Old South to the West and Southwest, and field-hand labor was no longer so necessary. The figures tell the dramatic magnitude of the out-migration. Between 1910 and 1920 the five states of the Deep South—South Carolina, Georgia, Alabama, Mississippi, and Louisiana—lost 400,000 blacks through out-migration.

The Depression of the 1930s cut off employment opportunities in the North and stemmed the flow of in-migrants to the cities. But the resurgence of industry during World War II again accelerated the pace of migration, and it continued into the 1950s and 1960s. Mississippi's black population declined more than 100,000 during the decade 1960–1970, and there were also absolute losses (in spite of high birth rates) in Alabama and South Carolina.

This was an extremely substantial migration, but it should be kept in perspective—particularly since there is a tendency to exaggerate it. Between 1910 and 1960 somewhat under 5 million blacks left the South, largely for the big cities of the North. This is a great number of people but hardly compares with the waves of European immigrants that inundated our shores during the first years of this century. For example, a total of 8.8 million European immigrants entered the United States between 1901 and 1911 alone. Even today in urban areas there are far more foreign immigrants than blacks in-migrating. In fact, there are not enough rural Southern blacks left to have all that great an impact even if they all migrated out. Foreign immigrants, on the other hand, continue to flow into the United States at a pace of approximately 400,000 a year. Thus in-migration of Southern blacks to the cities should be kept in perspective, and the long-standing role of the American city as the home of the immigrant must be borne in mind. Population growth among black urbanites today is due to natural replacement.

### Black Residential Patterns Today

Today only half the nation's blacks (52 percent) live in the South, and four out of five blacks are urban. The estimate is that "if present migration trends continue, from 75 to 85 percent of the Negro population will live outside of the South."[4] Thus the black population has gone in a few generations from being overwhelmingly rural to being more urban than

[4]H. C. Hamilton, "The Negro Leaves the South," *Demography*, **1**:294, 1964.

the white population. While blacks make up 11 percent of the national population, they make up 21 percent of the population of central cities and 28 percent of the population of the twelve cities having a population over 2 million.

The image of the Negro as a Southern rural sharecropper migrating to the big city is a picture out of another age and time. Today, while just over half of all blacks still live in the South, they are now one of the most urban segments of the total population. Blacks are more concentrated in the large cities and SMSAs than whites. Three out of every five blacks (58 percent) live in the central city of a major metropolitan area, as compared with 28 percent of the white population. Blacks make up the majority of the population in four major American cities: Atlanta, Gary, Newark, and Washington, D.C. In nine other cities—Baltimore, Birmingham, Charleston, Detroit, New Orleans, Richmond, Savannah, St. Louis, and Wilmington—more than 40 percent of the population is black. When discussing

**Table 9-2 Population Distribution and Change, Inside and Outside Metropolitan Areas (SMSAs), 1950, 1960, and 1970**

| Area | Population, millions | | | | | |
|---|---|---|---|---|---|---|
| | Negro | | | White | | |
| | 1950* | 1960 | 1970 | 1950* | 1960 | 1970 |
| United States | 15.0 | 18.9 | 22.7 | 135.1 | 158.8 | 177.6 |
| Metropolitan areas | 8.8 | 12.8 | 16.8 | 85.1 | 106.4 | 121.3 |
| Central cities | 6.6 | 9.9 | 13.1 | 46.8 | 50.1 | 49.5 |
| Outside central cities | 2.2 | 2.8 | 3.7 | 38.3 | 56.3 | 71.8 |
| Outside metropolitan areas | 6.2 | 6.1 | 5.8 | 50.0 | 52.5 | 56.4 |

| Area | Change, 1960–1970 | | | |
|---|---|---|---|---|
| | Negro | | White | |
| | Number change, millions | Percent change | Number change, millions | Percent change |
| United States | 3.8 | 20 | 18.8 | 12 |
| Metropolitan areas | 4.1 | 32 | 14.9 | 14 |
| Central cities | 3.2 | 33 | .6 | −1 |
| Outside central cities | .8 | 29 | 15.5 | 28 |
| Outside metropolitan areas | −.3 | −4 | 3.9 | 7 |

*1950 data for metropolitan areas not strictly comparable to 1970 definition of SMSAs.
*Source:* Based on U.S. Department of Commerce, Bureau of the Census.

racial change, however, it must be remembered that the prophecy of black majorities in all major American cities is demographically impossible. To put it simply, there are not enough blacks for this to occur. Blacks are still only 11 percent of the total population, and 80 percent of all blacks are already urban.

The percentage of blacks in central cities is increasing. In 1970, 58 percent of the total black population lived in central cities—which represented a sizable increase over the 44 percent living in cities in 1950.[5] During the 1960s the black population of central cities increased by 3.2 million. These increases were most marked in the largest metropolitan areas. In the cities of 2 million and over there was a decline of 2.5 million whites and an increase of 1.8 million blacks.[6]

The flight of whites from central cities has reached alarming proportions in some areas. For example, the white population of Detroit declined by 345,000 between 1960 and 1970, and the exodus from Chicago decreased the white population by over half a million. During this same period the black population of most of the nation's cities shot up. Thus, the racial transformation of central cities was accelerated. As noted by the Bureau of the Census, the "increase in the black population of the central cities proved to be both large and widespread, thus changing the racial mixture substantially."

### Segregation

Segregation of racial and ethnic groups is not new to American life. Anti-immigrant and anti-Catholic political movements, from the Know Nothing Party of the nineteenth century to the Klu Klux Klan of the 1920s, attempted to keep newcomers "in their place" socially and physically. When the Irish Catholic Kennedy family moved into Hyannis Port, there was great unhappiness among many old-line Protestant families about what was happening to the neighborhood.

An obvious characteristic of American cities is that they are racially segregated, with certain areas restricted to whites and others relegated to blacks. Much of the concentration of blacks in central cities, and particularly in the older inner-city areas, is a reflection of migration patterns similar to those that affected earlier ethnic minorities; but for the black population there is the additional factor of race, which frequently overrides economics. The best data on how patterns of segregation are changing are provided by Karl and Alma Taeuber in their study of segregation indices of American cities for 1940, 1950, and 1960.[7]

[5]U.S. Bureau of the Census, "The Social and Economic Status of Negroes in the United States, 1970," *Special Studies,* series P–23, no. 38, U.S. Government Printing Office, Washington, D.C., 1971 p. 13.

[6]Conrad Taeuber, "Population Trends in the 1960s," *Science,* **176:**774, May 19, 1972.

[7]Karl Taeuber and Alma Taeuber, *Negroes in Cities,* Aldine, Chicago, 1965.

Their segregation index, called the "index of dissimilarity," uses the computer to analyze census data for blacks and gives an index figure representing the proportion of nonwhites that would have to move to another block in order to have a complete balance of the races. For example, in a city where 10 percent of the population is black, the index would have a value of zero if one-tenth of the households on each block were black and a value of 100 if there was total segregation. Thus, the index has a theoretical range of 0 to 100, with 100 representing complete segregation.

According to the Taeubers' findings, the average segregation index for 207 of the largest cities in the United States was 86.2 in 1960. This means that 86 percent of all nonwhites would have had to change the block on which they live in order to produce an unsegregated pattern. Of the 207 cities in the sample, each having a population of 50,000 or more, the value of the segregation index ranged from a high of 98.1 in Fort Lauderdale to a low of 60.4 in San Jose.

Regionally, the South had the highest segregation index (90.9); with that of the North Central region second (87.7), followed by the West (79.3) and the Northeast (79.2). The overall degree of national racial segregation has been relatively constant over the decades, averaging 85.2 in 1940, 87.3 in 1950, and 86.2 in 1960. In each of these years half the cities in the study had segregation-index values of 90 or above, and five out of six had index scores of 80 or above. High levels of segregation are an established national pattern.

Between 1950 and 1960—the most recent dates for which data were included—"cities in every Northern and Western division experienced average decreases in segregation while cities in all of the Southern divisions again experienced increases in segregation."[8] The extreme segregation of Southern cities is a modern rather than a long-standing trend. In the South of days gone by, social segregation was so rigid that spatial segregation was unnecessary. Especially in the older Southern cities, whites frequently lived in the big house on the street while blacks lived in the smaller house behind in the alley. Black servants lived on the premises.

Southern cities over the decades have been increasing their degree of racial segregation, while there have been decreases more recently in the North. In the South before the 1950s, there was no need for the whites to practice spatial segregation since the social distance between the races was so pronounced. More recently, however, with the social distance between blacks and whites decreased by legislation, the South has been adopting Northern racial patterns and substituting spatial distance for

[8]Taeuber and Taeuber, op. cit., p. 43.

**Table 9-3 Average Values of Indexes of Residential Segregation for Regions and Census Divisions, and Changes in Indexes, 109 Cities, 1940, 1950, and 1960**

| | | Average values of segregation indexes | | | | |
|---|---|---|---|---|---|---|
| Region and division | Number of cities | 1940 | 1950 | 1960 | Change 1940–1950 | Change 1950–1960 |
| Total, all regions | 109 | 85.2 | 87.3 | 86.1 | 2.1 | −1.2 |
| Northeast | 25 | 83.2 | 83.6 | 78.9 | 0.4 | −4.7 |
| New England | 7 | 81.9 | 81.9 | 75.8 | 0.0 | −6.1 |
| Middle Atlantic | 18 | 83.7 | 84.3 | 80.0 | 0.6 | −4.3 |
| North Central | 29 | 88.4 | 89.9 | 88.4 | 1.5 | −1.5 |
| East North Central | 20 | 88.3 | 90.0 | 88.4 | 1.7 | −1.6 |
| West North Central | 9 | 88.6 | 89.9 | 88.3 | 1.2 | −1.5 |
| West* | 10 | 82.7 | 82.9 | 76.4 | 0.2 | −6.5 |
| South | 45 | 84.9 | 88.5 | 90.7 | 3.6 | 2.2 |
| South Atlantic | 22 | 86.9 | 88.7 | 90.6 | 1.8 | 1.9 |
| East South Central | 9 | 84.8 | 88.1 | 91.4 | 3.3 | 3.3 |
| West South Central | 14 | 81.7 | 88.5 | 90.5 | 6.8 | 2.0 |

*Census divisions within the West are not shown, because there is only one city (Denver) included in the study from the Mountain Division.

*Source:* Karl E. Taeuber and Alma F. Taeuber, *Negroes in Cities*, Aldine, Chicago, 1965, p. 44, table 5.

social distance. As of 1940, the *least* spatially segregated city of the 109 cities for which data are available was Charleston, South Carolina, the Birthplace of the Confederacy.[9] As of 1960 the segregation index of Charleston had increased almost 20 points, to 79.5.

As a rough generalization one could say that in the South it was acceptable for blacks to live close to whites but not to rise to the levels of white social classes. In the North, on the contrary, it was all right to move up but not to move next door. Recently, a national rather than a regional pattern of segregation has been emerging owing to increasing rates of spatial segregation in the South and decreasing rates in the North and West. However, everywhere the index remains high. (See Table 9-3.)

As expressed by the Taeubers:

> Negroes are more segregated residentially than are Orientals, Mexican Americans, Puerto Ricans, or any nationality group. In fact Negroes are by far the most residentially segregated urban minority in recent American history. This is evident in the virtually complete exclusion of Negro residents

[9]Op. cit., p. 45.

from most new suburban developments of the past 50 years as well as in the block-by-block expansion of Negro residential areas in the central portions of many large cities.[10]

North or South, large city or small, high percentage of blacks or low percentage of blacks, Negroes have been rigidly separated from other Americans. Even Mexicans and Puerto Ricans, who are less advantaged economically than urban blacks, are less segregated. For blacks, race rather than income has been the factor that has most determined residential patterns. According to the National Commission on Civil Disorders:

> This nearly universal pattern cannot be explained in terms of economic discrimination against all low-income groups. Analysis of 15 representative cities indicates that white upper and middle-income households are far more segregated from Negro upper and middle-income households than from white lower-income households.[11]

Legally inforced racial segregation is a thing of the past, but the voluntary or involuntary black ghetto continues as a major factor in the composition of American cities.

### Social-Class Distribution

As regards spatial distribution by social class, blacks tend to follow the same pattern as whites. The larger and older cities of the North are much more likely to have status differentials favoring suburban over central-city residence.[12] Within cities, there is commonly an increase in the level of socioeconomic status for blacks with distance from the city center. Marston suggests that areas that are changing to black residency are always of higher status than established black neighborhoods, regardless of where they are located in the urban area.[13] However, Rose, did not always find this to be true. In his research, transitional areas closer to the city were sometimes lower-class or working-class, but transitional areas in more peripheral locations were areas of higher status than all black areas.[14]

[10]Op. cit., p. 68.

[11]"The Migration of Negroes from the South," *Report of the National Advisory Commission on Civil Disorders,* U.S. Government Printing Office, Washington, D.C., 1968.

[12]J. John Palen and Leo Schnore, "Color Composition and City Suburban Status Differences," *Land Economics,* **41:**87–91, February, 1965.

[13]Wilfred G. Marston, "Socioeconomic Differentiation within Negro Areas of American Cities," *Social Forces,* **48:**165–176, December, 1969.

[14]Harold M. Rose, "The Spatial Development of Black Residential Subsystems," *Economic Geography,* **48:**43–65, January, 1972.

In Northern cities black residential areas were a result of the "trickle-down" system by which blacks inherit housing previously occupied by whites. Generally these were areas of older housing within central cities. Patterns in the South were different until this generation, with housing being built specifically for blacks. Until relatively recently there was little transition of areas from white to black by means of "trickling down." Black neighborhoods in the South were often on the periphery of the city as well as centrally located with the result that in the South black suburbanites were not always of higher socioeconomic status than black central-city residents. Today the pattern of social-class distribution for blacks in the South is becoming more like the Northern pattern. That is, higher-status populations, both black and white, are more likely to be found on the periphery of the city.

### Social-Class Changes

In May, 1954, the Supreme Court handed down its historic decision in *Brown v. the Topeka Board of Education,* ruling that "separate but equal" schooling was not equal and thus violated the Constitution. Before 1954, there had been relatively little note of the role of black men and women in urban life. Two excellent works, Drake and Clayton's *Black Metropolis and Frazier's Black Bourgeoise*[15] dealt with the parallel shadow society erected by urban blacks who were excluded from participation in white social structures. Myrdal also wrote his massive study of relations between Negroes and whites in the America of that period: *An American Dilemma.*[16] Otherwise, there had been little more than passing reference to blacks. They were the "invisible men."[17] Blacks simply didn't fit, and thus writers and researchers dealt with them either by ignoring their existence or tacking on a parallel, but not overlapping, stratification pyramid to account for them. Blacks did not fit neatly into Warner's six-tiered stratification system or any other widely used system.

The period from 1960 to the present has seen a remarkable and dramatic upturn in the economic and social status of American blacks. Income figures in America have always been closely related to social status, and what the figures now show is that a slender majority of black Americans (52 percent) are middle-class. This fact, which has not yet significantly affected the racial rhetoric of either the right or the left, means that most of "common-sense" knowledge held by both blacks and whites regarding the economic position of Negroes is badly dated.

[15]St. Clair Drake and Horace R. Clayton, *Black Metropolis,* Harcourt, Brace, New York, 1945 and E. Franklin Frazier, *Black Bourgeoise,* Free Press, Glencoe, Ill., 1957.

[16]Gunnar Myrdal, *An American Dilemma,* Harper and Row, New York, 1944.

[17]See the novel by Ralph Ellison, *The Invisible Man,* Random House, New York, 1952.

The old stereotype of the poor, uneducated black just up from the Southern cottonfields to the big city is ludicrously out of touch with contemporary social and economic reality. This is not to say that blacks as a group are not economically deprived when compared with whites; there are still substantial, if lessening, differences between the two groups as aggregates. Outside the South, the income of blacks was 74 percent of that of whites in 1970. This is a considerable gap, but it is a difference that has been rapidly closing. According to data from the census of 1970, income before inflation for white families went up 69 percent while income for black families went up 99.6 percent. Family income among blacks had doubled during a single decade.

In this case, though, the aggregate figures present a misleading picture, for there are in reality two black populations, one that is increasingly becoming middle-class and one that is settling in as a semipermanent urban underclass. The 1960s and 1970s have been a period of unprecedented mobility for blacks, who before the changes in legislation and attitude of the 1960s would have been restricted by a discriminatory job ceiling.[18]

One-third of all black urban families in 1970 had incomes of $10,000 or more (this was true of one-half the white population). Younger and educated blacks are making substantial progress in achieving economic equality with whites. The future of the black college student is particularly bright. Outside the South, families consisting of a husband and wife have an income level of 88 percent of white income. Most significantly, outside the South differences in income between blacks and whites for husband-wife families where the head of the family is under thirty-five years of age have all but disappeared. Income for such younger families was 96 percent of white income in 1970—a considerable jump from the 78 percent of only a decade earlier. Younger black husband-wife families in the North have reached equality with white families. When younger families where both the husband and wife work are compared, the black families outside the South earn 104 percent of what comparable whites earn; ten years earlier, this figure was only 85 percent.[19] (However, black wives work more weeks per year than white wives.)

The data suggest that, contrary to common belief, many of the programs initiated during the time of the "war on poverty" and the "great society" were successful in bringing major progress for blacks—economically, educationally, and occupationally. The fact is that a

[18]For data on the effects of the job ceiling on an earlier generation, see St. Clair Drake and Horace Clayton, *Black Metropolis*, Harcourt, Brace, New York, 1945, Chap. 9, "The Job Ceiling," pp. 219–232.

[19]For a fuller discussion of changes in income levels of blacks, see Ben J. Wattenberg and Richard M. Scammon, "Black Progress and Liberal Rhetoric," *Commentary*, **55**(4):35–44, April, 1973.

majority of blacks are now at least approaching the middle class; and as the percentage of blacks completing college and apprenticeship programs continues to grow, so will the black middle class. Middle-class blacks may still live in largely black ghettoes, but they are middle-class ghettoes, not slum neighborhoods. Forty-two percent of blacks owned their homes in 1970, as compared with only 24 percent in 1940. The overall quality of the housing was, however, inferior to that of whites.

### The Black Lower Class

At the other end of the spectrum the picture is much grimmer. Here we find the elderly who are scarred by previous racial experiences and the young who by accident of birth—illegitimacy, poverty, the absence of the father—are unable to take advantage of the new opportunities. They are stationary, or making only minimal progress, and thus are slipping relatively farther behind not only white society but middle-class blacks as well.

> This group, this "other Negro America," has not been significantly touched by present racial adjustments. Its hopes were raised in the 1950s; but now it cannot even rationalize personal failure entirely in racial terms, for *Ebony* bulges each month with evidence that the affluent Negro America is making rapid strides. Basic progress in improving the economic position of Negroes depends upon reaching the "other Negro America."[20]

Infant mortality rates illustrate this division. Although for middle-class blacks infant mortality rates are roughly comparable to those for whites, the death rate for *all* black infants is twice that of children born to whites. In 1972 the infant mortality rate for blacks was 35.7 deaths per 1,000 while the rate for whites was 15.2 per 1,000. Since prenatal maternal care is directly related to infant mortality, there is a long way to go to provide adequate maternal health care for all citizens.

Unemployment is still a very serious problem for blacks: unemployment rates are roughly twice as high for blacks as for whites. Again, though, the overall figures hide great differences. In recent years there has been a collapse of traditional discriminatory patterns in much of the labor market, but this has done little for blacks with only marginal education and skills. For these the old saying "If you're white, all right; if you're brown, stick around; if you're black, stay back" still has force.

The extent of the problem of poverty is easy to document. In the central cities of the largest metropolitan areas (cities over 1 million), the

[20]Thomas F. Pettigrew, *Racially Separate or Together?*, McGraw-Hill, New York, 1971, p. 37.

Chicago has made great strides in slum clearance, but the cost in personal alienation has been high. (*United Press International.*)

overall rates of poverty in 1970 were 9 percent for whites and 24 percent for blacks.[21] This is hardly a figure to be proud of, but a decade earlier the proportion of the black population living below the poverty level was almost twice as high.

Paradoxically, welfare roles have been increasing while the rate of blacks in poverty has been decreasing. Of the 10.6 million persons receiving funds from the Aid to Dependent Children program in 1971, 4.8 million (45 percent) were black. Of the total black population, 21 percent were on welfare as opposed to only 7 percent in 1960. This increase in those receiving welfare represents not an increase in poverty but an increase in the likelihood that those in poverty will receive aid. Equally significant, today almost one-third of all black families (30.1 percent) are

[21]Bureau of the Census, "Trends in Social and Economic Conditions in Metropolitan and Nonmetropolitan Areas," *Special Studies*, U.S. Government Printing Office, Washington, D.C., 1970, pp. 70–71.

headed by females; twenty years ago, this figure was only one-sixth. Since families where the father is absent are far more likely to be poor families, it is increasingly the case that poor black families are families where a male head is absent.

There is a widening gap between black families headed by women and those headed by men. The Bureau of the Census reports that during the decade 1960–1970 there was, in metropolitan areas, a 50 percent reduction in the number of black families below the poverty line headed by men, while the number of poor black families headed by women increased 48 percent.[22] As Wattenberg and Scammon express it:

> The phrase "black female-headed families" is too often interchangeable with a more succinct term: "poor." In 1971, more than half (54 percent) of such families were living below what the government calls the "low-income level"; only 17 percent of male-headed families could be so designated. And the brutal fact is that from 1959 to 1971 the number of male-headed families in poverty decreased by more than half, while the number of female-headed families in poverty increased by a third. Thus, by 1971, almost six in ten black families in poverty were female-headed. As male-headed families exited from the poverty class, female-headed families entered it in growing numbers.[23]

Among black women who are heads of families, one-third work; the other two-thirds do not. The result of this can be seen in the income figures for black familes: one-fourth of all black families had a median income of only $4,396 in 1970. On the other hand, for black families under age thirty-five outside the South where both husband and wife worked there was no substantial difference from the income levels of similar white families.[24]

### Unemployment and Family Disorganization

Probably the most controversial and misquoted study of the relationship between unemployment and family characteristics is the so-called "Moynihan Report," prepared by Daniel Patrick Moynihan.[25] Moynihan's thesis was that "the family structure of lower-class Negroes is highly unstable, and in many urban centers is approaching complete break-

[22]Bureau of the Census, "Trends in Social and Economic Conditions in Metropolitan and Nonmetropolitan Areas," *Special Studies*, U.S. Government Printing Office, Washington, D.C., 1971, p. 1.

[23]Wattenberg and Scammon, op. cit., p. 39. Reprinted from *Commentary* by permission; copyright © 1973, by the American Jewish Committee.

[24]U.S. Bureau of the Census, "The Social and Economic Status of Negroes in the United States, 1970," *Special Studies*, U.S. Government Printing Office, Washington, D.C., 1971, p. 1.

[25]*The Negro Family: The Case for National Action*, Office of Policy Planning and Research, Department of Labor, Washington, D.C., 1965.

down."[26] To support his argument, Moynihan documents the rise in traditional indicators of social disorganization: the number on welfare is at a crisis level (one-third of all blacks in Chicago; nearly one-fourth of marriages among urban Negroes are dissolved (three times the figure for whites); nearly one-fourth of Negro births are illegitimate (the figure is over 40 percent for urban areas such as Harlem); and only a minority of black children reach age eighteen having lived all their lives with both parents. These facts are directly linked by Moynihan, and others, to the disastrous level of unemployment among black men, which, when combined with the pattern of matriarchal domination of family life set during slavery, leaves the lower-class black male without a significant family role—a pattern that is then transferred to young males who grow up without fathers or other successful male figures to serve as models.

Discussing the effect of matriarchal domination, Whitney Young stated:

> The effect on family functioning and role performance of this historical experience (economic deprivation) is what you might predict. Both as a husband and as a father the Negro male is made to feel inadequate, not because he is unlovable or unaffectionate, lacks intelligence or even a gray flannel suit. But in a society that measures a man by the size of his paycheck, he doesn't stand very tall in a comparison with his white counterpart. To this situation he may react with withdrawal, bitterness toward society, aggression both within the family and racial group, self-hatred, or crime.[27]

Thus, Moynihan's thesis was that there was an immediate and crucial need to strengthen the black family. Moynihan argued that the poor urban black family will not change until black males are able to play meaningful and respected roles—and that this in turn will not occur until unemployment among blacks is substantially reduced and black males can become significant wage earners. Whether or not one accepts the picture of the totally disorganized poor black family headed by a woman (and it is probably an overstatement), it is clear that employment is the major key to helping not just individuals but families break out of the cycle of poverty and welfare.

### The Future

Crystal-ball gazing is always risky, but the prognosis for the future of black Americans looks far brighter than it has looked in the past. Nationwide opinion polls reveal that blacks are more optimistic about the

[26]Op. cit., p. 5.

[27]Whitney Young, *To Be Equal*, McGraw-Hill, New York, 1964, p. 25.

nation's future than are whites. A 1970 *Time*–Louis Harris poll based on interviews with a nationwide cross section of 1,255 blacks of all social classes found that, while 31 percent agreed with the statement that blacks "will probably have to resort to violence to win rights," to a remarkable degree they also expressed strong confidence that life is improving and will continue to improve. Sixty-seven percent felt that things are "getting better than they were four to five years ago." Moreover, and more significantly, the means endorsed for making progress have a strong middle-class ring. For example, 97 percent felt that blacks will make real progress by getting more blacks better-educated; 93 percent, by starting more businesses owned by blacks; and 92 percent, by electing more blacks to public office. These are hardly revolutionary positions. Activities such as taking to the streets in protest and supporting militant leaders and organizations were far less likely to be seen as a way of making progress.[28] The results clearly indicate that the overwhelming majority of blacks do not want to overturn the system by revolution so much as to obtain a fair share of the benefits of the system. Blacks no longer will tolerate being excluded.

## MEXICAN AMERICANS

Mexican Americans[29] are rather unique as an American minority, for they—like the Indians—originally became a minority not by voluntary or involuntary migration from Europe or Africa but by being militarily conquered. They are one of the nation's oldest minorities while at the same time, somewhat contradictorily, being the newest minority in terms of numbers of immigrants from Mexico and in-migration to the cities.

The Bureau of the Census indicates that in 1970 there were about 4½ million persons of Mexican descent in the United States and over 9 million persons of Spanish heritage (including Puerto Rico, Cuba, and South America). Mexican Americans constitute about 3 percent of the population of the United States. The Mexican-American population is heavily concentrated in the Southwest and California, although there has recently been considerable migration to Northern industrial cities, particularly Chicago.

A commonly used classification system divides the Spanish-speaking community into three subcategories. The first of these is the *Spanish Americans*, who were the early residents of New Mexico and California

[28] *Time*, April 6, 1970, p. 29.

[29] There is no generally accepted term used by Americans of Mexican ancestry to describe the ethnic group. "Mexican American," "Spanish American," "Latin," and, among younger activists, "Chicano," are all used, and the preferred term differs from place to place. For convenience, we will generally use the term "Mexican American."

before the American conquest. Geographically and historically, this group differs from the later immigrants from Mexico. The second subgroup, the *Mexican Americans*, consists of immigrants from Mexico since Mexican revolutions of the early twentieth century who still have cultural and other affiliations with Mexico. Frequently, they are citizens of the United States. The third group, the *Mexicans*, are still more recent arrivals and are the furthest from "Anglo" society as far as acculturation is concerned. In addition to having a Mexican background, they are also citizens of Mexico and may, in fact, be illegal immigrants to the United States. There is a very rough status hierarchy implied in the above categorization. "Spanish" ancestry has traditionally been considered more prestigious than "Mexican" ancestry, and "Indian" ancestry is at the bottom. This attitude is not a reaction to the racial situation in the United States but rather has roots deep in the early colonial history of Mexico under the Spanish Crown. The Spanish colonial social system is discussed further in Chapter 14, "Latin American Cities."

In contrast to the Spanish-speaking population that has long inhabited New Mexico and portions of surrounding states, the majority of the present Mexican American population are fairly recent immigrants. The immigrants came north because there was a lack of economic opportunities in the labor-heavy Mexican economy and a demand for temporary farm workers in the United States. Particularly following World War II, the economic boom in the United States, coupled with the inability of the Mexican industrial economy to absorb all of its workers, led to both legal ("green-carders") and illegal migration northward to supply the shortage in American agricultural labor.

### Socioeconomic Status

Mexican Americans are clustered near the low end of the occupational scale. They still hold over half of the agricultural jobs in Texas and California, and the efforts of Cesar Chavez to organize Mexican American farm workers have strengthened the view of the typical Mexican American as a farm laborer. However, the "agribusiness" enterprises in California and Texas are rapidly replacing men with machines, and the development of new farm machinery will accelerate this process.

Economically, the Spanish-speaking population is as a whole somewhat better off than blacks. This general comparison, however, masks wide variations among those of different Spanish-speaking backgrounds. Puerto Ricans make slightly less than blacks, Mexican Americans make slightly more, and Cuban Americans—many of whom left Cuba with marketable skills—make considerably more.

In spite of the considerable diversity among the Mexican American population, it is often negatively stereotyped by other Americans as poor, complacent, fatalistic, not goal-oriented, emotional, superstitious, and traditional. "Anglo" (non-Mexican) society tends to assume, because there are so many lower-class Mexican immigrants, that all persons of Mexican descent are poor. According to the 1970 census, 23.5 percent of the persons of Spanish heritage were below the poverty level.[30] People of Spanish heritage constitute one-third of the poor of New Mexico and Texas. Only one-half of 1 percent of all Mexican American families had incomes over $25,000 in 1970—as compared with 7.3 percent of all Americans.

Unfortunately, their inferior social status and economic position have sometimes led Mexican Americans to internalize the negative stereotypes of the majority culture. "Recent surveys in San Antonio and Los Angeles show a tendency for Mexican Americans to agree with the negative judgments that the larger society has passed upon them."[31] To a remarkable extent Mexican Americans do share the Anglo stereotypes of Mexicans as living in the present, being emotional, expressive, and warm, and having stronger family ties than Anglos. For example, more than 80 percent of those interviewed in Los Angeles and San Antonio felt that Mexicans are more emotional than other Americans.[32] This can result in what sociologists call a "self-fulfilling prophesy," where a false or incomplete premise is believed and invokes a response that makes it come true. An example would be the belief by a teacher that Mexican American children cannot cope with abstract concepts: if the teacher, because of this belief, organizes his or her teaching to avoid abstract concepts, the result will be educational deficiencies. Mexican Americans have, in fact, had serious problems with the formal education systems of North America. In all states, Mexican Americans have lower median educational levels than blacks. Of all the states, California has the highest median educational level for Mexican Americans and Texas the lowest.[33] Nationwide, the median educational level of adult males is just over 8 years. Moreover, even in cities as far north as Chicago, the population of Spanish background has a school dropout rate higher than that of any other minority.

Census figures for 1970 indicate that only 12.5 percent of white urban

[30]U. S. Bureau of the Census, Census of Population, 1970, *General Social and Economic Characteristics,* PC(1)-C1, U. S. Government Printing Office, Washington, D.C., 1972, p. 358.

[31]R. Guzman, "Ethnics in Federally Subsidized Research: The Case of the Mexican American," in *The Mexican American: A New Focus on Opportunity,* Inter-Agency on Mexican American Affairs, Washington, D.C., 1967, p. 246.

[32]Joan W. Moore, *Mexican Americans,* Prentice-Hall, Englewood Cliffs, New Jersey, 1970, p. 8.

[33]Leo Grebler, *The Schooling Gap: Signs of Progress,* Advanced Report 7, University of California, Mexican American Study Project, Los Angeles, 1967.

males aged sixteen to twenty-one were not in school; the percentage for persons of Spanish heritage (Mexican and others) was 25.4 percent—twice as high. The percentage for Negroes (25.1) was about the same as that for people of Spanish heritage. American schools have been ill equipped to deal with students who are not fluent in English and have frequently shunted them aside as if they were poor learners or deficient in intelligence.

### Movement to Cities

The problem of adequate schooling and other problems of adjusting to the larger Anglo society have become more acute with the rapid urbanization of the Mexican American population during the last two decades. Traditional isolated towns and villages in New Mexico and other Southwestern states have been losing population, while the Mexican American population of cities such as Albuquerque, San Antonio, and Los Angeles has been increasing.

In the border states, only about one-fifth of the Mexican American population still lives in rural areas.[34] Today Los Angeles has more people of Mexican ancestry than any other city in the Americas, except Mexico City and Guadalajara. Clearly, the Mexican American's future is an urban future. The geographical movement out of the Southwest is not only migration out of a region; it is a symbol of the inevitable change from rural to urban residence and from rural to urban ways of life.

When we look at the entire Spanish-speaking population—not just Mexican Americans—the data indicate that Spanish-speaking Americans have become nearly as urbanized as blacks and much more so than Anglos. Half (51 percent) of the 9.3 million Spanish-speaking persons counted by the 1970 census lived in central cities, and most of the rest lived in metropolitan areas. Roughly 80 percent of the Mexican American population is urban. Chicago has a Mexican and Puerto Rican population of 300,000, of whom as many as 75,000 may be illegal immigrants.

Mexican Americans have as a group attracted less attention to themselves than other minorities such as blacks. The relative quiet of Mexican American city dwellers can be partially attributed to the fact that even low-level income, housing, and services in the United States city are still infinitely superior to the destitute barrios of the Mexican *municipios*. The United States offers relative opulence compared with the poverty of the suburban squatter barrios of Ciudad Juárez—the latter sometimes without electricity or water. And even in these Mexican border slums, the per-capita income is two or three times higher than in other regions of

[34]Moore, op. cit., pp. 55–56.

Cesar Chavez was able to organize not only Mexican American farm workers, but for a time the support of the liberal establishment. (*Bruce Anspach/Editorial Photocolor Archives.*)

Mexico.[35] Moreover, some persons of Mexican ancestry in the United States are illegal immigrants and thus do not seek attention in any way. Official figures place the number of Mexican immigrants entering the United States at roughly a quarter of a million a year; unofficial estimates place the number of *Mojados* (or "wetbacks") as high as 1 million.[36]

But all signs point to greater militancy among Mexican Americans in the future. The Chicano movement has awakened the Mexican American community, and particularly the young, to the potential of united community action. ("Chicano" is a contraction and corruption of "Mexicano"; it originally meant one who was unsophisticated, but now means one who has soul.) Perhaps the greatest achievement of the movement is the instilling of pride in one's Mexican heritage.

The more radical of the Chicanos have developed a loose ideology that rejects the striving of the Anglo society and glorifies the special virtues of *la raza* (a term which implies race or ethnic identity, and

[35]Ellwyn R. Stoddard, *Mexican Americans,* Random House, New York, 1973, p. 31.

[36]The term "wetback" is slang for a Mexican who enters the United States illegally by swimming across the border formed by the Rio Grande. Actually, throughout much of the year illegal immigrants can cross an almost dry riverbed.

separateness). However, the Chicano movement still tends to confuse ethnic characteristics with those of social class. Being a true Chicano is sometimes identified with living in a barrio and being fluent in essentially lower-class Spanish dialects. The result is that Mexican Americans who have middle-class life-styles are branded as "Tío Tomés" (Uncle Toms). If the Chicano movement is to succeed, it will have to incorporate middle-class as well as poor Mexican Americans into its structure. Upward mobility need not be defined as cultural desertion.

### Differences between Mexican Americans and Anglos

Mexican Americans, as a rule, put heavier emphasis on familism than Anglo society does—although the difference in the cities is lessening. Women are still expected to fill traditional roles as wives and mothers. Even in Northern cities like Chicago, the patriarchal ideal is still prevalent.[37] Higher education and careers for women are still frequently discouraged, although this pattern is far stronger in the Southwest than in the Northern cities.

It is, however, easy to exaggerate the extent and depth of Mexican American traditionalism. The overwhelming majority of Mexican Americans identify themselves as Roman Catholic, for instance, but at the same time an increasing proportion of Mexican American women use means of birth control disapproved of by the Catholic church. Of course, some differences do persist. Fertility rates among Mexican Americans are still extremely high, with an average family of 4.8 children in the 1960s. Only American Indians, another poor minority, have rates this high. Increasing urbanization and urbanism, plus socioeconomic mobility, should bring fertility rates of Mexican Americans more in line with those of the larger society over the next decade.

Today the Mexican American population is a young population. High fertility rates and the large number of young immigrants have resulted in a population much younger than the national population. According to the 1970 census, the median age of urban persons of Spanish heritage was 20.9 years—while the median age of urban whites was 29.0 years.

### Conclusion

For Mexican Americans, unlike blacks, there are wide variations in patterns of physical segregation. Outside of the border states economics plays a larger part than discrimination in determining residential patterns. In the Southwest there is a long history of prejudice against Mexican Americans, and long-standing patterns of behavior to be overcome; but

[37]See, for example, Gerald Suttles, *The Social Order of the Slum,* University of Chicago Press, Chicago, 1968.

elsewhere in the country there is a general unawareness of Mexican Americans as a group—a situation with positive as well as negative aspects. There is a failure to know of, and appreciate, the richness of Mexican culture; but at the same time there are no long-accepted patterns of discrimination against and segregation of Mexican Americans. Although segregation and discrimination do occur, they are not institutionalized to the extent that they are in the relationships between blacks and whites. With the increasing growth of the urban Mexican American middle class, equal-status contacts with Anglos will become more common. And greater socioeconomic variation among Mexican Americans may decrease the Mexican Americans' sense of their community as a distinct entity.

## AMERICAN INDIANS

By omission, we have in essence denied that the American Indian has a heritage other than that portrayed in old John Wayne movies on late-night television. Only recently have there been popular books telling history from the Indian's side, such as *Bury My Heart at Wounded Knee.* Such works have helped to restore our perspective,[38] but valuable as they are, they do not confront one basic problem: our tendency always to refer to the Indian in the past tense, as if he had disappeared with the buffalo and the frontier. He didn't disappear; he was simply ignored and forgotten.

American Indians—from Cherokee to Sioux to Algonquin—are heterogeneous in patterns of social organization and in their world view. The only justification for subsuming such diversity under the generic term "Indian" is that the white society has consistently done this for several centuries and has responded similarly to all groups it has labeled "Indian." Only in this sense can we speak of Indians as a unitary group.

### The Socioeconomic Picture

The Indians were our first minority, and they are today our most deprived. Indians, for instance, have the lowest life expectancy of all groups in the nation: only 46 years, or not much better than that of a Roman citizen during the period of the Roman Empire. In spite of improvements, the age-adjusted death rates for Indians are still 40 percent above the rate for all races in the United States. The infant mortality rate among Indians, although it too is improving, is shocking: 44 percent above the national

[38]Wounded Knee was the final episode of the Indian Wars. Here 300 Sioux were massacred by the army in 1890. It was also the site of an unsuccessful militant political occupation by Indians in 1973. Dee Alexander Brown, *Bury My Heart at Wounded Knee,* Holt, Rinehart, and Winston, New York, 1971.

average.[39] No other American minority group, including Southern blacks, has anywhere near such excessively high mortality rates. Only its high birth rate keeps the Indian population growing. And it *is* growing—for after an extended period of decline, the supposedly "vanishing red man" is vanishing no more. Between 1950 and 1970, the officially counted Indian population more than doubled—although this increase is partially due to more efficient methods of enumeration. The 1970 census counted 793,000 Indians in the United States.

As far as educational attainment is concerned, the situation is poor. The average adult educational level is tenth grade—usually in inferior schools. The suicide rate among Indians is twice that of other Americans. Economically, the situation is equally desperate. Median family income in 1970 was $5,832. A third of all families have an income below the poverty level.

The principal source of income on reservations is the government: over half the Indians who have jobs are employed—often at minimum wages—by the government. However, only about one-third of the men have permanent employment, while four out of every ten do not have any type of employment.[40] As a result, government welfare payments (A.D.C., etc.), surplus-food programs, and the Public Health Care programs play a major, if not dominant, role in the economic health of Indians on reservations. From the standpoint of the Indians, little has changed since the last century when corrupt officials of the Indian Agency stole the funds Congress had appropriated for food for Indians on the reservations. Today Congress continues to appropriate money, but it still has trouble filtering down to those who need it. The federal government spent just under $480 million on programs for Indian reservations in 1969.[41] However, the grossly overstaffed and inefficient, if not incompetent and politically corrupt, Bureau of Indian Affairs manages to spend the overwhelming bulk of its funds before any money gets to the Indians themselves.

Federal programs and assistance funds total over $1,000 per family on some reservations, but according to one generous estimate "a maximum of 20 percent of the total grants for many governmental programs ever reaches the reservations."[42] On the Pine Ridge Reservation in South

[39] Indian Health Trends and Services, Program Analysis and Statistics Branch of the Indian Health Service, Dept. H.E.W., Washington, D.C., 1969.

[40] Calvin A. Kent and Jerry W. Johnson, *Indian Poverty in South Dakota,* Bulletin 99, Business Research Bureau, School of Business, University of South Dakota, 1969, p. 20.

[41] Murray L. Wax, *Indian Americans: Unity and Diversity,* Prentice-Hall, Englewood Cliffs, N. J., 1971.

[42] Kent and Johnson, op. cit., p. 112.

Dakota—where an unsuccessful uprising by militants took place in 1973—more than 40 percent of the fullblooded Indian families had incomes below $1,000 per year.

American Indians are by far our poorest and most deprived minority. It is illustrative of their status that although Indians were made citizens of the United States in 1924, state laws denied them the right to vote in Arizona and New Mexico until 1948.

### Indians in Cities

Indians are increasingly deserting the reservations for the cities, since it is clear that the reservations offer only a future of illiteracy, poverty, and alcoholism, all too frequently terminated by an early death. For today's Indians, anything more than bare survival means migration to the city. Reservations are devoid of opportunity and hope. The Bureau of Indian Affairs has also been urging Indians to leave their reservations and resettle in urban areas.

Between 1930 and 1970, the minority group that experienced the greatest degree of urbanization was not, as is commonly thought, blacks but rather American Indians. As of 1930, only 10 percent of the Indian population lived in metropolitan areas; and as recently as 1960, seven out of ten Indians were estimated to be rural. Today, roughly 45 percent of the Indian population is urban, and a majority of the Indian population lives in cities at least part of the year.[43] Precise figures are unavailable, since for a variety of reasons the censuses have never adequately enumerated the Indian population. Indians have been moving to cities in general rather than to any one city. More than 60 cities in the country have more than 1,000 Indians each, but in no large city do Indians account for more than 3 percent of the population. The largest Indian populations are found in Los Angeles, Chicago, Minneapolis, Milwaukee, Phoenix, Albuquerque, and Tulsa.

The not uncommon pattern of shuttling between city and reservation gravely hinders effective urban organization. Nonetheless, there has been some organization. The small but militant American Indian Movement (AIM) is more urban-based than reservation-based. The failure of the leaders of AIM to rally reservation Indians contributed to the failure at Wounded Knee (Pine Ridge, South Dakota) in 1973. Tribal differences and lack of stable urban Indian populations have worked against the creation of tight ethnic social communities such as those of the Jews, Italians, and Poles of half a century ago.

Within the cities the Indians cluster together in poorer neighbor-

[43]Elaine M. Neils, *Reservation To City: Indian Migration and Federal Relocation,* Univ. of Chicago, Dept. of Geography Research Paper, No. 13, Chicago, 1974.

hoods, much as the European immigrants did until well into the twentieth century. However, persons whose ancestry is Indian but who have been assimilated into middle-class America may not identify themselves as Indians except under particular circumstances, such as the distribution of funds from selling tribal estates. These people have Indian ancestry, but in their behavior, attitudes, and daily life they are indistinguishable from their neighbors of European ancestry. These culturally assimilated Indians are sometimes referred to by other Indians as "apples"—"red on the outside and white on the inside." More than one-third of Indians now marry non-Indians.

Generally Indians have shied away from the civil rights and protest movements of other groups, since integration or movement into white society has never been their goal. Militant Indians are proud of their own culture with its own value system.[44] The European cultural background of most Americans stresses competition and mastery over nature, whereas Indian cultures generally value cooperation and harmonious living within nature. White men have emphasized the importance of ending the reservation system and breaking tribal lands up into individual family parcels. The desire of the Indians themselves to keep all lands in common, owned tribally rather than individually, runs counter to the norms and values of the majority population. The normative urban structure, with its strong orientation toward goals and achievement, is also at least ideologically at odds with the Indian value system. Those Indians who don't assimilate, either by choice or because of lack of opportunity, are the true "forgotten Americans." Indians who insist on culturally remaining Indians continue to have conflicts with white society.

## JAPANESE AMERICANS

Whenever one starts making generalizations about minorities, one is brought up short by the example of the Japanese Americans. For the Japanese Americans, who only three decades ago were possibly our most hated minority, are now accepted, successful, and prosperous citizens. Japanese Americans were at the outset largely agricultural workers; they are now heavily urban and have, by dint of effort and hard work, overcome seemingly insurmountable obstacles. According to the sociologist William Petersen:

> Barely more than twenty years after the end of war-time camps, this is a minority that has risen above every prejudiced criticism. By any criteria of

[44]Stan Steiner, *The New Indians*, Harper and Row, 1968.

good citizenship that we choose, the Japanese Americans are better than any other group in our society, including native-born whites. They have established this remarkable record, moreover, by their own almost totally unaided effort. Every attempt to hamper their progress resulted only in enhancing their determination to succeed.[45]

The current status of Japanese Americans is that of a minority group which has successfully overcome numerous handicaps. Figures for California, where about 60 percent of the mainland Japanese Americans (i.e., Japanese Americans outside Hawaii) live show that they have the highest educational levels of any group in the state and that their income levels are far higher than those of any other minority and second only to those of whites. Additionally, Japanese Americans have remarkably low rates of delinquency, crime, and even mental illness.

Obviously, Japanese Americans have been notably successful in adapting to the values, behaviors, and expectations of the American system. Harry Kitano suggests that the statement "Scratch a Japanese American and find a white Anglo-Saxon Protestant" is generally accurate.[46] What makes all this the more remarkable is that Japanese Americans have had to overcome severe discrimination—discrimination which included being forcibly driven from their homes and businesses during World War II and being incarcerated behind barbed wire in "relocation camps."

### The Issei and Nisei

The first significant Japanese immigration to the United States occurred during the 1890s. Before then, there were little more than 2,000 immigrants. Immigration developed slowly and never grew large by comparison with the mass migrations from Europe. The total immigration to 1900 was slightly over 30,000; from then to the Gentlemen's Agreement of 1908 with Japan, 110,000; and from 1908 until World War I, about 75,000. Following the passage of the Immigration Act of 1924, the number of arrivals averaged 385 per year.[47] By 1970 there were 591,000 Japanese Americans, 217,000 of whom lived in Hawaii. (See Table 9-4.)

The emotional impact of the immigration was far more severe than its numbers might imply. The Issei, or first-generation Japanese Americans, were viewed by many on the West Coast as a threat. Organized labor was particularly vicious in its attack, since its members saw the Orientals as

[45]William Petersen, "Success Story: Japanese-American Style," *The New York Times Magazine*, January 9, 1966, p. 20. © 1966 by The New York Times Company. Reprinted by permission.

[46]Harry H. L. Kitano, *Japanese Americans: The Evolution of a Subculture*, Prentice-Hall, Englewood Cliffs, N. J., 1969, p. 3.

[47]William Petersen, *Japanese Americans*, Random House, New York, 1971, p. 16.

**Table 9-4 Japanese Immigrants to Mainland United States, 1861–1940***

| Period | Number | Percent of all immigrants |
|---|---|---|
| 1861–1870 | 218 | 0.01 |
| 1871–1880 | 149 | 0.02 |
| 1881–1890 | 2,270 | 0.04 |
| 1891–1900 | 27,982 | 0.77 |
| 1901–1907 | 108,163 | 1.74 |
| 1908–1914 | 74,478 | 1.11 |
| 1915–1924 | 85,197 | 2.16 |
| 1925–1940 | 6,156 | 0.03 |

*Not including migrants from Hawaii after its annexation. The use of the term "immigrant" is not clear even in official statistics. The above table is for "immigrants" who intended to settle permanently as opposed to "non-immigrants" who did not.

*Source:* William Petersen, *Japanese Americans,* Random House, New York, 1971, p. 15. Calculated from U.S. Bureau of the Census, *Historical Statistics of the United States,* U.S. Government Printing Office, Washington, D.C., 1960, Series C-88, C-104; Yamato Ichihashi, *Japanese Immigration: Its Status in California,* Marshall Press, San Francisco, 1915, p. 9.

threatening their jobs. Samuel Gompers, the head of the American Federation of Labor (AFL) and himself an immigrant, told a convention of the AFL in 1904 that "the American God is not the God of the Japanese." A pamphlet against the Chinese he had coauthored in 1902, *Some Reasons for Chinese Exclusion: Meat vs. Rice, American Manhood Against Asiatic Cooliesm—Which Shall Survive?* was reworked when the Japanese were perceived as the new threat. It called for barring the Japanese by law, or, if that failed, by force of arms.

As a result of anti-Japanese agitation in California and panic over the "yellow peril," the United States and Japan agreed that Japan would voluntarily cut back Japanese immigration. California also passed anti-Japanese land laws which denied to all persons ineligible for citizenship the right to own agricultural land or lease it for more than three years. Since federal law until 1952 denied those born in Japan the right to become American citizens, the California legislation was designed to take land away from the successful Japanese American garden farmers. Many Issei responded by putting the title to their land in the name of their American-born children. This second generation is known as the Nisei. In 1920, California closed the loopholes in the 1913 law in a further attempt to prevent Japanese Americans from owning land. This law was upheld by the Supreme Court on the ground that since there was no treaty stipulating aliens' rights, each state could make its own laws. The Immigration Act of 1924, by excluding aliens ineligible for citizenship, effectively barred all further Japanese immigration to the United States.

### The Internment Camps

The entry of the United States into World War II on December 7, 1941, resulted in anti-Japanese hysteria. It was popularly believed that a Japanese Fifth Column existed, conducting sabotage on orders from Tokyo. Interestingly, considering their later political development, such well-known liberals as the late Earl Warren and Walter Lippmann were among the most vocal against the Japanese, while one of the few public officials to denounce the rumors of sabotage as "racist hysteria" was J. Edgar Hoover, the Director of the FBI.

The public clamor for action was met in February, 1942, when President Roosevelt, on the recommendation of advisors, signed Executive Order 9066. The order designated military areas from which military commanders could exclude persons because of national security. The order also authorized the construction of inland "relocation centers." It was quickly implemented. On March 2, 1942, General De Witt, Commander of the Western Defense Area, a man noted for his anti-Oriental feelings, ordered all persons of Japanese ancestry to be evacuated from the three Western coastal states and part of Arizona. He summed up his feelings with the statement, "Once a Jap, always a Jap." The evacuation order included children with as little as one-eighth Japanese ancestry. Two-thirds of those ordered to leave their homes were citizens of the United States. They were each allowed to take one suitcase with them as they were herded by army troops into assembly centers and then shipped to one of ten inland relocation camps. More than 110,000 of the 126,000 Japanese in this country were put in these concentration camps—regardless of their citizenship.

Interestingly, no such action was taken against those of German and Italian ancestry on the East Coast, nor was any action taken against the Japanese on the strategic island of Hawaii, where the Japanese made up a full 37 percent of the population. Long after the war, it was officially admitted that no Japanese American had committed a single subversive act anywhere within the United States. But for as long as three years many Japanese Americans lived in dismal tarpaper shacks in deserted, inhospitable areas of California, Arizona, Idaho, Wyoming, Utah, and Arkansas, surrounded by barbed wire and machine guns. The inmates were let out only on "seasonal leaves"—which was an euphemistic way of saying that they were used as cheap labor on local farms. Jobs in the camps paid from $16 to $19 a month. The Federal Reserve Bank of San Francisco estimated in 1942 the Japanese Americans' financial loss—abandoned or cheaply sold stores, farms, and businesses—at $400,000, 000. The United States government eventually paid settlement claims at the rate of 5 to 10 cents on the dollar.

Life in the camps radically changed the structure of Japanese American society. The second-generation Nisei who spoke English and were citizens quickly filled most of the local leadership positions, displacing the older Issei. Ironically, because there were no whites in the camps the Nisei could fill a host of leadership positions anti-Japanese discrimination on the West Coast would have made unavailable to them on the outside. After the war many Nisei chose to move East, where their skills and abilities had a better chance of recognition, rather than back to the more ghettoized West Coast.

One of the many paradoxes of this period was that the 442d Regimental Combat Team—the most-decorated American unit in World War II—was composed of Japanese Americans. More than 1,000 of the men in the 442d had enlisted directly from the internment camps to fight for the country that had forcibly removed them from their homes and livelihood. The 442d's war cry, "Go for Broke," is a part of American history. Less well known is the fact that the average IQ of the unit was very high (119) and that the 442d had more college graduates than any other comparable unit in the armed forces. The Nisei earned, in blood, the grudging respect of other GIs. In action in Italy and France, the unit suffered 9,486 casualties—or over 300 percent of its original infantry strength.

### Japanese Americans Today

Thirty years after the war and the internment camps, the Nisei have an unparalleled record of upward mobility. In 1940 over a quarter of all Japanese Americans were laborers; by the 1970s this figure was down to only a few percent. Among all nonwhite groups the Japanese rank first in income and education. The Sansei, or third generation, born since World War II, has become almost totally acculturated. Compared with other college students, they tend to be retiring and reticent, but not as conforming as their Nisei parents. Their fierce desire for success and upward mobility is often reflected in the choice of safe and secure professions such as engineering and business administration. Now that the Japanese Americans have arrived, the proportion of liberal arts majors not oriented so strongly toward jobs can be expected to rise among the next generation.

Compared with other Americans, Japanese Americans, particularly on the West Coast, still live largely in cohesive ethnic communities with a strong sense of group responsibility and group "image." The sense of group identity is reflected in the low delinquency and crime rates—rates that will almost inevitably rise as "American" behavior patterns replace those of the tightly bound ethnic community. The structural factors that led to the isolation of the Japanese American community continue to change, moving it in the direction of the larger society.

Soon after arrival the Japanese Americans lost almost all knowledge of the Japanese language, and over the years many of the less functional Japanese customs have been abandoned in favor of the more efficient American models. Another sign of change has been the amount of marriages outside the group. Marriage of Sansei out of the ethnic community has become more common, particularly away from the more traditional ethnic communities in California.

The breakdown of distinctive ways of life is a mixed blessing. On the positive side Japanese Americans now participate fully in all aspects of national life. However, it would be sad and more than a little ironic if in an urban world that is seeking a sense of community the Japanese Americans, who persevered and prospered because of their strong community and their cohesive family system, would now allow their distinctive culture to be eroded or abandoned.

Part Three

# Urban Planning and Redevelopment

Chapter 10

# Urban Renewal and Related Housing Issues

*Let there be one man who has a city obedient to his will, and he might bring into existence the ideal polity about which the world is so incredulous.*
Plato
*The Republic*

The United States government has an official housing policy, formulated in 1949, which states that it is the aim of the government to:

**1** Eliminate substandard and other inadequate housing through clearance of slums and blighted areas.

**2** Stimulate housing production and community developments sufficient to remedy the housing shortage.

**3** Realize the goal of a decent home and a suitable living environment for every American family.[1]

However, in the twenty-five years that this has been official policy, no one

[1]Martin Anderson, *The Federal Bulldozer,* The M.I.T. Press, Cambridge, Mass., 1964, p. 4.

has seriously taken these statements as guidelines for clear and decisive action; rather, they have been viewed as goals or objectives to be sought. Today, as when the policy was written into law, safe, decent, and sanitary housing at affordable prices within a suitable living environment remains but a dream for all too many Americans.

Housing in America has traditionally been considered a private rather than a public concern, and the whole concept of involvement by the federal government in the housing of its citizens is fairly recent in the United States. It is fair to say that the concept of government support for housing is far from universally accepted in the United States—a situation unlike that in Northern European countries, for example.

## GOVERNMENT INVOLVEMENT

The United States government first became involved in housing during World War I, when it built housing for defense workers. This involvement was temporary. It took the massive economic collapse of the Great Depression of the 1930s to involve the government permanently in the question of housing. During the Depression, residential construction dropped by 90 percent and downtown skyscrapers stood vacant. Even the prestigious Empire State building in New York City was unable to fill its many offices. Franklin D. Roosevelt's administration came into office committed to improving this situation and reviving the economy through federal intervention, a new and radical approach at that date. In order to get a sick housing industry on its feet and encourage "builders to build and lenders to lend" the government engaged in extensive "pump-priming" in the housing area. The Housing Act of 1937, for example, established a slum-clearance program and created the United States Housing Authority, which built some 114,000 low-rent public housing units before the program was ended during World War II. However, it was never clear whether the goal of the programs of the 1930s was to put men to work or to provide new housing for those lacking "standard" dwellings. Whatever the purpose, the result was that several deteriorating slums were cleared, and every substandard unit of housing that was cleared was replaced with a standard unit.

The program of the 1930s differed from later efforts in at least two respects: first, only public housing was built on the cleared land, not shopping centers or office buildings; and second, the housing projects were by and large successful—many of them are still well-maintained today. Their success can be attributed both to their design (few were over four stories high, giving the buildings the atmosphere of family apartment buildings where people knew each other) and to the fact that residents for the first two decades or so were largely workmen and craftsmen on WPA or other fill-in jobs. Projects at this time did not house the unskilled or the very poor on welfare.

## THE FEDERAL HOUSING ADMINISTRATION (FHA)

In order to get bankers to invest in mortgages during the Depression, the government, through the Housing Act of 1934, created the Federal Housing Administration to insure home loans. Following World War II, the Veterans Administration also made loans (VA loans) guaranteed by the government to veterans. Under such schemes, private lending institutions still decide who will get loans—the FHA or VA in effect insures the bank against loss if the buyer defaults. The theory is that this system encourages lending institutions to make loans to buyers whom they would otherwise reject. FHA loans can be made for the purpose of new construction, purchase, or rehabilitation of homes, but originally the program concentrated on financing the construction of new homes. About a third of the houses built in the first decade of the program (1934–1944) had FHA assistance. Since the FHA was interested only in gilt-edge collateral to back up its mortgages, these homes were substantially middle-class; and since there was little vacant land in the cities, houses insured by the FHA were built in the suburbs. From the 1930s to the present an indirect effect of the FHA program has been to encourage suburbanization. The regulations of the FHA strongly discouraged the issuing of mortgages for the rehabilitation of inner-city urban homes; and although this policy was changed in the late 1960s, loans for rehabilitating central-city homes are still only a small part of all FHA loans.

### A Hidden Housing Policy

Following World War II, the FHA and the VA became active in issuing mortgages to working-class and lower-middle-class families who wanted to buy homes. The FHA had a hidden, but extremely effective, national housing policy. The suburban tract developments that surround all our larger cities would have been impossible without the federal mortgage-insurance programs that in effect paid middle-class and lower-middle-class whites to desert the central cities for newly built government-insured houses with low interest and low down payments in the suburbs. The FHA program encouraged and subsidized white suburbanization, while at the same time the urban renewal program, which we will be discussing presently, was trying to hold these same middle-class white families in the central city. Moreover, the suburbs were zoned to exclude blacks and other "undesirables" who might lower property values and threaten the FHA's investment. Until 1950 FHA regulations expressly forbade issuing loans that would permit or encourage racial integration. Even after the formal regulations were changed, the policy itself was not seriously modified until the late 1960s. Government policy thus directly encouraged "white only" suburbs and held blacks in the inner city:

> From 1935 to 1950, the federal government insisted upon discriminatory practices as a prerequisite to government housing aid. The Federal Housing Administration's official manuals cautioned against "infiltration of inharmonious racial and national groups," "a lower class of inhabitants," or "the presence of incompatible racial elements" in the new neighborhoods. . . . Zoning was advocated as a device for exclusion, and the use was urged of a racial covenant (prepared by FHA itself) with a space left blank for the prohibited races and religions, to be filled in by the builder as occasion required.[2]

In the United States today we have anything but a laissez-faire housing policy. Almost all financing for new houses or apartments involves the federal government in one way or another. The federal government pours a minimum of $10 billion a year into direct and indirect subsidies of the housing market. The federal government directly allocates between $4 and $5 billion dollars a year to housing. Included in this figure are appropriations for urban renewal, public housing, interest on mortgage loans, and subsidy programs. Included in the indirect subsidies are the funds provided by the FHA and VA mortgage-guarantee programs. About half the outstanding mortgage debt on single-family homes is insured by either the FHA or the VA.[3] Most of the balance is financed through savings and loan associations or banks whose deposits are insured and whose investments are regulated by federal laws. Additionally, the American tax system (unlike that of Canada, for example) provides for tax deductions on money paid for interest on mortgages.

## URBAN RENEWAL

### Origins

Following World War II, there was general agreement that something had to be done to encourage building in the cities and to provide additional urban housing. It was apparent by the late 1940s that the downtown sections of cities were heading for economic troubles if they could not be redeveloped. The problem was particularly acute on the deteriorating

[2]Charles Abrams, *The City Is the Frontier,* Harper and Row, New York, 1965, p. 61.

[3]Bernard Weissbroud, "Satellite Communities," *Urban Land,* **31**:6, October, 1972.

fringe areas of CBDs. While the land was being used only for things like slum housing, it was nonetheless extremely expensive land. Compared with costs on the city's edge, the expense of buying, tearing down, and rebuilding in the inner city was not economically feasible for private developers.

The Housing Act of 1949 sought to solve these problems by providing federal government funding for urban renewal. But liberals and conservatives in Congress had radically different ideas of what government should do. The eventual result was a classic American compromise, the Housing Act of 1949. The housing act contained both a public housing section, which the liberals had lobbied for, and an urban development section, which some conservatives and businessmen had sought. The section on urban redevelopment helped overcome resistance to the section on public housing, and vice versa.

Commercial and financial interests in the central cities supported urban renewal because they saw the renewal areas as providing the downtown area with a buffer or *cordon sanitare* against encroachment by slums. Moreover, the occupants of the urban-renewal housing were expected to be families with substantial purchasing power and thus able to help stimulate retail trade. Urban renewal was seen as being both good for business and good for the city.

The urban redevelopment section of the Urban Renewal Act was a radical break with past housing policies in that it provided for the use of public funds to buy, clear, and improve the renewal site, after which the ownership of the land would revert to the private sector. When the renewal area was approved, the authorities were given the power to buy properties at market prices and, in cases where the owner refused to sell, to have the property condemned and compensation paid through the government's right of eminent domain. The Supreme Court ruled that this exercise of the right of eminent domain was constitutional.

Once the city acquired all the land in the renewal area, the existing buildings were destroyed (or rehabilitated under later modifications of the act) and the land was cleared. New streets, lights, and public facilities were then installed, and finally the land was sold to a private developer who agreed to build in accordance with an approved development plan.

The developer paid about 30 percent of what it had cost the local government to purchase, clear, and improve the land. This so-called "write-down" was the difference between what the land had cost the public and what it was sold for to the private developer. Two-thirds of the city's loss was made up in a direct cash subsidy from the federal government. Thus, the control of the program was, and is, basically local, while most of the government funds are federal.

Generally, an urban renewal project will proceed through the following ten steps:

**1** The submission and approval of a Survey and Planning Application to develop an urban renewal project.

**2** The undertaking of the necessary surveys to provide the data essential for programming the project, and developing the urban renewal plan.

**3** The submission and approval of project plans (application for a loan and grant to carry out the project).

**4** The acquisition of properties.

**5** The relocation of all families and businesses.

**6** Demolition of structures.

**7** The rehabilitation of any structures determined to be economically feasible for such treatment and permitted by the plan.

**8** The installation of all public improvements such as roads, sidewalks, utilities, schools, parking lots, and parks.

**9** The resale or other disposition of the cleared land to developers who have agreed to build in accordance with the provisions of the urban renewal plan.

**10** Finally, the completion of the new construction.[4]

### Rehabilitation

The Housing Act was revised in 1954 to provide for a more workable program. No longer did an area have to be a slum in order to qualify. It could be "blighted"—that is, a potential slum. The earlier act had, in effect, made it necessary to level everything. Now alternatives to the bulldozer were to be considered. Greater emphasis was placed upon rehabilitation of adequate existing structures and conservation of neighborhoods. Federal funds were made available to guarantee bank loans made for purposes of rehabilitation. This meant that areas that banks had "red-lined" for no new investment funds could now obtain funds before the area slipped to a point where there was no alternative to the bulldozer.

In order to qualify for federal funding, a city had to demonstrate that it had a "workable program" which contained items such as a housing code setting adequate to minimal standards, a plan for relocating those displaced, and some provision for participation by citizens. The 1954 act also allowed funds to be used for projects that were not predominantly residential.

Rehabilitation of existing structures theoretically made it possible for at least some of the original residents to remain in a renewal area. In

[4]Carl G. Lindbloom and Morton Farrah (eds.), *The Citizen's Guide To Urban Renewal,* Chandler Davis, West Trenton, N. J., 1968, p. 15.

practice, it frequently worked differently. Many of the poorer families within the area to be redeveloped were buying their homes through land contracts—a type of contract in which the buyer has fewer rights than a mortgagee and must pay higher interest—and were investing a sizable percentage of their monthly income in housing. This was and is particularly true of blacks. As a result, these families had little financial flexibility. They were not able to invest additional funds in their homes to bring them up to the rigorous standards required by the redevelopment agency, even when loans for improvements could be obtained at low interest. The end result was that the house was sold to a middle-class or upper-middle-class person who could better afford the cost of rehabilitating the property. Thus, though the houses remained, the tenants frequently changed.

Since the purpose of urban redevelopment is to change patterns of land use for the benefit of the city as a whole, there is no requirement that housing which is destroyed has to be replaced with housing for people with a similar income level. In fact, once the dwelling units within the renewal area have been demolished and cleared, the land can be used for a shopping center, a park, or an office building. Roughly 35 percent of all federal funds are now used for largely nonresidential projects, and the figure is rising.

Most of the housing built in renewal areas has been high-income or upper-middle-income apartments rather than apartments with low or moderate rent. This has been done with the intent of holding in the city, or luring back into the city, upper-middle-class whites, with their spendable—and taxable—incomes. Low-income housing has been either excluded or minimized because it would usually house the poor and possibly blacks, and their presence in the renewal area would discourage more affluent groups from moving into the high-rent units. Given contemporary housing costs, the old residents could not return to the redeveloped site without subsidization.

### Relocation

Probably the most glaring weakness of urban renewal programs has been the displacement of large numbers of low-income families without adequate provision for their relocation. Until criticism built up, a few years ago, to a point where it could no longer be ignored, little had been done to rehouse those who were forced to move from a renewal area. The problem was particularly severe for black families who had to find low-cost housing within other already crowded ghettoes. The neighborhoods receiving the influx were thus tipped in the direction of becoming slums themselves.

### Housing for the Poor?

Considerably more housing has been demolished than has been built or even planned. From 1949 to 1965 a total of 311,197 dwelling units were demolished on urban renewal sites, with only 166,288 units built or planned to take their place.[5] Federal law required that priority be given in any low-rent units to be constructed to those who were displaced. There was, however, no requirement that low-income housing be provided on the renewal site, and in fact very few renewal sites have been used for low-income housing, although the number is on the rise. The theoretical priority was a meaningless commitment, for the new building usually took over five years to construct and there was no requirement that any units be available for occupancy before a family was displaced. Nor was there any guarantee that the units available would be of the right size for the families being displaced. In practice, the implicit goal of renewal was to move the old residents out so that they could be replaced by middle-class or upper-middle-class groups.

Even when low-income housing was originally included in the renewal plan, it was not uncommon for it to disappear somewhere in the inevitable replanning before construction. For example, the successful and racially integrated Hyde Park–Kenwood project on Chicago's South Side, adjoining the University of Chicago, included 600 units of low-income housing in the original proposal. However, by the time the plans were finally approved, this had shrunk bit by bit to zero units. Hyde Park consciously made the decision to integrate racially but not economically, and this was agreed upon by the upper-middle-class blacks in the area. As beautifully put by the comedians Mike Nichols and Elaine May, both one-time residents of Hyde Park, "Here's to Hyde Park–Kenwood, where Negro and white stand shoulder to shoulder against the poor." There is more than a little truth in this, for while it has sometimes been charged that urban renewal is "Negro removal"—70 to 80 percent of the displaced families are blacks—it is more accurate to say that it is "poor folks' removal."

There is considerable dispute as to whether area residents displaced by urban renewal are able to find adequate housing elsewhere. It is generally agreed that during the first years of the urban renewal program, residents were dispossessed and ejected from their homes in a fashion that can only be characterized as ruthless. The residents of the West End of Boston, for example, found themselves bulldozed out of their old Italian community virtually before they knew what was happening. Far from being encouraged to participate in planning for the area, local residents were actively discouraged, since it had already been decided

[5]Jeanne R. Lowe, *Cities in a Race with Time,* Random House, New York, 1967, chap. 6.

that the existing low-rent area would be far more valuable to the city as an area of expensive high-rise apartments.[6] The result is essentially similar when removal is for the purpose of expressway construction (e.g., the Eisenhower, Kennedy, and Dan Ryan expressways in Chicago).

Within urban renewal projects relocation programs were, until recently, given the very lowest priority. As one housing authority put it: "There was a tendency to give families a few dollars and tell them to get lost."[7] Certainly, funds were not lavished on those who had to move. For instance, in the West End of Boston each family received $100 for moving expenses. Between 1949 and 1964 only one-half of 1 percent of all federal expenditures for urban renewal went to families and individuals; and this figure increases to only 2 percent if businesses are included.[8]

Defenders of rehousing policies point to a survey made in 1964 by the Bureau of the Census, of 2,275 families displaced by urban renewal in 135 cities. The survey showed that 94 percent had "standard housing." Robert C. Weaver has said that this survey refutes "frequent charges of widespread failure by urban renewal to meet its rehousing obligations for those it displaces." Coming from a black authority on housing who served as Secretary of the Department of Housing and Urban Renewal, such a statement has to be given considerable weight.

Nonetheless, critics continue to make valid points. Even in the study by the Bureau of the Census, a reading of the definitions indicates that 9 percent of the units defined in the special study as "standard" were also regarded, under regular Census criteria, as "deteriorating."[9] Moreover, the study by the Bureau of the Census appears to overrepresent small towns, where housing problems are generally less severe.[10]

### The Effects of Relocation

Data from the West End illustrate the controversy over what happens to those who have to move. According to the official figures, 97 percent of those relocated from the West End were properly rehoused in standard housing. On the other hand, a careful study by outside researchers found that only 73 percent were properly rehoused, and the researchers suggested that the figure was that high only because those being relocated were white and thus found it easier to obtain alternative housing.[11]

[6] Herbert J. Gans, *The Urban Villagers,* Free Press, New York, 1962.

[7] Lowe, op. cit., p. 206.

[8] Herbert J. Gans, *People and Plans,* Basic Books, New York, 1968, p. 263.

[9] "The Housing of Relocated Families," in J. Bellush and M. Hausknecht (eds.), *Urban Renewal: People, Politics, and Planning,* Doubleday (Anchor), Garden City, New York, 1967, p. 356.

[10] Chester W. Hartman, "A Rejoinder: Omissions in Evaluating Relocation Effectiveness Cited," *Journal of Housing,* **23**:157, 1966.

[11] Chester Hartman, "The Housing of Relocated Families," *Journal of the American Institute of Planners,* **30**:266–286, November, 1964.

Part of the West End of Boston before urban renewal. Much of the area consisted of three- and five-story apartment buildings. (*Daniel S. Brody/Editorial Photocolor Archives.*)

Two reasons have been suggested for the discrepancy between the findings of renewal officials and others. First, renewal officials collect their data after the very poorest have already left the renewal area for other slums. Second, officials use a very strict criterion of "blight" while trying to identify an area as needing clearance, but tend to use far more lenient evaluations when considering the housing into which those who were relocated have moved. It should also be noted that the procedure of having an agency evaluate its own performance is one beset with many pitfalls.

On one point everyone agrees: it costs money to move. For example, median rents for those leaving the West End of Boston jumped 59 percent. The Bureau of the Census study indicated that most increases were not that severe, although rentals did go from 25 to 28 percent of family income, a noticeable increase for low-income families.

Renewal has social as well as economic costs for those forced to leave their homes; indications are that the effects are most traumatic when the area to be renewed is a relatively tight-knit neighborhood. A study of the Italian West Enders of Boston found that after relocation 46 percent of the women and 38 percent of the men gave "evidence of a fairly severe grief reaction or worse" when interviewed about leaving the West End. Even two years after being relocated out of the area, 26 percent of the women were reported as remaining sad or depressed.[12]

The West End was a cohesive community, and it is possible that the effects of being forced to abandon this community where people knew one another, and where neighbors were sometimes also relatives, was greater than would be the case in a community more characterized by anomie, where residents felt isolated and alienated. On the other hand, it is also possible that those living in disorganized areas and not having a cohesive family organization may be hurt even more by the removal of the few stable relationships that exist in their lives.

### The Residents' Views of Renewal

Undoubtedly, there are people who welcome urban renewal in their neighborhood as providing them with an escape from an unstable and disorganized environment. But research clearly indicates that the overwhelming majority of the residents of areas slated for urban renewal do not view their neighborhood in an unfavorable light. Chester Hartman's research on the West End confirmed that residents liked their community. In his words: "Certainly there was an extremely high rate of global satisfaction with the West End as a residential neighborhood. . . . Only a small proportion . . . expressed unqualified negative feelings about the area."[13] Rossi and Dentler's findings for the residents of the Hyde Park–Kenwood renewal area in Chicago are similar. A survey of attitudes found that two-thirds of the residents had favorable attitudes toward the neighborhood and only 3 percent had unfavorable attitudes.[14] Barresi and Lindquist found, in research done explicitly upon attitudes toward renewal in Akron, Ohio, that social class was closely related to the way urban renewal was viewed by the residents of a renewal area. They state:

> Those who view urban renewal positively have all of the objective characteristics of the middle class. Members of this class characteristically accept the policy decisions of government. . . . Those who are negative toward urban renewal are objectively lower class. Members of this class have been found, in study after study, to be alienated toward government, suspicious of its motives, distrustful of the integrity of those who govern, and generally cynical regarding the system. In addition, these individuals, in this particular

[12]Marc Fried, "Grieving for a Lost Home," in Leonard J. Duhl (ed.), *The Urban Condition,* Basic Books, New York, 1963, pp. 151–171.

[13]Chester W. Hartman, "Social Values and Housing Orientation," *Journal of Social Issues,* April, 1963, p. 119.

[14]R. Rossi and R. A. Dentler, *The Politics of Urban Renewal,* Free Press, Glencoe, Ill., 1961.

> urban renewal area will be hard-pressed to find housing adequate to their needs at a price they can afford.[15]

Lower-class and working-class populations clearly suffer the most from urban renewal. Thus their opposition to a program that deprives them of their homes and neighborhood ties is not surprising.

### The Bureaucracy's View of Renewal

Middle-class administrators who have been trained to expect physical mobility as a part of their lives find it difficult to empathize with groups who have far stronger territorial ties. To the administrators, moving is a normal part of life; they themselves expect to move and tend to equate moving with bettering oneself. They don't see why people who get a chance to move out of "slums" into other housing shouldn't be grateful for the opportunity. The extent to which the lives of some ethnic and working-class groups are tied up in a particular community is simply not appreciated.

Fortunately, as a result of the criticism leveled against urban renewal programs, the situation is improving for those who are required to move. Aid in relocating and financial compensation have been increased; and there is now a more widespread knowledge of the human costs of renewal and more sensitivity on the part of the bureaucracy to the necessity for dealing with these problems—if for no other reason than simply to forestall criticism.

### Blacks and Leaving the Ghetto

It is now conceded even by proponents of urban renewal that some groups of ethnic working-class whites don't want to leave their long-established areas. However, it has generally been assumed that blacks welcome any opportunity to escape from declining neighborhoods into better housing. This was thought to be particularly true of middle-income blacks who could afford better housing in neighborhoods with good services and schooling. The data, however, do not always support this assumption. Blacks, like whites, often resist moving away from what they consider "their" neighborhood even when such a move, considered objectively, would result in better housing.

Lewis Watts and his associates interviewed a sample of 250 middle-income black families in the Washington Park (Roxbury) section of Boston. Since Washington Park was designated as a rehabilitation and

[15]Charles M. Barresi and John H. Lindquist, "The Urban Community: Attitudes Toward Neighborhood and Urban Renewal," *Urban Affairs Quarterly*, **5**:270–290, March, 1970.

renewal area the families in the sample had the options of staying where they were, moving to another section of the same neighborhood, or moving elsewhere in the Boston area. The study was begun with the "belief that Roxbury's Negroes would rush to embrace any opportunity to escape from the relatively segregated and declining neighborhood."[16] However, in spite of the availability of better housing elsewhere, less than half the families seriously considered moving out of the area. Such house hunting as did take place was not very serious. Sixteen months after the study began, only 4 percent of the sample had chosen to move out to integrated suburbs. More surprising: "Less than five percent of the families in a ten-month period actually inspected a dwelling outside Roxbury and the families used public and voluntary bodies very little to assist them in hunting outside the Washington Park community or its contiguous neighborhoods."[17]

There were a number of reasons why families chose to stay in the neighborhood. Housing in the area rents at bargain prices, and it would therefore cost more to live outside the ghetto. Low-cost housing is also characteristic of white ethnic inner-city neighborhoods. As one woman in Roxbury said:

> It's more economical to live in Roxbury. The cost would be much more in Newton, Arlington, or Lexington. Moreover, I am eight minutes from work. I am happy with my housing arrangement in Roxbury. I don't have to be concerned with driving my children into Roxbury so that they will have a social life as other suburban Negro families have to do.[18]

This woman's comments indicate the importance that is also placed upon the convenience of the community. A central location means that there is no need for daily long-distance commuting to work. The wife of a professional man earning a very high income put it this way:

> I believe the convenient, cheap, rapid transit system which makes it possible to commute to downtown department stores in five minutes compensates for drawbacks; and my husband prefers to remain in Roxbury where he is within walking distance of his office and near his clients.[19]

Additionally, many blacks felt a commitment to the community and were afraid of discrimination, particularly against their children, if they moved

[16]Lewis G. Watts et al., "The Middle-Income Negro Family Faces Renewal," in Joe Feagin (ed.), *The Urban Scene,* Random House, New York, 1973, p. 202.

[17]Watts et al., op. cit., p. 203.

[18]Watts et al., op. cit., p. 207.

[19]Ibid.

to a predominantly white neighborhood. It was felt that the children would have a better social life in Roxbury. Finally, the rehabilitation program was seen as an advantage to the community, since it selectively removed the worst housing.

Research generally supports the view that many inner-city residents do not want to leave their neighborhoods for better-quality housing either elsewhere in the city or in the suburbs. This is true in communities where the people feel an identification with their area and are convinced that its advantages—such as low-cost housing, convenience, and compatibility with neighbors—outweigh its liabilities.

This message has taken a long time to get through to outsiders such as city planners, mayors, and downtown business interests. Over the past two decades city administrations have destroyed hundreds of viable neighborhoods with the conviction that "it's really for their own good, you know." Perhaps it is about time to ask the residents of inner-city areas whether or not they want their neighborhood to be "improved."

### Other Critiques

During the last decade urban renewal has come under increasing fire from both ends of the political spectrum not only for failing to solve the problem of urban housing, but for making it considerably worse. Critics charge that in the attempt to change existing patterns of land use urban renewal programs have done irreparable damage to the social fabric of the city. Of the original coalition of planners, social activists, downtown businessmen, and local mayors who pushed for urban renewal, only the major downtown business interests and a dwindling number of mayors and planners still hold to the old faith. Almost all the social scientists and an increasing number of urban planners have become disillusioned with what has been wrought, and have become active opponents of urban renewal projects.

It is fair to say that most of the original supporters of the urban renewal program viewed the crisis of the city as an economic crisis. Downtown commercial properties were declining, and the city's tax base was being eroded by the exodus of middle-class whites to the suburbs. Slums surrounding the downtown business districts were seen as strangling these areas and choking off the access of middle-class shoppers to them. For economic reasons, urban political and business leaders wanted to replace poor people, who frequently also were black, with upper-middle-class residents, who almost invariably were white.

**Martin Anderson** A strongly polemical and often persuasive attack on the economics of federal urban renewal programs is presented by the conservative economist Martin Anderson in his book *The Federal*

*Bulldozer.* After studying the record of urban renewal during its first fifteen years, Anderson recommended that "no new projects should be authorized; the program should be phased out by completing, as soon as possible, all current projects. The federal urban renewal program conceived in 1949 had admirable goals. Unfortunately, it has not [achieved] and cannot achieve them. Only free enterprise can."[20]

Anderson maintains that the private housing market has done far more than urban renewal to improve housing. He notes that between 1950 and 1960, 12 million new housing units were built and 6 million disappeared without any government action. Urban renewal, on the other hand, destroyed considerable low-income housing, while most of the new buildings constructed in urban renewal areas were high-rise apartments—only 6 percent of the new construction was public housing. Thus, rather than eliminating slums, urban renewal merely moved them from one area to another.

Moreover, Anderson charges, urban renewal actually bleeds money from the city instead of producing needed revenue. He claims that the average project takes almost twelve years to complete, and during most of that time the land lies vacant and is therefore off the tax rolls. The old tax-paying structures are torn down; but until something else is built, the city is deprived of revenue. Anderson estimates that 50 percent of the construction put up on urban renewal sites would have been put up elsewhere in the city even if the federal urban renewal program did not exist.

Anderson's conclusions are weakened by the fact that his data do not include the more successful projects of the late 1960s, which became available after the publication of his book. Also, in using overall national data he overlooks the success of a number of renewal projects. Also, improvements have been made in the administration of the program regarding the relocation of residents, although there is still a distressing time lag between the destruction of the old neighborhood and the building of the new one. The vacant holes scarring our larger cities testify to the apparent sloth of redevelopment. There is unfortunately more than a little truth to the charge that the federal government is now the biggest grower of ragweed in the country.

**Jane Jacobs** Of the attacks on urban renewal, the most widely read has been that of Jane Jacobs.[21] Jacobs's main concern is how cities can generate sufficient diversity to sustain themselves economically and, more importantly, provide humane, vital, and safe neighborhoods for their increasingly traumatized citizens. She suggests that planners have

[20]Anderson, op. cit., p. 230.

[21]Jane Jacobs, *The Death and Life of Great American Cities,* Random House, New York, 1961.

misread urban needs and, thus, have destroyed older areas of urban vitality only to replace these lively congested neighborhoods with vapid, slab-like projects that become wastelands of dullness and regimentation sealed off from any contact with city life. Low-income projects fare even worse, becoming centers for delinquency and vandalism, and so unsafe that even adult men will not venture outside their heavily bolted doors after dark. Her somewhat unorthodox proposals for remedying this situation will be discussed later, in Chapter 11, "Urban Planning: United States and Europe."

**Scott Greer** A third and more scholarly critique is provided by Scott Greer, who says that much of the confusion and downright contradiction in present urban renewal programs is a result of the mixture of three different goals. These are: increasing low-cost housing while eliminating slums, revitalizing the central city, and (this last is the most recent goal) creating planned cities through community renewal programs.[22] There is no question that urban renewal has done little to increase low-income housing. As Greer put it: "At a cost of three billion dollars the Urban Renewal Agency (URA) has succeeded in materially reducing the supply of low-cost housing in American cities."[23] Greer maintains that any program for improving housing must include public housing, and it must include open occupancy in practice as well as theory so that blacks can move anywhere in the city and not simply be channeled into transitory areas which then become new black neighborhoods. Certainly it makes little sense to decrease the amount of low-cost housing in central cities. Greer argues:

> Aside from CBD development, the "gray areas" of the city are far too vast to be developed profitably. Nor, in general, is there any reason why they should be; they constitute a huge supply of housing, markedly better in quality than the neighborhoods where most of the Negroes and poor live in contemporary cities.[24]

Finally, it is only fair to say that the urban renewal program has had some notable successes, such as the comprehensive renewal effort in New Haven, the Southwest Project in Washington, D.C., the Western Addition in San Francisco, and Society Hill in Philadelphia. Also, very few of the renewal sites were originally active, attractive communities; the majority were blighted, dilapidated, filthy slums which no one wants

[22]Scott Greer, *Urban Renewal and American Cities*, Bobbs-Merrill, Indianapolis, 1965, p. 165.
[23]Greer, op. cit., p. 3.
[24]Greer, op. cit., p. 176.

to bring back. Even critics of urban renewal concede that the grossest mistakes were made by the earliest projects and that as the program has matured, it has profited from its earlier errors.

The debate over urban renewal is sometimes presented as if there is a choice between urban renewal and no change; but, by design or otherwise, cities are constantly changing. Cities are not static monuments; to live, they must change. The hope is that planned change will, in the future, produce more humane and livable neighborhoods for all the economic, social, and racial groups that make up the urban mosaic.

## PUBLIC HOUSING

Public housing was originally designed to provide standard-quality housing for those who could not afford decent, safe housing on the private market. One of the basic unwritten assumptions of the program was that by changing a family's residence you could also change the way they lived and the way they behaved.

Advocates of social planning originally supported public housing as a means of social uplift and betterment. The tearing down of slum housing was seen as a way of destroying the crime, delinquency, drunkenness, and lax morals that were considered to be associated with the slum housing. Once again, technology was going to solve social problems—a naïve belief of long standing in America. This can be characterized as a "salvation by bricks and mortar" approach.

The experience with public housing built during the 1930s tended to support this belief. Public housing during this period was filled mainly with lower-middle-class families who were there because, owing to the Depression family heads couldn't get work. In a tight housing market they could not find adequate housing elsewhere. As the Depression ended, the male heads of households obtained promotions or new jobs that pushed the family income levels above the maximum allowed for staying in the project. With other housing becoming more plentiful for whites after World War II, both in city and suburban locations, those who were working their way into the middle class sought new housing. As these families moved out, the projects gradually lost their sound working-class image.

In many cities working-class households were replaced by new, unskilled, and frequently minority households. Increasingly, families who lived in projects were headed by women without a husband present, and were on welfare without any reasonable expectation of mobility into the middle class. The lack of education and training of the newer project residents, coupled with regulations that placed low limits on how much a family could earn and still qualify for public housing, meant that those who could be upwardly mobile moved on while those who were not mobile stayed.

The policy of evicting the successful has also meant that in the largest projects successful male role models are virtually nonexistent. This has disastrous results for boys, who have few images of successful men who aren't dope pushers, policy operators, pimps, and the like. In city after city across the land public housing is concentrated in relatively few, usually black, neighborhoods. This is because "aldermanic courtesy" allows an alderman to veto public housing in his own ward, and white neighborhoods don't want blacks in public housing.

In addition to its long list of other problems, public housing is now in severe financial difficulty. Since rents in public housing projects are based on income, the welfare poor pay less rent than their predecessors did. Meanwhile, costs for security, maintenance, heating, and salaries of staff have been going up. The Brooke Amendment of 1969 was designed to take some of the pressure for increased rents off the tenants by providing that tenants in public housing would pay no more than 25 percent of their income for rent. A federal subsidy to the local housing authority was supposed to make up the difference. In practice it hasn't done so. The Nixon administration consistently failed even to ask Congress for the amount of subsidy needed. In 1972, for example, the amount needed to cover deficits and provide adequate services was $325.4 million. HUD actually asked for $170 million and spent even less. Since the housing authorities are forbidden, in effect, to raise rents, they are incurring large operating deficits. An inevitable result of this squeeze is that even less is spent on maintenance and security.

All too many inner-city projects have today become the residences of last resort for the permanent poor of the society. Under the circumstances, it is not at all surprising that public housing has become associated in the public mind with crime, welfare, and vice. The public has become disillusioned with the whole concept of public housing, since it obviously isn't remaking the present-day poor into middle-class citizens. Once professionals thought that if they could get problem families out of the slums, then fathers would stop drinking, mothers stop fooling around, and kids stop doping and stealing. It didn't work; as caustically expressed by one professional in urban affairs, "they're the same bunch of bastards they always were."[25]

Public housing, in its present form, has few supporters, liberal

[25]Michael Stegman, "The New Mythology of Housing," *Trans-Action,* 7:55, January, 1970.

or conservative, black or white, well-to-do or poor. Without conscious design, we have designed a public housing program that almost ensures its own failure.

## Profile of Failure

In 1951, *Architectural Forum* featured an article entitled "Slum Surgery in St. Louis" which described a public housing project "of 11 story apartment houses, which even unbuilt have already begun to change the public housing pattern." The complex of 26 or more buildings was to be laid out on a fully landscaped site incorporating the latest principles of design, which would "save not only people, but money."[26] The project, which came to be known as Pruitt-Igoe, was supposed to pave the way for a bright new era in public housing.

The central feature of the design was a "skip stop" elevator system that would stop only at every third floor, which would have an open gallery containing laundry facilities and storage bins. The galleries were to be "vertical neighborhoods," providing, in addition to the laundry and other facilities, a "close, safe playground." In order to increase neighborliness, no more than twenty families would use a gallery. The floors in between the galleries would consist only of apartments. The entire complex was to be located on a large site (57 acres) with a "river of green running through it, and no through streets."

Pruitt-Igoe was completed in 1955, with thirty-three buildings of eleven stories each. A few changes had been made. The plan to mix some town houses in with the high-density units was rejected on the basis of a cost-benefit analysis done by the Public Housing Authority. There were also other economies, such as eliminating the landscaping, not painting the cinder-block galleries and other public areas, eliminating public washrooms on the ground floor, leaving steam pipes uninsulated, and not providing screens for the gallery windows. Although the project won an award in 1958 for architectural design, by then very serious problems were beginning to emerge. The economies listed above had some unexpected consequences: children urinated in hallways, burned themselves on exposed pipes, and fell out of gallery windows.

The project had been designed for a racially mixed population —one-third white and two-thirds black—but a heavy influx of hard-core poor families with numerous social problems soon drove out all who could escape. Demographically, the project soon became inhabited mainly by black households headed by women, with a large number of

[26]"Slum Surgery in St. Louis," *Architectural Forum*, April, 1951, pp. 128–135.

children—five to twelve per household—and on welfare. Of the 10,736 people living in Pruitt-Igoe in 1965, there were only 900 men—many of them elderly—but over 7,000 children, of whom 70 percent were under twelve years of age.

Pruitt-Igoe has become a symbol of all that is wrong with public housing projects, with elevators battered and out of order, stairwells with lighting fixtures ripped out, galleries unused and unsafe, and laundry rooms that invite robbery and rape. Laundry rooms, stairwells, and halls in Pruitt-Igoe were used by adolescents for sex. Making many "conquests" was one of the few ways for a boy there to achieve status with his peer group, and the girls viewed sex as a way of achieving popularity and maturity. The mean age for becoming sexually active was thirteen, and half the girls in the project became pregnant at least once before age eighteen.[27] Mothers found it practically impossible to supervise children. They feared to go out of their apartments; and this was a reasonable fear: a survey of residents disclosed that 41 percent of the adults had been robbed, 20 percent physically assaulted, and 39 percent insulted by teen-agers.[28] The absence of resident men and the physically unsafe design features, such as the skip-stop elevators and the open galleries, resulted in a constant threat of mugging or rape for female inhabitants.

By 1972, only the most desperate of the poor remained in the dangerous, foul-smelling buildings. Occupancy was down to a total population of only 2,788 persons. One by one, the buildings were simply abandoned by their tenants. Even the most down-and-out welfare recipients were unwilling to tolerate the degradation and the constant threat of personal danger. Rehabilitating the buildings to make them fit for human habitation, it was estimated, would cost more than $40 million, and then there was no guarantee that addicts and vandals would not destroy and terrorize the buildings again.

In the fall of 1972, the Housing Authority took the drastic action of blowing up the two worst buildings and began dynamiting the top seven stories off others in order to convert them into more manageable four-story buildings. It was hoped that the resulting low-rises would be easier for the tenants to control against outsiders and would provide some sense of defensible space and physical security. This effort was not successful, and in 1973 the Housing Authority began to demolish the remainder of Pruitt-Igoe.

If there is a lesson to be learned from Pruitt-Igoe and numerous similar projects across the country, it is that public housing all too

[27]Lee Rainwater, *Behind Ghetto Walls*, Aldine, Chicago, 1970, p. 309.

[28]Rainwater, op. cit., p. 103.

Pruitt-Igoe was dynamited in 1973, bringing full cycle the history of projects that were designed to "change the public housing pattern." (*Paul Ockrassa.*)

frequently removes "nonhuman" problems such as leaking roofs, faulty electricity, and rats at the cost of isolating the residents from the rest of the society and frequently increasing the human problems. Designs based on low-rise buildings or town houses provide greater defensible space and make possible surveillance by adults, which can reduce crime rates and give residents an important sense of territory.[29] This point is discussed more fully in Chapters 11 and 12. However, architecture can never solve the basic problem of an economic system that creates an underclass and effectively isolates it from the rest of the society. Until this is changed, we are merely attacking symptoms rather than the disease. The ultimate problem is not housing but poverty.

[29]Oscar Newman, *Defensible Space*, Macmillan, New York, 1972.

## DIRECT SUBSIDIES

Recognizing the general failure of the previous public housing programs, the 1968 Housing and Urban Development Act provided direct subsidies for low-income families so that they could purchase homes and thus have a stake in their housing and their future. This was the so-called "Title 235" program; a companion "Title 236" program provided for rent subsidies so that the poor could afford to rent apartments rather than go into public housing. Both programs have had a checkered history, and as of 1974 had, in effect, been killed.

Much of the controversy regarding the Title 235 program was the result of bureaucratic sloppiness in the way the program was administered, and criminal collusion between real estate speculators and FHA employees. Under section 235 of the federal housing code, low-income families were to be aided in the purchase of homes approved by the FHA. However, abuses occurred in the program when speculators bought older houses in slum areas, made superficial improvements, threw on a coat of paint, and then applied to the FHA for approval. Through irresponsible processing, and sometimes criminal collusion, such houses were approved as meeting FHA standards, and then sold through the Title 235 program to poor families.

The way the scheme worked was that a real estate speculator bought a run-down, inner-city home for, say, $11,000 and then put a couple of thousand dollars worth of cosmetic repairs into the place. A low-income buyer who qualified for the $200 down payment was then found, and the FHA appraiser was bribed to value the house at, say, $19,000. The FHA then insured the mortage for $18,800; and the speculator made a fast $6,000 profit.

Once the speculator had his money, he was in the clear; but the poor family was stuck with a lemon. These houses soon began to need major repairs, such as new roofs and furnaces, that poor families could not afford. Unskilled in home maintenance, the new homeowners encountered many problems beyond their resources or capabilities. The perhaps inevitable result was that families abandoned their houses, mortgages were foreclosed, and the FHA found itself owning numerous houses with inflated purchase prices—houses that no one wanted, in areas where no one would buy.

The problem was particularly severe in Detroit and Philadelphia, where foreclosures were so common that as of 1974, HUD was the largest landlord. Because of continued foreclosures, the Federal Housing Authority has become the biggest slumlord in Detroit, with over 15,000 properties on its hands.

Nationwide, the General Accounting Office has reported that as of 1974 HUD owned more than 200,000 housing units in over 111,000 properties—houses and apartment buildings. The FHA has had to borrow over $3 billion from the United States Treasury in order to cover losses entailed by foreclosures on substandard inner-city homes. Half the debts were on homes covered by an FHA fund for high-risk mortgages, but the rest were supposedly covered with an insurance rate high enough to establish a reserve for losses.

The $3 billion loss will eventually have to come out of taxes, since FHA has no hope of reselling most of the properties. The cost of repairing the properties for resale is prohibitively high; and in areas such as the inner city of Detroit, there simply are no buyers.

Unfortunately, the Title 235 program was never given an adequate test, for from its beginning it was the victim of large-scale fraud on the part of contractors and real estate agents and incompetence on the part of government employees. In Detroit alone several hundred persons were indicted for bribery, falsifying credit reports, and other crimes related to the program.

The Title 236 program of the 1968 Housing and Urban Development Act, which provided subsidies for construction of rental housing, likewise ran into trouble. There were numerous complaints: apartments were criticized as being of inferior construction, poorly located, and more expensive than comparable conventional apartments. While much of the criticism came from quarters that are known to be hostile to the whole concept of subsidized housing, it is still true that the Title 235 and Title 236 programs did not get off to what could under any circumstances be considered a good start.

## OTHER SUBSIDIES

Housing subsidies nonetheless continue, but through older, indirect, rather than direct channels. For example, if the interest differential on insured housing loans from the FHA and the VA were 1 percent higher, the cost to property buyers would be over $3 billion a year. Also, as was mentioned earlier, the federal government indirectly subsidizes home ownership by allowing deductions on federal income taxes for real estate taxes and interest payments on mortgages. If the United States followed the Canadian practice of not allowing deductions for real estate taxes or interest payments on mortgages, the increase in the tax revenues would be $3 billion a year. The point here is not whether this is or is not a good policy; the point is that it is a subsidy.

Thus, the real question in establishing a national housing policy is not whether or not to have subsidies, but rather who should benefit from them. Existing subsidy programs benefit both the affluent (the larger the house, the larger the tax benefit) and the very poorest (through public housing and matching funds for welfare payments). High-income housing constructed on urban renewal sites has also benefited from the previously discussed "write-down." What is needed is housing subsidies for lower-middle-income families so that they can afford to purchase decent, good-quality housing. Presently such families—outside the South, where costs are lower—are all but excluded from the new housing market. If the present trends in housing costs continue for another decade, only the upper middle class and the upper classes will be able to afford to purchase homes. It is almost certain that at some point in the near future the United States will have to begin openly subsidizing middle-class housing, as most Western European countries now do. Housing costs continue to rise faster than incomes.

## MODEL CITIES

Model Cities was another of the social welfare programs of the 1960s that is now defunct. The idea was to take a specific, limited, economically disadvantaged section of the central city and pour money into it in order to upgrade and redevelop it. Theoretically, this was to be a total approach, with housing, education, social services, and police protection all coordinated, to avoid the piecemeal character of past programs.

A number of problems soon appeared, such as how redevelopment sites were to be picked, how participation by citizens was to be used, how to control the size of the administrative staff and the funds consumed, and finally how the needs of the local area could be salvaged amid endless bureaucratic delays and confusion both locally and in Washington. However, the major weakness of the Model Cities program, from the perspective of established politicians, was that it was successful in involving inner-city residents in the actual planning of programs and policies.

Originally, Model Cities programs got their funds directly from Washington and thus could bypass established local political machines. City mayors were quick to recognize this threat to their power and succeeded in having the funds channeled through their offices. Within a remarkably short time, the more innovative parts of the Model Cities program were dropped, and it became difficult to see how the program differed from the established city bureaucracy in either purpose, program, or staff. President Nixon's decision to kill the program merely put the official stamp on what had already occurred in practice.

## LAND CONTRACTS

Not having money is just one of the liabilities of the poor, and particularly the nonwhite poor, in attempting to obtain housing. For example, the poor frequently are forced to buy houses on land contracts rather than mortgages. The land contract differs from the mortgage used by middle-class and upper-class buyers in that under a land contract the buyer does not either build any equity in the property or assume ownership of it until he has completely paid off the loan. Under a land contract, if a buyer misses a single monthly payment he can legally be stripped of his entire investment. Under Illinois law, which is similar to that of most states, the purchaser can be evicted from his house within forty-five days of a default. A mortgage holder is frequently given up to two years to make up a default, or he can leave the house and take part of his investment with him. The buyer under a land contract has nothing until the last payment is made.

In inner-city ghetto areas, money for standard mortgages is generally scarce; consequently, buyers have no alternative to land contracts, which in addition to the disadvantages just noted entail very high interest rates. For instance, in the ghetto of Lawndale on Chicago's West Side over half of the homes purchased in the early 1960s were bought on land contracts. The FHA refused to insure any mortgages in the area until 1967. The following case illustrates how land contracts work:

An elderly black couple bought a property in Lawndale that had been bought a month earlier by a speculator for $12,000, with a down payment of $2000. The black couple gave the speculator $1,500 down and monthly payments of $190 for nineteen years at 7 percent interest (the common rate at that time was 5 percent). Thus the speculator, who had made a net investment of $500, will receive a total of $44,820 in interest under the land contract—not bad for a $500 investment. The courts ruled that it was all perfectly legal. Under such circumstances, it is easy to understand why ghetto residents feel cheated.

## BLOCK BUSTING

Another form of exploitation which affects both blacks and whites is the immensely profitable practice of capitalizing on the racial and economic fears of whites. Because whites are fearful when blacks move into a neighborhood (or when they believe that blacks will move in), they can be made to panic and sell their houses at a loss. The technique of bringing this about is called "block busting," and it can be used by unscrupulous real estate agents to produce immense profits, first when the whites panic and sell, and second when the pent-up demand for homes among blacks is exploited by selling these houses to blacks at highly inflated prices. Blacks trying to flee the ghetto and get good schools for their children frequently have little choice but to pay whatever the real estate agents charge—and they charge plenty. At hearings held by the New York City Commission of Human Relations, markups by block busters as high as 112 percent were revealed.[30]

Over the years the techniques have become more subtle, although the purpose—quick profits—has remained constant. In the 1950s real estate agents would actually temporarily move a black family on welfare into a neighborhood—naturally, a household with many children—in order to create the fear that the area would turn into a slum overnight. Real estate salesmen then quickly appeared at the doors of homeowners to suggest that they had better sell immediately, "before you lose everything." To encourage the doubtful, rumors were started about what happens to property values—and to wives and children—when blacks move in. One enterprising firm in Chicago even went through neighborhoods that they were block busting and placed "For Sale" signs in front of rental properties in order to create the impression that everyone was moving out. Of course, they didn't bother to talk to an owner before putting the sign up on his property. Houses where owners were away on vacation were particularly valued as targets of "For Sale" signs, since the signs would not be torn down for a week or two.

Today the approach is more subtle, but it is still effective. While many large cities have banned agents' "For Sale" signs and have laws against mentioning racial changes when looking for houses to sell, the laws do not really make much difference. Everyone knows what is meant when a salesman says, "You know this is a changing area, and you'd better sell your house while you still can." It is a sure tip-off that the modern version of block busting is taking place when a neighborhood is suddenly flooded by real estate agents contacting homeowners by telephone calls, visits, and letters to remind them that this is the time to sell.

Preying on the fears of white homeowners that the entry of blacks into the neighborhood will mean a drastic drop in property values, the agents will offer to buy a house at less than its appraised value, but for cash, if the sale is made immediately. Commonly, once a mood of panic is established in an area, shady real estate agents will tell reluctant sellers, "We can only guarantee to buy your home at this price for the next week: after that we can't guarantee anything."

Once whites sell at a loss and move out, their houses are quickly

[30]Lowe, op. cit., p. 238.

resold to blacks at more than the appraised value. Many middle-class black families want to get away from the neighborhoods and schools of the ghetto badly enough to pay these inflated costs. As block busting builds momentum, money for conventional mortgages dries up, banks "red line" the area, and land contracts and other less desirable financing methods become common. Newer incoming black families are typically less able to meet the inflated debt structures incurred in purchasing housing than earlier, more affluent blacks. The inflation of values beyond what the properties are actually worth leads both to the subdivision of property into smaller units, to produce income, and to high rates of default. Declines in costly maintenance are also common among the financially overcommitted buyers. Needless to say, absentee landlords who once kept up rental property now fail to modernize periodically, make improvements, or even keep up basic maintenance. This process is called "disinvestment" and eventually leads to a point where, with conventional mortgage money for improvements or modernization unavailable, and with all costs rising, there is economic pressure to abandon the property.

Block-busted neighborhoods do sometimes become stable black neighborhoods, but unfortunately this is not the usual pattern. The resentment of remaining whites whose neighborhood has been block busted creates a climate of hostility that is hard to overcome, particularly since the newcomers come from different areas themselves and are not socially cohesive. The departing whites who sold their homes at below market value move on to new neighborhoods, but remain deeply embittered because, as they see it, blacks moved into their neighborhood and as a result they lost money. Such people are violently opposed to blacks moving into their new neighborhoods or suburbs.

It is understandable that those who have been block busted are bitter, but what they do not generally realize is that the black newcomer is equally exploited. The block busters make their profits from fast neighborhood turnover; and the faster the turnover, the greater the profit. Laws against block busting exist in some communities, but they are generally weak and rarely enforced. Attempts to prevent panic selling are usually on an *ad hoc* basis and are not enough to discourage real estate firms that have a history of specializing in turning over neighborhoods for a profit.

## ABANDONMENT

A new and extremely severe problem in some larger cities is the increasing amount of abandoned housing in ghetto neighborhoods. Abandoned buildings have become common, particularly since the urban riots of the late 1960s. Landlords default on mortgages and simply walk away from apartment buildings that are no longer economically viable.

The abandoned hulks of buildings marring the core of many large cities are mute testimony that cracking down on the slumlords is not a sufficient way to provide decent and safe housing for the poor. It is estimated that in New York City over 105,000 housing units were abandoned between 1960 and 1969. Many other Eastern and North Central cities also have increasingly frequent abandonments.

The problems began in the 1950s, when areas began turning over racially, and at the same time money for conventional mortgages became unavailable. The result was that blacks were often forced to buy at inflated prices and on land contracts involving impossible financial commitments. Properties, particularly multiple dwelling units, were often illegally converted to additional apartment units in order to increase income. Absentee owners in particular tended to let improvements, and even necessary maintenance, slip, since they saw little long-term economic potential in these properties.

When tenants apply pressure by means of rent strikes and militant enforcement of city housing codes, the owners' interest further decreases. Court orders to convert buildings back to the original design (that is, with larger apartments), in addition to vandalism, rising costs of heating, increased taxes, and skyrocketing insurance rates, help push operating costs above rental income. When this point is reached, a landlord frequently stops paying property taxes as a last form of taking a profit. An area with a sharp spurt in tax delinquencies is frequently on the verge of abandonment.

Finally, when a landlord sees no more economic potential, he defaults on his mortgage and simply abandons the building. Once the landlord abandons a building, services are cut off and the tenants move to other housing. Within days, vandals strip the building of anything of value and professional looters pull up with trucks and rip out plumbing and heating systems. Fires set by vandals or others are common in such abandoned buildings.

A case in point is the Woodlawn area of Chicago, which was organized in the early 1960s by Saul Alinsky so that the area might help itself through neighborhood action to force landlords to maintain their property. Woodlawn is now pocketed with the burnt shells of buildings and empty lots where apartments once stood. Since 1968, the Woodlawn section has experienced wholesale abandonment of buildings, and following this a series of fires that has displaced half the population—some 30,000 persons. It is estimated that by 1973 over 20 percent of the community's housing had been abandoned. The population that remains is largely poor, unemployed, and on welfare. Those who can get out do so, leaving the poorest of the poor behind.

Sadly, abandonments are coming at a time when there is still a considerable housing shortage. The abandonments reflect the unwillingness or inability of the private housing market to shelter the poor in clean, safe, and wholesome housing in inner-city neighborhoods with a high incidence of social problems.

## FIFTH CITY: THE IRON MEN

All this does not mean that nothing can be done. A few neighborhoods have, against heavy odds, managed to rehabilitate abandoned buildings and make a go of them. One of the most remarkable is the Fifth City section of Chicago, deep in the heart of Chicago's West Side ghetto. The Fifth City community organization is doing the impossible: rebuilding both buildings and community pride in what has long been considered one of the worst and most hopeless areas of the city.

Fifth City encompasses an area sixteen blocks square with a population of 5,000. A full half of the residents are on public welfare, and the yearly income per family is estimated to be $4,200 (this figure is for 1972). Racially, the area is 98 percent black. In 1972 the boundaries of Fifth City's area of involvement were extended to include 15,000 more persons.

Fifth City is a community-run organization that has been sponsored and partially staffed by the Ecumenical Institute. It is presently engaged in the largest community rehabilitation project in the nation—rehabilitating 102 units in seven buildings at a cost of $2 million.[31] Only the shells of the old buildings are saved, and they are tuckpointed and sandblasted. Inside, everything is new—from the walls to the plumbing to the electrical system. Once completed, the rehabilitated apartments are rented to local residents at low but economic rents. All the buildings are owned and operated by the Fifth City Redevelopment Corporation, which is made up of people living in the Fifth City community. Amazingly, while much of the Fifth City area comprises deteriorating buildings or abandoned hulks which have been severely vandalized, not one of the rehabilitated buildings awaiting occupants has been vandalized: not even a window has been broken.

The Fifth City organization restores identity and pride as well as buildings. The community is symbolized by an iron sculpture built by residents; this "Iron Man," standing one and a half stories high, symbolizes the community's ability to take anything and still pull itself up. At

[31]This information is provided by Bruce Donnelly of the Fifth City Chicago Community Corporation and by the author's own observations.

present, the community runs its own local health clinic, servicing ninety to a hundred patients weekly, and has converted an abandoned metal shop into a modern, carpeted, well supplied, and well staffed pre-school for several hundred local children.

Community events such as songfests, art fairs, street festivals, summer barbecues, and yearly trips for adults and adolescents help intensify the consciousness of residents as being part of a unique community.

Local residents do much of the work themselves. The head of the local Vice Lords was on the construction crew that converted the factory into the school, and most of the teachers are now local women who have been put through a rigorous three-month training program.

The community even has its own financially stable consumer credit union and has constructed a small shopping center for local businessmen. For a six-unit shopping center, Fifth City purchased from the city a partially vacant lot and a burned-out store. The shopping center is run by local businessmen, who by keeping their stores in the area have already proved their business expertise and their dedication to the area. Adjoining the shopping center, Fifth City has plans to construct a three-story, thirty-unit walkup condominium to make possible a new image of home ownership and community pride.

The Fifth City organization would be the last to suggest that all problems have been solved, or that they will be solved in the near future. What it has done over a period of eight years is to make a start; it has brought a measure of pride to one of the city's most hopeless neighborhoods, one that was very badly scarred by the riots and burnings of 1968. The Fifth City community is rebuilding itself from the ground up. More important, its residents have something few slum dwellers have: pride and increasing power over their own lives. Every day some sixty children of elementary school age gather for the Fifth City after-school program, and for blocks one can hear: "Who's the one who builds the city? I am that iron man!"

Chapter 11

# Urban Planning: United States and Europe

*We will ever strive for the ideals and sacred things of the city, both alone and with many; we will unceasingly seek to quicken the sense of public duty; we will revere and obey the city's laws; we will transmit this city not only not less, but greater, better and more beautiful than it was transmitted to us.*
Oath of the Athenian city-state

Genesis 11:4 tells of one of the earliest attempts at urban planning:

> It came to pass as they journeyed to the East that they found a plain in the land of Shinar and they dwelt there. . . . And they said, "Come let us build us a city, and the tower the top of which may reach unto heaven; and let us make ourselves a name, lest we be scattered upon the face of the whole earth . . . .

As we all know, the Tower of Babel was not noticeably successful as a form of urban planning in spite of the fact that it did have full citizen participation. The hope is that some of mankind's more recent and more modest attempts will be more successful. As was indicated in Chapter 2, ancient cities were rarely based on a plan or even a general concept of what the city should be.

## ANCIENT GREECE AND ROME

The ancient Greeks, who appreciated organization and structure in other aspects of their lives, gave little attention to the physical arrangement of the communities in which they lived. In classical Greek cities the main thoroughfares were generally planned as processional avenues, but residential development was undisciplined and chaotic. Rhodes, with its avenues radiating from a center, was something of an exception. What planning did take place was limited to the central municipal area, containing the principal monuments, temples, and stately edifices. Greek colonial cities, such as Priene in Asia Minor, show far more concern for planning than the Greek mother cities, with their meandering lanes and maze-like paths that followed no discernable pattern or higher logic.

Aristotle tells us that Hippodamus of Miletus, who lived in the fifth century B.C., was an early city planner. According to Aristotle,

> Hippodamus, son of Euryphon, a native of Miletus, invented the art of planning and laid out the street plan of Piraeus. . . . He planned a city with a population of 10,000 divided into three parts, one of the skilled workers, one of farmers, and one to defend the state. The land was divided into three parts: sacred, public, and private supporting in turn the worship of the gods, the defense of the state, and the farm owners. . . . [1]

Note that provision was made for farming within the city walls, a most necessary consideration during periods when the city was under siege.

The Romans were somewhat more successful than the Greeks at planning their towns. Rome itself showed little evidence of planning, but provincial Roman towns, with their central square and gridiron pattern of residences, established a model that can be seen in most American communities today. The provincial cities were modeled after the pattern of encampment developed by the Roman legions. Since the provincial towns were basically military outposts, it is not surprising that civilian buildings followed the pattern of the military camp, particularly since much of the planning was done by military engineers. It has been said that these outpost towns were so similar that if a Roman centurion was dropped in the middle of any one of them, he could not tell which town he was in. The largest of the planned Roman cities was Constantinople, the

[1]Aristotle, *Politics, ii, 8 1267.*

"Rome of the East," which the Emperor Constantine built to glorify his reign and escape the fate of previous emperors at the hands of the Roman Senate and street mobs.

## MEDIEVAL AND LATER DEVELOPMENTS

The fall of the Roman empire in the West meant the death of urban planning for virtually a millennium. However, even during the Middle Ages, when gradual organic growth was most likely to be the rule, some of the newly reviving towns built by French, Italian, and German princes followed the planned pattern of the earlier Roman colonial settlements—a grid layout and a central square with a market.[2]

The Renaissance revived cities and thinking about cities, but few of the planners' conceptions for total communities ever became more than academic exercises. Since these conceptions were rather fanciful and artificial, and bore virtually no relationship to the haphazard but vital cities then in existence, it is perhaps just as well that they were rarely executed. Star-shaped cities were especially popular; Vincenzo Scamozzi designed a utopian city shaped as a twelve-pointed star and actually built a small city, Palma Nova, in the shape of a nine-pointed star in 1593. The star shape was not entirely fanciful, however, since in the age of cannons and gunpowder the points of a star could serve as bastions for directing the defenders' enfilading fire. But the planners usually designed unrealistic, static communities that completely ignored the needs of the inhabitants, as well as basic considerations such as topography. Stylized form rather than naturalness was the goal. The epitome of this insistence on symmetrical perfection was Versailles, the magnificent home of the French kings, whose gardens, palaces, and town were planned as a unit.[3]

The English also made their own attempts, largely unsatisfactorily, at town planning. In 1580 Queen Elizabeth proclaimed restrictions on London's growth that were designed to give the city a green belt of open land and thus prevent crowding and poverty.[4] This policy—which foreshadowed the twentieth-century green-belt towns discussed in Chapter 12—failed, although it was backed by royal statute. Probably the most noteworthy master plan was that designed by Christopher Wren for the rebuilding of London after the disastrous fire of 1666. His plan was, unfortunately, not adopted in the rush to rebuild the city.

During more recent centuries, the changes in the physical organiza-

[2]Howard Saalman, *Medieval Cities*, Braziller, New York, 1968, p. 114.

[3]Ralph Thomlinson, *Urban Structure*, Random House, New York, 1969, p. 205.

[4]Daniel R. Mendelker, *Green Belts and Urban Growth*, University of Wisconsin Press, Madison, 1962, p. 27.

The Paris skyline looking west from the Eiffel Tower shows the often unfortunate architecture of the past decade. (*Richard Wood/ Black Star.*)

tion of Paris must be listed among the more successful attempts at planning. Contemporary Paris, with its broad avenues and magnificent squares, is the result of seventeen years of rebuilding directed by Baron Haussmann under the sponsorship of Napoleon III (1852–1870). The beauty of Paris today is not accidental but the result of Haussmann's genius. Boulevards were cut through festering slums, and the city was planned for separate industrial and residential areas. However, the rationale for the changes was not solely aesthetic; the broad boulevards provided excellent fields of fire for cannon and divided the city into districts which could be more easily controlled and isolated in times of civil insurrection.

Unfortunately, under recent French governments the skyline of Paris has been disfigured by some of the worst-designed skyscrapers in Europe. The controversial skyscraper complex of La Defense is an example: its insurance company building blots out the view of the Arc de Triomph. The government has already turned much of the banks of the Seine, where Parisians once strolled and fished, into expressways.

## PLANNED CAPITALS

Modern planned capital cities have been mixtures of success and failure. Canberra, Australia, which was begun in 1918, is pleasing to the eye; but it is impossible to go anywhere in Canberra without using a car, owing to the strict segregation of the city into governmental, residential, and commercial areas. Canberra is sometimes referred to as the world's most inconvenient suburb.

Brasilia, the capital of Brazil, located 600 miles inland from Rio de Janeiro, has a different problem. The city is grand and impressive, but the visitor finds it hard to escape the feeling that it is not really meant to be lived in. Separate centers for government, commerce, and recreation are clustered along one axis of the city, while housing occupies the other main axis. Although Brasilia is proving successful in encouraging the economic development of the center of the country and infusing national spirit, it is less successful in generating that perhaps indefinable *human* response we experience in the great cities of the world. Officials of the Brazilian government resist being transferred to Brasilia; and those who are assigned there fly back to the far more lively Rio de Janeiro as often as they can afford to. Brasilia lacks human warmth and livability. While the design is unquestionably bold and creative, it is also somewhat stark and abstract. The city is a remarkable monument, but monuments are not always comfortable places in which to live.

## URBAN PLANNING IN THE UNITED STATES

City planning in the United States is usually regarded as a twentieth-century development, but as early as 1672 Lord Ashley instructed that Charles Town be laid out "into regular streets for be the buildings never so mean and thin at first, yet as the town increases in riches and people, the void places will be filled up and the buildings will grow more beautiful." The town was designed to form a narrow trapezoid four squares long by two squares wide, fronting on the Cooper River. Philadelphia was also laid out according to the gridiron pattern. Today, the area surrounding Independence Hall once again shows the original pattern as William Penn intended. North American colonial cities as disparate as Quebec in the North and James Oglethorpe's Savannah in the South began their existence as planned enterprises.

However, as is indicated in Chapter 14, "Latin American Cities," planning was furthest developed in the Spanish colonies. The sixteenth-century Laws of the Indies, promulgated by the Spanish Crown, clearly specified how the conquistadores should construct their cities. Every new town was to have a wide central plaza (the *plaza mayor*) bordered by the major religious and administrative buildings, which were to radiate outward from the *plaza mayor* according to a gridiron plan. Better residences were located near the center of the city; the poor lived on the periphery. The effect of the Spanish town-planning ordinances can be seen to this day in Latin American cities. The patterns thus established are almost the reverse of Burgess's pattern, which was by and large typical in the development and growth of North American cities.

### Washington, D.C.

There is little that can be said for North American town planning during the eighteenth and nineteenth centuries. Pierre L'Enfant's plan for Washington, D.C., is one of the few bright spots in the picture of urban planning after the Revolutionary War. L'Enfant's original design, produced in 1791, called for broad sweeping diagonal boulevards overlying a basic gridiron pattern with major monuments or buildings gracing capacious squares at the intersections of major avenues. Economic realities soon forced the effective abandonment of L'Enfant's overall plan, and L'Enfant himself was removed in 1792, after numerous disputes. His contention that his plan was "most unmercifully spoiled and altered" is largely accurate. For example, he planned a broad boulevard along the river, to be lined with gardens; but this has never been seen except on his own detailed maps. He even had a plan to divert the river, making it flow toward the Capitol, whence it would be routed over a forty-foot waterfall and then back to its original course.[5] It was probably fortunate, however, that this particular feature was never constructed.

For much of the nineteenth century Washington remained, in Charles Dickens's words, "a city of magnificent intentions." Washington's oppressively hot, unhealthful summers did not encourage year-round residence. At the time that Lincoln assumed the Presidency, Washington was still a half-finished quagmire, packed with congressmen, lobbyists, job seekers, prostitutes, gamblers, and hangers-on while Congress was in session, and deserted when it was not. Only near the end of the century did a revival of interest in L'Enfant's original plans give us the neoclassical style of government buildings found in the capital today.

One of the city's most notable legacies from L'Enfant is the numerous traffic circles. Any tourist who has ever had the folly to drive into the city is not likely to forget the traffic circles, which disorient even the most experienced drivers.

[5]Charles N. Glaab and A. Theodore Brown, *A History of Urban America*, Macmillan, New York, 1967, p. 253.

## Nineteenth-Century American Towns

During the nineteenth century little creative energy went into the design of the rapidly multiplying new towns. New western settlements merely replicated older urban traditions. Communities were built as if God had intended that streets be laid out in a grid, at right angles to each other. This was in fact a fairly useful model in the Midwest and on the prairie, but it was applied even when it was grossly inappropriate. If hills got in the way, for example, as in San Francisco, streets were simply cut up one side and down the other rather than following the natural contour of the land.

The gridiron pattern was well suited to the feverish speculation that accompanied the nation's early growth; most promoters of sites were speculators whose major interest in the new communities was quick profit. The Federal Land Ordinance of 1785 also encouraged the gridiron pattern, since it divided all lands west of the Appalachians in the public domain into units of 1 square mile to facilitate their sale to settlers.[6] Roads and the way they divide land are another strong influence on the pattern of development of a city. A circular pattern, with roads leading from the center like the spokes of a wheel, focuses attention on the center of the city. It is a system "beloved by chieftains, emperors, priests, and popes."[7] Washington, D.C., and Detroit, Michigan, were both designed on modified circular patterns. The gridiron system, with its square lots, has always facilitated subdivision and thus is the model used in industrial and other economically oriented cities in the United States and elsewhere (Johannesburg is an example outside the United States). According to Christopher Tunnard, "the open lot and speculation have always gone hand in hand."[8] This was certainly true of the development of North American cities.

It is interesting to note that by the early twentieth century the rectangular grid had come to be identified with the American city.

> It is in America that the persistence of uniform right-angled streets has been most marked. Here the universality of the plan's adoption, and the rigidity of adherence to it, has been such that Europeans, forgetting the long history of rectangular street planning refer to it now as the American method.[9]

In the new frontier towns, housing was as predictable as the pattern of streets. The same American businessmen who prided themselves on

[6]Edmund K. Faltermayor, *Redoing America,* Harper and Row, New York, 1968, p. 17.
[7]Christopher Tunnard, *The City of Man,* Scribner, New York, 1953, p. 121.
[8]Tunnard, op. cit., p. 77.
[9]C. M. Robinson, *City Planning,* Putnam, New York, 1916, p. 16.

their originality and inventiveness in business created towns that were dull and drab. For a discussion of life in the planned industrial community of Pullman, see Chapter 7.

### Planned Communities

Totally planned communities fared little better. Lowell, Massachusetts, for all its early promise as an idealistic, paternalistic community, quickly deteriorated into just another New England mill town. Pullman, Illinois, was designed in the late nineteenth century as an experiment in both well-managed labor relations and town planning. In the words of its founder and sole owner, George Pullman, "With such surroundings and such human regard for the needs of the body as well as the soul the disturbing conditions of strikes and other troubles that periodically convulse the world of labor would not be found here."[10] But Pullman proved to be socially unexciting and architecturally monotonous. Although when it was built in 1880 it had been well outside the city of Chicago, by the turn of the century it had been surrounded by the expanding city. Pullman is today best known because of a bitter strike which took place there in 1894 and which was finally put down by the National Guard.

Planned urban communities tended to quickly become satellites and then suburbs of the nearest central city since, on their own, they lacked both the economic and the social diversity necessary to keep them viable. Of the new communities organized around religious doctrines—New Harmony and Oneida, for example—only Salt Lake City has grown and prospered, possibly because it had, under Brigham Young, a very tight social organization, plus an excellent environmental situation along the trail to the California gold fields.

### Parks

One of the brightest aspects in the rather discouraging story of nineteenth century urban planning is the work of Frederick Law Olmstead. In 1857, after much controversy, he began the building of Central Park on 843 acres of wasteland on the outskirts of New York City. The site was hardly promising, for, as Olmstead described it, much of it was a swamp "seeped in the overflow and mush of pigsties, slaughterhouses, and boneboiling works, and the stench was sickening." Central Park not only served the function of providing "lungs" for the city, but it inspired other cities to copy New York's successful plan. Parks were built across the country, and some of them, such as Lake Park in Milwaukee, Wisconsin—which

[10]Stanley Buder, *Pullman*, Oxford University Press, New York, 1967, p. *vii*.

aesthetic grounds, but it did have a concept of the city as an integrated whole and a vision of what it could be. It was a solid and sincere attempt to consciously improve the urban environment.

### Tenement Laws

The turn of the century also saw a movement by social reformers to improve the quality of life in inner-city slums by enforcing building codes and passing model tenement laws to correct some of the worse abuses of the design and construction of older tenements. To reformers such as the famous Jacob Riis, the slum was the enemy of the home and of basic American virtues. To quote Riis:

> Put it this way: You cannot let men live like pigs when you need their votes as freemen; it is not safe. You cannot rob a child of its childhood, of its home, its play, its freedom from toil and care, and expect to appeal to the grown-up voter's manhood. The children are our to-morrow, and as we mould them to-day so will they deal with us then. Therefore that is not safe. Unsafest of all is any thing or deed that strikes at the home, for from the people's home proceeds citizen virtue, and nowhere else does it live. The slum is the enemy of the home. Because of this the chief city of our land [New York] came long ago to be called "The Homeless City." When this people comes to be truly called a nation without homes there will no longer be any nation.[11]

The answer at that time appeared clear: destroy the slum and you will destroy the breeding ground of social problems. Symptoms of social disorganization such as alcoholism, delinquency, divorce, desertion, and mental illness were to be cured, or at least greatly reduced, through the provision of better housing and more open spaces for the young. This belief in salvation by bricks and mortar fit in neatly with the American belief in the unlimited potential of technology.

Many greatly needed improvements in housing were made as a result of the campaigns of the turn-of-the-century reformers; but crime, violence, and alcoholism were not banished as a result. The relationship between housing and social behavior is complex and not amenable to simplistic solutions.

Nonetheless, our faith in technology refuses to die. Recently, the shutdown of much of the aerospace program prompted various naïve suggestions that the aeronautical engineers be put to work without further ado (or training) on solving the "urban crisis." That these men were specialists in aeronautics and had not even a rudimentary background in

[11]Jacob Riis, *The Children of the Poor,* Scribner, New York, 1892.

urban problems seemed unimportant to many people: technology *per se* was expected to solve all problems.

### The City Efficient and Zoning

The golden age of concern with, and reform of, urban social life, esthetics, and politics died with the entry of the United States into World War I. Wholistic visions of the city's future such as had been provided by the City Beautiful movement ran contrary to the laissez-faire atmosphere of the 1920s. As a result, the emphasis was gradually shifted from the "city beautiful" to the "city efficient," and urban planning was replaced by city engineering. During the 1920s, the city was viewed as an engineering problem, and planners became technicians concerned with traffic patterns, traffic lights, and sewer systems. The city was viewed as a machine, and the goal was to keep the machine running smoothly.

The concept of the city as an evolving organic unit was also overshadowed by the development of a new planning tool, zoning. Zoning, which became a force in the United States with the New York City Zoning Resolution of 1916, was originally seen as a device to "lessen congestion in the streets" and to "prevent the intrusion of improper uses into homogeneous areas."[12] "Improper" use of land meant not only industrial and commercial establishments, but also lower-class housing. It was an attempt, largely successful, to segregate land usage and freeze "noncompatible" uses out of upper-middle-class neighborhoods.

The effect of the first weak zoning laws was mainly negative: that is, to keep unwanted types of buildings from being constructed. Zoning laws had little retroactive effect. (Zone boundaries in many cases recognized the existence of "natural areas" described by the early human ecologists, and then went a step farther and tried to prevent further change in these areas.) The 1921 Standard State Zoning Enabling Act, which was issued by the federal government, advised state legislatures to grant the following power to the cities:

> For the purpose of promoting health, safety, morals, and the general welfare of the community, the legislative body of cities and incorporated villages is hereby empowered to regulate and restrict the height, number of stories, and size of the buildings, and other structures, the percentage of the lot that may be occupied, the size of the yards, courts, and other open spaces, the density of the population, and the location and use of buildings, structures, and land for trade, industry, residence, or other purpose.[13]

[12]Dennis O'Harrow, "Zoning: What's the Good of It?" in Wentworth Eldridge (ed.), *Taming Megalopolis*, Doubleday (Anchor), Garden City, New York, 1967, p. 762.

[13]Newman F. Baker, *Legal Aspects of Zoning*, University of Chicago Press, Chicago, 1927, p. 24.

Today Houston, Texas, is the only major city in the country without zoning laws. Houston does not look noticeably different from other cities, because the market mechanism allocates the downtown land to business and commercial usage while outlying land is used for residential purposes. It is not economically feasible to deviate from the normative pattern of land use. On the other hand, if someone really wanted to build a gas station next door to a private home, there would be no zoning regulations to prevent such an action.

### Master Plans

The idea of the "city efficient" was also evidenced in the master plans for city development that became the hallmarks of the city-planning agencies created in the largest metropolises. The purpose of the master plan was to coordinate and regulate all phases of city development; but in practice the preparation of the plan frequently became an end in itself, since the planners rarely had any real authority over the nature and direction of urban development.

That master plans were seldom carried out was generally beneficial to the public, for they were often static and stylized, without any solid relationship with the real city. The plans adorning the walls of city planning agencies rarely defined neighborhoods, for instance, on the basis of established social-class and ethnic composition unless these happened to coincide with pronounced differences in type of housing. Physical criteria were almost exclusively used. Transportation lines and physical boundaries were all too frequently used to determine the units into which the planners divided the city. In the words of Herbert Gans:

> The ends underlying the planners, physical approach reflected their Protestant middle-class view of city life. As a result, the master plan tried to eliminate as "blighting influences" many of the land uses and institutions of lower class and ethnic groups. Most of the plans either made no provision for tenements, rooming houses, second hand stores, and marginal loft industry, or located them in catch-all zones of "nuisance uses," in which all land uses were permitted. Popular facilities that they considered morally or culturally undesirable were also excluded. The plans called for many parks and playgrounds but left out the movie theater, the neighborhood tavern, and the clubroom; they proposed churches and museums, but no night clubs and hot dog stands.[14]

Case studies of the actual planning process indicate that planners

[14]Herbert J. Gans, "Planning, Social: II. Regional and Urban Planning," in David Sills (ed.), *International Encyclopedia of the Social Sciences*, Crowell Collier and Macmillan, New York, 1968, vol. 12, p. 130.

often made their recommendations on the basis of arbitrary considerations without fully examining or understanding the consequences.[15] The death blow for many a master plan was the upsurge of urban renewal and other development plans after World War II. These development schemes were frequently put forward by interest groups in business or government that had no interest in the master plan as such. Conflicts between the static master plan and specific development proposals with available funding were almost always resolved in favor of the specific proposals. Today planners themselves are questioning the utility of creating more master plans, unless the plans are directly related to, and can have influence on, the future development of the city.

### The Approach of Jane Jacobs

Among the critics of current urban planning practices, Jane Jacobs is probably the best known. She is diametrically opposed to zoning and other planning tools as they are currently applied.

Using as an example her own beloved area of Greenwich Village in New York City (she now lives in Toronto), Jane Jacobs argues that the mixed housing and commercial usages and the resulting congestion, factors which orthodox planners are said to deplore, are the very reason why the area has retained its buoyancy and unique character over time. Cities, she suggests, are natural economic generators of diversity and incubators of new enterprises, and attempts by planners to zone various activities into distinct areas only work toward dullness and eventual stagnation both economically and socially.[16]

Jane Jacobs says that four conditions are indispensable if diversity and liveliness are to be generated in a city:

> **1** The district, and indeed as many of its internal parts as possible, must serve more than one primary function; preferably more than two. These must insure the presence of people who go outdoors on different schedules and are in the place for different reasons.
>
> **2** Most blocks should be short; that is, streets and opportunities to turn corners must be frequent.
>
> **3** The district must mingle buildings that vary in age and condition, including a good proportion of old ones so that they vary in the economic yield they must produce. This mingling must be fairly closegrained.
>
> **4** There must be a sufficiently dense concentration of people, for whatever purposes they may be there. This includes dense concentration in the case of people who are there because of residence.[17]

[15]Martin Meyerson and Edward C. Banfield, *Politics, Planning, and the Public Interest,* Free Press of Glencoe, New York, 1955.

[16]Jane Jacobs, *The Death and Life of Great American Cities,* Random House, New York, 1961.

[17]Jacobs, op. cit., pp. 150–151.

By providing a mixture of functions—residence, work, place of entertainment—a district ensures that eyes are constantly on its streets, maintaining safety. This diversity of use further means that uniquely urban specialty shops can operate profitably, since there is considerable traffic past their doors. Short city blocks provide for alternative routes and use of different streets—with the result that a cross section of the public passes the doors of the smaller specialty operations. Old buildings are needed, since, as Jacobs puts it, "Old ideas can sometimes use new buildings. New ideas must use old buildings." New buildings are limited to enterprises that can support the high costs of construction and rent. Old buildings not only provide space for new enterprises; they also break the visual monotony, and they can house cozy stores that provide gossip and a place to leave your key as well as merely selling goods. Finally, the dense concentration of people in an area contributes to its vitality and liveliness. Jacobs suggests that it is not accidental that the district in San Francisco with the highest dwelling density is the popular North Beach–Telegraph Hill section. High building density does not, of course, necessarily mean crowding. Medium-density areas fail to provide liveliness and safety, and they have none of the advantages of low-density, semisuburban areas.

In Jacobs' view, the population and environmental characteristics of a neighborhood shape its social character:

> Great cities are not like towns, only larger. They are not like suburbs, only denser. They differ from towns and suburbs in basic ways, and one of these is that cities are, by definition full of strangers. . . . Even residents who live near each other are strangers, and must be, because of the sheer number of people in small geographical compass. The bedrock attribute of a successful city district is that a person must feel safe and secure among all these strangers. He must not feel automatically menaced by them. A city district that fails in this respect also does badly in other ways and lays up for itself, and for its city at large, mountains on mountains of trouble.[18]

A valid criticism of Jacobs is that her preoccupation with street safety makes her oblivious to other urban problems and values. She views the city as a place where people will do violence to one another unless restrained. One of her most knowledgeable critics, Louis Mumford, suggests that Jacobs puts so much emphasis on the necessity for continued street life because her ideal city is mainly an organization for the prevention of crime.

Mumford points out that according to Jacobs' view, "the best way to

[18]Jacobs, op. cit., p. 30.

overcome criminal violence is to create a mixture of economic and social activities such that at every hour of the day the streets will never be empty of pedestrians and that each shopkeeper, each householder, compelled to find both his main occupations and his recreations on the street, will serve as watchman and policeman, each knowing who is to be trusted and who not. . . ."[19] Mumford points out that London of the eighteenth century, violent and crime-ridden, met these prescriptions. Furthermore, the benefits of high density, pedestrian-filled streets, cross-lines of circulation, and a mixture of primary economic activities can be found in Harlem—where they do not reduce street or other crime. On the other hand, a dispassionate observer would have to concede that whatever else Harlem is, it is certainly not dull.

Lewis Mumford also argues quite forcefully that this emphasis on safety blinds Jacobs to other values in an urban environment. Convenience, aesthetic beauty, the absence of the noise of trucks crowding the street, the minimizing of the effects of pollution—all these factors are made subservient to safety. Mumford criticized Jacobs' approach in these words: "That beauty, order, spaciousness, clarity of purpose may be worth having for their direct effect on the human spirit, even if they do not promote dynamism or reduce criminal violence, seems not to occur to her."[20]

### The Use of Space

Understanding the symbolic uses of space can certainly be of practical use to architects and planners who want to use sociological information to increase the adequacy of their designs.

Public housing projects in particular can be designed to minimize rather than maximize feelings of deprivation and isolation from the community at large. Today it is clear that the traditional high-rise project is not only designed to be dull and monotonous but is also dangerous to the inhabitants. Large open areas outside the projects frequently become "no man's lands" after dark, while within the buildings the large corridors, washing rooms, and even the elevators are unsafe. Residents are helpless to prevent muggings and rapes and feel that the only area they can control, and thus feel safe in, is the space within their own apartments. (See the section on unstable slums in Chapter 6 and Chapter 10.)

Architectural design can do a great deal to increase the security and

[19]Lewis Mumford, "Home Remedies for Urban Cancer," in Louis K. Loewenstein (ed.), *Urban Studies*, The Free Press, New York, 1971, pp. 392–393.

[20]Lewis Mumford, "The Sky Line: Mother Jacob's Home Remedies," *The New Yorker*, **38**:168, December 1, 1962.

The older low-rise Brownsville project has a much lower crime rate and maintenance cost than the high-rise Van Dyke project across the street. (Photo by Oscar Newman, from *Defensible Space, Crime Prevention Through Urban Design*, Macmillan, New York, 1972.)

livability of projects. One of the simplest changes is to build low-rise buildings (six stories at most) where no more than a dozen families share the same stairwell and thus know who should or should not be present. Some other elements that can help in providing security are:

**1** The territorial definition of space in developments reflecting the areas of influence of the inhabitants. This works by subdividing the residential environment into zones toward which adjacent residents easily adopt proprietory attitudes.

**2** The positioning of apartment windows to allow residents to naturally survey the exterior and interior public areas of their living environment.

**3** The adoption of building forms that avoid the stigma of peculiarity that allows others to perceive the vulnerability and isolation of the inhabitants.

**4** The enhancement of safety by locating residential developments in

> functionally sympathetic urban areas immediately adjacent to activities that do not provide continued threat.[21]

The effect of proper planning can be seen in a comparison of the Brownsville and Van Dyke housing projects in New York, which are separated only by a street. The low-rise Brownsville buildings, although older, have significantly fewer problems of crime and maintenance than the high-rise Van Dyke buildings. This is in spite of the fact that the average density per acre of the two projects is virtually identical. The Brownsville projects, with their six-story buildings and three-story wings, are humanly manageable and controllable to a far greater degree than the thirteen- and fourteen-story Van Dyke projects across the street.

Internal space can also be designed to decrease alienation. Architects define spaces inside apartments, for example, in terms of the functions they serve: kitchens for cooking; bedrooms for sleeping; dining rooms for eating; and windows for letting in light and air. Urban residents, however, often have their own ideas of the functions of space. Windows, for example, are not only for air and light but also for observing and communicating with the street; living rooms may not be viewed as an area for entertainment but as sacred space to be used for formal family occasions.

In one experiment in designing housing for the Puerto Rican residents of tenement buildings in East Harlem, a local community group and an architect jointly redesigned apartments according to the needs of the residents.[22] On the basis of what they learned from interviewing the residents and from their own observations, they designed the apartments to avoid the large areas of undifferentiated space so desired by middle-class whites. The residents wanted a design where the apartment entrance would open directly into the sacred space of the living room and where the kitchen, contrary to middle-class preference, could be closed off from the rest of the house by a solid wall with a door. This is what the housewives themselves, and their families, wanted in their homes.

Unfortunately, this experiment was a rare occurrence. Working-class and lower-class people are seldom asked what they want in housing. Perhaps some of the horrible mistakes in public housing projects could have been avoided if someone had bothered to talk with those for whom the apartments were being designed.

[21]Oscar Newman, *Defensible Space*, Macmillan, New York, 1972, p. 9.

[22]John Zeisel, "Symbolic Meaning of Space and the Physical Dimension of Social Relations," in John Walton and Donald E. Carns (eds.), *Cities in Change*, Allyn and Bacon, Boston, 1973, pp. 252–263.

**Table 11-1 Van Dyke and Brownsville: Some Comparisons**

Comparison of crime incidents

| Crime incidents | Van Dyke | Brownsville |
|---|---|---|
| Total incidents | 1,189 | 790 |
| Total felonies, misdemeanors and offenses | 432 | 264 |
| Number of robberies | 92 | 24 |
| Number of malicious mischief | 52 | 28 |

*Source:* New York City Housing Authority Police Records, 1968.

Comparison of maintenance

| Maintenance | Van Dyke (constructed 1955) | Brownsville (constructed 1947) |
|---|---|---|
| Number of maintenance jobs of any sort (work tickets) 4/70 | 3,301 | 2,376 |
| Number of maintenance jobs, excluding glass repair | 2,643 | 1,651 |
| Number of nonglass jobs per unit | 1.47 | 1.16 |
| Number of full-time maintenance staff | 9 | 7 |
| Number of elevator breakdowns per month | 280 | 110 |

*Source:* New York City Housing Authority Project Managers' Bookkeeping records.

A comparison of physical design and population density

| Physical measure | Van Dyke | Brownsville |
|---|---|---|
| Total size | 22.35 acres | 19.16 acres |
| Number of buildings | 23 | 27 |
| Building height | 13–14 story<br>9–3 story | 6 story with some<br>3 story wings |
| Coverage | 16.6 | 23.0 |
| Floor area ratio | 1.49 | 1.39 |
| Average number of rooms per apartment | 4.62 | 4.69 |
| Density | 288 persons/acre | 287 persons/acre |
| Year completed | 1955 (one building added in 1964) | 1947 |

*Source:* New York City Housing Authority Project Physical Design Statistics.

*Source:* Oscar Newman, *Defensible Space,* Macmillan, New York, 1972, pp. 46–48, tables 5, 6, and 7.

## EUROPEAN PLANNING

Europe has a tradition of urban planning for the community welfare that goes back many years. Europeans, lacking the land resources of the United States, have been more concerned with conserving their resources and preventing unlimited growth. The tendency toward compactness and public ownership also means that the desires of the individual builder are more subject to the criteria of the public welfare.

Planning in some European cities is also due in part to the devastation of World War II. Where whole cities were reduced to rubble, as in Germany, it was necessary to rely on a strong government influence in rebuilding. The United States has never had to face the rebuilding of its centers on such a scale.

In North America, rebuilding is almost synonymous with urban renewal; and this invariably means the tearing down of older buildings and rebuilding using modern architectural designs and materials. In Europe, rebuilding has sometimes had quite a different effect. Much of the rebuilding of German cities following World War II has consciously attempted to return the destroyed areas to the same appearance that they had before the war. Urban renewal need not mean changing existing patterns: this decision is one for us to make. Poland, after considerable thought and debate, rejected a modern glass-and-concrete design for rebuilding the center of Warsaw after its total destruction. The Poles consciously reproduced the appearance of this section of Warsaw during the period of its medieval glory. Brick by brick, the medieval section has been replicated. The fact that in North America renewal has taken place in one direction does not mean that there are not other alternatives; it means, rather, that we have become locked into one way of viewing urban renewal and rebuilding.

### Control of Land

One advantage enjoyed by some European communities is control over their own municipal lands. Stockholm began buying land in 1904 outside the city limits, with the goal of providing both green space and room for future garden suburbs. Most of this land has since been annexed to the city, so that Stockholm is now in the favorable position of owning about 75 percent of the land within its administrative boundaries. The city rarely sells its land; instead, it leases the land on 60-year renewable leases to both public and private developers. The money earned from the leases pays off the cost of the loan used to buy the land; and the municipality has the additional advantage of directly profiting from increases in land values. The public, rather than private land speculators, thus profits from the increased value of the land. If the city wants the land after the 60-year lease is up, it must go to court and prove that the land is needed for the public interest, and then pay the leaseholder the value of any buildings on the property.

Since World War II, the city-owned land in Stockholm has been used to develop a system of subcenters or "mini-cities," built one after another along rapid-transit lines extending in five directions from the old city center. Each subcenter contains between 10,000 and 15,000 inhabitants and is served by its own community services, schools, and shops. Unlike the British New Towns, these subcenters emphasize easy access to the center city. Blocks of flats, frequently high-rises, are built 550 yards from the transit station; detached and terrace-style housing is built beyond up to about 1,000 yards from the station. Cars are routed through green areas surrounding the living areas.

Along each string of subcenters, "main centers" are built at appropriate intervals. Four such centers have already been built, and a fifth is under construction. Each main center, with a larger shopping mall, theaters, and a major transit station, has a supporting population of between 50,000 and 100,000 persons within ten minutes by automobile or public transit.

### Housing in Europe

Everywhere in Europe the housing shortage has been chronic since World War II and the "baby boom" that followed it. Today France, Germany, Holland, and Sweden all build more housing units per 1,000 population than the United States. The rate in Sweden is nearly double the rate in the United States. Nonetheless, even in Sweden there is an undersupply of housing. A newly married couple may have to wait several years for an apartment. The housing squeeze is compounded by rising standards of demand—more room, modern bathrooms, etc.—and the changing nature of the family structure that is swelling the demand for housing. In the Netherlands the average number of persons per housing unit has dropped from 5.6 in 1900 to 2.9 in 1970, and it is still going down. The same trend is taking place elsewhere in Europe: aged persons and young single people now have their own housing units, so that the need for additional units is increasing.

There is a positive side to the situation in Europe: most new residential building there is subsidized in one way or another in order to hold down costs and maintain quality. Germany and the Netherlands have elaborate programs for loans to nonprofit housing organizations; Great Britain has rent rebates for the poor; and Sweden has an annual housing allowance of about $200 for all families with two or more children.

Rents are subsidized and in most countries take less than 20 percent of a family's income: this is excellent by American standards. In the Netherlands and Germany, rents frequently do not exceed 10 percent of the family income. The extreme is found in the Soviet Union, where the rent for a small apartment for a family of four would absorb only 3.5 percent of the average monthly income of an industrial worker. Utilities would cost another 3.5 percent on the average. The drawback in the Soviet Union is that owing to a severe housing shortage the current "housing norm" (rationing of space) is only 7 square meters (approximately 21 square feet) per person.[23]

### The Dutch Approach

Americans who fear that certain regions of the United States are turning into unrelenting megalopolises should find it instructive to see how the Dutch are coping with similar problems. The Netherlands is a small country with a population of 13 million and a population density of 970 persons per square mile. If the United States had this population density, it would have a population of over 3 $^1/_2$ billion, or roughly the present population of the world. The problem in the Netherlands is aggravated by the fact that the majority of the Dutch population is found in a megalopolis about 100 miles in diameter, including Amsterdam, Rotterdam, and The Hague. This conurbation is known as the *randstad,* or "rim city."

Nonetheless, it is possible to reach the open countryside in half an hour's time from the center of any of the cities in the *randstad.* In spite of considerable population growth and a housing shortage since World War II, the Dutch lead remarkably uncluttered lives. Urban sprawl such as that found in the United States is virtually unknown. The line between town and country is sharply drawn. When a city such as Amsterdam stops, it stops abruptly. It is quite common at the city's edge to see massive blocks of high-rise apartments overlooking cows peacefully grazing in totally open fields. By building upward rather than outward, the Dutch have kept their towns compact, and valuable woods, lakes, and fields are kept as a reserve for the use of all.

The Dutch have been able to save much of their environment, and at the same time provide for an ever-expanding demand for housing, by building tall multiple-unit residential buildings. The use of high-rises is dictated by the shortage of land and the necessity to keep down costs of land. Almost without exception, single-family houses are built in rows.[24]

[23]Leon M. Herman, "Urbanization and New Housing Construction in the Soviet Union," *American Journal of Economics and Sociology,* **30**:216, April, 1971.

[24]*The Netherlands: Current Trends and Policies in the Field of Housing, Building, and Planning During the Year 1968,* Ministry of Housing and Physical Planning, The Hague, 1970, p. 18.

Many families in the Netherlands, particularly those with small children, prefer single-family houses; and the privately financed dwellings now being built are substantially of this type. However, only the more affluent segment of the population can afford the high building costs. The government in effect subsidizes both rents and building costs for those not able to carry the full cost. The Dutch feel that every family, regardless of income level, is entitled to reasonable housing. As a result, rents are low by comparison with those in the United States. After deduction for taxes and social insurance, the average Dutch family pays only about 10 percent of its income on rent.[25] This is a result of the government's policy of rental subsidies and loans for building new dwellings. The average rent of a new dwelling financed with a state loan is roughly 15 or 16 percent of the average gross income of an industrial worker.[26] Subsidies and rent supplements are periodically readjusted so that the poor and the working classes will not be priced out of the housing market.

The Dutch also believe in public ownership of urban land; about 70 percent of Amsterdam is now owned by the city. In The Hague the policy is somewhat different: only about 20 percent of the land is owned by the city, but it is strategically located so that it can be used to set the pattern of real estate prices for the city. The third major city of the Netherlands, Rotterdam, saw its downtown area reduced to rubble by Nazi dive bombers in 1940. The city began to reconstruct after the war, with the core of the city as a commercial, cultural, and administrative center. Dutch officials now concede that it was a mistake to rigidly segregate commercial and residential areas. The Lijnbaan, the downtown shopping mall which has received much praise, contains fine shops, sidewalk cafes, and several apartment buildings without vacancies. Rotterdam's land policy is somewhere between that of Sweden and that of the United States. The city retains ownership of industrial and commercial land, with the land being leased and rents reviewed every three to five years. Land to be used for housing, on the other hand, is sold outright after it has been determined that the land usage is in conformity with the overall development plan for the city.

A system of local, regional, and—finally—national controls prevents unwanted urban sprawl. New buildings simply cannot be constructed unless they conform to the detailed development plan prepared by each municipality. Plans for development are drawn up by the city; but they must be approved by provincial authorities, who have certain limited powers of review and veto. If a local development is in conflict with the regional plan, and if the difference cannot be resolved at that level, the

[25]Op. cit., p. 14.
[26]Ibid.

question then goes to the national level for a decision. There is no national plan, as such; rather, there are national guidelines which influence the regional plans and the detailed city development plans. An attempt is made to avoid rigidity, and plans are constantly being modified—within the national guidelines—to meet new situations and needs. Without some controls, the remaining green space between The Hague, Rotterdam, and Amsterdam would soon be filled, and a megalopolis would become inevitable.

## APPLICATIONS IN THE UNITED STATES

At present it is quite problematical whether Americans would be willing to give up their ever expanding suburban developments for the type of controlled growth found in Europe. Thus far, Americans have generally been unwilling to accept changes such as planned environments and leaseholds rather than outright purchase. The evidence to date indicates that, for better or worse, Americans are wedded to the concept of the single-family house situated on as large a plot of private land as possible. Supporting this view is a study by William Michelson which indicates that in the United States the overwhelming majority of urban dwellers prefer living in single-family houses.[27] Most people in this country are not attracted to the type of multiple dwellings advocated by planners and designers like Le Corbusier, or even to more modest proposals involving town houses. Families with children want houses with their own surrounding yards—preferably in the suburbs. Planners and people do not agree on the nature of the "ideal" community.

[27]William Michelson, "Most People Don't Want What Architects Want," *Trans-Action*, July–August, 1968, pp. 37–43.

Chapter 12

# New Towns and Transportation Planning

*We shape our buildings, and afterwards our buildings shape us.*
Winston Churchill

Throughout the centuries, men have had visions of creating new towns free from the fads and foibles of older cities. The term "utopia" originated as the title of a book (1516) by Sir Thomas Moore which gave his version of how a new land of towns should be organized. Here we shall emphasize new towns that have actually been built. In the first part of this chapter, we shall be concerned with new towns that have been built during this century, and in particular with the numerous English new towns that owe their intellectual roots to the vision of Ebenezer Howard. The second half of the chapter will concentrate on some transportation alternatives.

## NEW TOWNS

### British New Towns

Ebenezer Howard (1850–1928), an English court stenographer, proposed the building of whole new communities. His ideas appeared in a book called *Tomorrow, A Peaceful Path to Real Reform* (1898), which was later reissued under the title *Garden Cities of Tomorrow* (1902). Howard's new towns, which were called "garden cities," were not to be simply another version of suburbs. Rather, they were to be self-contained communities of 30,000 inhabitants which would have within their boundaries ample opportunities not only for residence but also for employment, education, and recreation.

Howard's garden cities were essentially a reaction against the urban abuses of the Industrial Revolution in England. His new towns were not to be extensions of the morally and socially polluted city but self-sufficient towns with all necessary amenities, enjoying the benefits of a healthful country life. In Howard's words:

> There are in reality not only, as is so constantly assumed, two alternatives—town life and country life—but a third alternative in which all the advantages of the most energetic and active town life, with all the beauty and delight of the country, may be secured in perfect combination.[1]

This combination would in turn spur "the spontaneous movement of the people from our crowded cities to the bosom of our kindly mother earth, at once the source of life, of happiness, of wealth, and of power." Thus the garden city was fundamentally antiurban in its basic conception. It was to solve the problem of the great cities largely by abandoning them and starting over with a fresh environment.

Sir Frederick Osborn, one of the major proponents of new towns, described them as follows:

> Howard's Garden City is to be industrial and commerical with a balanced mixture of all social groups and levels of income. Areas are worked out for the zones: public buildings and places of entertainment are placed centrally, shops intermediately, factories on the edge with the railway and sidings. Houses are of different sizes, but all have gardens and all are within easy range of factories, shops, schools, cultural centers, and the open country. Of special interest is the central park and the inner Green Belt or Ring Park, 420 feet wide, containing the main schools with large playgrounds and such buildings as churches.[2]

However, the most distinctive feature of the garden cities was that beyond the city itself there was an encircling "green belt" of natural fields and woodlands which were owned by the town and could never be sold.

[1]Ebenezer Howard, *Garden Cities of To-morrow,* Faber and Faber, London, 1902, pp. 45–46.
[2]Frederick J. Osborn, *Green-Belt Cities,* Schocken, New York, 1969, p. 28.

This green belt could not be encroached upon for housing, business, industry, or even farming—although it could be used for pasturage. Because of this feature, garden cities are also known as "green-belt cities." The green belt not only provided a way for the residents to enjoy nature: it also effectively was to prevent the city from growing beyond its planned limit of 30,000 inhabitants.

Nor was the internal design of the garden city left to chance. The whole town, including its pattern of roads, was planned with both the quality and the basic design of buildings controlled. The central 5 or 6 acres were to contain civic buildings, a library, lecture halls, and theaters. Stores and shops were nearby. This core was surrounded by rings of houses, each with its own yard. Neighborhood schools and churches were scattered throughout the city, and small parks connected the various neighborhoods. The outermost ring of the city was to contain industries and warehouses with direct access to rail lines. The rail lines did not penetrate the center of the city proper.

The town was totally preplanned and strict zoning was central to

Howard's Garden Cities were to be self-contained worlds. Note that in contrast to industrial cities of his time, the railroads did not come into the city proper. (Ebenezer Howard, *Garden Cities of Tomorrow*, London, Faber and Faber, 1945, p. 52.)

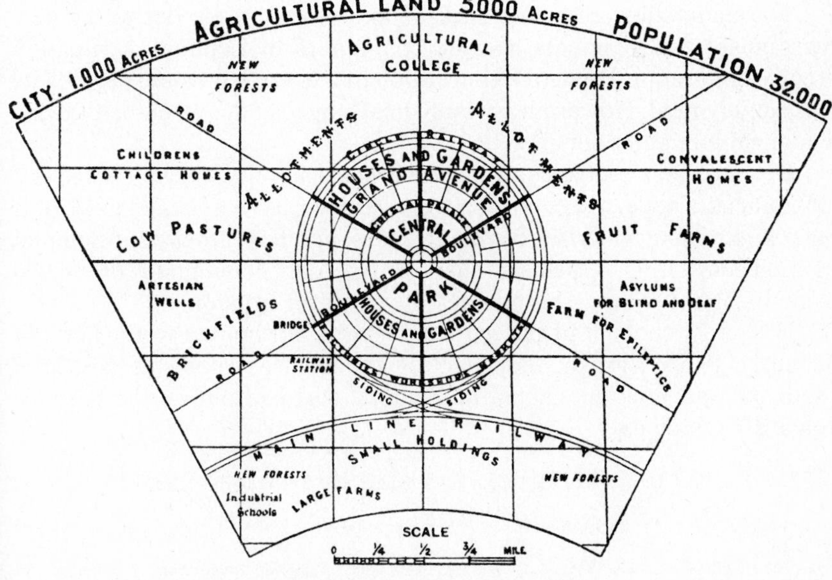


GARDEN CITY AND RURAL BELT

Howard's basic scheme. The residential city was divided into five neighborhoods or wards with approximately 5,000 population. Each was to have its own centrally located school and community subcenter and every attempt was to be made to keep all houses within walking distance of factories, schools, churches, shops, and of course, the open country.[3]

The whole site, including agricultural land, was to be under quasipublic or trust ownership, to ensure planning control through leasehold covenants. When the population outgrew the prescribed size and area, another new town was to be created with its own sacrosanct green belt. As with the ancient Greeks, problems of growth were to be handled by colonization rather than by extending city boundaries.

**Construction** The concept of garden cities would have gone the way of other utopian plans had Howard not been an activist as well as a visionary. In 1902, with the aid of the newly formed Garden City Association, he established the first garden city at Letchworth, some 30 miles north of London.[4]

This initial venture was plagued by many difficulties, the principal one being that the site selected was poor. Another problem was the difficulty of finding investors for a project that limited dividends to a maximum of 5 percent per year. In fact, it was twenty years before the shareholders received any dividends at all.[5]

The understandable reluctance of industry to move out to the new town meant that residents became commuters to London—a situation directly opposed to Howard's conception of a town that would provide its own employment. Howard was emphatically against the green-belt towns' becoming commuter suburbs.

Despite these problems, while the first garden city was still not out of the financial woods, a second, Welwyn Garden City, was begun in 1920. It too suffered financial crises for many years, but it eventually surmounted them. Today it is a pleasant and prosperous community of 44,000 residents about twenty-five minutes by rail from London.

Howard's concept of the garden city was not limited to England. In the early 1930s Lusaka, then part of the British colony of Northern Rhodesia, and now the capital of Zambia, was laid out on the basis of Howard's principles.[6]

[3]For a detailed discussion of the community's organization, see Osborn, op. cit.

[4]Frank Schaffer, *The New Town Story*, MacGibbon and Kee, London, 1970, p. 4.

[5]Lloyd Rodwin, *The British New Towns Policy*, Harvard University Press, Cambridge, Mass., 1956, pp. 12–13.

[6]John Collins, "Lusaka: The Myth of the Garden City," *Zambian Urban Studies*, University of Zambia, 1969.

**Government Involvement** Were it not for World War II, Howard's garden cities would probably have remained a quaint experiment. However, in the aftermath of World War II, with its extensive destruction in the heart of London, the British government became directly involved in the building of new towns through the New Towns Act of 1946. Advocates of new towns had long argued that they would provide a healthier, cleaner, safer, and more democratic environment. In the back of everyone's mind was also the fact that London had suffered grievously from bombing during the war and that new towns would disperse both population and industry at numerous smaller nodes rather than create one massive target in London. Furthermore, it was considered undesirable to rebuild badly damaged areas of London, such as the East End, at the old unsatisfactory population densities; new towns would help to absorb the surplus population. Government involvement in new towns meant that building on a grand scale was now possible, as a result of government financing.

Actually, the new towns were only one part of a four-part policy. The policy included; (1) a green belt around London to halt continuous metropolitan growth; (2) new towns to house the expanding urban population; (3) redevelopment of inner-city areas, conforming to higher standards than had existed previously; and (4) an attempt to control the location of employment and to prevent everyone from building in London.[7]

The first of the English government-sponsored new towns, Stevenage, was begun in 1947. Among other innovations, it had the first pedestrian shopping mall in Britain and neighborhoods designed to separate pedestrian walkways from contact with automobile and truck traffic. Today Stevenage is a pleasant and economically self-supporting community of 66,000. Its plans originally called for controlled growth to 190,000 inhabitants by the year 2000. Expansion to this size was turned down by the government, but smaller expansion has been authorized. Howard's arbitrary limit of 30,000 had to be discarded, as it did not provide a population large enough to create a lively, viable community. The ceiling was first raised to 75,000; but present planning calls for towns of 100,000, with "cluster cities" to hold 250,000 or more.[8] The concept of a city providing all its own employment has also been abandoned, in practice if not in theory, although the new towns are certainly not designed to be commuter suburbs; they are basically manufacturing

[7]Wyndham Thomas, "Implementation: New Towns," in Derek Senior (ed.), *The Regional City,* Aldine, Chicago, 1966, pp. 19–20.

[8]Osborn, op. cit., p. 2.

A noontime band concert enlivens the shopping mall of a British new town. (*Ian Berry/Magnum.*)

centers, with approximately half the population in industry and the other half in trade, the services, and the professions.

Houses and apartments built by the local new towns development corporations are not distributed on a first-come, first-served basis. Rather, priority is determined by a number of criteria, including employment by local or incoming industries and previous residence in one of the more crowded inner-city areas of London. Originally, following Howard's plan, almost all dwellings were rented, but successive British governments have been moving toward increasing the number of owner-occupied homes. As a means of encouraging home ownership, present renters are being offered the option of purchasing the property in which they presently live for 20 percent below market value.[9]

As of 1971, twenty-eight new towns had been completed in Great Britain, housing 1,667,000 persons. Nearly 1,800 manufacturing firms have been established in the towns since 1950, providing more than 160,000 jobs. New towns of up to 500,000 inhabitants are in the planning stage. It is well to remember that only 5 percent of Britain's housing construction after World War II has taken place in new towns; still, there

[9]For this and other information on policy, I am indebted to Mr. Frank Schaffer, Secretary of the Commission for the New Towns.

is a real commitment to new towns, with over $3.8 billion already invested in them. By the end of the next decade, the English expect to have nearly 4 million persons living in new towns, rather than jammed into cities where there would not be adequate jobs or living quarters.

**Problems** During the 1960s a great deal of attention was given by the British press to the loneliness and unhappiness felt by residents of new towns. The phrase "new-town blues" was coined to describe this situation. Empirical research, however, indicates that the opposite is more likely to be the case. The most extensive investigation of the question reported that

> . . . the creation of a new town with full social and economic planning results in an improvement in general health, both subjective and objective. Neurosis, the report concluded, is no greater in new towns than elsewhere. As they state it, "some people had indeed shown loneliness, boredom, discontent with environment and worries, particularly over money. It is easy enough for enterprising enquirers to find such people and attribute these symptoms to the new town. But a similar group of similar size can be found in any community, new or old, if it is sought.[10]

These findings were very similar to those of Herbert Gans, who studied Levittown, New Jersey, an American planned community and concluded that in general better rather than worse mental health was the rule.[11] Peter Willmott suggests that available British research indicates that many of the residents' problems are real but transitory. The studies which found problems were done on new arrivals. After settling in, the residents, and particularly their children, seem to have adapted successfully.[12]

A more serious problem and one not yet fully overcome by the British new towns is the identification of the towns as lower middle class. Professional, and even people at the level of junior managers, have generally shunned the garden cities—in spite of the fact that they offer excellent housing for the money. Social-class distinctions are still rather rigid in Great Britain, and a new town is not considered a prestige address. The new towns in general contain a high proportion of skilled manual workers.[13]

Moreover, according to one researcher, new towns have become *less*

[10]Lord Taylor and Sydney Chave, *Mental Health and Environment in a New Town*, Longmans, London, 1964, quoted by Schaffer, op. cit., p. 175.

[11]Herbert J. Gans, *The Levittowners*, Pantheon, New York, 1967.

[12]Peter Willmott, "Social Research and New Communities," in John Gabree (ed.), *Surviving in the City*, Ballantine Books, New York, 1973, pp. 252–272.

[13]Peter Willmott, "East Kilbride and Stevenage," *Town Planning Review*, **34**:312–313, January, 1964.

socially integrated over time. In Crawley—one of the new towns—a definite trend has been noted for middle-class people to work in the town but to live elsewhere.[14] This division of work and residence is the antithesis of Howard's original plan, according to which everyone would live and work in the same community. There are, however, other data which suggest that the absence of professionals and managers in the new towns reflects the situation of ten years ago, before the full range of new schools, shops, and reasonable amenities were available. Data from the British census appear to show that the social structure of the new towns is changing in the direction of the national average.[15] While the new towns are primarily industrial and commercial, and their social composition reflects this fact, they are not totally segregated according to class.

### European New Towns

Not only England but other European countries, including Sweden, Finland, the Netherlands, and the Soviet Union, built new towns after World War II. The Soviet Union has probably founded more new towns than any other nation—supposedly more than 800 between 1926 and 1963. About one-third of these were established in totally undeveloped areas. The Soviets' development of new towns has been generally explained as part of broad schemes for national development and the decentralization of industry. Many of their earlier new towns were connected with hydroelectric power projects and then expanded into manufacturing centers.[16]

In the Soviet Union, as in England, the new towns were planned to be separate from existing urban centers although related to them. Local industry was to provide sufficient employment so that few, if any, residents would be required to commute to the large city. Generally, these communities were originally designed to house a maximum of 60,000 to 100,000 people. In Sweden and the Netherlands, on the other hand, the new communities were designed to be closely tied to the central city, and to serve as residential—not employment—areas (see Chapter 11). New Scandinavian towns such as Valligby, Farsta, and Taby are basically residential and shopping areas. Unlike the British new towns, they are constructed along rapid-transit lines so that they will be an integral part of the city's life; they are not designed to be independent and self-contained employment units.[17] It is expected that most residents will work in the

[14]B. J. Heraud, "Social Class and the New Towns," *Urban Studies*, **5**:33–58, 1968.

[15]Schaffer, op. cit., p. 168.

[16]J. Clapp, *New Towns and Urban Policy—Planning Metropolitan Growth*, Dunellen, New York, 1971, p. 28.

[17]For a description of urban planning in Sweden, see Goran Sidenbladh, "Stockholm: A Planned City," in *Cities: A Scientific American Book*, Knopf, New York, 1965.

central city; consequently, rapid transit to the core of the central city is a basic feature of the design of these towns. Zoetermeer, a new town of 100,000 inhabitants 7 miles from The Hague, in the Netherlands, will be able to speed its residents to the center of The Hague in less than twenty minutes. Such new towns are really extensions of the older city into the countryside rather than attempts to create new rural utopian communities.

All European new towns have in common the fact that they were initiated, planned, and financed by the government. While there has occasionally been some financing from cooperatives, unions, or even private sources, the land and the facilities built on it have been owned either directly by the local government or by quasipublic corporations chartered by the national government to build and administer the town. Dutch planners also have the advantage that, since much of the land for new towns was drained from marshes, there is little dispute as to how the land is to be used.

Perhaps the most innovative new towns have been those designed by the Scandinavians. Scandinavian architecture is of particularly high quality. High-rise apartment buildings are usually used, not only because land costs are high but also to avoid suburban sprawl and to provide open spaces for recreation and enjoyment of the natural environment. In Sweden, Finland, and the Netherlands over 80 percent of the units are in blocks of flats. English new towns, on the other hand, have over 80 percent single-family homes.[18] Every attempt is made to put parking lots underground or otherwise out of sight, to preserve the environment. The increasing number of cars, however, seems to constantly outrun the planners' ideas about where to put them all. Still, by building compactly the planners ensure that much open space is left for woods, sports areas, and lawns.

The most ecologically conscious of the European new towns will be Vaudreuil, an hour's drive north from Paris along the Seine River. The French designers boast that it will be the first city fully planned to control all forms of pollution. All factories and other activities will have to conform to strict antinoise rules, and smoke from industries will go not into the air but into subterranean conduits. Refuse from homes will be disposed of through underground pipes to processing plants. The heat generated from the elimination of waste will then be used to supply part of the city's central heating needs. Vaudreuil is also unique in that other details of the community will not be fully planned. By avoiding the conventional zoning patterns the designers hope to avoid dullness and

[18]Pierre Merlin, *New Towns*, Methuen, London, 1971, p. 250.

stimulate variety and liveliness. Since factories will be quiet and nonpolluting, the planners see no reason to segregate them all in one restricted area.

Since the housing in new towns is constructed first and amenities follow, there is a problem of boredom and its consequences. Not everyone can adjust to the absence of night life and city excitement. Sweden's planned communities, for example, have had problems with alcohol and drugs—although these problems are hardly unique to new towns.

### American Experiments

Today, when European governments have directly taken the responsibility for planning and financing new towns, it is almost forgotten that during the 1930s the United States government also designed, financed, built, and for a decade managed three of the world's first green-belt towns for middle-class and lower-middle-class groups. The United States, however, has never had a national program for developing new towns as such. The building of these towns reflected specific measures that were being taken to combat the Depression of the 1930s. The government had three main objectives:

**1** To demonstrate a new kind of suburban community planning which would combine the advantages of city and country life.

**2** To provide good housing at reasonable rents for moderate-income families.

**3** To give jobs to thousands of unemployed workers which would result in lasting economic and social benefits to the community in which the work was undertaken.

The three American green-belt towns were Greenbelt, Maryland, outside of Washington, D.C.; Green Hills, Ohio, near Cincinnati; and Greendale, Wisconsin, just south of Milwaukee. They were basically experimental or demonstration projects. The towns were to have their own industry, as in the British model, but first a shortage of funds and then World War II kept them basically commuter suburbs. Following World War II, the private housing industry was able to convince Congress that having the government involved in the building and renting of low-rent homes was socialistic and dangerous to the free-enterprise system. As a result of Public Law 65 of 1949, all the homes built by the government were sold. The green belts surrounding the towns—which with the expansion of the central cities had become valuable land—were converted to other uses. Much of Greendale's green belt, for example, is now occupied by privately developed housing tracts and a large shopping center. It is more than a little ironic that when much of the world was trying to save its remaining green space surrounding cities, we were busy converting an existing green belt into a shopping center.

**Privately Built New Towns** Although the business of building cities is the largest single industry in the United States, we still construct our cities on a largely ad hoc basis. Thousands of small enterprises build our towns and cities, with little planning and even less research.

Privately built new towns were a phenomenon of the years after World War II. According to the Department of Housing and Urban Development, sixty-four new communities have been completed or substantially begun in the United States since World War II; forty of these were constructed during the 1960s.[19] These new towns are located in eighteen states, but half of them are in California, Florida, and Arizona. Four-fifths are within metropolitan areas; the remainder are mainly retirement communities for the elderly.

The best known of the American new towns are Reston, Virginia, just west of Washington, D.C., and Columbia, Maryland, near Baltimore on the way to Washington, D.C. Reston is more innovatively designed, but Columbia has been more successful in attracting new industry. Both Reston and Columbia are financed privately rather than by the government.

Reston, which was the brainchild of the developer Robert E. Simon, was taken over by Gulf Oil Corporation in 1967 because the town was not returning a profit. Economically, the town is now in reasonable health, although some residents say that there has been some slippage in the quality of architecture. Reston, like other privately financed new towns, and unlike the earlier ventures by the government, has a distinctly upper-middle-class character. Studies done in 1969 revealed that the average buyer in Reston was between thirty and forty years old, was the head of a family with two children, and had an annual income of about $17,000. (The mean national income in 1969 was $11,000). The income range in Reston was from $9,000 to over $60,000. In 1969, ground was broken for 198 units of federally subsidized moderate-income housing. But although Robert Simon had attempted to integrate the community economically by placing $25,000 and $45,000 houses side by side, the new management has abandoned this practice as not being economically sound. Mixed-income housing is desirable for social reasons, but it is apparently a drain on profits.

[19]National Committee on Urban Growth Policy, *The New City*, Praeger, New York, 1969, p. 114.

The new town of Reston, Virginia. Note the blend of high-rise and low-rise structures. (*Dennis Brack/Black Star.*)

Columbia, Maryland, the second new town near Washington, D.C., has so far been more successful economically than Reston. Architecturally, it is less successful; it resembles an ideal supersuburb, largely because the builders of the various sections were given a relatively free hand and built a mixture of their best-selling models. For example, a buyer can choose a standard interior and then decide whether the facade is to be Cape Cod, Nordic, or Georgian colonial. Columbia is, however, an extremely pleasant and well-planned community. Wooded areas and pathways run throughout the town.

Columbia, developed by the Rouse Company in a joint venture, covers 15,600 acres, and will eventually house 110,000 people. When complete, it will comprise an investment of about $2 billion. Like most new towns, it is organized into neighborhoods, each with its own elementary school and recreational facilities, including a swimming pool, a neighborhood center, and a convenience store. Three or four neighborhoods are combined to form a "village," which has an intermediate or middle school, a meeting hall, and large and more varied shops. These are all designed to cluster around a small plaza which has benches and a fountain. There is also a larger shopping center for the whole community in the downtown city center, which contains office buildings and larger department stores. Other innovations include a community college and a comprehensive full-care medical program in conjunction with Johns Hopkins Medical School.

As of 1971, Columbia had completed 300 moderate-income housing units which were federally subsidized. These units have not been clustered but are spread over five different sites to avoid the creation of a low-income ghetto. The subsidized rents ranged in 1971 from $99 a month for a one-bedroom apartment to $151.50 for a four-bedroom town house. Within the community, use of automobiles is discouraged by providing walkways and bicycle paths that are both more direct and not in physical contact with the highways. Nonetheless, the parking lots of the shopping centers are generally filled, and the corporation has had to discontinue the minibus service within the city because it did not attract enough customers. In 1972, Columbia enrolled its first forty-seven students—of a planned 1,500—in its Dag Hammarskjold College. Half of the original students were from foreign countries, and the college will actively seek an international student body.

**Critics** American new towns have had some political critics, the loudest of which have been mayors of large cities, who fear that new towns will drain away both interest and desperately needed funds from the central cities. Certainly the American new towns have a distinctively middle-class or upper-middle-class look. While Reston and Columbia both have subsidized housing for moderate-income families, the relative number of such units remains small. The towns are better balanced racially than economically. It is estimated that 15 to 18 percent of Columbia's population is black. New towns have yet to house substantial numbers of inner-city poor, but their record is certainly better than that of most central cities or suburbs.[20]

It is perhaps unreasonable to expect new towns to solve social ills

[20]Wolf von Eckard, "A Fresh Scene in the Clean Dream," *Saturday Review*, May 15, 1971, p. 22.

that have bedeviled society for generations. What the new towns can do is serve as testing grounds for innovations such as mixed-income neighborhoods, effective systems to prevent air and water pollution, and consumer-oriented mass-transit systems. Of course, to experiment meaningfully, funds are needed; and the reality is that these will not come from private developers who have to absorb such costs into the price of the houses they sell. If there is to be meaningful experimentation, governmental support must be available, as it is throughout Europe. Without governmental funding promising plans remain promising plans and nothing more.

**Future Prospects** Although new towns have considerable promise, it is unlikely that many private developers will be able or willing to finance them in the future. The initial front-end cash requirement is tremendous. Land acquisition cost $25 million at Columbia ($1,700 per acre), $13.2 million at Reston ($1,700 per acre), $32 million at Westlake Village, California ($2,700 per acre), and $40 million at Park Forest South near Chicago ($5,000 per acre).[21] Very few private developers can command that kind of money. Most American builders run relatively small operations: in 1970, there were more than 50,000 home-building concerns in the nation, none of which had as much as 1 percent of the market.[22]

In the United States, the Urban Growth and New Community Development Act of 1970 seeks to provide some of the necessary assistance to developers of public and private new towns. The most significant forms of assistance provided are: (1) federal guarantees backing debt obligations up to $50 million for any one project, up to 100 percent for public developers and 85 percent for private developers, to pay for land acquisition, initial development, and installing utilities; (2) planning grants to pay up to two-thirds of all planning costs for public developers and two-thirds of all costs in excess of normal planning costs for private developers; (3) federal loans to cover interest payments on the money developers have to borrow to pay front-end costs such as acquiring land and putting in utilities; (4) grants to local governments to help them through the first few years, when the cost of essential public services outruns the existing tax base; and (5) supplements to existing programs (such as assistance for sewers and water when these programs are part of a new town).[23]

Although this legislation is a big step forward, it still leaves far too

[21] Anthony Downs, "Private Investment and the Public Weal," *Saturday Review*, **54:**26, May 5, 1971.
[22] Joseph P. Fried, *Housing Crisis U.S.A.*, Praeger, New York, 1971, p. 152.
[23] Downs, op. cit., p. 26.

many loose ends to make the creation of new towns profitable to commercial developers. The developer still has to assemble the entire site through either purchase or option before he can even apply for federal aid to help fund the programs noted above. The financial obstacles to the building of new towns have been reduced, but they are still considerable. This is unfortunate, for new towns represent a major attempt to relate population, organization, technology, and environment in a way that produces a livable urban ecology. New towns such as Jonathan, 20 miles from Minneapolis, simply cannot survive without federal assistance. Jonathan, which began as a private development, had bogged down financially until in 1970 the Department of Housing and Urban Development guaranteed up to $21 million in loans for the first ten years of development. This was the first commitment of this sort under the New Communities section of the Housing Act of 1968.

The developers who built Park Forest—the community about which *The Organization Man*[24] was written—are now building a second new town in the suburbs south of Chicago, called Park Forest South. The community will, when completed in the early 1980s, be home for more than 100,000 persons. Over 4,000 acres of land have already been bought, and the cost of building the community will be in excess of $1 billion. A guarantee from the Department of Housing and Urban Development of up to $30 million in loans for planning and acquisition makes such long-term planning possible.

However, the communities just mentioned are the exception. If new towns are ever to be more than interesting isolated experiments, substantial involvement by, and subsidies from, the government will be necessary. A well designed new town that provides adequate services to its residents simply does not offer builders the same immediate profit as the traditional suburban housing tracts that ring our cities. In Great Britain, for example, only three of the new towns were making a profit as of 1971. The British expect that it will take fifteen years before the average new town will break even and twenty years before it becomes really profitable.[25] Few private investors have that sort of patience.

**Satellite Communities** Another, more moderate, alternative to present policies is the building of satellite communities. Small satellite communities can be built on the outskirts of existing metropolitan areas as an alternative to the traditional subdivision developments which sprawl

[24]William H. Whyte, Jr., *The Organization Man*, Doubleday (Anchor), Garden City, New York, 1956.

[25]Conversation with Frank Schaffer, Secretary of the Commission for the New Towns, Great Britain.

on the periphery of our major urban centers. Although provision of mass transit to the central city probably requires that new communities have at least 35,000 inhabitants, such communities could be constructed with as few as 8,000 to 10,000 persons. They are thus considerably smaller than "new towns." A community of 8,000 could be accommodated on a tract of under 200 acres, which is relatively easy to find on the outskirts of most metropolitan areas. Three thousand dwelling units—apartments or town houses—could be built at a modest density, twenty units to the acre on 150 acres of land. The additional acres could easily accommodate a school, a shopping center, and other community facilities.[26]

The purpose of such a community would be to provide reasonable housing for workers employed in outlying industries. Because of the high prices of housing in Northern and Western metropolitan areas, the satellite communities would have to consist partially of town houses and apartments. The apartments, however, could be sold as condominiums rather than as rental units.

## TRANSPORTATION

### Controlling Automobiles

The United States has become more conscious in recent years of the undesirable effects of overusing automobiles. But planning in northern Europe is ahead of planning in the United States as regards controlling the use of automobiles in key downtown areas in order to lower congestion and air pollution. The idea of banning the automobile from the central city is hardly new, but it did not become popular until recently. The growing problem of air pollution has created increasing concern over the effect of automobile exhaust in crowded downtown areas.

So far, the results of creating vehicle-free zones have been better than anticipated. Street-level pollution has declined while retail sales have remained strong. Shoppers have replaced vehicles on the streets of forty-seven German cities—twenty-eight of which have introduced pedestrian areas and traffic restraints since 1967. Traffic is now excluded from selected downtown sections of twenty cities in the Netherlands, fifteen in Denmark, fifteen in France, and eleven in Great Britain. Where once all gave way before the automobile, now pedestrians are increasingly being given the type of consideration that was previously reserved only for drivers.

The particular approach taken varies from city to city. Gothenburg, Sweden, and Bremen, Germany, permit only buses and streetcars to cross

[26]Bernard Weissbourd, "Satellite Communities," *Urban Land*, **31**:9, October, 1972.

A shopping mall in Stockholm, Sweden, separating pedestrians and vehicular traffic. (*Staffen Wennberg/Black Star.*)

the downtown area; all other traffic is shunted onto ring roads leaving and entering specific downtown areas by special routes. In Gothenburg, downtown traffic dropped 17 percent and levels of carbon monoxide were cut 80 percent in some areas. Downtown businesses were not hurt by the ban. Streets that were closed and turned into malls now provide interesting and comfortable shopping, as any tourist visiting Gothenburg (or Copenhagen) can testify. Vienna tried a somewhat different approach. In 1971, a zone for buses only, effective from 10:30 A.M. to 7:00 P.M., was created in the inner city. Deliveries by truck are allowed only between 7:00 A.M. and 10:30 A.M. Air pollution has been reduced 61 percent as a result of this plan, and the area involved is expected to be enlarged.

Banning all motor vehicles from the downtown area is not practical in large cities such as New York, Paris, or London. At the least, buses and taxis are necessary for transportation. New York is experimenting with curbs on traffic and with closing streets, such as Fifth Avenue, at least on a partial basis. Other American cities are also experimenting with various forms of pedestrian malls and new traffic patterns to discourage use of the automobile. New Orleans has greatly enhanced the attractiveness of the historic French Quarter by banning regular street traffic during daytime hours. Cities with high levels of pollution must meet the deadline (1975–1976) for air-quality standards established under the 1970 Clean Air Act. Meeting such standards is particularly difficult for a dispersed city, such as Los Angeles, that is built upon the assumption that everyone drives private automobiles everywhere. For such dispersed cities, gasoline rationing has been proposed as the only currently practicable means of substantially reducing pollution from automobiles, to say nothing of conserving energy.

Unfortunately, in spite of the growing concern over pollution and the urban environment, the number of automobiles continues to multiply. There are currently some 110 million automobiles on the road, and it is estimated that there will be 160 million by 1985. Automobile registrations are increasing at a rate of 3.5 times the birth rate, according to one estimate.[27] By the end of the 1970s, the volume of traffic is expected to increase to a point which will make today's traffic congestion seem minor. The volume is projected to go up 40 percent in Pittsburgh, 50 percent in Boston, 90 percent in Detroit, and 100 percent in Los Angeles.[28] Whether energy crises or environmental concerns will seriously modify the accuracy of this projection remains to be seen.

### Expressways

Urban expressways, which have accelerated suburbanization and changed the ecological structure of the metropolitan area, are increasingly becoming a dirty word to residents of central cities. In the 1950s, when the present program of urban expressways began, the roads appeared as a boon to both hard-pressed mayors and downtown merchants. Central-city businessmen liked the roads because they were a sign to local boosters that the city was again on the move—and, more important, the expressways were expected to raise downtown property values and lead to a rebirth of downtown shopping areas. Mayors welcomed the roads because they would reduce traffic congestion, halt the exodus to the suburbs, and provide a host of short-term construction jobs for the party faithful. About the only dissenting voices were those of the people who were to be displaced and whose homes were to be destroyed so the roads could be built. But no one really was listening to them. After all, federal funds were paying 90 percent of the costs of the expressway, and who could turn down a bargain like that?

Today there are increasing doubts about what has been created and a growing consensus that only for exceptional reasons should additional

[27]Senator Claiborne Pell, *Megalopolis Unbound,* Praeger, New York, 1966, p. 63.
[28]"Cars and Cities on a Collision Course," *Fortune,* February, 1970, p. 125.

expressways be built through urban areas. Mayor Daley's attempt to build a crosstown expressway through Chicago's West Side is an exception to the pattern. In cities from Boston to San Francisco, the expressways have uprooted established neighborhoods and detrimentally affected the cities' economic bases by taking tremendous amounts of property permanently off the tax rolls. Those displaced by the expressways frequently move out of the city, contributing their energies—and taxes—to the suburbs. Nor did the superroads lead to the rejuvenation of downtown retail trade. It turned out that the same road which could take someone downtown could also take him or her out to a new suburban shopping center—and the shopping center had the additional advantage of providing someplace to park the car. Expressways also greatly reduced the time necessary to get from a suburban home to a city job, thus nullifying one of the major advantages of central-city residence. Expressways directly accelerated the exodus from the city and the development of suburban housing tracts along the right of way. Thus metropolitan areas have come to take on the same shape—that of a star or the spokes of a wheel—that cities had at the beginning of the twentieth century. The difference—in addition to scale—is that in 1900 the spokes were railway or streetcar lines and today they are expressways.

Many of the first expressways were both necessary and useful; better mobility had to be provided. But the rationale for new central-city expressways has become increasingly questionable. In San Francisco, only a citizens' revolt stopped the construction of an ugly elevated freeway along the bay which would have destroyed one of the city's principal aesthetic advantages.

An example of a totally useless road is Boston's I–93 connector, which is universally agreed to have been a "$100 million misunderstanding." The expressway displaced hundreds of families and took six years to complete—and goes nowhere. Far from relieving the massive traffic jams from Boston's northern suburbs, I–93 is acknowledged to make them worse and more dangerous. City fathers, private citizens, the mayor, and even the governor have acknowledged that building this road was a huge mistake. The expressway stands, unused and unloved, a monument to the expressway-building euphoria of the 1960s. Mayor Kevin White's transportation advisor has suggested that the road simply be closed to all traffic. In his words: "I think it's better to admit the mistake and not use the damn thing."[29] Wags call the road "the world's longest bowling alley," but no one really knows what to do with it. Bostonians wish it would just go away. There was, however, one positive result: Governor Francis

[29]*Newsweek*, February 12, 1973, p. 32.

Sargent declared a moratorium on all building of highways in the urban areas of Massachusetts. In spite of the cries of the powerful highway lobby, no more six- or eight-lane roads are to be built through city neighborhoods. The emphasis in the future will be on providing adequate mass transit. The governor took a political gamble, cancelling $1 billion in planned urban expressways and barring any increase in parking areas in central cities.

The emphasis on mass transit is due not only to increased sentiment against expressways, but also to tough new federal antipollution standards. However, building up transit systems and freezing downtown parking may not be enough. Many of North America's major metropolitan areas may eventually have to face up to gasoline rationing.

### Rapid Transit

Despite considerable opposition from the highway and road-construction lobbies, there is increasing pressure for the government to encourage the building of rapid transit systems which would enjoy the same subsidies we now provide to trucks and private cars. The need for rapid transit systems is obvious. A single freeway lane can carry at most only 3,000 persons an hour (at an average occupancy rate of 1.5 persons per automobile). Buses can increase the capacity to 15,000 persons per hour. But rapid transit has a far higher capacity. A single rapid transit track is capable of carrying 60,000 persons an hour—the equivalent of 20 freeway lanes.[30] It is apparent that changes in social organization, such as laws encouraging rapid transit, are necessary if we are to use available transportation technology to save our environment. At present, 86 percent of the nation's commuters use private automobiles, 10 percent use buses, and only 4 percent use rail systems.

Commuters are reluctant to use rail transportation because many of the existing systems are antiquated and high-priced. The North Western commuter trains out of Chicago are known as one of the few reliable systems. In public-owned transit, the Bay Area Rapid Transit (BART) system in the San Francisco Bay area is capable of carrying up to 200,000 riders a day in clean, modern, comfortable, and quiet cars. Far too often, however, public transportation means poor transportation. No city in the United States has a subway system to match that of Montreal, where the cars are modern and have rubber-tired wheels. In spite of unprecedented urban growth, mass transit systems have been forced by economics to cut back on routes and services. There were 15.2 billion riders on various

[30]John B. Ray, *The Road and the Car in American Life*, M.I.T. Press, Cambridge, Mass., 1971, p. 281.

San Francisco Bay Area's BART system is a far cry from the antiquated subway and elevated systems of the East Coast. (*Photophile.*)

mass transit systems in 1930, but by 1970 this figure had been more than halved, to 7.3 billion riders. Without adequate public subsidy, the use of mass transit will decrease even further. Europeans do not expect local transit lines to make a profit; public transportation is viewed as a common utility or service that benefits all. Americans are only now coming to see the metropolitan area as an economically integrated unit demanding public transit.

A great deal of the present problem in mass transit can be traced to a decision made by Congress in 1956 to solve the transportation crisis of that date by authorizing 41,000 miles of freeways to be built over a period of sixteen years at a cost of $41 billion.[31] The highway lobby, a nationwide interest group of tire companies, gasoline companies, truckers, highway department officials, and the American Automobile Association, succeeded in their lobbying for a highway trust fund, outside the regular federal budget, which could be used only for the purpose of building more highways. A federal tax on gasoline, tires, and other transportation related goods and activities keeps the fund quite solvent.

For over a decade and a half no funding of any sort was provided by

[31]Wilfred Owen, *The Metropolitan Transportation Problem*, The Brookings Institute, Washington, D.C., 1956, p. 213.

the highway trust fund for aid to mass transit systems. In effect, the government subsidized and encouraged the use of private automobiles over mass transit. The results have been predictable: in the first fifteen years after the passage of the legislation to subsidize freeways, over 200 bus companies went out of business. In 1970, there were 357 fewer transit companies, 25,500 fewer vehicles, and significantly fewer passengers for mass transit than there had been in 1950.[32] This was in spite of a national population increase of over 50 million. The decision to support the technology of freeways and the private automobile has resulted in today's environmental and energy problems. Today we are at last allotting funds for mass transit, but the sums are still meager compared with the subsidies for automobiles and trucks.

[32]Leslie Tass, *Modern Rapid Transit,* Carlton Press, New York, 1971.

Part Four

# Urbanization in the Third World

Chapter 13

# The Developing World: Introduction and Overview

*Men make the city, and not walls or ships without men in them.*
Thucydides

*What is the city but the people?*
Shakespeare

Two-thirds of the world's population resides in developing countries, and it is in these countries that the most dramatic changes in the levels of urbanism and urbanization are currently taking place. At the present rate of growth in developing countries, large-city populations *double* every 13.5 years. Put in raw numbers, the developing world added 260 million city inhabitants to the world's population between 1950 and 1970. During this same period, the population of cities of 100,000 or more grew in developing countries at the spectacular rate of 67 percent per decade.[1]

[1]Kingsley Davis, "Burgeoning Cities in Rural Countries," in Scientific American's *Cities: Their Origin, Growth, and Human Impact*, Freeman, San Francisco, 1973, p. 220.

This rate of urban growth is far in excess of that experienced by North America and Europe during their greatest periods of urban expansion in the nineteenth century. Moreover, there is no sign that the pace is slackening. Projections made by the United Nations indicate that a full 85 percent of the world population increase that will take place between 1970 and 2000 will take place in developing countries, much of it in the cities.

While the developing world is still overwhelmingly rural, it already contains over one-third of the world's urban population and some of the world's largest cities. The urban population in developing countries is now greater than that of all the world's cities as recently as 1950. Urban populations in the developing world are expanding and will continue to expand well into the next century; and while each city and nation is in some way unique, the developing world as a whole shares certain characteristics.

## EFFECTS OF POPULATION GROWTH

Any discussion of developing countries and their cities must begin with some understanding of the amount and meaning of current rates of population growth. During the period from 1960 to 1970, the developing world, if China is included, increased in total population by half a billion persons. The medium estimate of population growth made by the United Nations is that the developing countries, not including China, will double from 1.8 billion people in 1970 to 3.6 billion in the year 2000. For Latin America alone the population projected for 2000 is almost 2 1/2 times its size in 1970.[2] Increases of this magnitude are certain to create almost unbearable pressures for food, better living conditions, more education, and more employment.

Zero population growth may be a potential reality in Europe, the United States, and Japan; but it is still only a slogan in the developing world, where the combined population of the various countries is currently increasing by more than 50 million persons a year. This means an additional 50 million persons a year who must be fed, clothed, housed, and otherwise provided for before the developing countries can even begin to improve the quality of life for those already present.

Much of the present population explosion, with its yearly national population increases of 2 1/2 and even 3 1/2 percent (2 percent doubles a population in only 35 years; 3 1/2 percent, in less than 20 years) can be traced to the importation from the West of basic information about public health and medicine. After World War II, death rates were reduced

[2]Irene B. Taeuber, "Population Growth in Less Developed Countries," in Philip M. Hauser, *The Population Dilemma*, Prentice-Hall, Englewood Cliffs, N. J., 1969, p. 42.

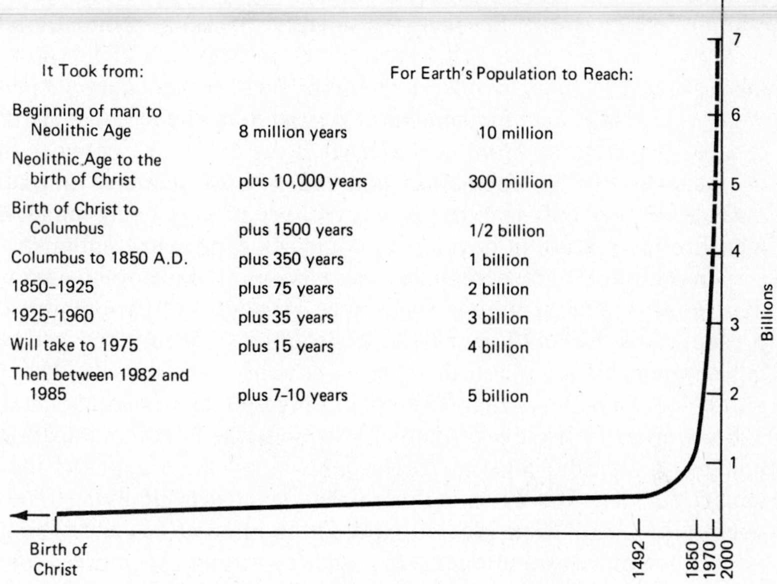


The world population explosion, and the urban population explosion, is largely the product of the last 200 years. (Shirley Foster Hartley, *Population Quantity vs. Quality,* Englewood, N. J., Prentice-Hall, 1972, fig. 1–2, p. 5. By permission of Prentice-Hall, Inc.)

drastically and at little cost but were not accompanied by other changes in the social or economic fabric of the societies. Malaria, for example, was largely eradicated by the decision of a handful of officials in government ministries to spray DDT from airplanes. On the other hand, the decision to restrict the number of births must be made by millions of individual couples, who then have to be provided with proper information and contraceptives so that they can effectively carry out their decision. Even when a society favors small families, it is not always possible to implement such values.

National population increases greatly exacerbate already serious problems, including problems of economic development. Funds that could be devoted to economic development are instead consumed in providing minimal subsistence and service to an ever-increasing number of people. Rather than investing capital, some developing nations are forced to spend it in order to meet, even marginally, the needs of their growing populations. Developing countries "have forty to forty-five percent of their population under age fifteen as contrasted with a maximum of twenty-five to thirty percent in the highly industrialized countries."[3] The accepted rule of thumb is that the percent of national income which must be invested merely to keep productivity from declining is some three times the annual percent rate of increase in the labor force.[4] In other words, if the labor force is growing by 3 percent a year, it will take a net investment of 9 percent of the national income just to keep productivity from declining. It is the difference between the rate of increase of the population and the rate of increase of industrial production that tells whether or not real progress is being made. By this measure the picture in developing countries is not very optimistic.

In addition to the economic demands put on developing countries by new mouths to feed, there are also increasing demands from those already present. This "revolution of rising expectations" occurs because increasing numbers of people in developing countries—and particularly in the cities—become aware that their condition of poverty is not the immutable natural order of life everywhere. Developments in communication technology—first radio and now even television—have exposed the urban underclasses to the existence of higher standards of living. The urban populations, with their greater exposure to alternatives and their greater awareness of nontraditional ways of life, have expectations for themselves and their children; and governments that ignore these expectations do so at their own risk.

## RICH COUNTRIES AND POOR COUNTRIES

Developing countries vary in their rates of development, but they all suffer in varying degrees from common problems such as low industrial output, low rates of savings, poor roads and communication, a high proportion of the labor force engaged in agriculture, insufficient medical services, inadequate school systems, high rates of illiteracy, poor diets, and sometimes malnutrition. The developing countries contain two out of three of the world's people, but they account for only one-sixth of the world's income, one-third of the food production, and one-tenth of the industrial output.[5]

It is thus quite clear that the term "developing country" is a euphemism. Various other terms, such as "modernizing country," "Third World country," and "noncommitted country," have been used, and they sometimes reflect ideological differences, but essentially they are all polite ways of saying "poor country." While the difference between the

[3]Ansley J. Coale, "Population and Economic Development," in Hauser, op. cit., p. 61.

[4]Coale, op. cit., p. 70.

[5]Irwin Isennberg, *The Developing Nations: Poverty and Progress,* Columbia University Press, New York, 1969, p. 13.

developed and the underdeveloped countries is usually phrased less harshly, the major distinction is that one category includes the "haves" and the other the "have-nots."

This rich-poor classification cuts across conflicting ideological systems. Developed nations, whether capitalistic or communistic, whether in Europe, Asia, or the Western Hemisphere, all have urban-industrial economies. Developing countries are so named because of their relationship to the economic power of the developed countries, which are used as the standard of comparison. "Development" is thus a relative rather than an absolute state. Newly developing countries are underdeveloped in the context of an economic comparison with Europe, the United States, or the Soviet Union. Whether the indigenous economic organization of a developing country is simple or complex—and in many cases it is extremely complex—it is invariably a traditional system and not a modern industrialized urban economy.

Economically, the developing nations of Asia, Africa, and Latin America—unless they have oil or other valuable resources—find themselves locked into a system where prices for the raw products they produce remain relatively stable while the cost of imported goods skyrockets. Such nations are seeking to achieve industrial development while the marketplace in which they must operate is largely controlled by the developed nations.

Moreover, data indicate that for many developing nations the status of "underdevelopment" may become relatively permanent; for while the poor nations are not getting poorer—as a whole—the rich nations are certainly getting richer. As a result, the gap between the developed and developing nations is increasing rather than decreasing. A survey of 150 nations by the Department of Social and Economic Affairs of the United Nations shows that in the decade 1960–1970 the per capita output of the developed countries rose 43 percent compared with an increase of only 27 percent in the developing countries.

## EMPLOYMENT, INDUSTRIALIZATION AND ECONOMIC DEVELOPMENT

Of all the common problems faced by the cities in developing countries, the problem of providing employment is, next to that of population growth, the most severe. The situation is quite different from that faced by the economically advanced Western countries during their earlier periods of urban-industrial expansion. In the era of Western industrialization during the last century, farmers and peasants were drawn to the city because of the economic opportunities it offered. Jobs, both in manufacturing and services, were generally available; and there was a solid demand for unskilled, if low-paid, workers. This was true both in Europe and North America.

The experience of the developing countries has been quite different. Workers flood into the cities, not because of the availability of jobs, but because the situation in the rural areas and small villages is even worse. People are being pushed to the cities by rural overpopulation rather than being drawn there by urban economic expansion.

In the vast majority of developing countries, the modern sector of the economy is only a small portion of the whole. Thus, in spite of some gains in industrial productivity and some increases in the gross national income, the rate of unemployment remains high. Industrialization starting from the low base found in the developing world has only a marginal effect on employment even when the *rate* of industrialization is relatively high.[6] Modern industrialization, unlike that in the United States during the latter part of the nineteenth century, does not require tremendous numbers of unskilled laborers. In developing countries it is common for the urban unemployment rate to be one-fourth of the labor force, and underemployment among those who do have jobs is also widespread.

## SQUATTER SETTLEMENTS

Another serious urban problem of developing countries is the mushrooming of shantytowns of squatters around major cities. Nowhere in the developing world has the growth of housing been able to keep pace with the urban population explosion. Consequently, principal cities are usually surrounded by "suburban" shantytowns that house the most recent newcomers to the city. These slums are called *barriedas, favelas, bustees,* or *bidonvilles* in various countries, but everywhere their function is the same—to house those who have the least resources and nowhere else to go. In many cities squatter settlements house over one-third of the total urban population.

Shanties and shacks are built in random fashion out of whatever refuse material the builder can salvage. Old packing crates, loose lumber, and odd pieces of metal are somehow patched together to provide a shelter. Since shantytowns almost by definition are illegally occupying the land on which they are built, they cannot demand city services. Streets, police and fire protection, and—most important—sanitary services are usually nonexistent. Water almost always has to be carried from the nearest public tap. Schools are rare. Electricity is the most commonly found utility, since wires can easily be strung from shack to shack.

[6]Gunnar Myrdal, *Asian Drama,* vol. 2, Pantheon, New York, 1968, pp. 1174–1175.

Venezuela is typical of developing countries in that its growing cities are surrounded by squatter settlements. *(Alain Keler/Editorial Photocolor Archives.)*

Health problems are exacerbated by the crowding and lack of proper disposal for sewage and refuse, and by the fact that the settlements are frequently built on the least desirable terrain, such as city dumps, marshlands, or hillsides. Attempts by the government to remove squatters are invariably unsuccessful: if one slum is destroyed, another is built overnight with the refuse from the earlier settlement. When no other city housing is available, there is little alternative to the squatter settlements.

The problem of providing housing for migrants is not, however, unique to the Third World. In spite of its massive housing program, the Soviet Union still must use shantytowns to house part of its urban population. In France, the *bidonvilles* ("tin-can towns") surrounding Paris house some 100,000 homeless North Africans and Portuguese migrants in haphazard wood-and-cement structures that lean one against another under their corrugated iron roofs. Abandoned buses provide homes for the more fortunate.

Squatter slums will remain as part of the urban scene in the developing world for many decades unless there is a precipitous decline in migration to the cities and a massive increase in foreign aid from more fortunate nations—and no one predicts that either of these conditions will be met.

## DENSITY AND ECONOMIC DEVELOPMENT

It should be noted that there is no clear relationship between density *per se* and the level or rate of economic development. High agricultural density is usually seen as a sign of underdevelopment, and high urban densities may or may not be desirable, depending on the level of economic development.

High densities of rural, and particularly agricultural, labor indicate inefficient agricultural production and a surplus of manpower which is either unemployed or underemployed. In closed extractive economies—such as farming, lumbering, and mining—the employment of a high proportion of the labor force in such pursuits means smaller average holdings. India, for example, employs about 70 percent of its labor force in agriculture, with an average holding of about 2 acres for every person of working age (fifteen to sixty-five years of age). Since the possibility of bringing new lands under cultivation is limited, any increases in agricultural densities inevitably mean less land per person.

In developed urban areas, where nonextractive industries dominate and a large volume of trade is possible, density is frequently an advantage rather than a liability. The industrial ring cities of the Netherlands and the Rhine River urban complex of Germany both have extremely high densities and high standards of living. Hong Kong provides an even more extreme example. Hong Kong has a population of 4 million crowded on a land area of 398 square miles: this comes out to about 10,000 persons per square mile. Nonetheless, Hong Kong has for years managed to increase its GNP at a rate far in excess of the rest of the world. Hong Kong has practically no natural resources, but it is blessed with a literate, energetic, and trained labor force. Its extremely high population density has not prevented Hong Kong from achieving one of the highest levels of per capita income in Asia.

This in no way suggests, of course, that high densities automatically result in high income levels and economic expansion. However, high density *can* be an advantage to a highly organized and heavily industrialized economy. The city concentrates large numbers of people in one place and thus minimizes what has been called "the friction of space." Production can be concentrated in one place; the city itself is a massive factory. Technological breakthroughs in transportation and communication also are means of overcoming the friction of space and allow the city to export both to its rural hinterland and to other urban areas.

In the noneconomic sphere, population concentration also permits and encourages specialized educational, cultural, and scientific organizations. Accumulations of personal and capital resources necessary for the emergence of such organizations can be found only in the city. The requirements of urban living also produce new problems, such as housing, sanitation, and the prevention of crime; and the necessity of dealing with these problems leads to an emphasis on innovation and rational problem solving.

The requirements of contemporary urban life and those of industrialization complement one another. Both emphasize the importance of adapting to changing conditions. Urbanization and industrialization are not the same thing, but it is not surprising that industrialism in the Third World is directly associated with the growth of urban areas and the spread of urban ideas.

## OVERURBANIZATION

Closely related to the question of density is that of overurbanization. The term "overurbanization" generally implies the belief that a particular developing country has too high a proportion of its population residing in cities, at densities detrimental to health, morals, and general well-being. Most important, "overurbanization" commonly is take to mean that the urban population of a nation is too large in relation to the extent of its economic development. Egypt, for instance, is far more urbanized than its degree of economic development would lead one to expect: indeed, it is more urbanized than France or Sweden, both industrial nations. Some urbanists refer to Egypt, therefore, as being overurbanized.[7]

While there has been some attempt to keep the term "overurbanization" free of any connotation of values, the concept usually does have negative connotations: it suggests that overurbanization is both artificial and harmful to economic growth. As one United Nations publication expressed it:

> Thus the recent rapid rate of urbanization visible in Asian countries does not bespeak of a corresponding growth of industry but of a shift of people from low productive agricultural employment to yet another section marked by low productivity employment, namely handicraft production, retail trading, domestic services in urban areas.[8]

[7]See, for example, Kingsley Davis and Hilda Hertz Golden, "Urbanization and the Development of Pre-Industrial Areas," *Economic Development and Cultural Change,* **3**:6–26, October, 1954.

[8]*Urbanization in Asia and the Far East,* Proceedings of the Joint UN/UNESCO Seminar held in Bangkok, August 8–18, 1956, UNESCO, Calcutta, 1957, p. 133.

Certainly it is true that many rural peasants migrate to the cities not because jobs are available there but because high rural densities are forcing them off the land. People go to the city because there really is nowhere else to go, and the city at least offers the possibility of finding a marginal job or powerful sponsor. However, the whole picture is not as glum as the term "overurbanization" suggests, for the productivity of the rural in-migrants is higher in the city than in the rural areas, and per capita incomes in cities are almost universally higher than in rural areas.[9]

If the concept of overurbanization is meant to suggest the undesirability of rapid urbanization in developing countries, the argument is difficult to prove. Certainly the data do not support the belief that rapid urbanization slows or impedes economic development. Life may be difficult in the city, but it is not better in the countryside: and in the city there is at least always hope and the possibility of something better. Experts may debate the issue, but all over the world peasants are voting with their feet in favor of city life.

It can be argued that the rapid growth of cities is a positive sign of the social and economic development of an area.[10] The city is not only the first area to reflect change, but also a source of change. City growth is correlated with the change from agriculturalism to industrialism, with economic rationality, with lower birth and death rates, with increased literacy and education—in short, with the whole process of modernization. Insofar as urbanization is associated with the development of a modernized mode of life, the problem in much of the developing world is not overurbanization but underurbanization.

## PRIMATE CITIES

A characteristic common to most developing countries is the "primate" city. A primate city is a principal city overwhelmingly large in comparison with all other cities in the country. In some countries, the primate city may be of major international size while the next largest city is hardly more than a town; the primate city is frequently the only city of note.[11] Commonly, within developing countries there is no hierarchy of cities of various sizes such as that found in developed nations, and primate cities most frequently occur in countries with relatively low overall levels of urbanization. Ethiopia, for example, is 95 percent rural and has few

[9]N. V. Sovani, "The Analysis of Over-Urbanization," *Economic Development and Cultural Change,* **12:**113–122, January, 1964.

[10]See, for example, Kingsley Davis and Anna Casis, "Urbanization in Latin America," *The Milbank Memorial Fund Quarterly,* **24:**186, April, 1946.

[11]Mark Jefferson, "The Law of the Primate Cities," *Geographical Review,* **29:**226–232, April, 1939.

The ultramodern Government Square of Nairobi, Kenya, with the inevitable symbol of Western influence, the Hilton Hotel. *(Editorial Photocolor Archives.)*

towns; but its capital city, Addis Ababa, has over 1 million inhabitants.

Most primate cities owe their origin and development to European colonialism. Cities such as Accra, Nairobi, Saigon, Hanoi, Singapore, and Hong Kong do not have long histories as urban places but rather were created consciously by colonial powers in order to establish bases from which they could exercise administrative and commercial control. They were established as little "Europes-in-Asia" or "Europes-in-Africa." Thus, they were usually located along the coasts in order to facilitate communication with, and transportation of raw material to, the mother country. From the very first, the orientation of the primate city was toward other cities in the developed countries rather than toward its own hinterland; and this pattern of commerce and culture coming from the outside has largely endured to this day.

Primate cities are most likely to be found when one of three circumstances exists. First, they occur in countries that were political and economic dependents of other countries. Second, they may occur in countries which now are small but once had extensive areas (examples are Vienna, Austria, which once controlled the Austro-Hungarian Empire; and Dakar, which was until the early 1960s the administrative center for French West Africa). Third, they occur in countries where the extent of economic development does not require cities of middle size.[12] A study based on worldwide data found the existence of primate cities to be associated with a number of other circumstances. These were: (1) dense populations in small areas; (2) low per capita income; (3) export-oriented and agricultural economies; (4) a colonial history; and (5) a rapid population growth.[13]

The concentration of population and economic activity in primate cities presents some typical features throughout the developing world:

**1** In the earlier stages, the economies of such cities were primarily export-oriented, and the cities also specialized in political and administrative activities. Today, manufacturing and services are the primary economic activities.

**2** Economic advantages result from the concentration of industry. Thus, income from peripheral areas finds its way to the metropolitan area. The higher rate of return attracts more capital: and this in turn leads to more enterprises, particularly services.

**3** The concentration of industrial activities—and above all the accompanying services—increases employment. Skilled manpower is attracted from peripheral locations. Thus, the city represents an advantage in terms of quality as well as quantity.

**4** Concentration of population and economic activities goes hand in hand with the centralization of administrative activity. The decision-making power of the primate city increases, while that of outlying cities and towns decreases. The center thus receives the lion's share of the available investment funds.

**5** The basic infrastructure of the nation is heavily determined by the requirements of the major city. This in turn encourages further concentration.[14]

[12]Brian J. Berry, "City Size Distribution and Economic Development," *Economic Development and Cultural Change,* **9:**573–581, July, 1961.

[13]Arnold S. Linsky, "Some Generalizations Concerning Primate Cities," *Annals of the Association of American Geographers,* **55:**506–513, September, 1965.

[14]Based on information in "Some Regional Development Problems in Latin America Linked to Metropolitanization," *Economic Bulletin for Latin America,* United Nations, New York, **17:**58–62, 1972.

Growth and economic development lead to further concentration, which in turn leads to further growth. Without anyone's really planning it that way the primate city comes more and more to dominate the rest of the country economically, politically, and socially. Government, education, and commerce all are located in the principal city, and this concentration produces further concentration. Urban-bred civil servants and teachers are reluctant to give up the advantages of the relatively cosmopolitan city for the backward rural hinterland. The new political independence of former colonies has only accelerated this trend, for the capital of a new nation takes on additional symbolic significance, and political officials and hopefuls now concentrate there.

A number of negative effects of such concentration have been noted. Hoselitz notes the suggestion that these cities are parasitic because they (1) rob the countryside of valuable manpower, (2) consume all available investment funds, (3) all but prevent the development of other cities, (4) dominate the cultural pattern and lead to the breakdown of the traditional culture, and (5) tend to have a high rate of consumption as opposed to production.[15]

### Value of Concentration

While some of this may be true, the overall impression is a distortion. Many smaller developing countries simply cannot support more than one major city at their present state of development. In time a structure of intermediate-size cities will no doubt emerge, but meanwhile there frequently is no alternative to the primate city. Whatever its faults, the primate city is the center of economic and social change. The movements for independence received their ideas and their support from the urban population; and the present governments, even in rural countries, are overwhelmingly led and staffed by urban dwellers. The very idea of a civil service is an urban concept. Hoselitz has argued for the primate cities as follows:

> The primate cities of Asia are the most important centers of cultural change, especially in those fields which vitally affect economic development; advance education, new forms of business organization, new administrative practices, and last but not least new technologies find a fertile soil in them, their intermediate position between East and West, their contact with world markets of commodities and ideas, their land of many traditional bonds make them into eminently suitable vehicles for the introduction of new ideas and new techniques.[16]

[15]Bert F. Hoselitz, "The City, The Factory, and Economic Growth," *American Economic Review*, **45:**166–184, May, 1955.

[16]Bert F. Hoselitz, "Urbanization and Economic Growth in Asia," *Economic Development and Cultural Change*, **6:**43, October, 1957. By permission of the University of Chicago Press.

Incomplete data indicate that the influence of the largest city over other urban places and rural areas is increasing rather than declining. This is true not only in Asia and Africa but also in Latin America. In Latin America, even in countries such as Colombia which formerly possessed some degree of regional balance, there is a clear trend toward concentration in a single metropolitan area.[17] In Chile, the primate city of Santiago grew in spite of a national policy of decentralization. Not only did Santiago's population grow at a faster rate than other cities (7 percent), but the city's gross domestic product also grew at a faster rate (6.7 percent, as opposed to 4.9 percent for the country, between 1960 and 1968).[18] The only known exception in Latin America to the pattern of primate cities is Mexico, where the high growth rate of Mexico City is being outdistanced by some vigorous smaller cities.[19] Almost everywhere else in the Third World, primate cities are becoming increasingly dominant.

## CONCLUSION

The expansion of an urban-industrial way of life into traditional societies not only is permitting the developing countries to expand their populations; it is changing their entire way of life. Urban-industrialization is not gradually transforming traditional societies throughout the world; rather, it is bursting them asunder and upsetting traditional attitudes, beliefs, customs, and behaviors. Scholars and politicians can debate whether or not these changes are for the better, but what is certain is that urban-industrial growth means change—a great deal of change.

[17]"Some Regional Development Problems in Latin America Linked to Metropolitanization," *Economic Bulletin for Latin America,* United Nations, New York, **17**:77, 1972.

[18]Op. cit., pp. 64–68.

[19]United Nations Commission for Latin America, "Urbanization and Distribution of Population By Site of Locality," in Gerald Breese (ed.), *The City in Newly Developing Countries,* Prentice-Hall, Englewood Cliffs, N. J., 1969, p. 196.

## Chapter 14

# Latin American Cities

*All are most beautiful, of a thousand shapes, and all accessible, and filled with trees of a thousand kinds and tall, and they seem to touch the sky; and I am told that they never lose their foliage, which I can believe, for I saw them as green and beautiful as they are in Spain.*

Christopher Columbus
*Letter to Ferdinand and Isabella of Spain on the first voyage, February 15 to March 4, 1493*

Any discussion of urbanization in the developing countries invariably points out that most Third World cities are the result of conscious decisions by European colonial powers, and that as a result most of the cities are relatively new—having been founded during the expansionist period of the late nineteenth century. But while this pattern may fit Africa and Asia, it most certainly does not apply to the situation in Latin America. Latin America already had grand cities at the time the Pilgrims were beginning to learn from the Indians how to raise corn.

## SPANISH COLONIAL CITIES

The Spanish designed their colonial cities—largely during the sixteenth century—to be remarkably similar in both ecological plan and functional purpose. Growth and development over the centuries have blunted many of the original similarities, but elements of the first cities still remain. The purpose of the cities was to serve as administrative centers and garrison posts for the Spanish military forces. The city was the center from which the mining or agricultural hinterland was to be controlled and the funnel through which wealth was to flow to the mother country. Spanish colonial cities did not enjoy the virtual independence of most of the early English towns in North America. Administrative decrees were promulgated from Spain. The Spanish Crown discouraged commercial or manufacturing activities that would make the colonial city any less dependent on Spain. The colonial pattern was practically completed by 1580, when sixteen of the twenty largest cities of today had been founded. Socially and commercially, the city looked toward Spain rather than toward its own hinterland. Cities were placed on the land; they did not grow out of it. Control and wealth were concentrated in the city. Before the period of independence (about 1825), there was little change in the social or economic organization of the colonial cities. None of them developed into manufacturing centers. The limited manufacturing and processing that did exist, such as the production of syrup and molasses and the spinning and weaving of cotton and woolen cloth, took place on the *haciendas* and other large landed estates.

The decrees governing the colonies were written in Spain by the Council of the Indies; home rule was unknown. These policies had two objectives, according to Smith: "(1) to make the colonies into producers of gold, silver, and precious stones; and (2) to limit their consumption of manufactured goods strictly to those produced in Spain, shipped in convoys from Spanish ports, and destined for a few strongly fortified seaports, of which the principal ones were Vera Cruz, Cartagena, and Callao."[1] The effect of all this was a throttling of trade and commerce as a basis for urban life in Latin American cities under Spanish domination. The merchant, who enjoyed such a prominent position in the social structure of New England, did not have equal influence in the Spanish colonies. The seaports were heavily fortified entrepots for receiving the manufactures of Spain in the annual convoys and assembling the treasure that was to be shipped to Spain on the return voyage.

[1]T. Lynn Smith, "The Changing Functions of Latin American Cities," *The Americas*, **25**:74, July, 1968.

## Physical Structure of the Cities

Physically, the Spanish colonial cities were well planned in accordance with ideas expressed by Charles V and Philip II. Legislation specified that cities be founded on unoccupied land near rivers, and that they be laid out in a manner permitting expansion.

As has been mentioned, most of the Spanish colonial cities were founded during the sixteenth century, and all except the very first were laid out according to the detailed plans set forth in the Laws of the Indies. The regulations provided for a central plaza surrounded by the cathedral and major governmental buildings. The *solares,* or house lots, were of uniform shape, and the city was laid out in a grid with intersections at right angles. Houses and grounds were to be surrounded by walls, and because of this the early cities frequently appeared to be more heavily inhabited than was actually the case. Since the cities were to serve as fortified strong points performing administrative functions for the surrounding hinterland, they were not always ideally located from the standpoint of transportation; Mexico City was located on an island in the middle of a lake. Political rather than economic considerations weighed most heavily in the location of cities. Even the legal rank of a city was a matter decided in Spain rather than in the New World.

The Spanish government did everything possible to retain a rigid class system. One edict even reserved all the top administrative, religious, and political positions for *peninsulares,* or those born in Spain. Those born in the colonies, regardless of their wealth or family position, were relegated to a secondary status—a factor that directly motivated local leaders to instigate the rebellion against Spain.

Colonial Spaniards had little interest in the countryside. Newcomers preferred to remain in the cities with their fellows. The frontier settlement or agricultural village held little of interest for these people. Farming was left to the Indians while the Spanish landlords resided in the colonial cities.

Fortunately, the grid layout of the cities offered considerable flexibility: the boundaries could be expanded as more room was needed. Additional grids were easily added by extending the straight streets and adding more identical blocks. The focus on the central plaza meant that there were no markets, walls, or storehouses at the periphery of the city to impede expansion.[2] The large lots (which the law required be enclosed by walls) initially resulted in a relatively low population density. Later,

[2]Ralph A. Gakenheimer, "The Peruvian City of the Sixteenth Century," in Glen H. Beyer (ed.), *The Urban Explosion in Latin America,* Cornell University Press, Ithaca, N. Y., 1967, p. 50.

subdivision of lots occurred, and this—and the cutting of new streets midway between existing streets—allowed the city to increase its density with relative ease.

Brazilian cities differed from the model just described in that they were not built to any standard plan such as that provided by the Law of the Indies. Cities in Brazil were few, with little influence, since the Portuguese, unlike the Spaniards, preferred to live a semifeudal existence on their estates in the country. Portuguese policy also kept towns such as Santos, Bahia, Recife, and even Rio de Janeiro small and impotent. Their splendid natural ports were open only to ships from Portugal, and this trade was not sufficient to turn these towns into real cities.

## Policy and Traditions

The differences in ecological patterns between the North American and South American cities are frequently attributed to Spanish colonial policy as typified by the Laws of the Indies.[3] However, Leo Schnore suggests that factors more powerful than "Iberian values" were apparently at work: "The fact of the matter is that the 'traditional Latin American pattern' could be observed in cities of the New World prior to the Spanish conquest."[4] He cites historical and archaeological evidence that among the pre-Colombian Aztec and Maya civilizations the elites tended to live in the centers of the great cities. This opinion is supported by a number of scholars. To quote two of them:

> The fundamental unit of the town settlement, with its core of civic and religious buildings, is dominant in all periods and in all but the most remote and inaccessible localities. Landa's classic description of the town of Yucatan can be applied with only minor variations to most of the known archeological history within the area of high culture in Meso-America: "Before the Spaniards had conquered that country, the natives lived together in towns in a very civilized fashion. . . . In the middle of the town were their temples with beautiful plazas, and all around the temples stood the houses of the lords and the priests, and those of the most important people. Thus came the houses of the richest and of those who were held in the highest estimation next to these, and at the outskirts of the town were the houses of the lower class."[5]

[3]See George A. Theodorson (ed.), *Studies in Human Ecology,* Row, Peterson, Evanston, Ill., 1961, pp. 326–327.

[4]Leo F. Schnore, "On the Spatial Structure of Cities in the Two Americas," in Philip Hauser and Leo Schnore (eds.), *The Study of Urbanization,* Wiley, New York, 1965, p. 369.

[5]Edwin M. Shook and Tatiana Proskouriakoff, "Settlement Patterns in Meso-America and the Sequency in the Guatemalan Highlands," in Gordon R. Willey (ed.), *Prehistoric Settlement Patterns in the New World,* Wenner-Gren Foundation for Anthropological Research, New York, 1956, pp. 93–100.

It is worth noting that Bishop Landa's account of Yucatan was first published in 1566. Apparently well before the Spaniards arrived, the distribution pattern of the social classes was set.

Gideon Sjoberg generalizes this pattern beyond the confines of Latin America: he suggests that it is a universal pattern of urban land usage in the nonindustrialized world—past and present. Sjoberg describes the preindustrial model as follows:

> Concentrated in the city's "central" area (often coterminous with the physical center, but not necessarily so) are the most prominent governmental and religious edifices and usually the main market. . . .
>
> The preindustrial city's central area is notable also as the chief residence of the elite. . . . Advantaged members of the city fan out toward the periphery, with the very poorest and the outcasts living in the suburbs, the farthest removed from the center. . . . [6]

In Sjoberg's words, the available materials "all confirm the universality of this land use pattern in the non-industrial civilized world."[7] This is an overstatement, but the overall pattern Sjoberg describes is no doubt accurate.

## EVOLVING PATTERNS

### The Basic Pattern

While one must be cautious of overgeneralizing, the common pattern for nonindustrial cities has been for the elites to preempt the center of the city while the poor are left the outer areas. Before the introduction of modern transportation technology, and before industrialization contaminated central areas with its noise, noxious fumes, and congestion, the central area of the city was the most pleasant and the most convenient area. This is where the elite built their homes, frequently with extensive grounds and almost always behind high walls that effectively isolated the home from the confusion of the streets and markets outside.

The pattern of high socioeconomic status in the center has also been found in North American cities before industrialization, particularly in the Old South. Heberle gives a clear account of the development of these cities:

> It seems to be characteristic for the older, smaller cities in the South that the

[6]Gideon Sjoberg, *The Preindustrial City: Past and Present*, Free Press, Glencoe, Ill., 1960, pp. 96–98.

[7]Sjoberg, op. cit., p. 98.

Plaza de los Armos in Lima, Peru, dominated by the Catholic Church. *(Alain Keler/Editorial Photocolor Archives.)*

> homes of the socially prominent families were to be found just outside the central—and only—business districts. . . . As the city grew and as wealth increased, the "old" families tended to move toward the periphery—following the general fashion of our age. . . . The old homes are then converted into rooming houses and "tourist homes."[8]

A review of seven of the most prominent sociological studies of Latin American cities indicates that the "traditional" model with its central plaza and with groups of higher socioeconomic status occupying the center rather than the suburbs, is true of all but the newest cities of Latin America.[9] According to Leo Schnore, the data suggest that the residential structure of cities evolves in a predictable direction and that this pattern is observable both in North America and, more recently, in Latin America:

[8]Rudolf Heberle, "Social Consequences of the Industrialization of Southern Cities," *Social Forces,* October, 1948, pp. 34–35.

[9]Schnore, op. cit., p. 366.

> Given growth and expansion of the center, and given appropriate improvements in transportation and communication, the upper strata might be expected to shift from central to peripheral residence, and the lower classes might increasingly take up occupancy in the central area abandoned by the elite. Despite mounting land values occasioned by the competition of alternative (nonresidential) land uses, the lower strata may occupy valuable central land in tenements, subdivided dwellings originally intended for single families, and other high-density "slum" housing arrangements.[10]

## "POET"

The ecological complex of *population, organization, environment,* and *technology* (POET) help us understand these changes. A population has to reach a certain size before highly segregated patterns of land use can be expected to develop. Sorting out people by socioeconomic status into separate neighborhoods and functional specialization can occur only when there is a large total population. The rate of growth is also significant; stagnant or slowly growing centers are not likely to resemble rapidly expanding cities. Variations in the racial and ethnic composition of a population can also affect spatial distribution, independent of economic factors. In growing cities subpopulations that are being augmented by new in-migrants can be expected to be more distinct than groups that are more socially and economically assimilated.

Of the four broad factors mentioned above (POET) we are most interested in social organization as being dependent on the other three. Preindustrial cities are generally segregated into homogeneous communities based upon ethnic, religious, language, and tribal criteria. Anyone observing the cities of developing countries is struck by the segmented nature of urban life, with different areas remaining socially—and sometimes occupationally—isolated from one another. Organizationally, the city itself is not the operating unit; rather, the city provides an unbrella for many relatively self-contained subsystems. Even when there are no physical walls and gates between areas of the city, there are lines of demarcation known to every resident.

Economic organization is also of great importance. The introduction of industrialization almost invariably leads to the development of separate factory districts, and the nature of industrialization determines the residential character of surrounding land. Few rich men build their homes in an expanding factory district. Industrialization also changes the "traditional" class system of rich and poor associated with preindustrial

[10] Schnore, op. cit., pp. 373–374.

cities, and the growth of a middle class clearly affects the spatial distribution of residential populations within the city.

Environmental factors, such as the presence or absence of highlands or bodies of water, certainly affect the spatial development of cities. However, while unique physical features have obviously shaped the growth and development of some cities, there is a surprising degree of uniformity in spatial structure from country to country, culture to culture, and continent to continent.

Technology is the variable that has done most in recent times to change the configuration of cities. As was indicated earlier, railroads and steam power did much to produce the nineteenth-century American city. Since the 1920s the automobile has permitted a form of population dispersion that was impossible earlier. The telephone and other advances in communication technology have meant that interrelated functions can be spatially separated without loss of contact and control. In Latin American cities, the elite preempted the more central areas for their residences, since these were the most accessible sites in an era of primitive transportation technology. Technological changes—automobiles, good roads, extension of power and sewage lines—have drastically reduced the attractiveness of the central city as a place of residence. Upper-class suburbanization is now emerging in Latin America on the pattern of North America.

### Early Social and Economic Structure

Following independence in the early decades of the nineteenth century, there was little or no change in Latin American social or economic structure. It was a period of consolidation, when the larger established centers continued to concentrate their economic and political power. In some ways independence, by politically separating the various new nations, encouraged the capital cities to become more provincial rather than more metropolitan.

The development of a middle class was inhibited by the stunted economic growth of the cities. Merchants and businessmen were looked down upon socially; for membership in the elite, one's income was expected to come from land holdings rather than manufacture or trade. As a result, the city—in contrast to cities in North America—was a political rather than an economic center:

> Political considerations and motivations, rather than economic or social, have historically controlled urbanization in Latin America. The city has, therefore, often emerged as an imposition, an appendage, tacked onto a relatively underdeveloped agricultural countryside—the military centers of

> the Aztecs, the political centers of the Incas, the political towns of the Spaniards, the political capitals of the nineteenth century republican cities of Latin America. Not only has the city not grown out of the economic needs or in relation to the socioeconomic development of its surrounding area; it has until very recently been divorced from the national reality.[11]

The growth of the middle class in the nineteenth century, when it did occur, was due in large part to the technological changes in transportation previously mentioned, and to immigration. The railroad and later the highway opened up new territories, territories that could be developed with the newly emerging agricultural technology. Also, in the latter years of the nineteenth century, waves of European immigrants brought about the formation of new urban institutions. Simultaneously, a new professional middle class and an urban bureaucracy began to develop.

However, this middle class, the most important group in economic growth and industrial development, further weakened its possible influence by allying itself with the upper classes and against the urban proletariat. Upper-middle-class professional groups were either excluded from the decision-making process or became so involved with the establishment that they ceased to be a force for political change. The urban middle class, which so dominates political life in North America and Europe, has had relatively little influence on national policy in most Latin American nations.

Politics in Latin America are still in a state of flux, with coup and counter coup often being an established way of life. In some countries, democratic forms are merely a facade to cover authoritarian regimes. Latin America throughout its history has lacked the type of democratic political stability that would contribute to the emergence of a substantial urban middle class.

## RECENT URBAN GROWTH

The Latin American cities of today are far from the sleepy towns of the turn of the century. Urbanization in Latin America is currently proceeding at a phenomenal rate. As recently as 1950, 39 percent of the population lived in places of 20,000 or more, but this figure had risen to 50 percent in 1960 and was expected to be 57 percent in 1975.[12] Another estimate for 1975, made by the Centro Latinoamericano de Demografia (CELADE), is almost identical: 56.5 percent. What this means is that Latin America is currently experiencing the most dynamic and critical phase of the process

[11]James Scobie, quoted in Glenn H. Beyer, op. cit., p. 63.
[12]Carmen A. Miro, "The Population of Latin America," *Demography*, **1**:21–24, 1964.

Modern Mexico City, as seen from Plaza Insurgentes. *(Herb Taylor, Jr./Editorial Photocolor Archives.)*

of urbanization. Within the period of a lifetime Latin America's being transformed from a rural, agriculturally oriented continent to one that is predominantly urbanized and urban-oriented. The process of urbanization, which took over a century in North America, is being compressed into a few short decades in Latin America.

Most North Americans still think of Latin America as a basically rural continent. Certainly, they don't think of it as being more urbanized than Europe; but that is in fact the case. Data compiled by the United Nations indicate that in 1970 the extent of urbanization in South America was 54 percent, or just above that in Europe: 53 percent (the figure for North America was 64 percent). Latin American cities are growing at an annual rate of 4.5 percent a year, compared with a much slower rural growth rate of only 1.4 percent a year. As recently as 1960, only four countries had more than 60 percent of their population living in cities; by 1975, this figure was up to eleven countries. In 1930 Latin America had only one city of over a million; by 1980 this number is predicted to increase to twenty-six. The greatest growth has been in the very largest cities. Latin America is a continent of primate cities, with 20 percent of its population in cities of over 100,000 inhabitants. Mexico City first reached the 1 million mark in 1930; today it has over 6 million inhabitants, and by 1980 the population in its metropolitan area may exceed 10 million.

Lima, Peru, street life complete with Coca-Cola sign. *(Alain Keler/ Editorial Photocolor Archives.)*

Figures for the entire continent, of course, cloud variations among nations. The range of urbanization in Latin American countries is great. Haiti has under 10 percent of its population in places of 20,000 or more, while Argentina, Chile, and Uruguay are among the most urbanized countries in the world. Figures for 1970 compiled by the United Nations show that Uruguay has more than 80 percent of its population living in cities and 40 percent in cities of 100,000 or more. Venezuela and Cuba are also highly urbanized. Because European and North American countries with equal levels of urbanization have much higher indices of industrialization—such as per capita consumption of energy, percent of the labor force in nonagricultural employment, level of education, and per capita income—it is sometimes maintained that Latin America is "overurbanized" for a developing region.

Taken as a whole, Latin America is considerably more urbanized than other Third World regions. It is far more urbanized than Asia and Africa, and during the 1950s it surpassed all regions except Oceania (Australia, etc.) in both rate of growth and size of the urban increment to the population.[13] The rate of growth is now probably higher in African

[13]John D. Durand and Cesar A. Pelaez, "Patterns of Urbanization in Latin America," in Gerald Breese, *The City in Newly Developing Countries*, Prentice-Hall, Englewood Cliffs, N. J., 1969, p.184.

cities, but the urban population explosion in Latin America has not slowed. Latin American cities, and particularly the largest primate cities, are growing at a rate that considerably outpaces the ability to provide urban services.

### Sources of Growth

The explosive growth of the cities comes from two sources. The first is natural increase. Cities in Latin America currently have relatively low death rates, owing to the utilization of modern programs of public health, sanitation, and vaccination. And birth rates are still high. Although high birth rates are generally a reflection of rural rather than urban norms, high fertility—which was necessary for survival in the countryside—has been transferred to the city. Children who in the past would have died now survive—and of course require an ever-increasing number of schools, jobs, and urban services.

The second source of growth is in-migration from rural areas. The contribution of migration varies from country to country, but it accounts for as much as half of the urban growth in countries such as Brazil and Venezuela.[14] Rural populations, while not growing as fast as urban populations, are still increasing, and the rural economy simply cannot support the increased numbers. Moreover, rural industrialization is decreasing the number of farm laborers required.

As has been noted before, rural dwellers are pushed from the land, rather than drawn to the cities by opportunities for employment there. Rural unemployment is simply being transferred to the cities. The annual increase in the rural population of Latin America is such that each year jobs on the land should be found for over half a million new workers.[15] The chance of finding employment for so many workers in the already overloaded agricultural sector is, however, minimal. There is already a considerable surplus in the rural labor force. According to one expert: "Under-employment in Latin American agriculture is so evident to anyone with first-hand knowledge of the agrarian situation that it is difficult to take seriously the academic debates about whether or not it exists. The CIDA studies showed that, by any common-sense definition of under-employment, from one-fifth to over one-third of the workers in Latin American agriculture are practically surplus."[16]

[14]Louis J. Ducoff, "The Role of Migration in the Demographic Development of Latin America," *The Milbank Memorial Fund Quarterly,* **43:**203, October, 1965.

[15]*Estudio Economico para America Latina,* ECLA: United Nations, 1966, pp. 41–51.

[16]Solon L. Barraclough, "Rural Development and Employment Prospects in Latin America," in Arthur J. Field (ed.), *City and Country in the Third World,* Schenkman, Cambridge, Mass., 1970, p. 106.

### Future Prospects

The largest cities continue to grow beyond the point where size and concentration produce economic advantage. In the present context it makes little sense to debate whether the cities should continue to grow or whether it would be better for the peasants to remain on the land. Whether or not planners think people should remain in rural areas, they are not going to do so. For good or ill, the cities are going to continue to grow in the foreseeable future.

Economically, it probably does not make sense to try to hold the peasants in the country or in small towns. It is sometimes argued that if rural life can be made more attractive, people will be less likely to abandon rural areas for the opportunities and advantages of the city. However, the costs of modernizing the rural sector are prohibitively high, particularly when the cities also need modernization. Rural electrification, for example, is far more expensive than providing electricity for urban slum dwellers. The same amount of money can do more for more people if it is spent in the city than if it is spent in the country. Because funds are limited, "community development" is more effectively directed toward urban populations, who by their very presence in the city have already indicated a willingness to make the changes required by the modernization process.

## CHARACTERISTICS OF URBAN INHABITANTS

Latin America is typical of the "Third World" in that half or more of the inhabitants of its largest cities are migrants from elsewhere. The Colombian census of 1964 revealed that half the inhabitants of Bogota and two-fifths of the inhabitants of other cities were in-migrants.[17] Half of the residents of Santiago are in-migrants. In Latin America, migration to cities tends to be more permanent and less seasonal than in other developing regions.[18] The city-bound migrants, like those elsewhere in the world, tend to be largely young adults. Older people are less prone to leave villages or rural areas for the opportunities and bright lights of the city.

This heavy migration of young persons, plus the population explosion—which, of course, adds only young people to the population—means that there are proportionately few people over the age of forty in the urban population. The impression of outsiders that "everyone seems

[17]"Some Regional Development Problems in Latin America Linked to Metropolitanization," *Economic Bulletin for Latin America,* United Nations, New York, 1972, p. 70.

[18]Philip M. Hauser (ed.), *Urbanization in Latin America,* UNESCO, Paris, 1961, p. 45.

so young" is borne out by the empirical data: it is common to find 40 percent or more of the population under fifteen years of age. This pattern will change somewhat as birth rates drop.

In Latin America, the pattern of sex distribution in urban areas differs from that of other developing regions. Most developing countries have an excess of males over females; Latin America has more females than males. In this respect, it is more similar to economically developed Western areas. While there is general agreement that there are more females, there is no agreement why this is the case. Perhaps the greater degree of urbanization and economic development in Latin America, compared with developing countries elsewhere in the world, accounts for the difference.

### Squatter Settlements

There is no universally accepted view of the squatter slums that ring all the great cities of Latin America. Some observers emphasize the squalor and disorganization of the squatter settlements (this is the majority view); some argue that these settlements are in effect evolving into reasonable low-income suburban housing areas (this is the minority position). Frequently, it seems that what a writer describes is not shaped as much by what he sees as by his philosophy and political beliefs. There is no unanimity.

The peripheral slums grow like mushrooms (in Chile they are called *poblaciones callampas,* which means "mushrooms") because of the population explosion and the migration of peasants from the land in search of a better life. In the metropolitan areas of Peru, the number of squatters increased from 45,000 in 1940 to 958,000 by 1960. The total population of Lima is estimated to be 4,994,788 persons as of 1975, of which 1,217,700—24.3 percent—live in *barriadas.*[19] In Caracas, the capital of Venezuela, over 35 percent of the total metropolitan population is living in squatter settlements.

In spite of government resettlement programs, it is clear that shantytown squatter settlements will be part of the Latin American urban scene for the foreseeable future. As long as the urban population continues to increase because of high birth rates and migration to the cities, the cities will continue to add more people than they can house. The Peruvian government has been more candid than most in admitting that it is unable to reduce the urban housing deficit because public investment must be directed toward developing national objectives.

One of the most interesting documents on the life of the poor in the

[19]Estimates from Peruvian national figures, 1970.

squatter shantytowns is the supposed diary of a dweller in the *favela* outside Sao Paulo, Brazil. The following are excerpts from her diary for one day in July:

> July 16 I got up. . . . I went to get the water. I made coffee. I told the children that I didn't have any bread, that they would have to drink their coffee plain and eat meat with *farinha.* I was feeling ill and decided to cure myself. I stuck my finger down my throat twice, vomited, and knew I was under the evil eye. The upset feeling left and I went to Senor Manuel, carrying some cans to sell. Everything that I find in the garbage I sell. He gave me 13 cruzeiros. I kept thinking that I had to buy bread, soap, and milk for Vera Eunice. The 13 cruzeiros wouldn't make it. I returned home, or rather to my shack, nervous and exhausted. I thought of the worrisome life that I led. Carrying paper, washing clothes for the children, staying in the street all day long. Yet I'm always lacking things, Vera doesn't have shoes and she doesn't like to go barefoot. For at least two years I've wanted to buy a meat grinder. And a sewing machine.[20]

The picture conjured up by such accounts is one of fecund, festering slums filled with dirty shacks and having no sanitary facilities, no garbage collection, and no hope of improvement. Here is another graphic account of the notorious *barriadas*:

> . . . so bestial, so filthy, so congested, so empty of light, fun, color, health, or comfort, so littered with excrement and garbage, so swarming with barefoot children, so reeking of pitiful squalor that just the breath of it makes you retch.[21]

At the other extreme, John Turner suggests that while there is some truth in the conventional image, and while some inhabitants of squatter settlements are indeed wretchedly poor, there are "many squatter settlements that are socially developing and physically self-improving suburbs rather than slums."[22] Probably the most balanced picture of the *barriadas* is provided by William Mangin's description of the same areas surrounding Lima described above:

> At worst a *barriada* is a crowded, helter-skelter hodge-podge of inadequate straw houses with no water supply and no provision for sewage disposal;

[20]From the book *Child of the Dark: The Diary of Carolina Maria de Jesus*, p. 18. Translated by David St. Clair. Copyright © 1962 by E. P. Dutton & Co., Inc., and Souvenir Press Ltd. Published by E. P. Dutton & Co., Inc., and used with their permission.

[21]James Morris, *Cities*, Harcourt Brace Jovanovich, New York, 1964, p. 227.

[22]John F. C. Turner, "Squatter Settlements in Developing Countries," in Daniel P. Moynihan (ed.), *Toward a National Urban Policy*, Basic Books, New York, 1970, pp. 256–257.

parts of many are like this. Most do have a rough plan, and most inhabitants convert their original houses to more substantial structures as soon as they can. Construction activity usually involving family, neighbors, and friends is a constant feature of *barriada* life and, although water and sewage usually remain critical problems, a livable situation is reached with respect to them.

For most of the migrants the *barriada* represents a definite improvement in terms of housing and general income, and Lima represents an improvement over the semi-feudal life of the Indian, *cholo,* or lower-class mestizo.[23]

## Urban Adjustment

The differences among writers are even more extreme when they address the issue of the life lived by the inhabitants of shantytowns. One view is that the inhabitants of the squatter settlements are set apart from the other city residents not only by their poverty but by their traditional rural orientation. Their rural backgrounds and continued rural ties mean that they remain essentially peasants, but peasants who by force of circumstance live in what is defined as an urban area. The implicit, if not explicit, assumption here is that the problem is how to integrate these nonurban people into a complex modern economic system.

A second position is that the rural character of the immigrants is considerably overemphasized and that problems of adjustment are far less severe than is commonly supposed.

The view of the city as a disorganizing force has been best expressed by sociologists such as Wilber Moore and Philip Hauser in their various writings—in particular, those done for the United Nations.[24] The general position is that the urban migrant finds himself in a marginal position in the city. Economically, he almost always enters the labor force at the bottom, and here he is in competition with thousands of others possessing the same low level of skills. More important, the migrant is socially cut off from others not only by his lack of a job but by his clothes, his language, and his customs. Emotional stress is built into a situation where the migrant has to decide which of his traditional practices to preserve and which to discard. Moreover, he is provided with few criteria for making such decisions. The resulting tension and strain are considered to be associated with antisocial behavior such as alcoholism, crime, drug addiction, and mental illness.[25]

[23]William P. Mangin, "Mental Health and Migration to Cities: A Peruvian Case," *Annals of New York Academy of Sciences,* **84:**911–917, 1960.

[24]See Bert F. Hoselitz and Wilber E. Moore (eds.), *Industrialization and Society,* UNESCO-Mouton, Paris, 1963; and Philip M. Hauser (ed.), *Urbanization in Latin America,* UNESCO, Paris, 1961.

[25]Wilber E. Moore, "Industrialization and Social Change," in Bert F. Hoselitz and Wilber E. Moore, op. cit., p. 343.

The family is also severely modified by urban life, according to this view. Customarily, it is claimed that there is an inevitable deterioration and disruption of traditional family life and a continual erosion of control by the family over individual members.[26]

Politically, slum dwellers are said to sell their vote to whoever delivers the greatest favors. The whole electoral process is said to be so remote from their lives that they are unlikely to perceive constitutionalism as a whole as having any relevance to them. Their lives are so close to the edge of disaster that gradualist and abstract orientations toward the future are not likely to develop.[27] According to this view, the in-migrant slum dweller is a ruralite awash in an urban sea—and he doesn't swim very well. When he can pick up work, he works; when he can't, he hustles, begs, or steals. While he dreams of success, his real goal is simply to get by for another day.

This picture has much in common with descriptions of the immigrants' problems of assimilation into the slums of North American cities. Louis Wirth, as you recall, defines urbanism as the mode of life of people who live in cities and are subject to its influence. These influences, it is said, act to destroy primary groups, weaken family ties, loosen the bonds of kinship, and lessen neighborliness. The result is impersonality, superficiality, anonymity in personal relations, and the substitution of large secondary organizations for the declining role played by kith and kin. To say that this is a pattern of disorganization may be an overstatement; but it is certainly a pattern of change. The disruption of family life through divorce and desertion, rejection of traditional religion, delinquency and alienation among the young, and a generally fragmented social world were some of the consequences associated with life in the slums of North American industrial cities. The newcomers, whether Irishmen, Poles, Russian Jews, or Mississippi blacks, went through a period of disorganization in which old ways were shed and new urban ways acquired. The move to the city was frequently not easy. Many families and individuals were not able to withstand the emotional as well as the physical wrenching and tearing.

### Culture of Poverty

A different view was taken by the late social anthropologist Oscar Lewis. While accepting the cultural distinctiveness of the *favela* and *barrio*

[26]For a summary emphasizing the negative effects of urban life on the individual and the family, see Gerald Breese, *Urbanization in Newly Developing Countries,* Prentice-Hall, Englewood Cliffs, N. J., 1966, pp. 86–90.

[27]See Daniel Goldrich, "Toward the Comparative Study of Politicalization in Latin America," in D. Heath and R. N. Adams (eds.) *Contemporary Cultures and Societies in Latin America,* Random House, New York, 1965, p. 369.

populations, Lewis did take issue with the generalization that these squatters and recent arrivals from the country have the same characteristics—personal isolation and social disorganization—that were associated with newly arrived North American slum dwellers. Lewis's studies described a "culture of poverty," with the poor having a provincial, locally oriented culture, whether they live in the country or in the city. Being severely deprived, slum dwellers have little ability to defer gratification, are strongly oriented to the present, and exhibit fatalism and resignation. Physically, they live in the urban area, but actually they are "enclaves within the city," isolated from the larger society.[28]

The idea of a "culture of poverty" with a strong orientation to the present rather than to the future helps explain why even slum dwellers who strike it rich by winning national lotteries seldom remain well off. Rather than invest their windfall conservatively to provide for the future, they frequently spend it to live like kings until it is gone, and then return to life in the shanty slum.

Describing his own research in Mexico City, Lewis summarized his findings as follows:

> **1** Peasants in Mexico City adapted to city life with far greater ease than one would have expected judging from comparable studies in the United States and from folk-urban theory.
>
> **2** Family life remained quite stable and extended family ties increased rather than decreased.
>
> **3** Religious life became more Catholic and disciplined, indicating the reverse of the anticipated secularization process.
>
> **4** The system of *Compadrazgo* [close ties between a child's natural father and the child's godfather] continued to be strong, albeit with some modifications.
>
> **5** The use of village remedies and beliefs persisted.[29]

Testing these findings several years later in an inner-city slum area only a short walk from the central square of Mexico City, Lewis found support for his earlier conclusions. Lower-class residents showed much less personal isolation or anonymity than one would expect on the basis of the common North American model. People moved their residences only within a very restricted area. Lifetime friendships and day-to-day contact with the same people were common. A high proportion of the residents of any particular housing settlement were related by ties of

[28]Oscar Lewis, "Urbanization Without Breakdown: A Case Study," *The Scientific Monthly,* **75:**31–41, 1952; and Oscar Lewis, "The Culture of Poverty," *Scientific American,* **215**(4):19–25, 1966.

[29]Oscar Lewis, "The Folk-Urban Ideal Types," in Philip Hauser and Leo Schnore, *The Study of Urbanization,* Wiley, New York, 1965, pp. 494–495.

kinship or friendship. Extended family ties were strong, particularly in emergencies, and most marriages occurred within the neighborhood unit.

The *vecindad,* or housing settlement, acted as a shock absorber for new rural in-migrants "because of the similarity between its culture and that of rural communities."[30] The family structure, diet, dress, and systems of belief differed little between people of rural origins and those of urban origins:

> The use of herbs for curing, the raising of animals, the belief in sorcery, and spiritualism, the celebration of the Day of the Dead, illiteracy and low level of education, political apathy and cynicism about government, and the very limited membership and participation in both formal and informal associations were just as common among persons who had been in the city for over thirty years as among recent arrivals.[31]

Thus, in Lewis's view, the urban-born and the rural-born slum dwellers share a common culture of poverty. One researcher has said that *barriada* residents "differ from the rest of the urban population more in the degree of their poverty than in their origins."[32]

### The Myth of Urban Rurality

Other researchers insist that the culture of the squatter slum dwellers is not rural at all, but essentially urban in its adaptation to the confusion, inequality, and lack of opportunity they experience in the city at large. Such researchers explicitly reject concepts such as "the culture of poverty." For example, on the basis of their work in Rio de Janeiro and Lima, Anthony and Elizabeth Leeds are extremely critical of what they refer to as "the myth of urban rurality." They maintain that the rural migration into the cities is not simply a movement of primitive peasant farmers. Rather, the in-migrants include people who have lived in large towns and villages, men who have been in the army, men who have worked abroad, and men with skills, trades, and experience in providing personal services which are needed in the city. The Leeds suspect that many of the so-called "rural values," including things such as "peasant shrewdness," also have considerable utility in an urban setting. They reject any explanations which assume that rural values persist unchanged:

> Interviews with the few people we identified as having come specifically

[30] Lewis, in Hauser and Schnore, op. cit., pp. 495–496.

[31] Ibid.

[32] Andrew C. Frank, "Urban Poverty in Latin America," *Studies in Comparative International Development,* **2**:76, 1966.

> from rural village areas of Brazil or Portugal directly contradict these assumptions more often than they confirm them. In a number of cases, the person in question appears to have adapted exceedingly rapidly to the urban and favela ambivalence and grasped vigorously what it offered. Thus, for example, the "rural" president of one favela association who had gotten training in electrical work, plumbing, and other construction skills had carried out a clever embezzlement once in office and stayed in a full term to boot, and had invested in land in the State of Rio De Janeiro where land values are appreciating rapidly.[33]

Four factors are said to operate in the selection of persons out of the total population to live in *favelas:* (1) true marginality, (2) stress, (3) economizing, and (4) taste.[34] "True marginality" refers to situations in which persons are able to manage in neither the legal nor, in some cases, the illegal economy of the city. Particularly in times of economic recession, those who are marginal to the labor supply find that they cannot get work. Robbery and thefts increase at such times, but not everyone can be successful even as a criminal. Some people are only able to vegetate, surviving somehow by begging and handouts.

"Stress" refers to situations resembling true marginality but in which the person involved is better able to manage because of greater internal or external resources. However, unpredictable situations such as loss of a job, the loss of the breadwinner, or prolonged sickness can put a family in a serious bind.

"Economizing" refers to situations where stable but limited resources have to be spread to take care of many needs. In order to achieve a goal such as moving oneself or one's children up the socioeconomic scale, the decision may be made to remain in a squatter shack (paying no rent or taxes) and to save one's money for other uses. Money can thus be saved, or even invested, rather than being eaten up by housing costs. In the *favela* it is also possible to raise garden vegetables and even some chickens. This pattern of economizing is part of the family history of the European immigrant groups who settled North America. For many in the inner city, it is still an active pattern.

Finally, "taste" refers to the situation in which someone simply prefers to live in a squatter settlement. The squatter settlement may be preferred because it is a place where one can be comfortable and free from the stresses of middle-class life. A man with a common-law wife or wives may prefer not to live in an area where there would be social

[33]Anthony Leeds and Elizabeth Leeds, "Brazil and the Myth of Urban Rurality: Urban Experience, Work, and Values in 'Squatments' of Rio De Janeiro and Lima," in Arthur J. Field (ed.), *City and Country in the Third World,* Schenkman, Cambridge, Mass., 1970, p. 233.

[34]Leeds and Leeds, op. cit., p. 243.

pressures. Also, those engaged in marginal occupations such as prostitution or petty crime find the *favela* more hospitable than other areas of the city. Finally, a person who would be a nobody elsewhere in the city might prefer to remain in a slum where he can be a big man.

Leeds and Leeds provide a useful counterweight to the more common view of the squatter slum as continuing an essentially rural cultural pattern. However, they do tend to somewhat glorify squatter settlements and to overstress the urban character of their inhabitants.

As the differences of opinion noted above indicate, the squatter settlement, like North American suburbs, can be many things to many people. Descriptions of such areas are probably most useful if viewed as logical constructs in which certain characteristics of an area (poverty, for instance) can be emphasized in order to compare and contrast the ideal construct with an actual existing locality.

## CONCLUSION

There is little question that the move from the country to the city has a considerable impact upon the migrant's way of live. However, what strikes many observers living in developing countries is not the difficulty of the adjustment to urban life, but rather the speed and facility with which the rural migrant becomes a city slicker. It is easy to forget that the urban dwellers with whom we are comparing the new migrant were quite likely migrants themselves. Half the population of many Latin American cities were originally migrants, and this figure is higher for many African and Asian cities. Within a few months of his or her arrival, it is often very difficult to tell the migrant from someone who has spent years in the city. A balanced picture must include both the problems, adjustments, and disorientation confronting the migrant and the reasonably successful adjustment most migrants make to their new surroundings.

Chapter 15

# African Urbanization

*There is always something new out of Africa.*
Pliny

Africa is currently the least urbanized of the continents. As of 1970, only one out of five people in Africa—21 percent—lived in urban places; and only one out of nine—11 percent—lived in cities of 100,000 or more inhabitants. At the same time, however, Africa is the continent with the highest rate of increase in urban population. Between 1960 and 1970, its urban population increased 4.7 percent.[1] This was the overall rate; some cities are in fact growing even more rapidly, with yearly population increases of 7 to 10 percent. These are among the highest rates in the world and would severely tax the capabilities of even the most economically advanced countries.

The population of the continent as a whole, which in 1971 was

[1] *The World Population Situation in 1970*, United Nations, New York, 1971, p. 65.

estimated to be 351,734,000, is increasing at an overall rate of 2.6 percent a year.[2] This overall rate, while lower than the rate of increase in the cities alone, is still sufficient to double the population of the continent before the year 2000. The rate of increase is this high because birth rates are among the highest in the world while death rates (although still high) are falling. As death rates continue to decline faster than birth rates, it is quite likely that Africa's rate of natural increase will go up rather than decline. Currently, only Latin America—which has high birth rates and already low death rates—shows a higher rate of natural increase. Family-planning programs are all but nonexistent in Sub-Saharan Africa, with the exception of Ghana and Kenya. Programs that do exist are small and poorly funded, since population growth is still not seen by most governments as threatening the standard of living. More visible economic development projects are given a higher priority than population control. Indeed, a few African nations still have official policies encouraging more rapid population growth.

## REGIONAL VARIATIONS

African cities vary greatly; the major regional distinction is between those of North Africa and those of Sub-Saharan Africa. North Africa is the most urbanized of the African regions. All the countries bordering the Mediterranean Sea have between 20 and 40 percent of their population in places of 20,000 or more inhabitants. This is not at all surprising when one considers the great civilizations this region has produced and its superior location for the development of trade centers. Away from the coast, much of the land of North Africa is either mountainous or arid desert and hardly suited for urban growth. Thus the population is highly concentrated in a limited area.

West and Central Africa lie in the middle range of African urbanization—which is very low by world standards—with between 5 and 20 percent of their population in cities. The larger cities are located along, or within easy access to, the coast. Their founding and development can almost always be tied to their role as colonial entrepot cities. Of the West African countries, Nigeria has by far the most cities.

East Africa is the least urbanized part of the continent. It does not have a tradition of cities: only Zambia, with its unique Copper Belt towns, has more than 10 percent of its population in cities.[3] Tanzania, for

[2] *Demographic Handbook for Africa,* United Nations Economic Commission for Africa, Addis Ababa, 1971, p. 12.

[3] *World Population Prospects 1965–1980,* United Nations Economic Commission for Africa, Addis Ababa, 1969, pp. 56–57.

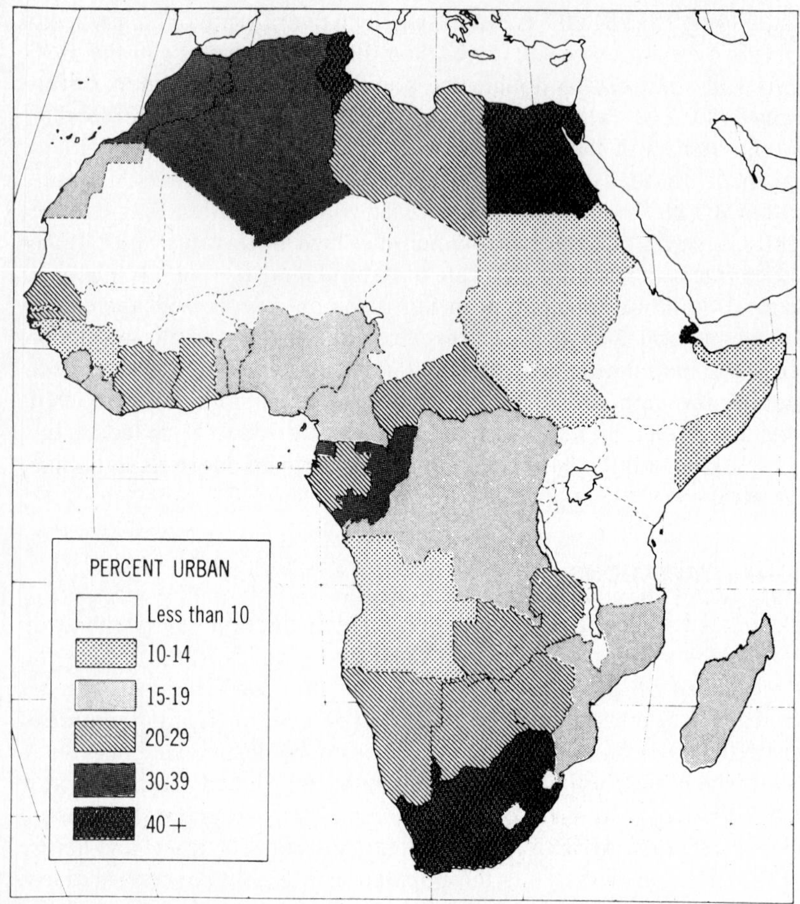


Although national boundaries distort the picture, we can see that African urbanization is concentrated along the North, West, and South coasts of the continent. (William A. Hance, *Population, Migration, and Urbanization in Africa,* New York, Columbia University Press, 1970, p. 221.)

example, has roughly 5 percent of its population in cities, and only 2.2 percent in cities of 100,000 or more—in this case, the capital city of Dar es Salaam. The situation in Tanzania is similar to that in other East African countries:

> Urbanization is growing steadily and at a rate far in excess of rural growth, but it is still insignificant. Less than 5 percent of the total population of the mainland is urbanized. In Zanzibar the percentage is 27, but even this high

figure gives an overall percentage of just over 5 for the whole United Republic. The predominantly rural character of the country is further emphasized by the fact that only one-third of the towns have populations exceeding 10,000. Dar es Salaam, the capital and principal seaport, with a population of almost 300,000, towers above them all.[4]

The Republic of South Africa is easily the most urbanized and industrialized nation on the continent, with 45 percent of its population in urban places. At the other extreme is the small landlocked country of Burundi, which has only 2.2 percent of its population in urban places; Burundi is the least urbanized nation in the world.

## THE PRECOLONIAL PERIOD

One sometimes hears a great deal of nonsense about African cities before the nineteenth-century colonial period. Until a decade or two ago, a reading of the literature gave the impression that there were few, if any, indigenous African cities south of the Sahara. This was due partially to a colonial mentality which did not admit the possibility that "backward natives" were capable of building cities and partially due to a lack of serious research on African history.

Scholars from Arabian Africa also have been prone to minimize the contributions of black Africa. For instance, one writer suggests that "historic (or ancient) capitals are confined to Arab Africa" and "'Native' (or Medieval) capitals are in fact a transition between the historical and colonial capitals. . . . Culturally, they are universally associated in one way or another with intrusive, alien influences, mainly Arab and generally Asian."[5]

More recently, the pendulum has been swinging in the opposite direction. The trend has been to find ancient "cities" and "urban civilizations" everywhere. Trading centers such as Timbuktu (whose current population is approximately 6,000) have been elevated to the status of major metropolises, a position they occupied for only relatively short periods of time, if at all. On the other hand the region did produce cities, some of which had considerable importance.

Of all African cities, those of North Africa have the longest urban traditions. Alexandria was founded, with its present name, by Alexander the Great in 332 B.C., but settlements on that location go back at least another 1,000 years before that. During the height of the Roman Empire,

[4]J. Cameron and W. A. Dodd, *Society, Schools and Progress in Tanzania*, Pergamon Press, Oxford, 1970, p. 9.

[5]G. Hamdan, "Capitals of the New Africa," *Economic Geography*, **40**:239–241, July, 1964.

The ancient city of Timbuktu today is a poor desert town. *(Michael Renaudeau/De Wys.)*

North Africa was dotted with important cities, some of which may have contained as many as 25 percent of the population of their regions.[6] With the decline of the Roman Empire these cities suffered the same fate as Roman cities in Europe. Over time, most of them disappeared—although, again as in Europe, newer cities now sometimes sit over the ancient ruins.

Elsewhere in Africa, many cities were first built during the peak of Moslem power. The revival of trade in the tenth century benefited not only North African cities such as Fez and Algiers but also Sub-Saharan towns, including Kano in Northern Nigeria. The Yoruba towns of southwest Nigeria also emerged at about this time, as did caravan centers such as Timbuktu. During the following centuries a number of primarily West African kingdoms created capitals, but most of these capitals had short histories. Segou in Mali, Labe in Guinea, Zinder in Niger, and Kumasi in Ghana all rose and fell. These cities primarily served their kingdoms as market and trade centers. Then as now, East African cities were less numerous, with only a few Moslem towns, found generally along the coast of the Indian Ocean. Present cities such as Mogadishu in

[6]William A. Hance, *Population, Migration, and Urbanization in Africa,* Columbia University Press, New York, 1970, p. 211.

Somalia and Mombasa in Kenya prospered as Moslem trading centers. These towns served almost until the present century as centers for the trading in goods and buying slaves from the interior for shipment to Arabia.

## THE COLONIAL PERIOD: EUROPEAN INFLUENCE

The first Europeans to come to Sub-Saharan Africa were the Portuguese. During the sixteenth century, they founded the first European settlements, which were little more than fortified trading posts where goods from the interior could be collected and stored for shipment to Europe. Attempts by the Portuguese to extend their influence inland were unsuccessful. Their early successes in Ethiopia, for example, were short-lived, and Portuguese missionaries and traders were later expelled from that country.

Until the colonial period of the late nineteenth century, Europeans showed little interest in colonization. Cape Town in the Republic of South Africa, for example, was established by the Dutch East India Company only as a station to provide meat, fresh produce, and water to the Dutch ships on the way to the Indies.[7]

The seizure of land in black Africa by Europeans accelerated during the last quarter of the nineteenth century. Britain, France, Germany, Belgium, and Portugal all rushed in to carve up the continent into colonies administered by Europeans. The important African cities of the present are largely the products of this colonialism, since each colony had to have an administrative capital. The major cities, founded during the colonial period, with the dates of their founding, are: Accra, Ghana (1876); Abidjan, Ivory Coast (1903); Port Harcourt, Nigeria (1912); Brazzaville, Congo (1883); Kinshasa, Zaire (formerly Leopoldville, Belgian Congo) (1881); Yaounde, Cameroon (1889); Kampala, Uganda (1890); Nairobi, Kenya (1899); and Johannesburg, South Africa (1886). Of the major new towns founded during this period, only Addis Ababa in Ethiopia (1886) and Omdurman in Sudan (1885) were indigenous creations.

Most of the cities of Africa are in actuality far newer than the dates mentioned above would indicate, for rapid increases in the populations of Sub-Saharan African cities did not begin until roughly thirty years ago. Until World War II, most African cities were relatively small. Nairobi, one of the most modern of all African cities, had a population of only 20,000 in 1920 and only 33,000 in 1930. The population jumped to 200,000 in the 1950s, and today it is in excess of 600,000. The pattern is similar,

[7]H. M. Robertson, *South Africa,* Cambridge University Press, London, 1957, pp. 3–4.

and in many cases even more spectacular, in other African cities. Kinshasa, for instance, has tripled its population in the last two decades. In spite of these increases, Africa still remains—as has been noted—the least urbanized of the world's major regions.

## COMPARISON OF AFRICA AND THE WEST

The geographer William Hance has assembled from a variety of sources a number of characteristics differentiating between urban growth in Africa and urban growth in the West at a hypothetically comparable period. These differences are presented not so that "value judgments" can be made, but in order to highlight certain aspects of African urbanization that differ from the Western experience. The points of difference Hance notes are as follows:

> **1** The rates of growth, particularly of the major cities, are much more rapid in Africa. Some have achieved their present position in one-fifth to one-tenth the time required in Western Europe.
>
> **2** There is less correlation—association—between the cities' rate of growth and the measures of economic growth in their countries.
>
> **3** The growth of urbanization is often not paralleled by a comparable revolution in the rural areas.
>
> **4** A less favorable ratio of population to resources in rural areas means that the push factor is more important than it was in Europe. That is, people pour into the cities not because the city needs workers, but because the countryside is overpopulated.
>
> **5** The linkage of some cities with their domestic hinterlands is less developed, while the ties of these cities to the outside world and their dependence on it remain striking.
>
> **6** There is relatively less specialization in the African cities. The division of labor is less developed.
>
> **7** There are generally higher rates of unemployment. Here the European cities had the advantage of being able to drain off large numbers of people who might have become redundant, to the New World. The African cities have no such convenient safety valve.
>
> **8** Differences in outlook and values may slow the adjustment to the city and reduce the tempo of its economic life, as, for example, the reliance on the extended family for support and the absence of the Protestant Ethic with its emphasis on hard work, achievement, and success.
>
> **9** There is a dual tribal and Western structure in many African cities.
>
> **10** Migrants to the town differ in several important respects: almost all are unskilled, their level of educational achievement is relatively lower though above average as far as the source areas are concerned, and almost all arrive without capital resources.

**11** Heavier responsibility is placed on governments, local and national, to provide for the urban residents. In the West, private enterprise normally met the needs for new housing, while local governments had a tax base adequate to provide the public services. Not so in Africa, where the demands of government are far more onerous and almost none are capable of meeting them.[8]

The reference to a "dual structure" in point 9 has to do with the simultaneous existence of tribal customs and Westernized ways of life. For example, the use of penicillin to cure infection exists alongside the belief that fevers are caused by the evil eye. Generally, Western ways tend to dominate in the economic sphere, while in the social and family sphere traditional customs retain their old strength. A college graduate may choose his job, but in many places his father still chooses his bride.

## PRIMATE CITIES

The decade of the 1960s saw thirty-two former colonial territories emerge as independent nations. Within these nations, the preeminent centers for innovation and modernization are the largest cities. The term "primate city" is clearly appropriate to the pattern of urbanization found in the independent black nations of Sub-Saharan Africa. The cities—and most particularly the capital cities—are the dominant economic force, the seats of government, the cultural centers, and the hubs of transportation and communication networks. The primate city is the manufacturing center, the break-of-bulk transportation node, the major market, and the financial center.

The dominance of the primate cities is easy to document. Dakar, which has only 16 percent of the population of Senegal, consumes 95 percent of all the electricity in the country and accounts for three-quarters of its commercial and manufacturing workers and over half its employees in transportation, administration, and other services. Lagos, although it is only one of the cities of Nigeria and contains only about 1 percent of the nation's population, still manages to account for 46 percent of the electricity consumed, 56 percent of the country's telephones, and 38 percent of the registered vehicles.[9]

The importance of the primate cities is heightened by the economic separation of the major city from the surrounding countryside. Africa is noted for a sharp break between the modernizing city and the tribal "bush." Urban influences are confined largely to the cities themselves.

[8]Hance, op. cit., pp. 293–294.
[9]Hance, op. cit., pp. 209–210.

There is little of the American pattern, in which the city gradually tapers off and becomes the countryside. Going a few miles into the bush can take someone not only away from built-up areas but also away from the major influence of modernization.

The physical size and structure of the primate city is the most visible sign of its dominance; but its social role as the breaker of the cake of custom is even more significant. The primate cities "are not merely the focal points where the break with tradition can be seen most clearly but also the centers in which a major restructuring of African society as a whole is taking place."[10] Just how deep into the countryside major restructuring has penetrated is, of course, open to some dispute. But that change is taking place in the cities is accepted by all.

The association between the growth of cities and the rise of African independence movements has been commented upon by many observers. Twenty years ago, a political scientist noted that "it is above all in these new urban societies that the characteristic institutions and ideas of African nationalism are born and grow to maturity."[11] In Africa the city is the incubator of social change. More than on any other continent, the city not only towers over the countryside but controls it economically, educationally, politically, and socially.

## INDIGENOUS CITIES

Cities in Africa can be classified by means of cultural, tribal, religious, or even economic function criteria; but the most visible and most widely accepted distinction is between the indigenous cities—those founded by Africans—and the more numerous cities founded by Europeans. True, it is sometimes difficult to make clear-cut distinctions, since many cities have both indigenous and European components; and one must remember that generalizations may not wholly apply to specific cases. However, the differences between the two types of cities are notable. The physical layout of each type of city is intimately related to its cultural and social characteristics. The physical structure and social organization of a city clearly reflect one another.

Indigenous cities are most common in North and West Africa. In East Africa, towns not founded by Europeans—such as Mombassa, Zanzibar, and even Harar in eastern Ethiopia—were generally founded by Moslem Arabs. We shall discuss Addis Ababa, the most notable exception to this statement, later in this chapter. In West Africa, the most noted

[10]Peter C. Gutkind, "The African Urban Milieu: A Force for Rapid Change," *Civilizations*, **12**:185, 1962.

[11]T. Hodgkin, *Nationalism in Colonial Africa*, Muller, London, 1956, p. 18.

The old city of Kano, Nigeria, is in sharp contrast to the center of the capital of Lagos, Nigeria. *(Editorial Photocolor Archives.)*

cities of African origin are the Yoruba cities of Nigeria. Many of these cities have fairly large populations, although there is a continuing scholarly debate whether these were and are true cities or extremely large agglomerations of basically agricultural villages. These are referred to in the literature as "rural cities," "city villages," or "agrotowns." In any case, the Yoruba cities had the largest populations in Sub-Saharan Africa before the colonial period. Ibidan as of 1850 had roughly 70,000 inhabitants; the Nigerian census for 1963 showed ten Yoruba towns with populations exceeding 100,000.

Ecologically indigenous cities are not as sharply differentiated as Western cities. In the indigenous city the main focus is the central market, which is commonly quite large and frequently out of doors rather than

The central business district of Casablanca reflects its colonial heritage. *(De Wys.)*

housed in buildings. Nearby are the quarters of the chief or ruling prince. The main mosque is also centrally located in Moslem cities.[12] Historically, surrounding this central core were the quarters of the lesser chiefs and nobles. These areas contained not only the nobles but also their retainers, soldiers, and followers. Each quarter was a self-contained city within the larger city. Much of this legacy persists today.

Frequently, quarters are divided on the basis of tribal or religious affiliation. Walls and gates sometimes separate the quarters from one another. Within a quarter, there is no overall plan or scheme. Streets wind in an irregular pattern and are suitable only for walking or animal traffic, since the lanes are narrow and buildings come right up to the passageway. Structures are rarely more than two stories high and constructed of local materials. Congestion is common and sanitation facilities are minimal.

As these indigenous towns came under the control of colonial powers, a new administrative area on the European style was frequently appended to the periphery of the old city, and a major road or two would

[12]Hance, op. cit., pp. 249–250.

be cut through the old city to connect its center with the offices of the colonial administrators. Rarely did the indigenous city and the colonial city blend. Each was a separate entity; and though existing side by side, they frequently even followed different laws, with Western legal systems applying only in the European quarters. In time, the European quarters expanded to include modern commercial and business districts. In a few cases, the modern city came to completely surround the old city. The Casbah in Algiers, for example, has long been completely enclosed by a modern city largely created by the French. Rail lines, of course, went only into the European quarter.

## CITIES FOUNDED BY EUROPEANS

The colonial cities founded by Europeans differed in almost every respect from the indigenous cities. They did not grow out of the local culture. Rather, the layout of the city, its social and political organization, and even its architectural styles came from Europe. The government housing in Accra, Ghana, with its wide lawns and large single-family houses, looks like nothing so much as Victorian England. The centers of colonial cities were exclusively for use and residence by Europeans. Nighttime curfews frequently prevented the entry of Africans into the European sections, and the entry of Europeans into the African sections.

The colonial city was organized around the central business district, which in addition to stores and other business offices also included the administrative offices of the colonial government. Streets were usually wide and crossed at right angles in a grid pattern. A description of Stanleyville (now Kisangani) is typical:

> The physical layout of the town could be seen as both an expression and a symbol of the relations between Africans and Europeans. European residential areas were situated close to, and tended to run into, the area of administrative offices, hotels, shops and other service establishments, while African residential areas were strictly demarcated and well removed from the town centre.[13]

The "African" or "native" quarters or locations in the colonial city were almost always on the outskirts. Africans who worked in the European center were in effect commuters from suburban locations—although, in this case, the suburbs were high-density slums. This is, of course, the complete reverse of the pattern in American industrial cities as described in Chapter 4.

[13]V. G. Pons, cited by A. L. Epstein, "Urbanization and Social Change in Africa," *Current Anthropology*, **8:**(4)277, 1967.

By far the most extreme examples of the effects of patterns of social organization on the ecology of a city can be seen in the Republic of South Africa. Here the government policy of *apartheid,* or forced racial segregation, has resulted in a conscious division of the major cities into African, European, Indian, and "Coloured" (mixed race) areas. Each of the populations is allotted specific areas in which, and only in which, they can purchase property. For South Africa, race overrides all other criteria in determining the spatial development of the city.[14]

## SQUATTER SLUMS

*Bidonvilles* (tin-can cities) are a standard part of the "suburban" landscape of every growing African city. They house up to one-third of the total urban population. The rapid population growth of recent years, along with the push from the land, has resulted in an explosive expansion of the urban population—without a proportionate increase in city housing.

As a result, *bidonvilles* are a fact of city life, from Casablanca in the North (180,000 residents in shantytowns) to Lusaka in the South (90,000 in shantytowns). Most governments simply do not have the resources to engage in massive housing programs. Even a relatively affluent country such as the Ivory Coast has not been able to begin to meet the housing demand. Compounding the problem is the inability of the increasing urban population to pay even the minimal rents that government-built housing would require. Food and clothing generally absorb from two-thirds to nine-tenths of a newcomer's income.[15] That doesn't leave much for extras such as decent housing. Shantytowns with homes of packing crates, scrap metal, or mud and wattle will be part of the urban scene for years to come.

## HOUSING AND URBAN PLANNING

Second only to employment, the most pressing problem in African cities is housing. Various approaches have been taken to reduce the number of shantytowns and squatter slums surrounding the major cities, but none of these programs has come near to solving the problem.

Some West African governments have tried to stem the migrant tide by passing legislation providing for the repatriation of unwanted new workers back to their villages and setting stiff prison terms for those who return to the city. Repatriation has not proved successful: workers either

[14]Leo Kuper, Hilstan Watts, and Ronald Davies, *Durban: A Study in Racial Ecology*, Jonathan Cape, London, 1958.

[15]Hance, op. cit., p.286.

drift back to the city or are replaced by others. Other governments have tried to increase the attractiveness of rural villages and to settle unemployed urban populations in new, self-contained communal villages. Both of these approaches are quite expensive, and as a result seldom move beyond the planning or pilot-project stage. Such schemes have difficulty competing for scarce governmental funds. Moreover, the pressures driving younger people to the cities are social as well as economic and are not likely to be solved by such government programs as can be presently implemented.

The construction of low-cost houses or flats cannot come near to meeting the need for new housing. Abidjan in the Ivory Coast is doing better than most: it constructs roughly 1,200 government units annually, but the need is for between 6,000 and 8,000 units annually. As a result, governments are coming more and more to accept the idea of aiding in the construction of reasonably planned slums which at least have minimal urban amenities such as an available water supply, roads, and group sanitary facilities for the disposal of human waste.

Zambia is adopting the so-called "site and service" scheme, by which a township is laid out and a prospective builder is given a plot and a loan of $50 to buy necessary building materials, such as cement for the floor or a corrugated iron roof. After that, the builder is for all intents and purposes on his own. The rationale underlying this approach is that the goal of the government should not be to build housing but to raise the standard of living. Slum dwellers don't need more prodding to improve their living conditions; what they need is more money. As a shanty dweller gets a decent job and begins to make some money, he begins to improve his housing on his own.

Even professional planners have made some notable mistakes in the type of housing they have built. Nigeria is an example: when building housing for slum dwellers, it built single-family houses on the European model. These represented the type of home the Nigerian planners themselves liked. The slum dwellers, however, preferred a more communal existence, with all homes opening onto a common courtyard. The people for whom the houses were designed considered the separated single-family houses cold and unfriendly.

There are, of course, urban planning problems other than housing. Lagos, Nigeria, for instance, has a major problem having to do with the nature of the site on which the original city was constructed. Lagos was originally located on a narrow island close to the coast. This made considerable sense when the concern was defending a trading post. But today the island is the most densely populated section of the city, and the lagoon separating it from the mainland is a stinking, polluted sewer. For years there was only one bridge connecting the island and the mainland. Today there is a second new bridge, but the traffic jams at rush hour are worse than anything in the United States. At peak traffic hours, it can take forty-five minutes just to get over the bridge. Urban problems apparently can be exported to developing countries more rapidly than urban solutions.

## THE ECONOMIC PICTURE

Colonialism may be dead, but its economic effects linger on. Overdependence on a single crop or mineral resource leaves many countries vulnerable to fluctuations in world market prices. Ghana was set back by almost a decade of depressed cocoa prices; Ethiopia is subject to fluctuations in the price of coffee; Liberia is subject to fluctuations in the price of crude rubber; Zambia depends on the price of copper. It is difficult to plan a development budget on the basis of fluctuating world prices.

Economically, Africa as a continent is not doing well. It is generally assumed that a developing country should expand economically at a rate of at least 3 percent a year. According to this minimum criterion, twenty-eight African countries, containing some 72 percent of the population of Africa, have been growing economically at a rate far too slow to be considered even marginally satisfactory.[16] In fact, thirteen countries, comprising 22 percent of the African population, have had *negative* economic growth rates.[17] Poor planning and excessive reliance on foreign capital, which is not always available, have contributed heavily to this unsatisfactory economic performance.

The picture is no better in the agricultural sector. Agriculture still occupies a preeminent economic position in most African countries. It occupies about 77 percent of the economically active population. The growth in food production, however, has been disappointing. African food production grew at a rate of about 2 percent a year during the 1960s. However, owing to increases in the population, on a per capita basis there was actually a *decline* of 0.2 percent annually in available foodstuffs.[18] This stagnation in a crucial area is generally attributed to traditional and inefficient methods of farming. As a result, nations whose economies are based on agriculture find themselves in the unfortunate position of importing foodstuffs.

[16]*Africa Social Situation: 1960–1970,* Prepared for the African Population Conference, Accra, Ghana, December, 1971, by the Economic Commission for Africa, p. 8.

[17]Ibid.

[18]Op. cit., p. 11.

Industrial growth has also been slower than was hoped for a decade ago; but here the increases have been relatively steady, if unspectacular. Almost everywhere, the industrial base remains small, reflecting a colonial history of producing raw materials rather than finished manufactures. Industrialization is slowed by the smallness of internal markets, the shortage of skilled and experienced manpower, and the lack of capital. However, the picture differs from country to country. Nigeria, for one, has made major strides in developing its oil resources. Generally, the rate of industrial development is closely tied to the availability of investment funds.

Economically, African countries are, with some notable exceptions, among the poorest on earth. Furthermore, the gap between them and the developed nations of the West is getting larger every year. The United Nations Economic Commission for Africa estimated the average gross domestic product (at 1971 market prices) at about $150 per capita, excluding South Africa. The highest income level is found in Libya ($1,950). Libya, of course, has oil. Burundi, Rwanda, and Upper Volta are at the other end, with figures around $50. Comparable figures for the United States, the United Kingdom, and Japan are $4,645, $1,953, and $1,631 respectively.[19]

It would be pleasant to predict a better future for all the developing African countries, but the economic facts of life indicate that this is unrealistic. A few years ago, for example, Somali overthrew a corrupt feudalistic regime and replaced it with a socialistic state intent on modernization. Unfortunately, this has really made little difference as far as economic development is concerned, since regardless of its form of government Somalia has virtually no resources. So long as its major export is bananas, Somalia is going to remain an impoverished country. Developing countries that have few natural or other resources are almost certain to see the gap between themselves and the developed world widen rather than close unless the present pattern and rate of investment and aid are radically increased. Further, increases in the cost of importing necessary oil and gasoline, which have disrupted the economies of developed countries, have all but destroyed the economies of some developing nations.

## URBAN FUTURE

Regardless of the extent of economic growth, continued urban growth is clearly the pattern for as far into the future as anyone cares to project. There really is little alternative. Many of the semiarid agricultural and

[19]Op. cit., p. 19.

grazing areas of East Africa are already overused. Remaining in the area of one's birth, and further raising the density of the area, is not a reasonable alternative for those who hope to better their way of life. The opening up of new lands not previously used for settlement requires costs far out of proportion to the possible returns. The cost of providing necessary services—water, roads, schools, housing—would be extremely heavy. In East Africa it would also involve a political decision to destroy many of the remaining game parks and wildlife refuges, since there is little other land that is not already being used.[20]

The following description of the situation in Tanzania could be applied equally well to the social, political, and economic situation in other African countries.

> Death rates have fallen and the population is now estimated to be growing at 2.1 percent a year. This means that almost 45 percent of the population is under sixteen, and raises immediate political issues. The economy will have to expand in the industrial and cash-crop sectors if these people are not to be either unemployed workers in the cities or subsistence farmers. Many youths are migrating to the towns, producing a severe strain on the social services. Unemployed or semi-employed youth, loitering in the streets or waiting around TANU offices for small jobs, begin to be a political problem. Party leaders are aware of them; but harranguing against loiterers, telling unemployed youth to go and farm, and even restricting people's freedom to come to Dar es Salaam has not dissuaded youth from accumulating in the towns.[21]

Finding employment for the masses in the cities is an increasingly serious problem. Urbanization is clearly the wave of the African future, but whether it will mean economic development is still problematic.

## SOCIAL COMPOSITION

The recent explosive growth of urban areas means that the majority of the adults in the cities were not born there but are in-migrants. The African city is a city of newcomers. In Abidjan, the capital of the Ivory Coast, only 29 percent of the total population, and only 7 percent of those over twenty years of age, were actually born in the city. Research by the author shows that 44 percent of the population of Addis Ababa, Ethiopia, were born in the city. But this figure gives a misleading impression, since more than 70 percent of those listed as born in Addis Ababa are in fact

[20]For a discussion of some of the problems in Kenya, see Dick Oloo (ed.), *Urbanization: Its Social Problems and Consequences*, Kenya National Council of Social Service, Nairobi, 1969.

[21]Henry Bienen, *Tanzania: Party Transformation and Economic Development*, Princeton University Press, Princeton, N. J., 1970, p. 265. Reprinted by permission of Princeton University Press.

children under fifteen years of age. Over three-quarters of the population over fifteen years of age were born outside the city and are thus migrants.

The sociologist Louis Wirth's view of the city as a place where social relations are dominated by the labor market and contacts with others are superficial, impersonal, and transitory is only partially accurate as a description of African urbanism. There is no question that many of the disorganizing aspects of urbanism posited by Wirth can be found in any large African city. Family life sometimes breaks down, and prostitution is common. The latter situation is partially due to urban sex ratios, which are typified by disproportionate numbers of males. The situation is reasonable in West Africa, where in the cities there is a ratio of roughly 95 females to every 100 males. However, in Middle Africa there are only about 85 females per 100 males; and in parts of East Africa there are only 55 to 75 females per 100 urban males. The situation is most extreme in South Africa, where government policy prevents workers from bringing their wives to the cities with them. The resulting abnormal family situations encourage drunkenness, violent crime, and rape. The situation is not unlike that found in the towns of the American West before the arrival of the homesteaders with their families.

Since its civil war, Nigeria has had a serious problem with violent crime, and in 1972 public executions were begun there in an attempt to halt the spiraling crime rates. East Africa, particularly Uganda, has also been plagued by an increase in assaults and crimes of violence. However, while the situation is serious, matters have still not reached the state of, say, New York City—except perhaps in some of the South African townships, where normal family life is extremely difficult, owing to distorted sex ratios discussed above.

However, the impact of urbanization is not always predictable. Tradition and modern ways often blend. An example of such blending is the use of both courts and traditional agents to resolve conflicts.[22] Problems of psychological maladjustment appear as a rule to be far rarer than Wirth's thesis would suggest. The town may be a new experience, but since a major proportion of the townsmen were once migrants themselves, almost every newcomer knows someone in the city who will take him in and who will help him adjust to urban life. Family ties and wider kinship ties are surprisingly strong and resilient to urban pressures. Relatives are expected to take the newcomer in and provide for his basic needs until he can get on his feet. If the migrant does get a job, he is then expected to contribute to providing for the family.

[22]Michael J. Lowy, "Me Ko Court: The Impact of Urbanization on Conflict Resolution in a Ghanaian Town," in George Foster and Robert Kemper (eds.), *Anthropologists in Cities*, Little, Brown, Boston, 1974, pp. 153–177.

In most cases, far from being subject to indifference and social isolation, the migrant is quickly integrated into the life of the quarter—a place where there are numerous others of the same tribe, and probably even the same village. Outside observers are struck by the ebullience, gusto, and camaraderie found in African towns, particularly in West Africa. A description of Dar es Salaam, the capital of Tanzania, fits other African cities equally well:

> It would be difficult to find a single African who arrived in Dar-es-Salaam knowing not a soul. . . . Almost every African who decides to come comes to a known address, where lives a known relation; this relation will meet him, take him in and feed him and show him the ropes, help him seek a job . . . until he considers himself able to launch out for himself and take a room of his own.[23]

This pattern is, if anything, more prevalent in West Africa, where the pattern of life is more open and friendly toward newcomers.

Also aiding the migrant's adjustment is the African pattern of remaining in the city for months or even years and then returning to the countryside for a period of time before migrating back to the city. Migration out of the cities during rainy seasons or harvest seasons is common in some countries.

It is well to keep in mind that the pull of the town is not uniform for all groups. The Masai of Kenya, although pressured by the Kenyan government to rationalize their agriculture and adopt modern ways, have consistently rejected town life in favor of their traditional rural culture. The Ila of Zambia have also rejected urbanization and modernization. Both tribes seem to be an embarrassment to their national governments because they don't want to "modernize." The Kenyan government plans to divide up the Masai communal lands and give each family individual plots. A similar program was tried by the United States government to modernize the American Indians, with the result that many Indians lost their lands. There are indications that the same fate awaits the Masai. It is quite possible that by the year 2000 the self-reliant virtues and warrior strengths of the Masai will be praised in every local schoolbook; but by then the Masai culture doubtless will have been effectively destroyed.

## MIGRATION

During the colonial period workers were frequently compelled to move from their tribal areas to areas where they were needed for mining, agriculture, or construction. The Belgians used forced labor to build the

[23]J. A. K. Leslie, *A Social Survey of Dar es Salaam,* Oxford University Press—The East African Institute, London, 1963, p. 33.

Congo-Ocean railway, which was completed in 1934 at a cost of over 15,000 African lives. The British also used, until the 1920s, a system of compulsory service known as the "Kasanvu System."

The forced systems are gone, but large-scale migration is still an integral part of the economy of several African nations. Economic exploitation still forces natives in South Africa to become migrants, and the Firestone rubber interests in Liberia continue a system of labor recruitment involving payments to local chiefs for so many men delivered. "Paramount chiefs are assigned quotas and are paid for sending laborers to the plantations. The quotas established in the late 1920s have not been revised appreciably since that time."[24] While force is not used, many migrants still have little choice: not to go is not to eat. Migration also has political implications. Malawi's political accommodation to South African racial policies clearly has an economic basis. Funds sent home by Malawians working in South Africa keep the small country of Malawi economically afloat.

Except in South Africa, where mass yearly movements of indentured labor are still common, mass migratory movements other than to the city are becoming less common. One reason is that independent African states have become concerned over alien migrants taking jobs while citizens remain unemployed. Ghana and the Ivory Coast both have policies of restricting foreign migration. Occasionally Zaire and other countries round up foreigners in their cities and send them back across the borders. It is difficult to generalize, however, because patterns of migration are not uniform throughout the continent. The patterns obtaining in West Africa sometimes differ markedly from those in East or Central Africa.[25]

## TRIBALIZATION

Urbanization is supposed to weaken traditional bonds, but it can be argued that urbanization in Africa has strengthened rather than weakened tribal identification.[26] Some scholars maintain that the immigrant, rather than being "detribalized," is "supertribalized" as a result of coming into contact, for perhaps the first time, with people from other cultures. Tribal origin usually replaces kinship as a symbol of belonging. This is an expansion of identity from the parochial to the more general.

Gideon Sjoberg suggests that the role played by cultural or tribal subsystems in modernizing societies is analogous to that played by

[24]Robert W. Clower et al., *Growth Without Development: An Economic Survey of Liberia*, Northwestern University Press, Evanston, Ill., 1966, p. 158.

[25]M. Banton, "Social Alignment and Identity in a West African City," in Hilda Kuper (ed.), *Urbanization and Migration in West Africa*, University of California Press, Berkeley, 1966.

[26]William John Hanna and Judith Lynne Hanna, *Urban Dynamics in Black Africa*, Aldine-Atherton, Chicago, 1971, p. 107.

immigrant enclaves in the American city of several decades ago. Cultural, ethnic, tribal, class, or occupational groupings perform a number of functions not only for the newcomer but for the society at large. First, the tribal, ethnic, or other group introduces the newcomer to others in the city and indoctrinates him into the ways of the city. Information on such matters as where to live, how to get a job, and how to avoid the police is transmitted to the migrant in order to aid his adaptation to the city. Second, the subgroup, being originally itself a part of the rural culture, maintains within the city many rural customs and traditions. While learning the new ways, the migrant will still have some contact with his past. Third, because migrants return to rural areas for periods of time, and because there is a pattern of visiting between rural villages and the city, the customs and ways of the city (urbanism) are spread to villages—so that patterns of urbanism are gradually being diffused throughout rural areas.[27]

Kinship and tribal affiliation provide bridges by which the migrant crosses into the urban arena. Being a member of a tribe gives a newcomer an immediate identification that is recognized by everyone. It tells him how to behave, and it provides a more or less ready-made group of associates, friends, and even drinking partners. While tribalism may have negative effects in a country seeking to develop national rather than tribal loyalties, on the individual level tribal membership eases the adjustment to city life.

It has been an unfortunate aspect of the history of modern Africa that this expansion of identity often stops at the ethnic or tribal level. National as opposed to tribal identification is still comparatively weak. In country after country, the ruling elite are all of the same tribe. For example, ex-Emperor Haile Selassie and virtually all Ethiopians of importance are from the Amhara tribe. Similarly, President Jomo Kenyatta of Kenya surrounds himself with his fellow Kikuyus. After a coup—whether in Uganda, Ghana, or elsewhere—the first act has usually been to dismiss senior army leaders from other tribes and appoint in their place the fellow tribesmen of the coup leader. Tribal rivalries can even lead to civil war: an example is the Nigerian civil war, in which the Ibo tribe attempted unsuccessfully to become an independent, separate state, Biafra. Leaders often call for "detribalization" but do not always practice what they preach, if one can judge by the limited ethnic makeup of their own governments. It is among the educated young that the sense of national dedication is strongest.

[27]Gideon Sjoberg, "Cities in Developing and in Industrial Societies: A Cross-Cultural Analysis," in Philip M. Hauser and Leo F. Schnore (eds.), *The Study of Urbanization*, Wiley, New York, 1965, pp. 226–227.

## TRIBAL ELDERS AND NEW ELITES

One way the city promotes social change is by undermining the position of rural-based tribal elders. A tribal background offers little precedent for confronting urban problems. A young man migrating to the city can frequently make more than a tribal elder, and rural patterns of communal sharing break down under a system of individual wages. Independent young men, no longer constrained by tribal customs, are more willing than elders to confront and exploit innovations. The tribal elder knows little of how the urban social and economic order operates and can offer only minimal assistance to those entering city life; indeed, his advice may be disfunctional for solving urban problems. A man who is considered a person of status and prestige in the bush or village may be little more than another unemployed worker in the city. The strength of the traditional elite lies in the countryside; their influence in the city is minimal.

Very little of what has been said thus far applies to the emergent African upper classes. Young, well trained, and frequently critical of the past, they are the antithesis of the tribal elder. The urban elites are young, frequently only in their thirties. Their schooling has often taken place abroad: at Oxford or Cambridge if the country was formerly British; in Paris if the country was formerly French. Many of the urban elite left their home countries while still adolescents for education abroad. They are trained as doctors, lawyers, teachers, and other professionals, and their backgrounds are in many respects more typically European than African. Their tastes in food, clothing, and housing, and their general life-style, are distinctly cosmopolitan, with a European orientation. For example, while they may listen to the national radio station, they almost certainly get their daily news of the outside world from the BBC World Service. Income differences between this urban elite and the African urban poor are even greater than in developed nations such as the United States and the Soviet Union. In West Africa, a university graduate just entering a government bureaucracy can expect to earn ten times more than an urban laborer.[28] Being strongly oriented toward the future, the urban elite seek to push their countries into the modern world and have little patience for the slow, older ways of the traditional tribal elites.

## ASIANS

Cities in East and South Africa have had, in addition to African and European populations, a large minority of residents from the Indian subcontinent, who are always referred to in Africa as "Asians." Original-

[28]P. C. Lloyd, *Africa in Social Change,* Penguin Books, Baltimore, 1967, p. 150.

ly most came as indentured laborers to construct the railways. Many stayed on as residents. During the later colonial period, the Indians occupied a middle stratum in East Africa between British administrators and African workers. Indians served as lower-level civil servants, and most importantly as entrepreneurs and small businessmen. They were heavily represented in commerce and the professions. Virtually all small shopkeepers in Kenya, Uganda, and Tanzania were Asians until these countries forced their expulsion. The Indians in East Africa had separate markets, separate residential districts, and a separate social life within their own tightly knit community. Social interaction between Asians and Africans was rare, and intermarriage even rarer. The educational levels of Asians, while lower than those of the whites, were considerably higher than those of the African population. After the independence movements of the early 1960s, the political as well as economic influence of the Indians temporarily increased. Because of their training, they quickly filled many of the positions vacated by the British.

However, their wealth, clannishness, and political influence drew increasing antagonism from the larger African population, and during the late 1960s East African countries began to expropriate the Asians' property and expel them. The most extreme case was Uganda, where in 1972 all Asian property was seized without compensation and all Asians were forcibly expelled. With the exception of South Africa, where the Indians still occupy a legal and social position between the whites and the natives, most Indians have now left Africa or are in the process of leaving.

## STATUS OF WOMEN

It is difficult to make generalizations about the position of women in Africa, since this varies from country to country and from one tribal and cultural group to another. Still, several overall statements can be made. It is generally safe to say that norms, attitudes, and values in Africa have a long history of strongly favoring male dominance. It is also clear that, regardless of other factors, cities are far more equalitarian in practice than the countryside. Urban populations are young, new to urban life, and more flexible than their rural counterparts.

In Ghana "mammy wagons" (small buses) dominate local transportation and much of the retailing of food and other goods is controlled and operated by women. Ghanaian women are noted throughout the continent for their organizing skills. Even in North African Moslem cultures, where the status of females has been traditionally inferior, great changes are taking place in the education of women and participation by women in national life.

Everywhere, the move to cities tends to be a liberating experience. In the bush and in rural villages, the position of women is set by custom; but in the city, with its new occupations and skills, the occupational structure is more flexible. Urban occupations may be so new that they are not yet sex-defined. Skills and professional training of all sorts are usually in short supply, so that the woman who has had the benefit of education and training can generally use her training. On the other hand, those females (or males, for that matter) without specific skills or abilities are likely to remain locked into poverty. While it is true that trained women participate in the social and economic life of the city to an extent unknown in the countryside, it is also true that for lower-class women without husbands there frequently is little alternative to prostitution and other marginal economic enterprises.

Further clouding the situation is the problem of distinguishing between the normative beliefs regarding the position of women and the actual practice in the cities. Ethiopia has a well-earned reputation as one of the most conservative African states—an emperor surrounded by semifeudal nobles—and the status of women as prescribed by custom, church law, and the legal code is inferior. But upper-class Ethiopian women have far more power than is at first apparent, since they legally control all their own property. The husband does not gain control of his wife's possessions and property at time of marriage (this is unlike the English common-law practice). Thus if divorce occurs—and over six out of ten unions do end in divorce—when the woman goes, so does her property. It is perhaps a suggestive sign of the actual rather than official status of women that among the more affluent families who own automobiles, the woman is as likely to be using the car as the man.

## A CASE STUDY OF AN INDIGENOUS CITY

A better understanding of the qualitative as well as quantitative aspects of African urbanization can be gained by looking at one city, Addis Ababa in Ethiopia. Addis Ababa is a primate city; its population was estimated at 1,025,800 in 1973. Addis Ababa contains 57 percent of Ethiopia's urban population—but only 3.4 percent of its total population. The second-largest city, Asmara, had a population of 176,410 in 1967.[29] No other city had as many as 60,000 inhabitants. In spite of the rural nature of Ethiopia, Addis Ababa is one of the very largest cities of Sub-Saharan Africa. Excluding the Union of South Africa, only Kinshasa in Zaire and Lagos and Ibadan in Nigeria have larger populations than Addis Ababa.[30]

Addis Ababa, sometimes called the capital of Africa because of the

[29] *Demographic Handbook for Africa*, op. cit., p. 46.
[30] Op. cit., pp. 41-48.

presence of the United Nations Economic Commission for Africa and the Organization of African Unity, has a unique history among African cities. Unlike most other Sub-Saharan African metropolises, it is authentically African. Although founded in 1886 at the height of the European colonial expansion in Africa, the city was a totally Ethiopian creation.

Addis Ababa (the name means "New Flower") was not originally intended to be a permanent city. Rather, it was founded by Emperor Menilik II as a temporary capital. Having no urban tradition, the Ethiopian emperors moved their capital from time to time as military factors, weather, or exhaustion of local resources (food and firewood) dictated. Addis Ababa—which was Menilik's eighth capital—was laid out as an armed camp. The Emperor chose for his *guebi,* or palace, a hill above the northern thermal springs and then allotted various surrounding quarters, known as *sefers,* to his leading nobles. Social organization was strongly feudalistic. Each *sefer*—literally, "camp"—included the residence of an important noble plus all his warriors, troops, retainers, and slaves and their families. No distinctly upper or lower class areas were initially developed, as was the case in cities founded by Europeans. The effect of this original organization as an armed camp can still be clearly seen in the city's social, economic, and ethnic arrangements.

The high altitude of the city—8,000 to 8,500 feet—has meant a general absence of malaria, cholera, and tsetse flies. On the other hand, it has also meant a long, cold rainy season with related pulmonary disorders, and large numbers of fleas. The high altitude, with its thinner air, also poses problems of adjustment for foreigners—but not for Ethiopians, who are acclimated to life in the rugged highlands.

Early visitors to Addis Ababa universally commented that it resembled a large straggling village more than a city.[31] Further contributing to this impression of a large floating camp were fluctuations in the city's population. The normal population around 1910 was roughly 60,000; during the rainy season, it sometimes dropped to as low as 40,000.[32] When an important chief came to the capital, he brought his entire army and household with him. There are reports of chiefs who brought 100,000 to 150,000 men with them, and even as late as 1915 it was not unusual for a governor to bring 30,000 to 50,000 men along as a personal guarantee of safety.

As the city grew, its eastern side surrounding the palace gradually developed into the administrative center, while the western zone surrounding the old market place, or *mercado,* became the commercial

[31]Docteur Merab, *Impressions d'Ethiopie,* vol. 2, Leroux, Paris, 1921–1923, p. 11.

[32]Richard Pankhurst, "Notes on the Demographic History of Ethiopian Towns and Villages," *The Ethiopian Observer,* **9**:71, 1965.

center. Because the ruling Amhara tribe despised any type of commercial activity or trade, business activities were relegated to subordinate tribes. The Amhara concentrated their attentions on ruling, farming, and mounting expeditions to the south to capture more slaves.

Haile Selassie I ruled the country, first as regent and then as emperor, since 1916. He officially decreed the end of slavery in the early 1920s, but this was not observed to any large degree inside the city and virtually not at all outside. It is estimated that 25,000 of the 60,000 inhabitants of the city were slaves in 1910. Today slavery in the true sense is gone from all but the most remote areas. However, the descendants of slaves—the Shanquellas, Sidamo, Gurages, and some of the darker-skinned Gallas—still are at the bottom of the social ladder; the men serve largely as *zabanias* (guards for houses and walled compounds) and the women as domestic maids or *mamitas* (children's nurses).

The Italians occupied Ethiopia from 1936 to 1941. They envisioned Addis Ababa as the capital of their Sub-Saharan African empire and engaged heavily in building, constructing the country's first road network—five roads radiating outward from the capital. These roads, which still make up the basic road network, ensured that Addis Ababa would become the transportation and administration center of the country. The Italians also constructed a new market area, known as the Piazza, east of the traditional market and built a road from this new market to the small railway station at the southern end of the city. The southern end of the city, which is somewhat lower in altitude and thus warmer, was set aside as the Italian residential area. A southward movement has been characteristic of the city since this time. Most of the newer European-style villas and high-rise apartments that have been constructed during the past decade are in the southern area.

Today the radius of the city is about 4 to 5 miles with the most heavily built-up area roughly in the center. Although its present population is 1 million, Addis Ababa still essentially retains its nonurban character. According to a survey taken by the Etho-Swedish Building College, over 90 percent of the housing units are still constructed of *chica*—a mixture of earth, straw, and water plastered around eucalyptus poles. Over 90 percent of the units surveyed by the College had mud floors; this creates serious health problems during the rainy season, since the floors are generally lower than the outside land.[33] The ever-present and fast-growing eucalyptus trees also serve to give the city a small-town appearance by masking the houses. The trees do a yeoman service, since they provide firewood for all heating and cooking, lumber for building,

[33]"Survey of Housing Conditions I and II: Totals and Average," mimeograph, Etho-Swedish Institute of Building and Technology, May and July, 1962.

A small market in Ethiopia. Note that most of the tukels (houses) have had straw roofs replaced with galvanized iron. *(Mary Doody.)*

and wood for furniture. Even the leaves are used in baking the Ethiopian bread, called *injera.*

The rural feeling of the city is also no doubt due to the fact that it is a city of rural migrants. Three-quarters of the population over fifteen years of age were not born in the city.[34] Presently in-migration to the city is in the neighborhood of 7 percent a year. Jobs are very difficult to obtain, and many people work as domestic servants. Servants of *forengi* (a term applied to Europeans or Americans, and sometimes to other Africans) frequently have servants themselves to care for their children. Young boys are seen everywhere as street beggars while young country girls frequently are sold to, or otherwise end up in, the many hundreds of *tej* houses, which offer potent local beer and also serve as houses of prostitution. Handicraft industries are only slowly developing, since handicrafts have traditionally been associated with inferior status. Weavers, for example, are sometimes alleged to be possessed by the devil and to have the evil eye. Such beliefs inhibit the development of craft industries.

[34] J. John Palen, "The Volume and Implication of Migration Into Addis Ababa," paper read at VIII World Congress of Sociology, Toronto, 1974, p. 11.

In terms of its functional base, Addis Ababa is still primarily a political and administrative center. All major Ethiopian government agencies, all foreign embassies, the United Nations Economic Commission for Africa, and the Organization of African Unity are located in the capital. Recently there have been noticeable increases in the transportation, communications, manufacturing, and education sectors. Industrialization is growing but is still at a relatively infant stage, with all capital goods being imported. Retail trade is also growing but is oriented largely to Addis Ababa itself.

Transportation to and from the city is still primitive, particularly for goods. Passenger jets fly several times a week to Europe, but heavy industrial or consumer goods must be brought to the city over a narrow-gauge single-track railroad built almost sixty years ago by the French to connect Addis Ababa with the port of Djibouti, located in the only remaining French African colony, the Territory of the Afars and Issas. Each day thousands of donkeys also bring wood, hay, and produce into the city from surrounding areas, but they are being supplanted by large, overloaded trucks.

Addis Ababa is both a feudal city and a modern city. It is an overgrown village and the headquarters of the prestigious United Nations Economic Commission for Africa. It is a city with Mercedes-Benz automobiles where the per capita income is $69 a year. It has high-rise apartments, but still no sanitary sewers. For better or worse, it represents the future.

Chapter 16

# The Middle East

*Woe to them that join house to house. Woe to them that lay field to field till there be no place.*

Isaiah 5:8

The area we commonly refer to as the "Middle East" does not easily fit into either the category of Asia or that of Africa. Technically, most of what we call the Middle East is in Asia Minor, with some overlap into Africa (for example, Egypt). In terms of history, culture and development, the Middle East is a distinct area, with patterns of urbanism and urbanization that cannot usefully be lumped together with the different patterns of Asian or African cities.

The Middle East is sometimes referred to as the "cradle of civilizations." This is not an exaggeration, for the great ancient civilizations of Mesopotamia, Egypt, and the Levant all developed in this relatively small geographic area. The early development of this area was discussed briefly in Chapter 2. In this chapter, the emphasis will be on the cities of the

Middle East from the Islamic period to the present, for the social and spatial organization of present cities in the area is directly related to their preindustrial past. In terms of economic development as well as geography, the Middle East occupies a position somewhere between the countries of Western Europe and those of Asia and Africa.

Scholars today agree that Islamic civilization has been predominantly an urban civilization.[1] In the words of Lapidus, "From the beginning of recorded history Middle Eastern cities and civilization have been one and the same."[2] The city was the center of political, social, and cultural activities. This was true in spite of the fact that many of the countries still are not unified and tribal factors are important.

It is clear that Middle Eastern cities differed in significant respects from the medieval corporate city and the autonomous city-state of the classical world. The medieval European city with which we are familiar grew out of a feudal land-based system; its charter defined its rights *vis-à-vis* the rural manors which were the real centers of power. European medieval cities developed on the fringes of power and were forced to develop their own political structure because they did not fit into the dominant agriculturally based system. They had to evolve their own laws and customs, often in opposition to those of the countryside. Middle Eastern cities, on the other hand, in many cases had urban histories that went back to antiquity. The city was not on the fringe of the system; it was the system. Cities in the East had traditionally been administrative or trade centers within large urban-oriented empires. The caliph, like the earlier Roman emperors, lived in the city, not in the countryside in fortified rural castles.

The laws of the city were those of the entire territory. Since laws were written in the cities, there was no need for autonomous laws and regulations for cities—and thus no independent group which could legally challenge the caliphate as the Western middle class challenged its rulers by developing constitutional law. The city was not viewed as a rival of the hinterland: the city was superior and dominant. City authorities enforced the laws and collected the taxes. Thus there was no need for independent municipal governments of the type developed in Western Europe. Rather, the Middle Eastern cities resembled Asian cities in lacking independent formal organizations.[3] The legally autonomous city with its own corporate charter, as defined by Max Weber, was a product of Europe.[4]

[1]S. M. Stern, "The Constitution of the Islamic City," in A. H. Hourani and S. M. Stern (eds.), *The Islamic City,* Bruno Cassirer, Oxford, 1970, p. 25.

[2]Ira M. Lapidus, *Middle Eastern Cities,* University of California Press, Berkeley, 1969, p. v.

[3]J. Gernet, *"Note sur les villes chinoises au moment de l'apogee islamique,"* in A. H. Hourani and S. M. Stern, op. cit., pp. 77–85.

[4]Max Weber, *The City,* D. Martindale and G. Neuwirth (trans.), The Free Press, Glencoe, Ill., 1958, p. 88.

## PHYSICAL AND OTHER CONSIDERATIONS

Roughly four-fifths of the Middle East is either desert or arid mountains, and this basic environmental fact greatly influenced, if it did not determine, the location of cities. In addition to the limitations of the environment, political and military considerations influenced the location of Islamic cities. During the Roman Empire and earlier, the great cities were almost always seaports—Alexandria, Antioch, and Carthage, are examples. The Moslems did not follow this ancient pattern: they shunned the sea and instead built an inland empire. This was partly from choice—the origins of Islam were in the interior rather than on the more sophisticated coast—but also partly from military necessity. Arab armies were successful on land, but the Mediterranean Sea was controlled by others—first by the hostile Byzantine Empire and later by the equally dangerous Italian city-states.

As a result, the Moslems built an interior empire and previously great cities such as Alexandria shrank to the status of frontier outposts. The great Moslem cities, such as Damascus, Baghdad, Cairo, Tehran, Jerusalem, Mecca, and Medina, were all inland. Some, such as Kairouan and Fustat, were originally Arab camps at the edge of the desert; others, such as Damascus and Yazd, had been handling desert traffic for centuries; still others, such as Samarra, Baghdad, and Cairo had once served as royal cities; and a few, such as Jerusalem and Mecca, were religious centers.

## ORGANIZATION OF THE CITY

Wherever the city was located, it had to have an agricultural hinterland to supply its daily needs. In addition, the peasants—many of whom actually lived within the protection of the city walls and cultivated adjacent lands—needed the technical skills, such as the canalizing and storing of water, and the military security, particularly from roaming nomads, provided by an urban population. Some cities, like Damascus, still have agriculturists living within the city and working the fields outside.[5] This is directly opposite to the American pattern, which has people living outside the city and working within it.

Traditionally, Islamic cities had a number of physical features in common. First, located in the most dominant natural defense position within the city would be the citadel. This was the military heart of the city, the place where, if necessary, a last-stand defense could be made.

Second, every major city also possessed a royal compound or

[5]Charles Issawi, *The Economic History of the Middle East*, University of Chicago Press, Chicago, 1966, p. 216.

Before the modern era, the cost of moving goods was extremely high. A market in Saudi Arabia, today an oil-rich nation. *(University of Louiseville.)*

enclave. Sometimes this was located in the very heart of the city, and sometimes on virgin land; but wherever it was placed, it invariably grew and absorbed surrounding properties. The royal compound contained not only the palace, treasury, and other directly related operations; it also was the center for all administrative offices. In addition, there were also barracks for the house guards and personal troops whose loyalty could be counted on in times of revolt or attempted coup.

Finally, there was the central market area or grand bazaar, which included not only the shops and stalls of the various craftsmen, tradesmen, and merchants but also the major mosques and the all-important religious schools. The citadel and palace are now tourist sights, but the grand bazaars continue to serve an important commercial function. Various sections of the bazaar are devoted to specific goods or products: all the spice shops are found in one section, another specializes in shoes, another in clothing, and another in copper or brass metalwork. Silversmiths and goldsmiths also have their own special locations. The grand bazaar of Cairo covers over a square mile of the city center.

Internally, Islamic cities have traditionally been divided into quarters that resemble village communities. Most of one's daily life would be lived within a quarter; there were relatively few institutional ties cutting across district lines to bind various quarters together. Guilds, merchant associations, and professional organizations, which were so important in medieval European cities, were all extremely weak.[6] What little organization that did cross the boundaries of quarters was created by the *ulma,* the learned religious elite that later came to exercise political and social power as well. The schools of law of the *ulma* were socially, religiously, and physically central.

Within the various quarters there were wide differences in social, economic, and political power. There were no specifically upper-class districts. Residence in quarters was based on adherence to particular religious or political positions. Ethnic minorities, specialized crafts, and even foreign merchants might have their own quarters. Some of the more suburban quarters were composed largely of people of recent village or nomadic origin—again, a contrast to the North American pattern.

## POPULATION GROWTH

Most contemporary Middle Eastern cities are underdeveloped by Western standards, yet in their days of glory they easily outshone anything found in medieval Europe. During the Middle Ages the Islamic world produced an urban culture that stretched from Fez to Damascus. Cairo in the fourteenth century was the most populous city in the world, perhaps containing within her extended boundaries almost 500,000 inhabitants.[7] At this time the major European cities were barely one-tenth this size.

The seventeenth and eighteenth centuries were a period of decline for most Moslem cities. Cities generally began to expand again during the latter part of the nineteenth century. The growth of Cairo demonstrates this pattern. During the first half of the nineteenth century, the population of Cairo dropped to its lowest point—about 200,000. Then it began to grow again, reaching 600,000 at the turn of the century, 1 million by 1927, and 2 million by 1947; today it is well over 5 million. Each year, more than 100,000 inhabitants are added.

In recent years, much of this growth has been the result of a push from the land which is due to the rural population explosion. It has not been due—as in the West—to any rapid expansion of economic oppor-

[6]Lapidus, op. cit., p. 49.

[7]Janet Abu-Lughod, "Varieties of Urban Experience: Contrast, Coexistence and Coalescence in Cairo," in Lapidus, op. cit., p. 162.

tunities in the city. Consequently, some observers characterize cities such as Cairo as "overurbanized" and underindustrialized.[8]

Overall, the accelerating rate of growth of Middle Eastern cities can be attribted to three factors: (1) the population explosion, which has produced not only urban growth through natural increase but also migration of surplus population from the land to the cities; (2) the discovery and exploitation of oil and the financial independence it has brought to some countries in this area; (3) the impact of World War II and its aftermath, with the beginning of political independence and the use of the power of the state to promote industrialization and economic modernization.

## MODERNIZATION AND DEVELOPMENT

The industrial growth of Middle Eastern cities resulted from the imposition of a tiny modern sector upon the traditional society.[9] Since the major impetus and capital were provided by Europeans, the modern sector long remained isolated from the traditional economy. Estimates made from information provided by censuses indicate that even today over half the employed males in Cairo are within the traditional rather than the modern economy.[10] There has not been a gradual blending of the traditional into the modern; rather, modern fixed-price stores compete with nearby traditional markets where prices are the result of bargaining.

There is no pattern of economic and social change common to all Middle Eastern cities. Tel Aviv, for example, differs enormously from Baghdad, Damascus, or even Jerusalem. The development of Tel Aviv as a primate city can be explained in great part by the emergence of Israel as a nation-state. Founded in 1909 as a Jewish "garden city" separated from the Arab city of Jaffa, Tel Aviv grew rapidly, particularly after World War II. Its reservoir of trained professional and managerial talent aided its transformation into a major industrial commercial center. Tel Aviv has expanded its metropolitan area until now it encompasses numerous formerly independent surrounding towns. After Jerusalem came under Israeli administration as a result of the Six-Day War in 1967, Tel Aviv was no longer the only Israeli city; but its economic primacy is yet to be challenged.

The cities of the Middle East may be ancient, but as the example of

[8]Kingsley Davis and Hilda Hertz Golden, "Urbanization and the Development of Pre-Industrial Areas," in Paul K. Hatt and Albert J. Reiss, Jr. (eds.), *Cities and Society*, Free Press, New York, 1957, pp. 120–140.

[9]Abu-Lughod, op. cit., p. 164.

[10]Abu-Lughod, op. cit., p. 166.

The old city, or Arab half, of Jerusalem looks much as it did centuries ago. *(George Rodger/Magnum.)*

Cairo indicates, most of their growth has come during this century. Most cities have more than doubled their size during the past decade or so. Beirut has annexed surrounding towns, and Baghdad and Kuwait have grown far beyond the old city walls. In Kuwait, old quarters have been

Tel Aviv is a modern Western city. Unlike Jerusalem, it is a business rather than a religious or historic center. *(Israel Government Tourist Authority.)*

razed and new apartments and villas built. The city has more than quadrupled in size—largely owing to the great affluence produced by Kuwait's oil revenues.

## SPATIAL ECOLOGY

In the absence of urban planning, growth of the cities has not followed any discernible pattern. Commercial, residential, and industrial usages all intermingle. Newer housing sections tend to be located on the periphery, but modern housing is also being built in central locations. There may even be mixed usages within the same building. In cities such as Beirut, the lower floor is used for stores or businesses, the next few floors are used for business offices, and the upper floors are middle-class apartments. Slum dwellers live both in inner-city mixed residential and industrial areas and in shantytowns on the city's edge. Some nations have also built high-rise government housing for the poor on the suburban fringes.

Theories of urban ecological organization developed in America have little relevance to the Middle East. If one looks at the ecology of Cairo, it is apparent that Burgess's concentric-zone theory has little utility there.[11] Contrary to the American pattern, in Cairo the areas of high social status are centrally located, and close to both the old and the new central business districts. Housing patterns still largely follow the traditional preindustrial model rather than the industrial model.

## COMPARISONS AND CONCLUSIONS

In making comparisons with other regions of the world, and particularly with North America, certain differences should be remembered. First, Middle Eastern cities are generally small by Western standards. They do not have the size that earlier American sociologists of the Chicago School more or less presupposed as an inevitable adjunct of urbanization.

Second, Middle Eastern cities are not industrialized centers in the Western sense. The cities are commercially oriented, but the way of life is far less bureaucratic than in industrialized states.

Third, the Middle Eastern cities have been growing at rapid rates. As a result, many of the city dwellers exhibit characteristics and behavior patterns that reflect their rural or village background. Urbanism as a way of life, with its emphasis on complex secondary organizations, is not characteristic of much of the urban population. Family ties, kinship, ethnic group, and primary group still have a great deal to do with determining the nature of the life one will lead. In Cairo, more than one-third of the residents were born outside the city. Migrants do not simply pick up urban ways; they also, in effect, ruralize the cities. Many city dwellers still are tied to rural customs and culture. Migrants shape the city as much as the city shapes them. Assimilation is a two-way street.

Fourth, formal institutions, such as civic associations, labor unions, and charitable organizations, rarely play more than a minor role in

[11]See, for example, S. S. Hassan, "The Ecology and Characteristics of Employed Females in Cairo City," a paper presented at the Seminar on Demographic Factors in Manpower Planning in Arab Countries held at the Cairo Demographic Center, November, 1971; and Janet Abu-Lughod, "Testing the Theory of Social Area Analysis: The Ecology of Cairo, Egypt," *American Sociological Review*, **34**:198–212, April, 1969.

The outdoor cafes of the Middle East serve as both business settings and social clubs. *(Marc Riboud/Magnum.)*

adjusting the migrant to the city. Informal organizations or subsystems based on tribal, cultural, or ethnic identification are far more important. In Middle Eastern cities the role of the coffee shop is central. Men conduct much of their social and business lives from coffee shops. Frequently the proprietor and all the patrons come from the same rural village. Thus the coffee shop is a place where news of the village can be exchanged and assistance can be given to newcomers. The coffee shop is more of a social than an economic institution.[12]

Fifth, while the cities may be growing, the majority of the national population is still rural. Urban ways have not replaced traditional ways outside the cities. Even in such an urban and relatively urbane city as Cairo, an automobile ride of three-quarters of an hour can take one not only out of the city, but also out of this century. Along the Nile, camels still carry goods, water buffalo still plow the fields, and farmers use wooden water wheels to irrigate their fields, as has been done for centuries. The existence of large cities should in no way be confused with the existence of an overall contemporary urban culture.

[12]For a description of this pattern in Cairo, see Janet Abu-Lughod, "Migrant Adjustment to City Life: The Egyptian Case," *American Journal of Sociology,* **67**:22–32, July, 1961.

Chapter 17

# Urbanization in Asia

*The civilization under which people are restricted and controlled by a material environment from which they cannot escape, and under which they cannot utilize human thought and intellectual power to change the environment and improve conditions, is the civilization of a lazy and nonprogressive people.*

Hu Shi

Of all the regions of the world, it is Asia about which one must be most careful when attempting to make generalizations on urbanization, because patterns of urbanization in China, Japan, India, and Southeast Asia all have different historical roots. These areas do, of course, have some things in common; but any generalization must be applied with some care to individual cities.

What can be said is that Asia has a great tradition of city life and numerous cities whose histories go back many centuries. In fact, until 200 years ago Asia contained more city dwellers than the rest of the world combined.[1] And if present demographic trends continue, by the year 2000

[1]Rhoads Murphey, "Urbanization in Asia," *Ekistics,* **21**:8, January, 1966.

Asia will again have more city dwellers than any other continent. While precise data are hard to obtain—particularly on the size of Chinese cities—it is still clear that at least one-third of the total urban population of the world is found in Asia. Asia has more large cities and a larger number of people—but not a larger *percentage* of people—in cities than either Europe or America.

Despite this, the majority of Asia's population still consists of village-based agrarians; only a minority live in true urban places. Overall, figures compiled by the United Nations for 1970 indicate that 21 percent of the population of Asia can be found in urban places of 20,000 or more and 15 percent in cities of 100,000 or more. This low level of overall urbanization places Asia just above Africa as regards the percentage of the population that is urbanized. Asia is still overwhelmingly a rural continent. The greatest degree of urbanization is found in the East Asian region (28.6 percent urban); this region includes Japan, which is almost three-quarters urban.[2]

All this means that while Asia is still predominantly rural, at the same time it has some of the world's largest cities. A relatively low proportion of the population lives in urban places, but these places are frequently immense. Shanghai, with almost 11 million people in the central city alone, is the world's largest city; Tokyo, which has 9 million people, is second and the Tokyo-Yokohama metropolitan area has 20 million inhabitants. Bombay, Calcutta, and Peking are also among the world's largest cities.

It has been suggested that Asia is in the position of being "overurbanized" while at the same time its momentum of urbanization is increasing. Heavily populated Asian urban areas continue to attract large numbers of immigrants because, even with all its crowding and problems, city life is better than the rural alternative. Overurbanization, however, as we have suggested in earlier chapters, is a loaded term. The degree of overurbanization is measured against Western industrial standards and Western levels of per capita income, which are unrealistic standards of comparison for much of the world.

## THE STRUCTURE OF INDIGENOUS CITIES

Asian cities other than those founded and developed by Westerners display a spatial organization having much in common with the preindustrial city (discussed in Chapter 2). Indigenous Asian cities of the past were predominantly political and cultural centers and only secondarily eco-

[2] *The World Population Situation in 1970,* United Nations, New York, 1971, p. 64.

nomic centers. The function of traditional capital cities was to serve not as economic centers but as symbols of the authority, legitimacy, and power of the national government. Administrative functions were everywhere more important than commercial or industrial functions.

Cities were located inland, near the centers of their empires, except in Japan and parts of Southeast Asia, where this was not practical. Such inland cities were centers physically as well as socially and were also far safer from attack than coastal cities. Peking, Delhi, and Ankor are classic examples: they served as symbols of legitimate authority and were planned with monumental architecture, such as temples and palaces, that would emphasize this role. In China and sometimes in India the city was walled; in Southeast Asia it usually was not; and in Japan walls never existed.

## COLONIAL CITIES

The history of Western-type cities is quite different from that of indigenous cities. Western-type cities were imported to the East by European adventurers who entered the area seeking trade. These cities, in contrast to the traditional preindustrial cities, were primarily oriented toward trade and commerce and thus were located along seacoasts in order to facilitate trade and communication with the mother country. Originally small trading sites, perhaps with a small fort for protection, these cities are now among the largest in the world. Hong Kong, Singapore, Shanghai, Calcutta, and Bombay all began as foreign-dominated port cities.

The physical structure of these cities clearly reveals their non-Asian origins. During the colonial period, Europeans and Asians were segregated into separate housing areas, with the European colonial sections clearly resembling Western cities in their street development, architecture, and overall use of space. Asian quarters of the cities developed in more traditional ways and at considerably higher densities. While the overwhelming majority of the population were Asian, even during the height of the colonial period, the skylines and particularly the centers of these cities show the unmistakable hand of Western influence.

Cities such as Shanghai, Singapore, and Hong Kong had model Western economies that emphasized manufacturing as well as commerce. Although they occupied Asian soil, their real social and economic roots were in England. Urban institutions were transplanted from Europe, since the traditional society lacked the required economic and commercial organization. Today cities such as Hong Kong and Singapore are famous throughout the world for their industrial products and the experience and skills of their businessmen.

The differences between the various major Asian regions are so considerable that these major cultures must be discussed separately. India, China, and Japan will receive special treatment as will the geographical area of Southeast Asia.

## INDIA

Since it is impossible in a section of one chapter to discuss all relevant aspects of Indian culture and their impact on urban life, we will limit our discussion basically to a description of some of the physical differences between Indian and Western cities.

### Land Use: Foreign and Indigenous Influences

Contemporary Indian cities are a combination of indigenous and foreign influences. However, even today these two cultures have remained distinct from one another, so that in Indian cities one can distinguish the European from the traditional sections by physical criteria. In the cities created by foreigners, such as Bombay and Calcutta, the differences may be seen within the various sectors of the city. Where a native city already existed, as was the case with Delhi, the British built their European city (in this instance, New Delhi) next to the existing city. During the British colonial period native sectors of the various cities were even administered differently. Bangalore, for instance, was divided for purposes of administration into Bangalore City on the west side and the Civil Station and Military Catonment on the east side.[3]

Traditional Indian cities used their land quite differently from the cities founded by Europeans. The native cities had central business districts, but these differ both in size and function from the Western model. The CBDs of the Indian cities are quite small by Western standards. Also, they are not highly specialized in only one or two functions, such as retailing and services, as is characteristic of the Western model. The center of the CBD in Indian cities is the central market. Surrounding the central market—which is made up of numerous small shops selling a variety of goods for personal or household use—are streets specializing in certain merchandise such as goldware, brassware, furniture, and clothing. Intermixed throughout these streets are small hotels, small manufacturing plants, residences, moneylenders' shops, lawyers' offices, and even wholesale merchants.

Speaking of the CBD of Calcutta, one researcher observes:

[3]Noel P. Gist, "The Ecology of Bangalore, India: An East-West Comparison," *Social Forces*, **35**:357, May, 1957.

The Badshahh royal mosque in Lahore, Pakistan, built by the Moghul emperor Aurangzeb. (*United Nations.*)

> The very small area of this zone, in comparison with any Western city of magnitude, the gigantic volume of administrative, commercial and other activities and services carried on daily in this area, and the comparatively little urban renewal, building activity, and vertical extension, are features in strong contrast with those of Western Metropolises.[4]

Industrialization is not a major function of the indigenous city. When industrialization does exist, most of it is on a small scale and of the cottage type, and it is widely dispersed over the city and intermixed with residential and commercial uses. Large-scale industry is generally decentralized because of the availability of transportation—rail lines and highways—and open land on the periphery. Even public institutions such as the municipal building (city hall), the post office, and the telephone exchange tend to be dispersed rather than in the CBD. In brief, land is

[4]N. R. Kar, "Urban Characteristics of the City of Calcutta," *Indian Population Bulletin*, April, 1960, p. 55.

haphazardly given over to a variety of uses; particular activities are not concentrated in particular locations. Western models do not apply.

The areas built by Europeans present quite a different picture. British areas of new cities such as the "civil lines," which contained civil government headquarters and the homes of the administrators, and the "cantonments"—military reservations—are today still in marked contrast to the indigenous city. Where the native city is grossly overcrowded and its streets and lanes are filled with carts and people running every which way, the European sections were designed and still remain as quiet neighborhoods where spacious houses are graciously separated by large lawns and trees. Malaria was thought to be caused by bad air (*mal air*), so the British constructed their residential areas with ample space for air circulation between homes.

Since independence, many of the "civil lines" areas have fallen into a respectable shabbiness, but they are still a world removed from the old city. Density figures clearly document the difference between the old and new areas. The gross density is 13.2 persons per acre in New Delhi, but 213.3 persons per acre in Old Delhi.[5] The high figure for Old Delhi, moreover, is not for an area of apartment buildings but for one of one- and two-story buildings.

### Housing for the Poor

Much of the poorest population lives not in the city proper but on the periphery. As is the case in Latin America and Africa, on the perimeters of Indian cities are found squatter shantytowns, or, as they are known in India, *bustees.* These densely packed slums are among the worst in the world. The poverty and squalor are extreme. The hundreds of thousands of urban newcomers who overcrowd the shack towns live almost always without any of the urban amenities, such as municipal water or sewage disposal. Migrants pour into the city because there is no hope in the countryside; but the city has no way of absorbing their labor. India today has millions more workers than it can effectively use. The level of industrialization and economic development has been far exceeded by the rate of growth of the urban population. India had some 600 million people as of 1972 and each year is adding 13 million more—or the total population of Australia. As a result of the population explosion, the quality of life in Indian cities is likely to get worse before it gets better.

Calcutta, India's largest metropolitan center, contains some 7 million

[5]Gerald Breese, *Urbanization in Newly Developing Countries*, Prentice-Hall, Englewood Cliffs, N. J., 1966, p. 62.

Calcutta residents sleeping in their only homes, the street. (*Marilyn Silverstone/Magnum.*)

people, most living in abject poverty. Over three-quarters of the population of the city proper live in overcrowded tenements and squatter slums. According to official estimates, two-thirds of the population live in buildings constructed of unbaked brick and 57 percent of the families live in a single room.[6] The congestion, filth, garbage-filled streets, and general deterioration of the city have been frequently commented on by both scholars and travelers.

Living conditions in Calcutta are among the worst in the world; the city has a minimum of 300,000 homeless residents who eat, sleep, breed, live their lives, and die on the streets without even the shelter of a squatter shack. As the population increases, conditions are almost certain to become even more squalid. Calcutta is well on the way to becoming the most hopeless city in the world. "The teeming masses of Asia" is a cliché, but unfortunately it describes reality in the cities of the Indian subcontinent. Calcutta has "become a metropolis without benefit of the industrial revolution that gave rise to cities in advanced nations."[7] Without major industrialization and a more equitable distribution of wealth, the future of Calcutta is as clouded as that of the Indian nation as a whole—of which it is the largest urban concentration.

### Prognosis

India suffers from far too many people—600 million at present: 808 million projected for 1985. The cities are filled with villagers patiently camping out on the city streets, to the point where the cities resemble large-scale refuge camps. The introduction of modern public health practices and the partial eradication of malaria, smallpox, and plague have drastically reduced infant mortality rates (staggeringly high in the past), and over the last thirty-five years life expectancy has been increased from twenty-six years to about forty-one years.

Between 1961 and 1971, the population rose by 110 million. Forty-one percent of the population is under fifteen years of age. When these young people come of age, there will be a still more extreme population crisis, for while the life expectancy has been getting longer in India, the quality of life has not been improving. Population growth is such an overwhelming problem that all attention must be turned simply to providing enough food. Other problems, such as improving the quality of life, increasing education, and improving housing, necessarily are neglected. Questions such as those about saving the environment are not even asked.

[6]Nirmal Kumar Bose, "Calcutta: A Premature Metropolis" in Scientific American, *Cities: Their Origin, Growth, and Human Impact,* Freeman, San Francisco, 1973, p. 251.

[7]Bose, op. cit., p. 251.

## CHINA

China took its last national census in 1953; thus there is a great lack of recent data on Chinese urbanization. What little is known refers more to the decade of the 1950s than to the most recent period.[8] Because of the lack of hard data, even the most general statements regarding the extent of urbanization may be subject to considerable error. It is not so much that the Chinese have been withholding data as that reliable statistical information for the decades since the 1950s does not exist. It is to be hoped the opening of China to the West which began in 1972 will lead to the development of accurate information on the nature of China's urban growth.

The Chinese census of 1953 indicated a total population of 583 million. The last official population figure released by the Chinese was 647 million in 1957. According to projections by the United States Bureau of the Census, the low estimate for the population of China in 1975 was 869, million, and the high estimate was 932 million.[9] It is estimated that China is presently increasing at a rate of roughly 2 percent a year; but an increase of even 1 percent a year would give China a population of over 1 billion by the year 2000. Roughly one out of every four children born this year will be Chinese.

The population of China is concentrated in the southern and eastern sections of the country. The People's Republic of China has an area of about 3,800,000 square miles, with 96 percent of the population living on 40 percent of the land area.[10] The greatest density is found in the Yangtze Valley, where there are 2,000 to 2,500 persons per square mile.

### Western Influences

The first manufacturing and industrial cities of China were the treaty ports, under Western influence, and frequently directly administered by Westerners. During the nineteenth century, Chinese coastal cities were physically controlled and occupied by European, and later Japanese, administrators and troops.

The European powers were able to force the weak and ineffectual Manchu dynasty to give foreigners virtually total control over the economic, political, and social life of the major Chinese cities. Europeans

[8]Among the best overviews are M. B. Ullman, "Cities of Mainland China: 1953 and 1958," *International Population Reports,* Series P–95, Washington, D.C., 1961; and John S. Aird, "The Size, Composition and Growth of the Population of Mainland China," *International Population Reports,* Series P–90, Washington, D.C., 1961.

[9]U.S. Department of Commerce, Bureau of the Census, *Estimates and Projections of the Population of Mainland China: 1953–1986,* U.S. Government Printing Office, Washington, D.C., 1968, International Population Report Series, P–91, no. 17, pp. 42–47.

[10]Aird, op. cit., p. 5.

lived in separate newer sections of the cities which were policed by European troops. Foreigners could not be tried for crimes in Chinese courts. In Shanghai, the largest and most prosperous of the treaty ports, the teeming Chinese city was separated from the foreign section by a fine park. Signs at the borders of the park stated, "No Dogs or Chinese Allowed." Even the capital of Peking had its "legation quarter" for foreigners, near the central Imperial City. However, the number of foreign residents was never particularly large. In Canton, China's major southern city, foreigners at their height numbered only 894 out of a city population of over 1 million.[11]

The Nationalist government which replaced the Manchu dynasty in the early decades of this century was strongly urban-oriented. It was made up of an urban military and upper-class elite which continued the traditional practices of taxing and coercing the peasants to support the urban-based government. The communists, on the other hand, led by Mao Tse-tung, based their strength on the peasants. After years of internal struggle and the civil war of 1947 to 1949, the communists came to power and established a republic on a form modified from that of the Soviet Union.

### Extent of Urbanization

Presently, one-fifth of China's population resides in cities. Estimates made by the United Nations put the urban population of China at 164 million in 1970.[12] If this estimate is correct, China now has more persons living in cities than any other country of the world. Moreover, the cities of mainland China are estimated to be presently increasing at a very high rate: 4.4 percent a year.[13] If China does not yet have the world's largest urban population, it soon will. It already has the world's largest city: Shanghai.

Since the establishment of the People's Republic in 1949, there has been a massive shift of population from rural to urban. Between 1949 and 1956, some 20 million Chinese migrated from rural areas into the cities. More recently the government has been trying to reverse this flow and send surplus urban population into the countryside. During the Cultural Revolution of the late 1960s, unemployed Red Guards, labor battalions, and those guilty of ideological sins were shipped by the trainload to the countryside. Many of these migrants made poor adjustments to their new surroundings and drifted back into the cities. However, since the ending of the disorders of the Cultural Revolution and the restoration of

[11]Ezra Vogel, *Canton Under Communism*, Harvard University Press, Cambridge, Mass., 1969.
[12]*The World Population Situation in 1970*, United Nations, New York, 1971, p. 62.
[13]Op. cit., p. 65.

discipline, the government policy of moving surplus population out of the cities has been more successful.

### Rural Resettlement of Urban Youth

China, virtually alone among the developing countries, has been able to deal effectively with the problem created when urban areas grow faster than the opportunities for urban employment. Other governments have failed to halt migration to the cities and to return jobless immigrants to the countryside; but China has been successful because it possesses a strong political leadership and an effective administrative structure to carry out the dictates of its leaders.

In 1963, following the economic crisis brought on by the failure of the "Great Leap" campaign, the government decided to stabilize the urban population at 110 million, considered a manageable figure.[14] In order to do this, it was decided to "rusticate," or return to the countryside, urban school graduates; this would lessen the pressure on the urban economy and help promote agriculture and indigenous industry in rural areas. Today a combination of extreme pressure and ideological conviction, results, in many urban-educated youths volunteering for permanent resettlement in the countryside. "Volunteers" include all graduates of urban secondary schools and universities who have not been accepted at an educational institution at the next higher level or have not been assigned to a post in urban industry or service units.[15] In the words of a call by Mao Tse-tung in December 1968:

> It is very necessary for the educated youth to go to the countryside to be reeducated by the poor and lower-middle peasants. Cadres and other people in the cities should be persuaded to send their sons and daughters who have completed junior or senior middle school, college or university, to the countryside. Let us mobilize. Comrades throughout the country should welcome them.[16]

It is estimated that within two years of this call, between 10 and 15 million youths "volunteered" to move permanently to rural villages.[17] Some estimates (as of 1973) run as high as 25 million. If this is an accurate picture, the migration involved is one of the greatest in history. Most of the youths come from the largest industrial and educational centers, such as Peking, Tientsin, Shanghai, and Canton. According to Chinese reports,

[14]Pi-chao Chen, "Overurbanization, Rustication of Urban-Educated Youths, and Politics of Rural Transformation," *Comparative Politics*, April, 1972, p. 374.

[15]Pi-chao Chen, op. cit., p. 365.

[16]Ibid.

[17]Pi-chao Chen, op. cit., p. 369.

Shanghai alone had shipped close to half a million young intellectuals to the rural countryside by the end of 1969. In effect, educated young people are being massively transferred from the cities, which cannot yet absorb their labor and employ them productively, to the countryside where their talents are badly needed.

**Shanghai**

Shanghai was born out of Western commercial enterprise and organized its economy along Western lines. It was largely imposed upon the existing peasant civilization.[18] Within a decade of its opening to foreign trade in 1843, Shanghai had become a physical and economic embodiment of nineteenth-century European urban thought. In nineteenth-century Shanghai, with its extraterritoriality (land held by foreigners which was not legally considered Chinese territory), foreign concessions, and foreign gunboats, the modern industrial world of European rationality came face to face with the traditional, inefficient, seclusionist ways of the Chinese Empire.

For the Chinese planners of today, the physical development of Shanghai has been complicated by several factors. For example, in their attempts to plan the development of Shanghai, the Chinese Communists have had to overcome the effects of the previous pattern of mixed foreign domination. Each of the foreign settlements had not only its own administration and police but also its own pattern and width of streets. Developing a uniform citywide street pattern has required widening existing streets as well as extending others by tearing down buildings and houses. The total length of city streets has increased more than ten times—from 200 miles to over 2,000 miles—over the period from 1949 to 1972.[19]

Shanghai's dominant position as the industrial center of the nation has also complicated plans for industrial dispersion. Today Shanghai has more than 1.5 million industrial workers employed in industries such as steel, machine tools, shipbuilding, chemicals, motor vehicles, and textiles. Efforts have recently been made to disperse industrial sites to outlying areas, but they have been handicapped by shortages of transportation and capital. Outlying areas raise vegetables and fruits for the city. The mass of industrial activity is located within the city proper, with resulting pollution and transportation congestion. The pollution and congestion from automobiles is minimal, however, since there are few cars to be found on the streets.

[18]For a description of Shanghai before communism, see Rhoads Murphey, *Shanghai—Key to Modern China,* Harvard University Press, Cambridge, Mass., 1953.

[19]Hung-Mao Tien, "Shanghai: China's Huge 'Model City,'" *Milwaukee Journal,* December 16, 1973.

Downtown Shanghai. Note the prerevolutionary buildings and the absence of automobile traffic. The traffic policeman in the elevated perch controls the street lights. (*Rene Burri/Magnum.*)

The absence of automobiles also limits the distance one can live from one's workplace. In order to get to work, the populace uses a crowded bus system—said, however, not to be as overcrowded as that in Tokyo—and bicycles. There are over 1 million bicycles in the city, but many families still do not own one and the demand outruns the supply.

At the time of the revolution, Shanghai, like other Chinese cities, was faced with a massive housing problem. Years of war and turmoil had left the poor to exist in shacks and straw huts along the streets and the river bank. These hovels are now gone, and some 95 residential villages have been constructed. Although the housing is crowded—from 43 to 48 square feet per person, according to Chinese officials—apartments are reported to be neat and well maintained.[20] Within the city, water, sewers, and electricity are available to virtually every family, and 300,000 families are reported to have gas stoves. An average working family pays from $1.50 to $3 a month for rent, which is roughly 4 to 8 percent of the family income.[21]

[20]Hung-Mao Tien, loc. cit.
[21]Hung-Mao Tien, loc. cit.

### Peking

Today Peking, which has been the capital of China almost continuously since 1267 A.D., occupies an area of over 4,000 square miles and has a population of over 6 million.[22] The city is a combination of the ancient and the very modern, with the suburban districts being mostly farming villages that have been organized into communes. A factory sector is being developed in the eastern and southern suburbs. Because of the absence of private transportation on a large scale—although the city does have 1.5 million bicycles—every attempt is made to construct new factories near housing for the workers. Older housing is less satisfactory than new housing, which usually consists of brick buildings four to six stories tall. A family of four or five persons generally lives in an apartment consisting of two rooms plus a kitchen, a bathroom, and a small foyer. All the newer apartments have running water, water heaters, and flush toilets.[23] The shape of the future can be seen in housing development in Ho-p'inh-li, a suburb of Peking, which contains not only primary and middle schools, but also nurseries, hotels, and other facilities.

### Summary—China

As a result of drastic measures, such as the resettlement of urban young people in rural areas, China has been able to contain its urban crisis. Reports from travelers all indicate that China has been more successful than countries such as India in providing for its urban population. In many cities of the developing world, there is massive unemployment, sometimes in excess of 25 percent; but this does not appear to be a problem in China. While life is highly regimented by Western standards, it also is quite tolerable. The starvation and street begging that were a common sight in China before 1949 no longer exist. Great wealth and great poverty have both been abolished, and the average worker, it is generally agreed, lives better and more securely than ever before.

According to all reports, the people are well fed and adequately, if uniformly, clothed. The cities are said to be clean and free of crime; mugging, robbery, and rape are rare. The drug traffic, prostitution, and gambling are also said to have been virtually eliminated.[24] Certainly most Chinese live better than they did under the Nationalists. One cannot avoid comparing the cities of China, with their clean, cared-for streets and well-fed people, with the cities of India, with their filthy streets and poverty-stricken beggars.

[22]Hikotaro Ando, *Peking,* Dodansha International, Tokyo, 1968, p. 41.
[23]Arthur Galston, "Peking Man (and Woman) Today," *Natural History,* November, 1972, p. 28.
[24]Galston, op. cit., p. 31.

### A Note on Hong Kong

The British Crown Colony of Hong Kong, on the Chinese mainland, has a particularly severe housing problem. The small colony—398 square miles—has virtually no unused land, while its population, augmented by refugees from mainland China, has continued to grow. Massive housing projects have sprung up all over the once-barren colony, but even this very active building program has not been able to keep up with increases in population. Government figures show that 600,000 persons, or roughly 15 percent of the population, still live in squatter huts made out of anything that the occupants can throw together. The poor sanitation facilities of these squatter slums, coupled with the highest densities in the world, mean that diseases such as the "Hong Kong flu" of several years ago can spread through the slums like wildfire. Since there is no room for expansion outward, the crowding can only get worse. Already, there are over 4 million people living at a population density of roughly 10,000 per square mile. Nevertheless, the level of living in Hong Kong is one of the highest in Asia.

## JAPAN

Japan has an urban tradition even longer than that of India as regards the role of the city in regional and national life. Japan's urban tradition goes back at least to the fifteenth century. The so-called "castletowns" formed a basic urban stratum upon which later cities have been built.[25] Tokyo and Osaka were originally castletowns.

### The Extent of Urbanization

The forced opening of Japan, in the nineteenth century, to Western influences led to a boom in city building. Cities such as Tokyo, Nagoya, and Osaka grew, first as trading centers, and later as manufacturing and commercial cities. Industrialization and urbanization took place so completely that today Japan is the first Asian nation to equal—and in some cases, surpass—Western levels in these two areas. The United Nations reports that Japan as of 1970 was almost three-quarters urban (72.4 percent), a figure which is essentially the same as that for the United States.[26] Moreover, the urban population of Japan is remarkably concentrated, with an overall national density of 600 persons per square mile and 45 percent of the total population occupying only 1 percent of the land

[25]J. W. Hall, "The Castle Town and Japan's Modern Urbanization," *Far Eastern Quarterly*, 1955, pp. 37–56.

[26]*The World Population Situation in 1970,* United Nations, New York, 1971, p. 64.

area. In 1960, 24.5 percent of the population (a remarkable figure) already lived in places of 1 million inhabitants or more.

### Suburbanization

Suburbanization has been a fact of urban life for fifty years in Japan. Slums and low-income housing are located on the least desirable land; in the case of Japan, the land which is least desirable is either marshy areas subject to flooding within the city or land outside the city boundries. A long trip to work in Japan is the penalty of the poor rather than the prerogative of the rich as it is in the United States. The destruction of World War II considerably accelerated suburbanization. One-third of the city of Osaka was destroyed, including 40 percent of all its housing units. Although ownership of automobiles, and its consequent pollution, is growing, the commuting to and from suburbs is still largely done by rail, not by private automobile. Upper-class suburban areas can be expected to increase in the future.

### Tokyo-Yokohama

The Tokyo-Yokohama metropolitan area is the world's largest, with over 20 million people. Since the middle 1950s Tokyo has been adding 275,000 persons each year to its metropolitan population, with a full three-quarters of this increase representing migration from elsewhere in Japan. Tokyo-Yokohama is not only the world's largest metropolitan area; it is also probably the world's most congested and polluted. Air pollution is so severe that it directly causes scores of deaths each year. Workers in some industries automatically use gas masks while drug stores have machines dispensing oxygen. The level of water pollution was graphically demonstrated when a Tokyo newspaper printed on its front page a photograph that had been developed solely by dipping the negative in a chemically polluted river.

Transportation is in similar condition. Subways are so overburdened that uniformed "pushers" are employed to stand on the platforms to shove and force additional people into the already overcrowded subway cars. At street level the situation is hardly better; Tokyo has the worst automobile congestion in the world. Roads are in dismal shape; the school systems are overburdened; there are long waiting lists for apartments; and all public services are overworked and inadequate. Virtually the entire shore of Tokyo Bay is given over to industrial uses which are built on land reclaimed from the sea. Islands in the bay are currently being filled in using garbage from the city, which has resulted in serious water pollution.

Pushers are employed in Japan to shove additional people into already overcrowded cars. (*Martha Cooper Guthrie/Editorial Photocolor Archives.*)

### Conclusion—Japan

In discussing Japanese urbanization it is important to remember that while Japan is an Asian country, its levels of urbanization and industrialization are far closer to those of Europe and North America than to those of the rest of Asia. The strengths and problems of Japanese cities are largely those of developed Western metropolises. Japan, along with the small enclaves of Hong Kong and Singapore, has both a level and a pattern of urbanization highly atypical of Asia in general.

Many current urban problems in Japan are a result of the decision of the Japanese after World War II to concentrate all their efforts on industrial production for export. Only minimal attention and resources were devoted to "social overhead" such as sewage systems, water systems, housing, and urban transportation. As late as 1962, over 1.5 million households in Tokyo had no sewer facilities. The result is that today Japan has a massive backlog of demands for urban services.

The picture, however, is not as grim as these considerations alone would indicate, for while Japan has large problems, it also has great resources. Japan has the technology, the skilled manpower, and the financial resources to rebuild and remake its cities; and there is increasing evidence that a commitment to raise living standards is being made. Japan is a developed country with a mature economy which faces the same problems of pollution, energy, and so forth as other developed countries, although on a somewhat larger scale. Japan has the ability and resources to cope with its urban problems; what it now requires is the will to make the commitment. The problem is one of social organization rather than technology.

## SOUTHEAST ASIA

Urbanization is not part of the tradition of Southeast Asia. Unlike China, India, or Japan, it had no indigenous urban areas. Most cities in Southeast Asia are a product of European colonial expansion, Chinese enterprise, or a combination of the two: "In almost every country in Southeast Asia, with its 220 million people of which about 25 million live in cities, there are large cities, but every one of these is the product of a merging of European colonialism with Chinese urbanness.[27]

Cities in Southeast Asia are relatively new. Few date back more than a century or so. Primate cities, particularly ports, are common. Most of the cities are clearly divided into Western and non-Western districts. The

[27]Norton S. Ginsburg, "Urban Geography and 'Non-Western' Areas," in Philip M. Hauser and Leo F. Schnore (eds.), *The Study of Urbanization*, Wiley, New York, 1965, p. 332.

Western sector has a recognizable business district, but the remainder of the city more closely resembles traditional cities elsewhere in Asia. Cities are further divided along ethnic lines, with the Chinese district being the most obvious. Much of the commercial life of the city may in fact center in the Chinese district. As elsewhere in Asia, the migrants to the city cluster on the outskirts of the town. Suburbanization as such is little developed, partially owing to the inadequacy of the transportation network.

As is true elsewhere in the developing world, shantytowns are a severe problem, with their shacks of wood, cardboard, and pieces of galvanized iron. In Manila, the problem is particularly acute: it is estimated that there are 130,000 squatters in Manila, and these people, living in subhuman conditions, make up roughly one-fourth of the population. Their shacks are built along the 24 miles of silted-up and garbage-filled *esteros,* or drainage canals, built by the Spanish to take sewage into the sea. During severe storms the squatters' trash and garbage clog the sluices and contribute to the flooding of the city. The government is trying to relocate the squatters at the Carmona resettlement site 25 miles south of Manila. Upon arrival at Carmona each family is given a lot, building materials, and food for one month. One problem, however, is that the jobs are still in Manila, and it costs roughly 40 cents—one-fourth of the minimum daily wage—to commute to the city.

### Saigon: An Expanding Primate City

A brief examination of the growth of Saigon will highlight some of the factors influencing the growth of Southeast Asian cities in general.

Saigon's urban history began in 1859, when the French captured a village of native huts, none of them permanent structures. On this site the French built Saigon as an administrative capital, laying out the streets in the grid pattern. The Chinese quarter and marketplace, known as Cholon, developed simultaneously with Saigon. Thus Saigon became the French colonial capital for Cochin China, later named Vietnam, while Cholon was the Asian city. Early growth in Saigon was orderly, while Cholon grew haphazardly. The two areas were merged by the French in 1932 for administrative purposes.

Before World War II, the largest population group in Saigon was the Chinese.[28] From about 300,000 inhabitants in 1940, the population increased to an estimated 1,400,000 by 1953.[29] Roughly 60 percent of Cholon, and 30 percent of the entire city, was Chinese at this time.

[28]Norton S. Ginsburg, "The Great City in Southeast Asia," *American Journal of Sociology,* **60:**459, March, 1955.

[29]D. W. Fryer, "The Million City in Southeast Asia," *Geographical Review,* **43:**477, October, 1953.

Continued warfare and unrest in the countryside increased the flow of refugees from the hinterland, and by 1967 the population of Saigon was approaching 3 million. This made Saigon one of the world's most congested cities. Currently, over 3 million people live in a city built for 700,000. The tinderbox slums of Cholon are particularly vulnerable to catastrophes such as fire. Huts of sheetmetal, scraps of wood, and cardboard are packed one upon another. In the mid-1960s a fire destroyed 2,000 shacks and left 30,000 people homeless. With the departure of American troops, Saigon was left with an average of two motor scooters per family but a grave deficiency in housing and other urban needs.

## AUSTRALIA

Finally, there is Australia, a country that is in, but not of, Asia. Australia's 13 million people are heavily concentrated in the cities of the southeastern corner of the nation. Five million people inhabit the two metropolitan areas of Melbourne and Sydney alone. Although Australia is demographically the most highly urbanized nation in the world, its physical appearance is far different from what one usually associates with urbanization. Four out of five Australian families own their own single-family houses, and Australian sociologists refer to their country as "the first suburban nation." Almost nothing that can be said about Australia applies to the rest of Asia, and vice versa.

## CONCLUSION

Everywhere in Asia urbanization and urbanism are rapidly, if not spectacularly, increasing. Even in China, where government policies strongly encourage stable population, the cities are inevitably going to grow, since the Chinese government is also encouraging industrial development and trade.

Today, individual cities are frequently immense but the overall level of urbanization is still low in all major Asian nations except Japan and Australia. This is certain to change. Looking at Asia as a whole, it is quite reasonable to assume that by the year 2000 four out of every ten Asians will be city dwellers.

Generalizing beyond this point for the entire region is impossible, since the outstanding characteristic of the continent is its diversity. Many of the urban problems may be similar, but the solutions have differed widely both in their content and in their degree of success.

Japan is by far the most urbanized of the large nations of Asia and has the greatest resources, both technical and economic, that can be brought to bear on specific problems such as housing, sanitation, and transportation. China has immense human resources which it has been able to effectively mobilize to attack problems of rapid urban growth. India, on the other hand, has been relatively ineffective in providing the minimal necessities of urban life. For the average poor urbanite in India, the quality of life may well get worse during the remaining years of this century.

The only virtual certainty is that urbanism and urbanization are more and more becoming the Asian, as well as the American and European, way of life.

Part Five

# Conclusion

Chapter 18

# Toward the City's Future

*He that will not apply new remedies must expect new evils; for time is the greatest innovator.*

Sir Francis Bacon

Urban life is, as every mayor of a large city is constantly reminding us, in a state of turmoil, trouble, and transition. The city of the 1920s, 1930s, and 1940s is dying, and a new postindustrial urban form is being born. However, how fast this new urban society will emerge and what physical and social form it will take are matters of considerable doubt and dispute.

## POPULATION CHANGES

### Urban Growth

As has been indicated throughout this book, the world is presently urbanizing at a remarkable rate, with no end of the process in view. Today we live in an urban world, a massive change from the beginning of the nineteenth century, when only 3 percent of the world's population lived in places of 5,000 or more. Kingsley Davis suggested two decades ago that "there is no apparent reason why [the world] should not become as urbanized as the most urban countries today—with perhaps 85–90 percent of the population living in cities and towns of 5,000 or more and practicing urban occupations."[1] Today there is no reason to fundamentally question Davis's prediction.

In the United States recent downward trends in the birth rates have apparently convinced some people that there is no longer any problem of population increase. This is a risky assumption for Americans, and even more so for the world in general. For example, even assuming that the United States will quickly achieve a replacement level of fertility—two children per family—the population of the country will continue to grow during all of our lifetimes and into the second half of the twenty-first century. The current net population increase, even with our present birth rates, is about 400,000 per year. Projections by demographer Norman Ryder, which are based upon the smallest ultimate population size compatible with a uniform number of future births, project a population of 262.5 million people in the United States by the year 2000. By 2060 the population would reach its maximum size—297.9 million, an increase of 46 percent over 1970.[2]

Thus growth is definitely part of the future of America. In fact, of the 60 million people—this is a minimum—that will be added to the American population between 1970 and 2000, approximately 80 percent will live in urban areas. This is an additional metropolitan population almost as large as the total population of France. For the immediate future the Bureau of the Census estimates that there will be a minimum of 13 million more households in 1985 than in 1975. This is a greater increase than occurred in the fifties and one-third greater than the rate from 1960 to 1970.

## Urban Dispersion

One answer for the inevitable housing crisis is the creation of new towns and cities. The National Commission on Urban Growth has recommended the creation of 100 new towns of about 100,000 each and 10 new cities of 1 million each to absorb part of this growth, but unless there is a major change of national will and commitment, the bulk of the new urban population of this century will most likely be housed in additional developments on the edge of already existing metropolitan areas. This is a

[1]Kingsley Davis, "The Origin and Growth of Urbanization in the World," *American Journal of Sociology*, **60**:437, March, 1955.

[2]Norman B. Ryder, "The Future Growth of the American Population," in Charles F. Westoff (ed.), *Toward the End of Growth*, Spectrum Books, Prentice-Hall, Englewood Cliffs, N. J., 1973, p. 87.

sobering thought, particularly for those already dismayed by the extent of contemporary urban sprawl.

Another possibility is a renaissance of the central city. Gasoline prices will curb the previous demand for peripheral locations in the exurbs, and may incline those who had been accustomed to driving everywhere to patronize central-city shops and places of entertainment. The population for which central-city residence is the most attractive is the younger adult-oriented households with adequate income. The generally poor quality of city schools is immaterial to this population, but they do demand a relatively crime-free neighborhood with housing in good condition and easy access to transportation. The rehabilitated "New Town" area on the North Side of Chicago is an excellent example of an expanding white, middle-class, adult-oriented community. Further contributing to the growth of such areas is the increasing number of younger married couples without children.

Rebirth of central cities will probably be restricted to areas of the type described above. It is highly unrealistic to expect the combination of housing demand and energy problems to do much for inner-city ghettos. Those who have fled these areas for the suburbs are not going to move back. Even if there were no racial conflicts, the poor housing and lack of urban services and amenities in the inner city would still make these core areas undesirable. No increase in the cost of gasoline will bring middle-class movement into such areas. The effect of a growing population of adults and energy problems is likely to be selective rather than general. Some areas of the city will experience revival; but these will, as was stated above, be largely areas inhabited by white middle-class adults.

### Migration to Urban Places

Central-city population size may be stabilizing, but overall metropolitan areas will continue to expand. For 200 years the combination of heavy immigration from abroad and internal movement from farm to city has given the city a growth rate far in excess of the countryside. Will the curbing of mass immigration and the virtual disappearance of the rural population, as a major population group, mean the end of migration? Definitely not. As one authority has stated:

> Movement of people among cities will surely continue, and may well accelerate, yet it does mean that the very triumph of the city will eliminate something which has been part of urban life since cities began: the attraction of the farm boy to the metropolis, and his transformation into an urbanite. . . .
>
> We can expect the migrant from the farm—and even the small town—to

> virtually disappear. For a great many reasons it is unlikely that the rural migrant from overseas will replace him. A constantly mounting proportion of the new arrivals will be lifelong urbanites from other American metropolitan areas.[3]

Migration today is increasingly between one metropolitan area and another, with the poorer migrants more commonly going from central city to central city. The more affluent move from the suburbs of one metropolitan area to the suburbs of another metropolitan area without touching the cities themselves. Aggregate movement in the United States is toward the North and the West—particularly the West. The great interior of the country is sending migrants to both coasts. The movement is toward deep water—the Atlantic and Pacific oceans, the Gulf of Mexico, or the Great Lakes. Today more than two out of five Americans live in a metropolitan area abutting deep water. This movement toward the periphery of the nation and toward deep water results, of course, in ever-greater concentrations of population in metropolitan areas while densities in rural and small-town areas decrease. The effects of such concentration are already all too visible in parts of California and Florida. It would be tragic if the mistakes made after World War II, which produced urban sprawl in Los Angeles and San Jose, for example, were unthinkingly repeated elsewhere. But there is not a great deal of evidence that most community planning is taking place on other than a piecemeal, *ad hoc* basis.

## CHANGING EMPLOYMENT PATTERNS

During the first three-quarters of this century the work role has played a vital part in most adults' lives. The work role not only placed a person in society, it also in large part determined the pattern of an individual's social participation. This all may be in the process of changing as we enter postindustrial society: that is, a period in which the vision of the good life will include more than unlimited economic growth; in which a greater proportion of time will be devoted to providing services and less to producing goods; and in which a smaller proportion of the population and a smaller proportion of time will be required to support the production of essential goods. This may cause serious adjustment problems in a society oriented toward acquisition of goods through competition.

One certain result will be an increase in the demand for leisure-time facilities and recreational activities. This demand will be fueled in part by greater affluence and in part by the greater availability of free time among

[3]Charles Tilly, "Migration to American Cities," in Daniel P. Moynihan (ed.), *Toward a National Urban Policy*, Basic Books, New York, 1970, chap. 13, pp. 153 and 165.

most of the population. Working hours for professionals may not decrease, but the work week of those who punch time clocks certainly will—particularly among union workers. Four-day work weeks, although not yet standard, have already moved well out of the experimental stage. Decade by decade the nature of the work force is inexorably changing. In each decade a higher level of skill is required for entrance-level employment. The kind of raw, unskilled labor—often immigrant—that was needed at the turn of the century is now largely unnecessary. To put it bluntly, the nation no longer needs a large number of unskilled workers. As a result, probably at least 5 percent of the contemporary labor force is, to use the apt British term, redundant. Increasing automation will raise the percentage of unneeded workers during the remaining years of this century.

New jobs do replace older, obsolete ones, but almost invariably the new jobs demand greater training and higher qualifications than the jobs being phased out. In 1956, white-collar jobs for the first time became more numerous than blue-collar jobs. While we are increasingly substituting technology for muscle power, society has yet to cope with the question of how to handle those not needed in the labor force. Our present unsatisfactory answer is a bureaucratic, expensive, and debilitating welfare system—a system which supports at least one-tenth of the population of most large central cities. Welfare programs came into existence largely during the Depression, when unemployment was considered a temporary rather than a semipermanent condition. Today it poorly suits the needs of both society and the individual.

One alternative might be to expand government and quasigovernment services to offer employment to all those needing it. This would not only meet the needs of individuals and families more adequately than the semipauperization represented by welfare but could also provide for a more pleasant and humane urban life. In order to provide jobs, mail service could, for example, be expanded to provide morning and afternoon deliveries of mail to residences—as in fact was done in the cities until recent decades.

Fortunately, there is evidence that—at least for blue-colar workers—the question of employment or unemployment may not be as important as was previously thought. In an extensive study of the sociological ramifications of the abrupt shutdown of a major automobile plant, it was found that "the loss of a job, particularly when it is not one's fault, may not be as important as the fact that unemployment symbolizes the loss of other out of plant goals."[4] Only when unemployment resulted in significant economic loss did the workers become seriously alienated or

[4] J. John Palen, "Belief in Government Control and the Displaced Worker," *Administrative Science Quarterly*, **14**:592, December, 1969.

seek government control. The research indicated that if unemployed workers have some alternative source of financial support—as, for example, unemployment compensation, savings, or outside income—being unemployed by itself is not as serious a problem as white-collar professionals have automatically assumed.

For those workers who do not identify with their jobs but merely tolerate them as a means of achieving other goals, and particularly for older displaced workers, it may not be necessary to provide new jobs, but only a reasonable income level. Given the resources of the nation and the expense and limited success of retraining displaced workers, a combination of public work programs and a system of negative income taxes would be in the best interest of the individual and the nation.

### Women in the Work Force

Another area in which the labor force can be expected to change is the proportion of working women. Since the 1920s an increasing proportion of women have been entering the labor force; today, nearly two out of every five American workers are women. Most of these women are married, and half of them are over thirty-nine years of age. Three-quarters of all employed women hold full-time jobs. By 1970, working women represented 42 percent of all women over age sixteen in the population, close to double the figure for 1920. In the past women were concentrated in traditionally female occupations, such as teaching, clerical work, nursing, and retail trade. Today women are moving into a broad range of occupations, and this trend can be expected to accelerate in the future as fewer and fewer jobs remain sex-defined.

## CHANGING METROPOLITAN POLITICAL SYSTEMS

Organizationally, metropolitan areas are in a state of confusion and disorganization. Present home rule provides for local control at a substantial price. The political system itself becomes a major obstacle to effective planning. A multiplicity of city, suburban, county, township, regional, state, and federal bureaucracies all must intermesh if the metropolitan area is to be serviced effectively and at minimum cost, and this rarely works as well in practice as in theory. The interminable squabbling between city mayors and suburban political officials is one index of the ineffectiveness of the present system. The New York conurbation (admittedly an extreme example) includes people from three different states and some 1,400 different jurisdictions of one sort or another.

One alternative would be to abandon most local jurisdictions and move in the direction of one metropolitan-area government such as those found in Dade County, Florida (Miami); Nashville, Tennessee; and Toronto, Canada. However, in spite of the generally favorably reports on these consolidations, there is little real agitation or political pressure in most major American urban areas for adoption of this system.

Another approach is a two-tiered, or two-level, system which would move certain decision-making powers and organization to the level of a county or SMSA while other functions would be handled by dividing the entire area—including the central city—into political units the size of suburbs, which would handle local problems. Schmandt has envisioned such a plan:

> What is necessary, therefore, is to move in two directions. One is to create the kind of urban governmental mechanism that is capable of handling the major maintenance functions of a metropolitan aggregation, playing the coordinating role essential to a specialized and large-scale community, and guaranteeing the "openness" of the opportunity structure. The other is to establish local governmental units of such size that the individual will have meaningful opportunity to participate in and control those public activities which directly and immediately affect his neighborhood and his life style. The first objective will require the creation of a metropolitan or regional government with territorial jurisdiction over the entire urbanized area; the second will necessitate the division of the central city into smaller political units of 100,000 to 150,000 population, each with governmental structures and power similar to those of the suburban municipalities. Under this plan, the counties and all special districts within the urban region would be abolished as governmental entities; the other local units—the suburban municipalities and suburban school districts—would continue in existence as at present, although some industrial concentrations, because of their importance to the total community, would be placed under the jurisdiction of the larger government. Elections to the regional council would be by district, with the chief executive selected at large.[5]

Under the larger metropolitan unit would be placed functions common to the urban system as a whole, such as water supply, waste disposal, expressways and streets, control of air and water pollution, museums, public hospitals, and major recreational facilities. On the other hand, local matters such as education, enforcement of housing codes, and recreation would be left to the local community. As for education, there is no reason why local central-city areas should not have their own school boards and school policies, just as suburbs presently do. Given the present low

[5]Henry J. Schmandt, "Solutions for the City as a Social Crisis," in J. John Palen and Karl H. Flaming (eds.), *Urban America*, Holt, Rinehart and Winston, New York, 1972, p. 363.

quality of most central-city schools, more localized control could only improve the situation.

Police departments, I believe, should also be organized on a local basis—with a common radio network and other specialized facilities—while fire protection should be provided on a metropolitan basis. It makes little sense for suburban fire departments to duplicate expensive equipment; furthermore, the area that a fire-station services should be determined by the needs of a population rather than by political boundaries. Police, on the other hand, have a day-to-day contact with the community that firemen do not. Small, locally administered departments such as those found in suburbs today are most likely to provide a setting in which the police and the community can come to know and respect one another. Large bureaucratic departments in which patrolmen are shifted from district to district seldom are able to establish rapport with citizens. This is especially true of many black inner-city areas, where the police are objects of overt hostility and are viewed by the residents as an occupying army. In such a situation, the police generally respond in kind. What would happen to the extremely high crime rates in these areas if locally controlled police forces replaced the present system? A new system would certainly be worth trying, in selected cities and as a closely monitored experiment.

However, dissatisfaction with past policies and practices has yet to create sufficient pressures for change. There is little chance that such new approaches will receive serious consideration by policy makers; in this they will resemble other rational approaches to reform suggested in the past. For the immediate future we appear to be doomed to continue with overlap and confusion; we can only hope that voluntary cooperation among the various governmental units within metropolitan areas will increase.

## PHYSICAL CITY PLANNING

Urban planning, to many people, almost automatically means physical planning; but physical planning is never free from social implications—the two are always intertwined. Moreover, our view of the future influences our contemporary behavior. As Scott Greer has expressed it:

> It is my assumption that images of the future determine present actions. They may or may not determine the nature of the future—that depends on a much more complex set of circumstances. But willy-nilly much of our behavior is postulated upon images of a possible and/or desirable future.[6]

[6]Scott Greer, *The Urbane View,* Oxford University Press, New York, 1972, p. 322.

### Utopias

One of the most significant of the images of the future, Ebenezer Howard's visionary "garden cities," was discussed in Chapter 12. Howard designed a system of compact, self-contained cities of limited size that were designed to attract residents away from large cities such as London. Other planners, of course, had their own visions of utopia. Frank Lloyd Wright's model (1934) of a decentralized garden city called "Broadacres" was even more explicitly antiurban than Howard's. Wright proposed that each individual in his "urban" model be allotted at least 1 acre which he or she would be expected to farm. Wright's attitude toward contemporary cities was anything but friendly. Significantly, his book *The Living City* ends with material excerpted from Ralph Waldo Emerson's *Essay on Farming.*[7]

A different type of "city of tomorrow" was Le Corbusier's "radiant city." This was to be composed of a center of towering skyscrapers surrounded by parks and open spaces. Residences, similarly, would be in tall, thin apartment superblocks surrounded by greenery.[8] Brazilia, the new capital of Brazil, although not designed by Le Corbusier, followed his general plan: it has a unified high-rise center and residential superblocks united by a radial system of freeways. However, as was indicated in Chapter 11, Brazilia is too uncomfortably monumental for most people, who prefer for living the chaos of a Rio de Janeiro.

Sometimes physical planning for the future seems to be a fanciful, "brave new world" kind of academic exercise. The vision of Buckminster Fuller is an example: it cuts our ties to the physical earth and to mundane things such as water mains and sewers by means of recycling packs that we could wear on our backs like the astronauts' life-support systems. The urban architectural critic Wolf von Eckardt discusses Fuller's idea as follows:

> The box regenerates our wastes and water and even reconditions our air and provides us with light and heat. If only we strap those little black boxes to our backs, he says, we can all disperse over the world's mountains and deserts, telecommunicate with each other, and dispense with crowded settlements. Fuller, needless to say, did not acquire his astounding, sophisticated knowledge from video screens on lonely mountaintops. He acquired it in the lively bustle, the intellectual interchange, and the accumulation of wisdom that crowded human settlements stand for.[9]

[7]Frank Lloyd Wright, *The Living City,* Mentor-Horizon, New York, 1958.

[8]Le Corbusier, *The Radiant City,* part I, Pamela Knight (trans.), parts II and VI, Eleanor Levieux (trans.), parts III, IV, V, VII, and VIII, Derek Coltman (trans.), Grossman-Orion, New York, 1967; this is a translation of the French version, *La Ville Radieuse,* 1933.

[9]Wolf von Eckardt, "Urban Design," in Daniel P. Moynihan (ed.), *Toward A National Urban Policy,* Basic Books, New York, 1970, chap. 9, p. 113.

Constantinos A. Doxiadis's prescription for planning an organized community likewise is radically removed from the situation in contemporary cities. Doxiadis proposes a city of 2 million, organized into communities of 30,000 to 50,000—each within an area of 2,000 yards by 2,000 yards. Services, schools, stores, businesses, and parks would all be organized so that residents could walk to them; public transit and highways would be around the communities. Movement from community to community within the city would be by means of "deepways"—underground highways.[10]

Another fanciful model for future cities is the architect Paolo Soleri's "arcology," a compact three-dimensional city. Soleri places heavy emphasis on building a city vertically, layer on layer, and on using "miniaturization," or a more compact form, which he believes is the rule of evolutionary development.[11] Dantzig and Saatz take this idea of vertical compactness a step further and propose a compact vertical city that makes round-the-clock use of all facilities.[12]

While such planned utopias challenge the imagination, they also frequently appear rather sterile and lifeless. They often seem better suited to guided tours than to day-in, day-out habitation. To theorize about the future is one thing; to want to live in it is another. For example, Buckminster Fuller claims that plastic domes, similar to that covering the Houston Astrodome, can now be constructed, permitting a controlled climate and environment. Cities covered by domes could theoretically be built in otherwise hostile environments such as desert regions or even the smog-filled Los Angeles Basin. Inside the domes, artificial light, controlled heating and cooling, and even synthetic grass can be provided. The question is whether or not we really want to live with synthetic lawns.

On the other hand, viewing the future as a lineal multiplication of the past is not only far less interesting but over the long run almost certain to be inaccurate. It would be rather depressing if our only dream for the future of the metropolitan area was of an endless growth of subdivisions and shopping malls. If we do not plan our cities differently, they will continue to develop the way they have been developing for the last fifty years: do we really want that? The choice for the future is not between planning and no planning, for our cities today are in fact the result of planning—even if it is only low-level planning of individual pieces of property or individual buildings. The question thus is not whether or not

[10]For an overview of Doxiadis's thought, see C. A. Doxiadis, "The Coming Era of Ecumenopolis," *Saturday Review,* March 18, 1967, pp. 11–14.

[11]Paolo Soleri, *Arcology, The City in the Image of Man,* M.I.T. Press, Cambridge, Mass.,1969.

[12]George B. Dantzig and Thomas L. Saatz, *Compact City: A Plan for a Liveable Urban Environment,* Freeman, San Francisco, 1973.

St. Louis' Climatron contains rare botanical collections. The early glass and steel geodesic dome was designed by R. Buckminster Fuller and completed in 1960. (*United Press International.*)

planning should be done, but rather on what level it should be done—the individual level or some more general level.

### Planning of the Middle Level

Planners and social critics must get away from the all-or-nothing approach by which we exercise our imaginations either in grand fantasies or not at all. The trick is to find the line between speculative fancy and unimaginative elaboration of the past. This is another of those things that are far simpler in theory than in practice, for novel and innovative schemes are all too often considered unrealistic and dismissed out of hand. As Machiavelli accurately observed centuries ago, "There is nothing more difficult to carry out, nor more doubtful of success, nor more dangerous to handle than a new order of things."[13]

What we need, in my judgment, is far more ideas and schemes of the middle range. For example, New York has experimented with closing Fifth Avenue to traffic for certain periods and having a municipal summer

[13]Niccolo Machiavelli, *The Prince,* W. K. Marriot (trans.), J. M. Dent, London, 1958, p. 29.

theatre company putting on plays in the street from its own portable stage built on a truck.

Most schemes of this sort are neither overelaborate nor expensive. The major argument against any such lower- or middle-range experimentation is frequently "We've never done anything like that before."

For instance, one of the most interesting architectural innovations in housing design seen in recent years is Moshe Safdie's "Habitat," erected for Expo '67 in Montreal. Safdie's design of modular systems-built boxes piled irregularly upon one another was originally hailed by some observers as the answer to the urban housing problem. The modular units were prefabricated and shipped to the construction site; the irregular placement of the units provided not only for variety but also for balconies and private space. The result was a rare combination of both privacy and a sense of community. Unlike most modern apartment buildings, Habitat gave the immediate impression of being concerned with human needs and designing buildings to these needs rather than simply stuffing people into space. Unfortunately, "Habitats" have turned out to be both more expensive and less practical than was hoped. In addition to the financial difficulties, there is also a less clearly expressed but nevertheless deep

Habitat, designed by Moshe Safdie for Expo '67 in Montreal, was an attempt to provide private space for apartment dwellers and get away from the conventional slab-sided high-rises. (*United Press International.*)

reluctance to try anything as different from conventional apartment buildings as Habitat.

A number of middle-range transportation alternatives such as closing streets have been discussed in Chapter 12. A pet scheme of mine is the "Borrow a bike" plan. The idea is quite simple: the city would simply put up numerous clearly marked municipal bicycle racks and fill them with city-owned bicycles. This scheme was, in fact, proposed in Amsterdam but rejected by conservative officials. Anyone could use any bike from any rack, the only requirement being that he or she eventually return it to one of the racks. The bikes would be simple, straightforward, one-speed models painted a distinctive common color. There would be little point in stealing them, since in any event they would be freely available as transportation to anyone who wanted them. Some people would undoubtedly lock their "own" bikes, but if enough bikes were available, this would not be an important problem. Certainly some riders would move on to purchase their own more elaborate models, so that the scheme would probably increase rather than decrease sales by private dealers—just as Henry Ford's cheap Model T spurred the purchase of more elaborate automobiles. Bicycles could be manufactured and assembled at minimal cost by the city itself, employing persons on welfare who want jobs but have only minimal skills. The advantage of such a scheme is that it would reduce pollution, reduce gasoline consumption, ease traffic, and increase the physical—and probably emotional—health of the population. The disadvantages would be the initial cost of bicycles (although costs of repairing streets should compensate for this over the long run) and the fact that in some cities the bikes would probably not be much used through the winter months. Also, even if the plan saved the city money, some residents would no doubt complain that it was socialistic nonsense and that the city has no business giving people bicycles. Perhaps they have a point, but if American city dwellers used bicycles as much as the residents of Amsterdam or Peking, there would be fewer problems with pollution and with energy crunches.

Finally, it is crucial to remember that whatever our formal plans for the city of the future, much of what it will actually become is the result of untold numbers of diverse decisions made by different individuals. As Jane Jacobs has said:

> . . . most city diversity is the creation of incredible numbers of different people and different private organizations with vastly differing ideas and purposes, planning and contributing outside the formal framework of public action. The main responsibility of city planning and design should be to develop—insofar as public policy and action can do so—cities that are

congenial places for this great range of unofficial plans, ideas and opportunities to flourish, along with the flourishing of the public enterprises.[14]

## THE "URBAN CRISIS" THEORY

As recently as 1930 a planner could exult over the harmonious combination of urban and rural elements in Los Angeles and describe the city as "a federation of communities coordinated into a metropolis of sunlight and air."[15] No one makes such claims today. All around, one hears that the city is not only going to hell but going to hell at an ever more rapid pace. It is an accepted cliché that we live in an age of urban crisis. Crime, violence, pollution, ugliness, congestion, and alienation are all attributed in one degree or another to urban life. Certainly there is no lack of prophets to passionately catalog our urban ills. As Lewis Mumford says:

> Nobody can be satisfied with the form of the city today. Neither as a working mechanism, as a social medium, nor as a work of art does the city fulfill the high hopes that modern civilization has called forth—or even met our reasonable demands.[16]

Constantinos Doxiadis states it somewhat differently but reaches a similar conclusion—urban collapse:

> We must face the fact that modern man has failed to build adequate cities. In the past his problems were simpler, and he solved them by trial and error. Now human forces and mechanical ones are mixed and man is confused. He tries and fails. We say he will become adapted. Yes, he is running the danger of becoming adapted, since adaptation is only meaningful if it means the welfare of man. Prisoners, too, become adapted to conditions! For man to adapt to our present cities would be a mistake, since he is the great prisoner. Not only is man unsafe in his prison, but he is facing a great crisis and heading for disaster.[17]

Even the National Commission on Causes and Prevention of Violence gets into the act with the picture of central business districts occupied only by police patrols during night time hours and high-rise apartment buildings walled off by security devices from the rest of the city.[18]

[14]Jane Jacobs, *The Death and Life of Great American Cities,* Vintage-Random House, New York, 1961, p. 241.

[15]R. M. Fogelson, *The Fragmented Metropolis: Los Angeles 1850–1930,* Harvard University Press, Cambridge, Mass., 1967, p. 163.

[16]Lewis Mumford, *The Urban Prospect,* Harcourt Brace Jovanovich, New York, 1968, p. 108.

[17]C. A. Doxiadis, op. cit., p. 11.

[18]National Commission on the Causes and Prevention of Violence, *Violent Crime: The Challenge to Our Cities,* Braziller, New York, 1969, pp. 69–70.

### A Dissenting View

Still, there is reason to doubt that the situation is really as bleak and hopeless as it is often portrayed. Is the city really irredeemable? The conventional wisdom that the city is in a state of crisis is strongly challenged by Edward Banfield:

> It is clear at the outset that serious problems directly affect only a rather small minority of the whole urban population. In the relatively new residential suburbs and in the better residential neighborhoods in the outlying parts of the central cities and in the older, larger suburbs, the overwhelming majority of people are safely above the poverty line, have at least a high school education, and do not suffer from racial discrimination. For something like two-thirds of all city dwellers, the urban problems that touch them directly have to do with comfort, convenience, amenity, and business advantage. In the terminology used here, these are "important" problems but not "serious" ones. In a great many cases, these problems cannot even fairly be called important; a considerable part of the urban population—those who reside in the "nicer" suburbs—lives under material conditions that will be hard to improve upon.
>
> The serious problems are to be found in all large cities and in most small ones. But they affect only parts of these cities (and only a minority of the city populations). In the central cities and the larger, older suburbs the affected parts are usually adjacent to the central business district and spreading out from it. If these inner districts, which probably comprise somewhere between 10 and 20 percent of the total area classified as urban by the Census, were suddenly to disappear, along with the people who live in them, there would be no serious urban problems worth talking about. If what really matters is the essential welfare of individuals and the good health of the society as opposed to comfort, convenience, amenity, and business advantage, then what we have is not an "urban problem" but an "inner-central-city-and-larger-older-suburb" one.[19]

Banfield goes on to say that nearly 90 percent of expenditures by the federal government for improving the cities—rather than just maintaining them—is directed into two programs: the improvement of transportation through the creation of a national expressway system, and the federal housing programs such as urban renewal, the FHA, and the VA. He contends that both of these mammoth government programs to aid the cities are directed mainly toward the problems of comfort, convenience, amenity, and business advantage. Insofar as they have any effect on the serious problems, it is, on the whole, to aggravate them.

[19]Edward G. Banfield, *The Unheavenly City*, Little, Brown, Boston, 1968, p. 11, 12. Reprinted with permission of Little, Brown and Company. These arguments are substantively restated with some additional documentation in Edward G. Banfield, *The Unheavenly City Revisited*, Little, Brown, Boston, 1974.

> In many important respects, conditions in the large cities have been getting better. There is less poverty in the cities now than there has ever been. Housing, including that of the poor, is improving rapidly: one study predicts that substandard housing will have been eliminated by 1980. In the last decade alone the improvement in housing has been marked. At the turn of the century only one child in fifteen went beyond elementary school; now most children finish high school. The treatment of racial and other minority groups is conspicuously better than it was. When, in 1964, a carefully drawn sample of Negroes was asked whether, in general, things were getting better or worse for Negroes in this country, approximately eight out of ten respondents said "better."
>
> If the situation is improving, why, it may be asked, is there so much talk of an urban crisis? The answer is that the improvements in performance, great as they have been, have not kept pace with rising expectations. In other words, although things have been getting better absolutely, they have been getting worse *relative to what we think they should be.*[20]

One needn't agree with Banfield's larger arguments or conclusions—some of which have been discussed in earlier chapters—in order to appreciate his iconoclastic approach, which doesn't accept it as given that cities are sliding into catastrophe.

## VARIOUS APPROACHES TO SOCIAL PLANNING

Approaches to social planning and problem solving range from the use of existing social mechanisms in conventional ways to attempts to radically restructure the entire system. Three general assumptions regarding problem solving and the resulting approaches to planning can be delineated: (1) conventional approaches, which assume that problems can be solved by existing mechanisms; (2) reformist approaches, which assume that the system needs some major modification; and (3) radical approaches, which assume that problems cannot be solved by the existing social system.[21]

Conventional approaches to planning and problem solving assume that the system itself is not in question. Inadequacies are attributed to the failings of individuals. An example might be responding to the Watergate scandal by blaming it all on bad advisors and poor personal judgments made by a few individuals. The appropriate traditional response would thus be to replace the offending personnel with new faces. Reassessment

[20]Banfield, op. cit., p. 19.

[21]An earlier form of this approach can be found in J. John Palen and Karl H. Flaming (eds.), *Urban America*, Holt, Rinehart, and Winston, New York, 1972, p. 335.

**Table 18-1 Strategies for Planning and Problem Solving**

| Assumptions regarding problem solving | General approach to planning | Resulting action taken |
|---|---|---|
| Most, if not all, problems can be solved by existing mechanisms | Conventional approaches (System needs minor modifications, fine tuning, or both) | New leadership, better administration shift in priorities, new legislation |
| Some problems cannot be solved by existing mechanisms | Reformist approaches (System needs some major modification; likely to see system itself as source of problems) | Mobilization of power bases outside existing party structures, quasilegal protests, civil disobedience |
| Most, if not all, problems cannot be solved by existing mechanisms | Radical approaches (System needs major revision or replacement) | Rejection of societal goals, extreme countercultural movements, revolution, planned violence |

*Source:* Based on J. John Palen and Karl H. Flaming, *Urban America,* Holt, Rinehart and Winston, New York, 1972, p. 335.

of priorities would also be an essentially conventional response. Here, the emphasis is upon the allocation of resources and weighting of priorities within the system rather than upon structural modification of the system itself.

Reformist responses, as outlined in Table 18-1, are characterized by ideological commitment to the goals and ideals of the society but not by attempts to achieve them through conventional means. Reformers are more likely to see the system itself as the source of the problem and to have little faith in correcting it by traditional means. They accept quasilegal methods falling outside the traditional system, as did members of the civil rights movements of the 1960s.

Radical views of the future differ from the conventional and reformist positions by rejecting, at least implicitly, the goals of the society as well as the means used to implement them. The existing system is judged to be so corrupt and repressive that the response is to destroy it and start over. Radical responses are almost always overtly ideological in their vision of the new utopia.

### Urban Policy

A response to the urban crisis that would fall into the first category is provided by Daniel Moynihan, who gives his national urban policy in ten points. Moynihan, a former urban counselor to President Nixon, stresses that an accumulation of government programs does not add up to a clearly thought-out urban policy. Existing hidden policies such as FHA loans for suburban homes that encourage racial discrimination or AFDC welfare policies that encourage broken homes and dependency must be recognized for what they are and changed. Clearly enunciated policies also have the advantage of spelling out explicit goals and allowing observers to assess progress toward these goals. Moynihan thus is not calling for radical reformation of the society but rather for a more rational organization of government to achieve explicitly described goals.

Moynihan's is basically a practical program of what could be done, not necessarily what will be done. Moynihan stresses three general themes: first, he calls for shifts in priorities; second, he calls for greater coordination between different levels of government and the public; and finally, he makes an appeal for a heightened aesthetic commitment to the city and to urban values. Moynihan's ten points of urban policy, in order of urgency and importance, are as follows (in slightly abbreviated form):

> **1** The poverty and social isolation of minority groups is the single most serious problem of the American city today. It must be attacked with urgency, with a greater commitment of resources than has heretofore been the case, and with programs designed especially for this purpose.
>
> **2** Economic and social forces in urban areas are not self-balancing. . . . A concept of urban balance may be tentatively set forth: a social condition in which the forces tending to produce imbalance induce counterforces that simultaneously admit change while maintaining equilibrium. It must be the constant object of federal officials whose programs affect urban areas to seek such equilibrium.
>
> **3** At least part of the relative ineffectiveness of the efforts of urban government to respond to urban problems derives from the fragmented and obsolescent structure of urban government itself. The federal government should constantly encourage and provide incentives for the reorganization of local government in response to the reality of metropolitan conditions. . . . The federal government should discourage the creation of paragovernments designed to deal with special problems by evading or avoiding the jurisdiction of established local authorities, and should encourage effective decentralization.
>
> **4** A primary object of federal urban policy must be to restore the fiscal vitality of urban government, with the particular object of ensuring that local governments normally have enough resources on hand or available to make local initiative in public affairs a reality.
>
> **5** Federal urban policy should seek to equalize the provision of public services as among different jurisdictions in metropolitan areas.
>
> **6** The federal government must assert a specific interest in the

movement of people, displaced by technology or driven by poverty, from rural to urban areas, and also in the movement from densely populated central cities to suburban areas.

**7** State government has an indispensible role in the management of urban affairs, and must be supported and encouraged by the federal government in the performance of this role.

**8** The federal government must develop and put into practice far more effective incentive systems than now exist whereby state and local governments, and private interests too, can be led to achieve the goals of federal programs.

**9** The federal government must provide more and better information concerning urban affairs, and should sponsor extensive and sustained research into urban problems.

**10** The federal government, by its own example, and by incentives, should seek the development of a far heightened sense of the finite resources of the natural environment, and the fundamental importance of aesthetics in successful urban growth.[22]

## The City as a Social Problem

One point upon which urbanists, including relative conservatives such as Moynihan and Banfield, generally agree is that the core problems of the city are social problems, particularly the problem of race and our reactions to it. If the racial problems of the city could be at least partially solved, then other problems could more effectively be addressed.

The difficulty is that we are frequently unwilling to admit the existence of social problems until they reach serious proportions, and even then we seek solutions through other than social reforms in the naive belief that "technology saves." Public housing projects and freeways are perhaps the two best-known examples of how we have, with disastrous results for the cities, attempted to provide engineering solutions for social problems. For example, the technology exists for building mile-high apartment buildings. The real question should not be "Is it possible?" but rather "Is it desirable?" Still, the faith in the ultimate technical solution persists. As Jeb Magruder, at one time a technology consultant for the White House, said:

> The cities have no place else to turn except to technical solutions. There is no political or social solution to providing more adequate energy, or waste disposal, or drug abuse. I want to see something better and technology can do it if we work at it.[23]

[22]Daniel P. Moynihan, "Toward a National Urban Policy," *The Public Interest,* Fall, 1969, pp. 8–19.
[23]*The New York Times,* July 29, 1972.

The answers even to questions about energy are, of course, far more social and political than technical. America's social orientation toward automobiles, its values concerning the environment, and even its political policies toward the oil monopolies determine whether the nation has an "energy crisis" far more than technology alone. The decision of an oil company not to build a needed refinery may be an economic or a political decision, or both, but it is not a technological decision. Of course, if one expects technology to solve all problems, even including drug abuse, then there really isn't any need to even consider modifying or changing the social, economic, or political system.

## THE "POSTCITY" AGE

### Superterritoriality

One futurist sees megalopolis as just the beginning of one world-wide city. Doxiadis sees population increases resulting in a world with urban settlements covering an area not just 7 to 10 times larger than they now do, but as much as 30, 40, or even 50 times as large. Moreover, he predicts that it is probable that all settlements will become interconnected to form a continuous system covering the inhabitable earth. In Doxiadis's opinion, there is no possibility of halting or changing the growth of this ultimate megalopolis he calls Ecumenopolis. He feels that stopping the trend toward Ecumenopolis is impossible for two reasons:

> **1** These are trends of population growth determined by many biological and social forces which we do not even understand properly, let alone dare countermand.
>
> **2** The great forces shaping the Ecumenopolis—economic, commercial, social, political, technological, and cultural—are already being deployed, and it is too late to reverse them.[24]

He further believes that the eventual creation of Ecumenopolis should be considered "an inevitability which we must accept." The challenge as he sees it is "to make the Ecumenopolis fit for Man."[25]

Fortunately, this prediction has little contact with empirical reality. Population growth is far from inevitable; and biological and social forces do not operate in response to mysterious and mystical "forces" beyond our knowledge. Whatever our urban areas become, they will be the result of our present and future actions—wise or unwise—not the result of unchangeable forces.

[24]C. A. Doxiadis, *Ekistics*, Hutchinson, London, 1968, p. 430.
[25]Ibid.

### Nonterritoriality

Others see the traditional city as passing away. In recent years, we have come to think less in terms of the city versus the country and more in terms of a larger urban-dominated community that often includes rural sectors. This new unit, commonly called the "metropolitan community," has evolved rapidly in the United States during the past half-century. Now some scholars believe that we are moving from metropolitan communities to a new "postcity" age. As Melvin Webber states this position, "We are passing through a revolution that is unhitching the social processes of urbanization from the locationally fixed city and region."[26] Webber maintains:

> A new kind of large-scale urban society is emerging that is increasingly independent of the city. In turn, the problems of the city place generated by early industrialization are being supplanted by a new array different in kind. With but a few remaining exceptions (the new air pollution is a notable one), the recent difficulties are not place-type problems at all. Rather, they are the transitional problems of a rapidly developing society-economy-and-polity whose turf is the nation. Paradoxically, just at the time in history when policy-makers and the world press are discovering the city, "the age of the city seems to be at an end."[27]

He suggests that we have failed to draw up a simple conceptual definition distinguishing between the spatially defined urban area and the social systems that are localized there. Because our cities have historically been spatially structured, we don't have the concepts or language to deal with the new situation. The resulting problems, Webber says, are serious ones, for we seek local solutions to problems that transcend local boundaries and are not susceptible to municipal treatment. Problems of poverty, crime, unemployment, and even transportation transcend any city or even cities in general.

Webber suggests that the future pattern can be discerned in the life-styles of the new cosmopolites who through frequent use of airlines and telephones have established new spatially dispersed networks of specialized knowledge. These cosmopolites are the producers of the information and new ideas that are transforming societies.

What is most open to dispute in Webber's analysis is that American society as a whole is inevitably evolving in the direction of the territorially unbound city dweller. He states:

[26]Melvin M. Webber, "The Postcity Age," *Daedalus*, **97**(4):1092, Fall, 1968.

[27]Webber, op. cit., pp. 1092–1093. Reprinted by permission of *Daedalus*, Journal of the American Academy of Arts and Sciences, Boston, Mass., Fall, 1968, *The Conscience of the City*.

> At one extreme are the intellectual and business elites, whose habitat is the planet; at the other are the lower-class residents of city and farm who live in spatially and cognitively constrained worlds. Most of the rest of us, who comprise the large middle class, lie somewhere in-between, but in some facets of our lives we all seem to be moving from our ancestral localism toward the unbounded realms of the cosmopolites.[28]

This is far from certain. It *may* be true for segments of the upper middle class; but, as we have seen in earlier chapters, upper-middle-class professionals tend to consistently underrate both the strength and the utility of territorially bounded urban life-styles.

### The Passing of the City?

Another contemporary reworking of the concept of the passing of the city is provided by John Seeley, who suggests that the Western nations have reached their highest point of development and institutional practices. He goes on to say: "If the view is correct, there is something tragicomic about sitting around 'planning' to secure, extend, and improve what is to be shortly swept away. . . . "[29]

To Seeley, what is significant about the city is not that it is a population center or manufacturing node but that it is the place where whatever is highest in the civilization is carried on:

> Just as the city is in normal times that place where the civilization reaches the highest point of its gradient, where the civilization is refined, developed, elaborated, and fed back to the hinterland, so in abnormal times the city is that place where its successor is being incubated, nurtured, fostered, or developed. And the conscience of the city lies at that *nucleus nucleorum*, wherever it may be, where most actively, most passionately, most devotedly, most integrally the foundations of the new civilizations are being in action and interaction conceived, incarnated, tested and worked out.[30]

Thus, the city as we know it will pass, to be replaced by a new and as yet undefined form.

> Very little will need planning—just enough control over the spread of cities and their ways to permit the conscience of the city to find itself chiefly outside these centers, to spread through the society which, by then, may be

[28]Webber, op. cit., p. 1095. Reprinted by permission of *Daedalus*.

[29]John R. Seeley, "Remaking the Urban Scene: New Youth in an Old Environment," *Daedalus*, **97**(4):1125, Fall, 1968.

[30]Seeley, op. cit., p. 1126. Reprinted by permission of *Daedalus*, Journal of the American Academy of Arts and Sciences, Boston, Mass., Fall, 1968, *The Conscience of the City*.

> ready, having reached its fevered climax, to abandon its delirium and search out a new way. That new way, I am confident, will not be, cannot be, in content, organization, aim, or spirit, anything like a continuation or culmination of what we have hitherto nurtured and known.[31]

Other sociologists who do not have the same certainty are dubious as to whether this prophecy of the passage of the city will come to be. Nor would many social scientists accept the idea that planning for cities is unnecessary, futile, and perhaps even harmful. Even with all the limitations of planning, most of us prefer to plan our urban futures on the basis of empirical knowledge rather than soothsaying or speculation. To paraphrase Mark Twain's famous remark, the reports of the death of the city have been greatly exaggerated.

[31]Seeley, op. cit., p. 1139. Reprinted by permission of *Daedalus*.

# Bibliography


## CHAPTER 1

Bierstedt, Robert: *The Social Order,* McGraw-Hill, New York, 1970.

Davis, Kingsley: "The Origin and Growth of Urbanization in the World," *American Journal of Sociology,* vol. 60, March 1955.

Eldridge, Hope Tisdale: "The Process of Urbanization," in J. J. Spengler and O. D. Duncan (eds.), *Demographic Analysis,* Free Press, Glencoe, Ill., 1956.

Hauser, Philip, and Leo Schnore: *The Study of Urbanization,* Wiley, New York, 1965.

Hinkle, Rosco C., Jr., and Gisela J. Hinkle: *The Development of Modern Sociology,* Doubleday, New York, 1954.

Meadows, Paul, and Ephraim Mizruchi (eds.): *Urbanism, Urbanization, and Change: Comparative Perspectives,* Addison-Wesley, Reading, Mass., 1969.

United Nations: *Urbanization in the Second United Nations Development Decade,* United Nations, New York, 1970.

## CHAPTER 2

Adams, Robert M.: "The Origins of Cities," *Scientific American,* September 1960.

Aristotle: *Politics,* Book VII, IV 7–8, B. Jowett (trans.), 1932 ed.

Braidwood, Robert J.: "The Agricultural Revolution," *Scientific American* reprint, September 1960.
Childe, Gordon: "The Urban Revolution," *Town Planning Review,* vol. 21, 1950.
———: *What Happened in History,* Penguin Books, London, 1946.
Coulanges, Fustel de: *The Ancient City,* Doubleday, Garden City, New York, 1956. (First published 1865.)
Creel, H. G.: *The Birth of China,* Reynal and Hitchcock, New York, 1937.
Curwin, E. Cecil, and Gudmund Hart: *Plough and Pasture,* Collier Books, New York, 1961.
Davis, Kingsley: "The Origin and Growth of Urbanization in the World," *American Journal of Sociology,* vol. 60, March 1955.
———, and Hilda Hertz: Unpublished manuscript (table) in Neil J. Smelser (ed.), *Sociology: An Introduction,* Wiley, New York, 1967.
Gans, Herbert: *The Urban Villagers,* Free Press, Glencoe, Ill., 1962.
George, Dorothy: *London Life in the Eighteenth Century,* Harper Torchbooks, New York, 1964.
Gibbon, Edward: *The Decline and Fall of the Roman Empire,* Dell, New York, 1879. (First published 1776.)
Glotz, Gustave: *Ancient Greece at Work,* Norton, New York, 1967.
Hawley, Amos H.: *Urban Society,* Ronald Press, New York, 1971.
Hiorns, Frederick: *Town Building in History,* Harrap, London, 1956.
Hoselitz, Burt F.: "The Role of Cities in the Economic Growth of Underdeveloped Countries," *Journal of Political Economy,* vol. 61, 1953.
July, Robert W.: *A History of the African People,* Charles Scribner's Sons, New York, 1970.
Langer, William L.: "The Black Death," in Scientific American, *Cities: The Origin, Growth, and Human Impact,* Freeman, San Francisco, 1973.
Lee, Rose Hum: *The City,* Lippincott, Chicago, 1955.
Lenski, Gerhard: *Human Society,* McGraw-Hill, New York, 1970.
Liebow, Elliot: *Tally's Corner,* Little, Brown, Boston, 1967.
Minor, Horace: *The Primitive City of Timbuctoo,* Doubleday Anchor, New York, 1965.
Mumford, Lewis: *The City in History, Its Transformations and Its Prospects,* Harcourt, Brace and World, New York, 1961.
Mundy, John H., and Peter Reisenberg: *The Medieval Town,* Van Nostrand, New York, 1958.
Petersen, William: *Population,* Macmillan, New York, 1969.
Pirenne, Henri: *Economic and Social History of Medieval Europe,* Harcourt, Brace and World, New York, 1936.
———: *Medieval Cities,* Princeton University Press, Princeton, N. J., 1939.
Plato: *The Laws,* Book V, 437, B. Jowett (trans.), 1926 ed.
Russell, J. C.: *Late Ancient and Medieval Population,* The American Philosophical Society, Philadelphia, 1958.
Saalman, Howard: *Medieval Cities,* Braziller, New York, 1968.
*Scientific American: Cities: The Origin, Growth, and Human Impact,* Freeman, San Francisco, 1973.

Sjoberg, Gideon: "The Preindustrial City," *American Journal of Sociology,* vol. 60, March 1955.

Smelser, Neil J. (ed.): *Sociology: An Introduction,* Wiley, New York, 1967.

Suttles, Gerald: *The Social Order of the Slum,* University of Chicago Press, Chicago, 1968.

Trigger, Bruce: "Determinants of Urban Growth in Pre-Industrial Societies," in Peter Ucko, Ruth Tringham, and G. W. Dimbleby (eds.), *Man, Settlement, and Urbanism,* Schenkman, Cambridge, Mass., 1972.

Ucko, Peter, Ruth Tringham, and G. W. Dimbleby (eds.): *Man, Settlement, and Urbanism,* Schenkman, Cambridge, Mass., 1972.

Weber, Max: *The City,* D. Martendale and G. Newwirth (trans.), Free Press, New York, 1958.

Wirth, Louis: "Urbanism as a Way of Life," *American Journal of Sociology,* vol. 44, July 1938.

## CHAPTER 3

Blake, Nelson M.: *A History of American Life and Thought,* McGraw-Hill, New York, 1963.

Bogue, Donald J.: *The Population of the United States,* Free Press, Glencoe, Ill., 1969.

Bowes, Frederick P.: *The Culture of Early Charleston,* University of North Carolina Press, Chapel Hill, 1942.

Bridenbaugh, Carl: *Cities in Revolt,* Knopf, New York, 1955.

———: *Cities in the Wilderness,* Capricorn Books, New York, 1964.

Bryce, James: *The American Commonwealth,* Putnam, New York, 1959. (First edition 1888.)

Cressey, Paul F.: "Population Succession in Chicago: 1898–1930," *American Journal of Sociology,* vol. 44, 1938.

Davis, William T. (ed.), *Bradford's History of Plymouth Plantation,* Scribner, New York, 1908.

Elazar, Daniel J.: "Urban Problems and the Federal Government," *Political Science Quarterly,* vol. 82, December 1967.

Ford, P. L.: *The Works of Thomas Jefferson,* Putnam, New York, 1904.

Frame, Richard: "A Short Description of Pennsylvania in 1692," in Albert Cook Myers (ed.), *Narratives of Early Pennsylvania, West New Jersey, and Delaware,* Charles Scribner's Sons, New York, 1912. Reprinted in Ruth E. Sutter, *The Next Place You Come To,* Prentice-Hall, Englewood Cliffs, N. J., 1973.

Glaab, Charles N.: *The American City,* Dorsey, Homewood, Ill., 1963.

———, and A. Theodore Brown: *A History of Urban America,* Macmillan, New York, 1967.

Glazier, Willard: *Peculiarities of American Cities,* Hubbard Bros., Philadelphia, 1884.

Green, Constance McLaughlin: *The Rise of Urban America,* Harper and Row, New York, 1965.

Hawley, Amos H.: *Urban Society,* Ronald Press, New York, 1971.

Hofstadter, Richard: *The Age of Reform,* Knopf, New York, 1955.

Hurd, Richard: *Principles of City Land Values,* The Record and Guide, New York, 1903.

Lipscomb, Andrew A., and Albert E. Bergh (eds.): *The Writings of Thomas Jefferson,* vol. X, The Thomas Jefferson Memorial Association, Washington, D.C., 1904.

McKelveg, Blake: *The Urbanization of America, 1860–1915,* Rutgers University Press, New Brunswick, N. J., 1963.

Mumford, Lewis: *Sticks and Stones,* Horace Liveright, New York, 1924.

Myers, Albert Cook (ed.): *Narratives of Early Pennsylvania, West New Jersey, and Delaware,* Charles Scribner's Sons, New York, 1912.

National Resources Committee: *Our Cities: Their Role in the National Economy,* U.S. Government Printing Office, Washington, D.C., 1937.

Petersen, William: *Population,* Macmillan, New York, 1961.

Schlesinger, Arthur M.: "The City in American History," *Mississippi Valley Historical Review,* vol. 27, June 1940.

———: *Paths to the Present,* Macmillan, New York, 1949.

Smith, John: *The General Historie of Virginia, New England, and the Summer Isles,* University Microfilms, Ann Arbor, Mich. (First published in London, 1624.)

Strong, Josiah: *Our Country: Its Possible Future and Its Present Crisis,* Baker and Taylor, New York, 1885.

Sutter, Ruth E.: *The Next Place You Come To,* Prentice-Hall, Englewood Cliffs, N. J., 1973.

Trollope, Anthony: *North America,* Lippencott, Philadelphia, 1862.

U.S. Bureau of the Census: U.S. Census of Population, vol. II, 1950, and vol. I, 1960.

Vidich, Arthur J., and Joseph Bensman: *Small Town in Mass Society,* Doubleday Anchor, New York, 1960.

White, Morton, and Lucia White: *The Intellectual Versus the City,* Harvard and M.I.T. Press, Cambridge, Mass., 1962.

Zink, Harold: *City Bosses in the United States,* Duke University Press, Durham, North Carolina, 1930.

## CHAPTER 4

Alihan, Milla A.: *Social Ecology,* Columbia University Press, New York, 1938.

Bell, Wendell, and Scott Greer: "Social Area Analysis and Its Critiques," *Pacific Sociological Review,* vol. 5, 1962.

Burgess, Ernest W.: "The Growth of the City: An Introduction to a Research Project," *Publications of the American Sociological Society,* vol. 18, 1924.

———: "Residential Segregation in American Cities," *Annals of the American Academy of Political and Social Science,* vol. 140, November 1928.

Caplow, Theodore: "The Social Ecology of Guatemala City," *Social Forces,* vol. 28, 1949.

Davie, Maurice R.: "The Pattern of Urban Growth," in George Murdock (ed.), *Studies in the Science of Society,* Yale University Press, New Haven, Conn. 1937.

*Demographic Handbook for Africa,* United Nations Economic Commission for Africa, Addis Ababa, 1968.

Duncan, Otis Dudley: Review of Shevky and Bell, "Social Area Analysis," *American Journal of Sociology,* vol. 61, July 1955.

———, and Beverly Duncan, "Residential Distribution and Occupational Stratification," *American Journal of Sociology,* vol. 60, March 1955.

Fava, Sylvia F. (ed.): *Urbanism in World Perspective,* Crowell, New York, 1968.

Firey, Walter: "Sentiment and Symbolism as Ecological Variables," *American Sociological Review,* vol. 10, 1945.

Gettys, Warner E.: "Human Ecology and Social Theory," in George A. Theodorson, (ed.), *Studies in Human Ecology,* Row Peterson, Evanston, Ill., 1961.

Gibbs, Jack (ed.): *Urban Research Methods,* Van Nostrand, New York, 1961.

Gottman, Jean: "The Skyscraper Amid the Sprawl," in Jean Gottman and Robert Harper (eds.), *Metropolis on the Move,* Wiley, New York, 1967.

———, and Robert Harper (eds.): *Metropolis on the Move,* Wiley, New York, 1967.

Haggerty, Lee J.: "Another Look at the Burgess Hypothesis: Time as an Important Variable," *American Journal of Sociology,* May 1971.

Harris, Chauncy, and Edward Ullman: "The Nature of Cities," *Annals of the American Academy of Political and Social Science,* vol. 242, 1945.

Hatt, Paul K., and Albert J. Reiss, Jr. (eds.): *Cities and Society,* The Free Press, New York, 1957.

Hauser, Francis L.:"Ecological Patterns of European Cities," in Sylvia F. Fava (ed.), *Urbanism in World Perspective,* Crowell, New York, 1968.

Hauser, Philip M., and Leo F. Schnore: *The Study of Urbanization,* Wiley, New York, 1965.

Hawley, Amos H.: *Human Ecology: A Theory of Community Structure,* Ronald Press, New York, 1950.

———, and Otis Dudley Duncan: "Social Area Analysis: A Critical Appraisal," *Land Economics,* vol. 33, November 1957.

Hillery, G. A.: "Definitions of Community: Areas of Agreement," *Rural Sociology,* vol. 20, 1955.

Hoyt, Homer: *The Structure and Growth of Residential Neighborhoods in American Cities,* U.S. Federal Housing Administration, U.S. Government Printing Office, Washington, D.C., 1939.

International Urban Research, *The World's Metropolitan Areas,* University of California Press, Berkeley, 1959.

Macura, Milos: "The Influence of the Definition of Urban Place on the Size of Urban Population," in Jack Gibbs (ed.), *Urban Research Methods,* Van Nostrand, New York, 1961.

Marston, Wilfred G.: "Socioeconomic Differentiation within Negro Areas of American Cities," *Social Forces,* vol. 48, December 1969.

McKenzie, Roderick: *The Metropolitan Community,* McGraw-Hill, New York and London, 1933.

Michelson, William H.: *Man and His Urban Environment,* Addison-Wesley, Reading, Mass., 1970.

Murdock, George (ed.): *Studies in the Science of Society,* Yale University Press, New Haven, Conn., 1937.

Newcomb, Charles: "Graphic Presentation of Age and Sex Distribution of Population in the City," in Paul K. Hatt and Albert J. Reiss, Jr., *Cities and Society,* Free Press, New York, 1957.

Park, Robert E.: *Human Communities,* Free Press, New York, 1952.

———, and Roderick D. McKenzie: "The City: Suggestions for the Investigation of Human Behavior in the Urban Environment," in Robert E. Park, E. W. Burgess, and Roderick D. McKenzie (eds.), *The City,* University of Chicago Press, Chicago, 1925.

———, E. W. Burgess, and Roderick D. McKenzie (eds.): *The City,* University of Chicago Press, Chicago, 1925.

Petersen, William: *Population,* Macmillan, New York, 1969.

Pinkerton, James R.: "The Changing Class Composition of Cities and Suburbs," *Land Economics,* vol. 49, November 1973.

Schnore, Leo F.: *Class and Race in Cities and Suburbs,* Markham, Chicago, 1972.

———: "The Myth of Human Ecology," *Sociological Inquiry,* vol. 31, 1961.

———: *The Urban Scene,* Free Press, New York, 1965.

———, and Joy K. O. Jones: "The Evolution of City-Suburban Types in the Course of a Decade," *Urban Affairs Quarterly,* June 1969.

Shevky, Eshref, and Wendell Bell: *Social Area Analysis,* Stanford University Press, Palo Alto, Calif. 1955.

Sjoberg, Gideon: "Cities in Developing and in Industrial Societies: A Cross-cultural Analysis," in Philip M. Hauser and Leo F. Schnore, *The Study of Urbanization,* Wiley, New York, 1965.

Smith, Joel: "Another Look at Socioeconomic Status Distributions in Urbanized Areas," *Urban Affairs Quarterly,* June 1970.

Theodorson, George A. (ed.): *Studies in Human Ecology,* Row Peterson, Evanston, Ill., 1961.

Thomlinson, Ralph: *Urban Structure,* Random House, New York, 1969.

Ullman, Edward: "Presidential Address, The Nature of Cities Reconsidered," *The Regional Science Association Papers and Proceedings,* vol. 9, 1962.

Van Arsdol, Maurice, Santo F. Camilleri, and Calvin Schmid: "The Generality of Urban Social Area Indexes," *American Sociological Review,* vol. 23, 1958.

Wirth, Louis: "Urbanism as a Way of Life," *American Journal of Sociology,* vol. 44, July 1938.

## CHAPTER 5

Anderson, Theodore R.: "Comparative Urban Structure," in *International Encyclopedia of the Social Sciences,* Crowell Collier and Macmillan, New York, 1968.

Atchley, Robert C.: "A Size-Function Typology of Cities," *Demography,* vol. 4, 1967.

Bollens, John C., and Henry J. Schmandt: *The Metropolis,* Harper and Row, New York, 1970.

Cassidy, R.: "Moving to the Suburbs," *New Republic,* Jan. 22, 1972.
1958 Census of Business: *Central Business District Statistics,* Summary Report, BC 58–CBD 98, U.S. Bureau of the Census, Washington, D.C., 1961.
Coale, Ansley J.: "Population and Economic Development," in Philip M. Hauser (ed.), *The Population Dilemma,* Prentice-Hall, Englewood Cliffs, N. J. 1969.
Colley, C. H.: "The Theory of Transportation," *Publications of the American Economic Association,* vol. 9, May 1894.
Davis, Kingsley: *World Urbanization 1950–1970, vol. II: Analysis of Trends, Relationships, and Development,* Institute for International Studies, University of California, Berkeley, 1972.
Dice, Lee R.: *Man's Nature and Nature's Man: The Ecology of Human Communities,* University of Michigan Press, Ann Arbor, 1955.
Duncan, Beverly: "Factors in Work-Residence Separation: Wages and Salary Workers, 1951," *American Sociological Review,* vol. 21, 1956.
Duncan, Otis Dudley: "From Social System to Ecosystem," *Sociological Inquiry,* vol. 31, 1961.
———, and Leo F. Schnore: "Cultural, Behavioral, and Ecological Perspectives in the Study of Social Organizations," *American Journal of Sociology,* vol. 65, September 1959.
———, et al.: *Metropolis and Region,* Johns Hopkins Press, Baltimore, 1960.
Forstall, Richard L.: "Economic Classification of Places over 10,000," *Municipal Year Book: 1967,* International City Managers Association, Chicago, 1967.
Gottman, Jean: *Megalopolis,* Twentieth Century Fund, New York, 1961.
Hadden, Jeffrey K., and Edgar F. Borgatta: *American Cities,* Rand McNally, New York, 1965.
Harris, Chauncy: "A Functional Classification of Cities in the United States," *Geographical Review,* vol. 33, January 1943.
———, and Edward L. Ullman: "The Nature of Cities," *The Annals of the American Academy of Political and Social Science,* vol. 242, November 1945.
Hatt, Paul K., and Albert J. Reiss, Jr. (eds.): *Cities and Socity,* Free Press, New York, 1957.
Hauser, Philip M. (ed.): *The Population Dilemma,* Prentice-Hall, Englewood Cliffs, N. J., 1969.
Hawley, Amos H., Beverly Duncan, and David Goldberg: "Some Observations of Changes in Metropolitan Population in the United States," *Demography,* vol. I, 1964.
———: *Urban Society,* Ronald Press, New York, 1971.
Hill, Gladwin: "The Environmental Revolution Enters a Crucial Phase," *National Wildlife,* April–May 1973.
"How Shopping Malls Are Changing Life in United States," *U.S. News and World Report,* vol. 74, no. 25, June 18, 1973.
*Major Retail Centers,* Summary Report, BC 63–MRC–1, U.S. Bureau of the Census, Washington, D.C., 1965.
*Major Retail Centers in Standard Metropolitan Statistical Areas,* United States Summary, BC 67–MRC–1, U.S. Bureau of the Census, Washington, D.C., 1967.
National Resources Committee: *Technological Trends and National Policy,* U.S. Government Printing Office, Washington, D.C., 1937.

Palen, J. John, and Karl Flaming: *Urban America,* Holt, Rinehart and Winston, New York, 1972.

Reiss, Albert J., Jr., "Functional Specialization of Cities," in Paul K. Hatt and Albert J. Reiss Jr. (eds.), *Cities and Society,* Free Press, New York, 1957.

Robinson, W. S.: "Ecological Correlations and the Behavior of Individuals," *American Sociological Review,* vol. 15, June 1950.

*Small-Area Data Notes,* vol. 6, Department of Commerce Bureau of the Census, U.S. Government Printing Office, Washington, D.C., March 1971.

*Small-Area Data Notes,* vol. 6, Department of Commerce Bureau of the Census, U. S. Government Printing Office, Washington, D.C., October 1971.

U. S. Bureau of the Census, Census of Population: 1970, *General Social and Economic Characteristics,* Final Report, PC(1)-C1, U. S. Government Printing Office, Washington, D.C., 1972.

*United States Department of Commerce News,* Social and Economic Statistics Administration, U. S. Government Printing Office, Washington, D.C., April 21, 1972.

Vernon, Raymond: "Production and Distribution in the Large Metropolis," *The Annals of the American Academy of Political and Social Science,* vol. 314, 1957.

Weller, Robert H.: "An Empirical Examination of Metropolitan Structure," *Demography,* vol. 4, 1967.

## CHAPTER 6

Becker, Howard S., and Irving Louis Horowitz: "The Culture of Civility: San Francisco," *Trans-Action,* April 1970.

Bott, Elizabeth: *Family and Social Network,* Tavistock Publications, London, 1957.

Calhoun, John B.: "Population Density and Social Pathology," *Scientific American,* vol. 206, February 1960.

Clines, Francis: "Methadone Care Cutting Arrests, *New York Times,* September 3, 1972, p. 3.

Coles, Robert, and Jon Erikson: *The Middle Americans,* Atlantic-Little, Brown, Boston, 1971.

Conforti, Joseph M.: "Newark: Ghetto or City," *Society,* vol. 9, September–October 1972.

Downs, Anthony: "Alternative Futures for the American Ghetto," in John Walton and Donald E. Carns (eds.), *Cities in Change,* Allyn and Bacon, Boston, Mass., 1973.

Duhl, Leonard J. (ed.): *The Urban Condition,* Basic Books, New York, 1963.

Durkheim, Emile: *The Division of Labor in Society,* George Simpson (trans.), Free Press, Glencoe, Ill., 1960.

"Eight Cities Show a Crime Disparity," *The New York Times,* January 27, 1974, p. 34.

Fried, Marc: "Grieving for a Lost Home," in Leonard J. Duhl (ed.), *The Urban Condition,* Basic Books, New York, 1963.

———, and Peggy Gleicher: "Some Sources of Residential Satisfaction in an Urban Slum," *Journal of the American Institute of Planners,* vol. 27, 1961.

Galle, Omer R., Walter R. Gove, and J. Miller McPherson: "Population Density and Pathology: What Are the Relations for Man?" *Science,* April 7, 1972.

Gans, Herbert J.: "Urbanism and Suburbanism as Ways of Life: A Reevaluation of Definitions," in J. John Palen and Karl H. Flaming (eds.), *Urban America,* Holt, Rinehart, and Winston, New York, 1972.

———: *The Urban Villagers,* Free Press, Glencoe, Ill., 1962.

Germani, Gino (ed.): *Modernization, Urbanization, and the Urban Crisis,* Little, Brown, Boston, 1973.

Greeley, Andrew M.: *Why Can't They Be Like Us?: America's White Ethnic Groups,* Dutton, New York, 1971.

Greer, Scott: *The Urbane View,* Oxford University Press, New York, 1972.

Hartley, Shirley Foster: *Population Quantity vs. Quality,* Prentice-Hall, Englewood Cliffs, N. J., 1972.

Hatt, Paul K., and Albert J. Reiss, Jr.: *Cities and Society,* Free Press, New York, 1957.

Jacobs, Jane: *The Death and Life of Great American Cities,* Random House, New York, 1961.

Markham, James: "What's All This Talk of Heroin Maintenance?" *New York Times Magazine,* vol. 6, pp. 6–12, July 2, 1972.

Marx, Karl, and Friedrich Engels: *The German Ideology,* in R. Pascal (ed.), International Publishers Company, New York, 1947, pp. 68–69.

Matza, David: "The Disreputable Poor," in Neil J. Smelser and Seymour M. Lipset (eds.), *Social Structure and Mobility in Economic Development,* Aldine, Chicago, 1966.

Milgram, Stanley: "The Experience of Living in Cities," *Science,* vol. 167, March 13, 1970.

*The Milwaukee Journal,* January 16, 1973.

Munro, William B.: "City," in *Encyclopedia of the Social Sciences,* Macmillan, New York, 1930.

National Resources Committee: 'The Process of Urbanization: Underlying Forces and Emerging Trends," in Paul K. Hatt and Albert J. Reiss, Jr., *Cities and Society,* Free Press, New York, 1957.

Palen, J. John, and Karl H. Flaming (eds.): *Urban America,* Holt, Rinehart and Winston, New York, 1972.

Rainwater, Lee: "Fear and the House as Haven in the Lower Class," in J. John Palen and Karl H. Flaming (eds.), *Urban America,* Holt, Rinehart and Winston, New York, 1972.

Redfield, Robert: "The Folk Society," *American Journal of Sociology,* vol. 52, 1947.

———, and Milton Singer: "The Cultural Role of Cities," *Economic Development and Cultural Change,* vol. 3, 1954.

*Report of the National Advisory Commission on Civil Disorders,* U.S. Government Printing Office, Washington, D.C., 1968.

Robertson, John, and Norman Zinberg: *Drugs and the Public,* Simon and Schuster, New York, 1972.

Sennett, Richard: *Classic Essays on the Culture of Cities,* Appleton, New York, 1969.

———, and Jonathan Cobb: *The Hidden Injuries of Class,* Vintage Books, New York, 1973.

Simmel, Georg: *The Sociology of Georg Simmel,* Kurt H. Wolff (trans.), Free Press, Glencoe, Ill., 1950.

Smelser, Neil J.: *Sociology: An Introduction,* Wiley, New York, 1967.

———, and Seymour M. Lipset (eds.): *Social Structure and Mobility in Economic Development,* Aldine, Chicago, 1966.

Starr, Joyce R., and Donald E. Carns: "Singles and the City: Notes on Urban Adaptation," in John Walton and Donald E. Carns (eds.), *Cities in Change,* Allyn and Bacon, Boston, 1973.

Suttles, Gerald D.: *The Social Order of the Slum,* University of Chicago Press, Chicago, 1968.

Terkel, Studs: *Division Street: America,* Pantheon Books, a Division of Random House (Avon ed.), New York, 1967.

Thomas, William I., and Florian Znaniecki: *The Polish Peasant in Europe and America,* 5 vols., University of Chicago Press, Chicago, 1918–1920.

Toffler, Alvin: *Future Shock,* Random House, New York, 1970.

Ucko, Peter, Ruth Tringham, and G. W. Dimbleby (eds.): *Man Settlement and Urbanism,* Schenkman, Cambridge, Mass., 1972.

U.S. Bureau of the Census: "Consumer Income," Current Population Reports, ser. P–60, no. 80.

Walton, John, and Donald E. Carns: *Cities in Change,* Allyn and Bacon, Boston, 1973.

Wheatley, Paul: "The Concept of Urbanism," in Peter Ucko, Ruth Tringham and G. W. Dimbleby (eds.), *Man Settlement and Urbanism,* Schenkman, Cambridge, Mass., 1972.

Whyte, William F.: *Street Corner Society,* University of Chicago Press, Chicago, 1943.

Williams, Walter: "Cleveland's Crisis Ghetto," *Trans-Action,* September 1967.

Wirth, Louis: *The Ghetto,* University of Chicago Press, Chicago, 1928.

———: "Urbanism as a Way of Life," *American Journal of Sociology,* vol. 44, July 1938.

Young, Michael, and Peter Willmott: *Family and Kinship in East London,* Penguin Books, Baltimore, 1962.

Zorbaugh, Harvey W.: *The Gold Coast and the Slum,* University of Chicago Press, Chicago, 1929.

## CHAPTER 7

Bell, Wendell: "The City, the Suburb, and a Theory of Social Choice," in Scott Greer, Dennis L. McElrath, David W. Minar, and Peter Orleans (eds.), *The New Urbanization,* St. Martin's Press, New York, 1968.

Berger, Bennett M.: "The Myth of Suburbia," *Journal of Social Issues,* vol. 17, 1971.

———: *Working Class Suburbs,* University of California Press, Berkeley, 1960.

Blumenthal, Ralph: "800,000 Suburban Poor Suffer Amid Environment of Affluence," in Charles M. Haar (ed.), *The End of Innocence,* Scott, Forseman, Glenview, Ill., 1972.

Buder, Santley: *Pullman,* Oxford University Press, New York, 1967.

Clark, S. D.: *The Suburban Society,* University of Toronto Press, Toronto, 1966.

Cohen, Albert K., and Harold M. Hodges, Jr.: "Characteristics of the Lower Blue-Collar Class," *Social Problems,* vol. 10, Spring 1963.

Dobriner, William M. (ed.): *The Suburban Community,* Putnam, New York, 1958.

Farley, Reynolds: "Suburban Persistence," *American Sociological Review,* vol. 29, 1964.

Fava, Sylvia Fleis: *Urbanism in World Perspective,* Crowell, New York, 1968.

Gans, Herbert J.: *The Levittowners,* Vintage Books, New York, 1967.

———: "Urbanism and Suburbanism as Ways of Life: A Reevaluation of Definitions," in J. John Palen and Karl H. Flaming (eds.), *Urban America,* Holt, Rinehart, and Winston, New York, 1972.

Greer, Scott: *The Urbane View,* Oxford University Press, New York, 1972.

———: "The Urbanization of the Suburbs," in Louis H. Masotti and Jeffrey K. Hadden (eds.), *The Urbanization of the Suburbs,* Sage Publications, Beverly Hills, Calif., 1973.

———, Dennis L. McElrath, David W. Minar, and Peter Orleans (eds.): *The New Urbanization,* St. Martin's Press, New York, 1968.

Haar, Charles M. (ed.): *The End of Innocence,* Scott, Forseman, Glenville, Ill., 1972.

Hauser, Philip M.: *The Population Dilemma,* Prentice-Hall, Englewood Cliffs, N. J., 1969.

Hawley, Amos H., and Basil Zimmer: *The Metropolitan Community: Its People and Government,* Sage Publications, Beverly Hills, Calif., 1970.

Kramer, John: "The Other Mayor Lee," in *North American Suburbs,* Glendessary Press, Berkeley, Calif., 1972.

Lineberry, Robert, and Ira Sharkansky: *Urban Politics and Public Policy,* Harper and Row, New York, 1971.

Massotti, Louis, and Jeffrey Hadden: *The Urbanization of the Suburbs,* Sage Publications, Beverly Hills, Calif., 1973.

Michelson, William H.: "Most People Don't Want What Architects Want," *Trans-Action,* July–August 1968.

———: "Potential Candidates for the Designer's Paradise," *Social Forces,* vol. 46, 1967.

Pendleton, William W.: "Blacks in Suburbs," in Louis Massotti and Jeffrey Hadden, *The Urbanization of the Suburbs,* Sage Publications, Beverly Hills, Calif., 1973.

Riseman, David: "The Suburban Sadness," in William M. Dobriner (ed.) *The Suburban Community,* Putnam, New York, 1958.

Rose, Arnold (ed.): *Human Behavior,* Houghton Mifflin, Boston, 1962.

Rose, Harold M.: *The Black Ghetto,* McGraw-Hill, New York, 1971.

Schnore, Leo F.: "The Social and Economic Characteristics of American Suburbs," *Sociological Quarterly,* vol. 4., 1963.

———: "The Socio-Economic Status of Cities and Suburbs," *American Sociological Review,* vol. 28, February 1963.

Seeley, John, R., Alexander Sim, and Elizabeth Loosley: *Crestwood Heights,* Basic Books, New York, 1956.

Shoslak, A., and W. Gomberg (eds.): *Blue-Collar World,* Prentice-Hall, Englewood Cliffs, N. J., 1964.

Spectorsky, A. C.: *The Exurbanites,* Berkley, New York, 1958.

Spinrad, William: "Blue-Collar Workers as City and Suburban Residents—Effect of Union Membership," in A. Shoslak and W. Gomberg (eds.), *Blue-Collar World,* Prentice-Hall, Englewood Cliffs, N. J., 1964.

Stein, Maurice R.: *Eclipses of Community,* Harper and Row, New York, 1960.

Taeuber, Conrad: "Population Trends in the 1960s,' *Science,* vol. 176, May 19, 1972.

Taeuber, Karl E: "The Effect of Income Redistribution on Racial Residential Segregation," *Urban Affairs Quarterly,* vol. 4, September 1968.

———, and Alma F. Taeuber: *Negroes in Cities,* Aldine, Chicago, 1965.

U.S. Bureau of the Census: "Social and Economic Characteristics of the Population in Metropolitan and Nonmetropolitan Areas," *Current Population Reports,* ser. P–23, no. 37, U.S. Government Printing Office, Washington, D.C., 1971.

———: "The Social and Economic Status of Negroes in the United States, 1970," *Special Studies,* ser. P–23, no. 38, U.S. Government Printing Office, Washington, D.C., 1971.

———: "Trends in Social and Economic Conditions in Metropolitan and Nonmetropolitan Areas," *Current Population Reports,* ser. P–23, no. 33, U.S. Government Printing Office, Washington, D.C., 1970.

Warner, Sam B., Jr.: *Streetcar Suburbs,* Harvard University and M.I.T. Presses, Cambridge, Mass., 1962.

Wattel, Harold: "Levittown: A Suburban Community," in William Dobriner (ed.), *The Suburban Community,* Putnam, New York, 1958.

Wattenberg, Ben J., and Richard Scammon: "The Suburban Boom," in John Kramer (ed.), *North American Suburbs,* Glendessary Press, Berkeley, Calif., 1972.

Whyte, William H.: *The Organization Man,* Doubleday Anchor, Garden City, N. Y., 1956.

Zelan, Joseph: "Does Suburbia Make a Difference: An Exercise in Secondary Analysis," in Sylvia Fleis Fava, *Urbanism in World Perspective,* Crowell, New York, 1968.

## CHAPTER 8

Acker, Joan: "Women and Social Stratification: A Case of Intellectual Sexism," in Joan Huber (ed.), *Changing Women in a Changing Society,* University of Chicago Press, Chicago, 1973.

Aiken, Michael, and Paul E. Mott: *The Structure of Community Power,* Random House, New York, 1970.

Amory, Cleveland: *The Proper Bostonians,* Dutton, New York, 1947.

Anton, Thomas J.: "Power, Pluralism, and Local Politics," *Administrative Science Quarterly,* vol. 7, March 1963.

Babchuk, Nicholas, Ruth Morsey, and C. Wayne Gordon: "Men and Women in Community Agencies: A Note on Power and Prestige," in Nona Glazer Malbin and Helen Youngelson Waehrer (eds.), *Women in a Man-Made World,* Rand McNally, Chicago, 1972.

Baron, H. M., et al.: "Black Powerlessness in Chicago," *Trans-Action,* November 1968.

Blau, Peter M., and Otis Dudley Duncan: *The American Occupational Structure,* Wiley, New York, 1967.

Bottomore, T. B.: *Classes in Modern Society,* Vintage Books, New York, 1968.

Broom, Leonard, and F. Lancaster Jones: "Father-to-Son Mobility: Australia in Comparative Perspective," *American Journal of Sociology,* vol. 74, no. 4, January 1969.

Burgess, Ernest W.: "The Growth of the City: An Introduction to a Research Project," *Publications of the American Sociological Society,* vol. 18, 1924.

Burnight, Robert, and Parker Marden: "Social Correlates of Weight in an Aging Population," *Milbank Memorial Fund Quarterly,* vol. 45, 1967.

Campman, Robert: *The Share of Top Wealth-Holders in National Wealth,* Princeton University Press, Princeton, N. J., 1962.

Dahl, Robert A.: "A Critique of the Ruling Elite Model," *American Political Science Review,* vol. 52, June 1958.

———: *Who Governs?* Yale University Press, New Haven, Conn., 1961.

Flaming, Karl H., and J. John Palen: "Black Powerlessness in Policy-Making Positions," *Sociological Quarterly,* vol. 13, Winter 1972.

Gregory, Frances W., and Irene D. Neu: "The American Industrial Elite in the 1870's: Their Social Origins," in William Miller (ed.), *Men in Business, Essays on the Historical Role of the Entrepreneur,* Harper and Row, New York, 1962.

Gutman, Herbert G.: "The Reality of the Rags-to-Riches Myth," in S. Thernstrom and Richard Sennett (eds.), *Nineteenth-Century Cities,* Yale University Press, New Haven, Conn., 1969.

Hodge, Robert W., Paul M. Siegel, and Peter H. Rossi: "Occupational Prestige in the United States, 1925–63," *American Journal of Sociology,* vol. 70, November 1964.

Hollingshead, A. B., *Elmtown's Youth,* Wiley, New York, 1949.

———, and Fredrich Redlich: *Social Class and Mental Illness,* Wiley, New York, 1958.

Huber, Joan (ed.): *Changing Women in a Changing Society,* University of Chicago Press, Chicago, 1973.

Hunter, Floyd: *Community Power Structure,* University of North Carolina Press, Chapel Hill, 1953.

Jackson, Elton: "Status Consistency and Symptoms of Stress," *American Sociological Review,* vol. 27, August 1962.

Kahl, Joseph: *The American Class Structure,* Holt, Rinehart, and Winston, New York, 1957.

Keiser, R. Lincoln: *The Vice Lords: Warriors of the Streets,* Holt, Rinehart, and Winston, New York, 1969.

Lenski, Gerhard E.: "Status Crystallization: A Non-Vertical Dimension of Social Status," *American Sociological Review,* vol. 19, August 1954.

———: "Status Inconsistency and the Vote: A Four Nation Test," *American Sociological Review,* vol. 32, April 1967.

Lipset, Seymour M., and Reinhard Bendix: *Social Mobility in Industrial Society,* University of California Press, Berkeley, 1959.

———, and Hans Zetterberg: "Social Mobility in Industrial Societies," in Seymour M. Lipset and Reinhard Bendix, *Social Mobility in Industrial Society,* University of California Press, Berkeley, 1959.

Lundberg, Ferdinand: *The Rich and the Super Rich,* Bantom Books, New York, 1969.

Lynd, Robert, and Helen Lynd: *Middletown,* Harcourt, Brace, New York, 1929.

———, and ———: *Middletown in Transition,* Harcourt, Brace, New York, 1937.

Malbin, Nona Glazer, and Helen Youngelson Waehrer (eds.): *Women in a Man-Made World,* Rand McNally, Chicago, 1972.

Miller, William: "American Historians and the Business Elite," in *Men in Business, Essays on the Historical Role of the Entrepreneur,* Harper and Row, New York, 1962.

——— (ed.): *Men in Business, Essays on the Historical Role of the Entrepreneur,* Harper and Row, New York, 1962.

Palen, J. John, and Leo F. Schnore: "Color Composition and City-Suburban Differences," *Land Economics,* vol. 41, February 1965.

Polsby, Nelson W.: "How to Study Community Power: The Pluralist Alternative," *Journal of Politics,* vol. 22, August 1960.

———: "The Sociology of Community Power: A Reassessment," *Social Forces,* vol. 37, March 1959.

*Report of the National Advisory Commission on Civil Disorders,* U.S. Government Printing Office, Washington, D.C., 1968.

Rogoff, Natalie: *Recent Trends in Occupational Mobility,* Free Press, Glencoe, Ill., 1953.

Schnore, Leo F.: "The Socio-Economic Status of Cities and Suburbs," *American Sociological Review,* vol. 28, February 1963.

———: *The Urban Scene,* Free Press, New York, 1965.

Sewell, William H.: "Community of Residence and College Plans," *American Sociological Review,* vol. 29, February 1964.

Sexton, Patricia Cayo, and Brendan Sexton: *Blue Collars and Hard Hats,* Vintage Books, New York, 1971.

Smith, Joel: "Another Look at Socioeconomic Status Distributions in Urbanized Areas," *Urban Affairs Quarterly,* vol. 5, June 1970.

Thernstrom, Stephen: "Immigrants and WASPS: Ethnic Differences in Occupational Mobility in Boston, 1890–1940," in Stephen Thernstrom and Richard Sennett (eds.), *Nineteenth-Century Cities,* Yale University Press, New Haven, Conn., 1969.

———: *The Other Bostonians: Poverty and Progress in American Metropolis, 1880–1970,* Harvard University Press, Cambridge, Mass., 1973.

———: "Urbanization, Migration, and Social Mobility in Late Nineteenth-Century America," in Alan Trachenberg, Peter Neill, and Peter C. Bunnell (eds.), *The City: American Experience,* Oxford University Press, New York, 1971.

———: "Yankee City Revisited: The Perils of Historical Naivete," *American Sociological Review,* vol. 30, April 1965.

———, and Richard Sennett (eds.): *Nineteenth-Century Cities,* Yale University Press, New Haven, Conn., 1969.

Alan Trachenberg, Peter Neill, and Peter C. Bunnell (eds.): *The City: American Experience,* Oxford University Press, New York, 1971.

Udry, Richard J.: "Marital Instability by Race and Income Based on 1960 Data," *American Journal of Sociology,* vol. 72, 1966.

Walton, John: "A Systematic Survey of Community Power Research," in Michael Aiken and Paul E. Mott (eds.), *The Structure of Community Power,* Random House, New York, 1970.

Warner, W. Lloyd: *The Social Life of a Modern Community,* vol. 1 of the Yankee City Series, Yale University Press, New Haven, Conn., 1941.

——— (ed.): *Yankee City,* Yale University Press, New Haven, Conn., 1963.

Whyte, William Foote: *Street Corner Society,* University of Chicago Press, Chicago, 1943.

Wilson, Everett K.: *Sociology: Rules, Roles, Relationships,* Dorsey, Homewood, Ill., 1971.

## CHAPTER 9

Brown, Dee Alexander: *Bury My Heart at Wounded Knee,* Holt, Rinehart, and Winston, New York, 1971.

Dennis, Henry C. (ed.): *The American Indian 1492–1970,* Oceana Publications, Dobbs Ferry, N. Y., 1971.

Downs, Anthony: "Alternative Futures for the American Ghetto," *Daedalus,* vol. 97, no. 4, Fall 1968.

Drake, St. Clair, and Horace R. Clayton: *Black Metropolis,* Harcourt, Brace, New York, 1945.

Ellison, Ralph: *Invisible Man,* Random House, New York, 1952.

Frazier, E. Franklin: *Black Bourgeoise,* Free Press, Glencoe, Ill. 1957.

Glazer, Nathan, and Daniel Patrick Moynihan: *Beyond the Melting Pot,* M.I.T. Press, Cambridge, Mass., 1963.

Grant, Madison: *The Passing of the Great Race,* Scribner, New York, 1921.

Grebler, Leo: *The Schooling Gap: Signs of Progress,* Advanced Report 7, University of California, Mexican American Study Project, Los Angeles, 1967.

Guzman, R.: "Ethnics in Federally Subsidized Research: The Case of the Mexican American," in *The Mexican American: A New Focus on Opportunity,* Inter-Agency on Mexican American Affairs, Washington, D. C., 1967.

Hamilton, H. C.: "The Negro Leaves the South," *Demography,* vol. 1, 1964.

*Indian Health Trends and Services,* Program Analysis and Statistics Branch of the Indian Health Service, Department of H. E. W., Washington, D.C., 1969.

Kent, Calvin A., and Jerry W. Johnson: *Indian Poverty in South Dakota,* Bulletin 99, Business Research Bureau, School of Business, University of South Dakota, 1969.

Kitano, Harry H. L.: *Japanese Americans: The Evolution of a Subculture,* Prentice-Hall, Englewood Cliffs, N. J., 1969.

Marston, Wilfred G.: "Socioeconomic Differentiation Within Negro Areas of American Cities," *Social Forces,* vol. 48, December 1969.

Moore, Joan W.: *Mexican Americans,* Prentice-Hall, Englewood Cliffs, N. J., 1970.

Moynihan, Patrick: *The Negro Family: The Case for National Action,* Office of Policy Planning and Research, Department of Labor, Washington, D.C., 1965.

Myrdal, Gunnar: *An American Dilemma,* Harper and Row, New York, 1944.

Neils, Elaine M.: *Reservation to City: Indian Migration and Federal Relocation,* University of Chicago Department of Geography, Research Paper no. 13, Chicago, 1974.

Palen, J. John, and Leo F. Schnore: "Color Composition and City Suburban Status Differences," *Land Economics,* vol. 41, February 1965.

Petersen, William: *Japanese Americans,* Random House, New York, 1971.

———: "Success Story: Japanese-American Style," *The New York Times Magazine,* January 9, 1966.

Pettigrew, Thomas F.: *Racially Separate or Together?* McGraw-Hill, New York, 1971.

Reilly, William K. (ed.): *The Use of Land,* Task Force Report sponsored by the Rockefeller Brothers Fund, Crowell, New York, 1973.

*Report of the National Advisory Commission on Civil Disorders,* "The Migration of Negroes From the South," U.S. Government Printing Office, Washington, D.C., 1968.

Rose, Harold M.: "The Spatial Development of Black Residential Subsystems," *Economic Geography,* vol. 48, January 1972.

Samora, Julian: *Los Mojados: The Wetback,* University of Notre Dame Press, Notre Dame, Ind., 1971.

——— (ed.): *La Raza: Forgotten Americans,* University of Notre Dame Press, Notre Dame, Ind., 1966.

Steiner, Stan: *The New Indians,* Harper and Row, New York, 1968.

Stoddard, Ellwyn R.: *Mexican Americans,* Random House, New York, 1973.

Suttles, Gerald: *The Social Order of the Slum,* University of Chicago Press, Chicago, 1968.

Taeuber, Conrad: "Population Trends in the 1960s," *Science,* vol. 176, May 19, 1972.

Taeuber, Karl, and Alma Taeuber: *Negroes in Cities,* Aldine, Chicago, 1965.

———, and ———: *Negroes in Cities,* table 5, Aldine, Chicago, 1965.

*Time,* April 6, 1970, p. 29.

U.S. Bureau of the Census: "The Social and Economic Status of Negroes in the

United States, 1970," *Special Studies,* Ser. P–23, no. 38, U.S. Government Printing Office, Washington, D.C., 1971.

———: "Trends in Social and Economic Conditions in Metropolitan and Nonmetropolitan Areas," *Special Studies,* U.S. Government Printing Office, Washington, D.C., 1970.

———: Census of Population: 1970, *General Social and Economic Characteristics,* Final Report, PC(1)-C1, U. S. Government Printing Office, Washington, D.C., 1972.

Wattenberg, Ben J., and Richard M. Scammon: "Black Progress and Liberal Rhetoric," *Commentary,* vol. 55, no. 4, April 1973.

Wax, Murray L.: *Indian Americans: Unity and Diversity,* Prentice-Hall, Englewood Cliffs, N. J., 1971.

Young, Whitney: *To Be Equal,* McGraw-Hill, New York, 1964.

### CHAPTER 10

Abrams, Charles: *The City Is the Frontier,* Harper and Row, New York, 1965.

Anderson, Martin: *The Federal Bulldozer,* M.I.T. Press, Cambridge, Mass., 1964.

Barresi, Charles M., and John H. Lindquist: "The Urban Community: Attitudes Toward Neighborhood and Urban Renewal," *Urban Affairs Quarterly,* vol. 5, March 1970.

Bellush, J., and M. Hausknecht (eds.): "The Housing of Relocated Families," in *Urban Renewal: People, Politics, and Planning,* Doubleday Anchor, Garden City, New York, 1967.

Duhl, Leonard J. (ed.): *The Urban Condition,* Basic Books, New York, 1963.

Feagin, Joe (ed.): *The Urban Scene,* Random House, New York, 1973.

Fried, Marc: "Grieving for a Lost Home," in Leonard J. Duhl (ed.), *The Urban Condition,* Basic Books, New York, 1963.

Gans, Herbert J.: *People and Plans,* Basic Books, New York, 1968.

———: *The Urban Villagers,* Free Press, New York, 1962.

Greer, Scott: *Urban Renewal and American Cities,* Bobbs-Merrill, Indianapolis, Ind., 1965.

———: "The Housing of Relocated Families," *Journal of the American Institute of Planners,* vol. 30, November 1964.

———: "A Rejoinder: Omissions in Evaluating Relocation Effectiveness Cited," *Journal of Housing,* vol. 23, 1966.

Hartman, Chester W.: "Social Values and Housing Orientation," *Journal of Social Issues,* April 1963.

Jacobs, Jane: *The Death and Life of Great American Cities,* Random House, New York, 1961.

Lindbloom, Carl G., and Morton Farrah (eds.): *The Citizen's Guide to Urban Renewal,* Chandler Davis, West Trenton, N. J., 1968.

Lowe, Jeanne R.: *Cities in a Race with Time,* Random House, New York, 1967.

Newman, Oscar: *Defensible Space,* Macmillan, New York, 1972.

Rainwater, Lee: *Behind Ghetto Walls,* Aldine, Chicago, 1970.

Rossi, R., and R. A. Dentler: *The Politics of Urban Renewal,* Free Press, Glencoe, Ill., 1961.
"Slum Surgery in St. Louis," *Architectural Forum,* April 1951.
Stegman, Michael: "The New Mythology of Housing," *Trans-Action,* vol. 7, January 1970.
Watts, Lewis G., et al.: "The Middle-Income Negro Family Faces Renewal," in Joe Feagin (ed.), *The Urban Scene,* Random House, New York, 1973.
Weissbroud, Bernard: "Satellite Communities," *Urban Land,* vol. 31, October 1972.

## CHAPTER 11

Aristotle: *Politics,* B. Jowett (trans.), ii, 8 1267.
Baker, Newman F.: *Legal Aspects of Zoning,* University of Chicago Press, Chicago, 1927.
Buder, Stanley: *Pullman,* Oxford University Press, New York, 1967.
Eldridge, Wentworth (ed.): *Taming Megalopolis,* Anchor Doubleday, Garden City, N. Y., 1967.
Faltermayor, Edmund K.: *Redoing America,* Harper and Row, New York, 1968.
Gans, Herbert J.: "Planning, Social: II. Regional and Urban Planning," in David Sills (ed.), *International Encyclopedia of the Social Sciences,* Crowell Collier and Macmillan, New York, vol. 12, 1968.
Glaab, Charles N., and Theodore Brown: *A History of Urban America,* Macmillan, New York, 1967.
Herman, Leon M.: "Urbanization and New Housing Construction in the Soviet Union," *American Journal of Economics and Sociology,* vol. 30, April 1971.
Jacobs, Jane: *The Death and Life of Great American Cities,* Random House, New York, 1961.
Loewenstein, Louis K. (ed.): *Urban Studies,* Free Press, New York, 1971.
Mendelker, Daniel R.: *Green Belts and Urban Growth,* University of Wisconsin Press, Madison, 1962.
Meyerson, Martin, and Edward G. Banfield: *Politics, Planning, and the Public Interest,* Free Press of Glencoe, New York, 1955.
Michelson, William: "Most People Don't Want What Architects Want," *Trans-Action,* July–August 1968.
Mumford, Lewis: "Home Remedies for Urban Cancer," in Louis K. Loewenstein (ed.), *Urban Studies,* Free Press, New York, 1971.
———: "The Sky Line: Mother Jacob's Home Remedies," *The New Yorker,* vol. 38, no. 4, December 1, 1962.
*The Netherlands: Current Trends and Policies in the Field of Housing, Building, and Planning During the Year 1968,* Ministry of Housing and Physical Planning, The Hague, 1970.
Newman, Oscar: *Defensible Space,* Macmillan, New York, 1972.
New York City Housing Authority Project Physical Design Statistics and New York City Housing Authority Project Manager's Bookkeeping Records:

*Progressive Architecture,* Van Dyke and Brownsville Project—Comparison of Crime Incidents, Comparison of Maintenance, and a Comparison of Physical Design and Population Density, 1972.

O'Harrow, Dennis: "Zoning: What's the Good of It?" in Wentworth Eldridge (ed.), *Taming Megalopolis,* Doubleday Anchor, Garden city, N. Y., 1967.

Riis Jacob, *The Children of the Poor,* Scribner, New York, 1892.

Robinson, C. M.: *City Planning,* Putnam, New York, 1916.

Saalman, Howard: *Medieval Cities,* Braziller, New York, 1968.

Thomlinson, Ralph: *Urban Structure,* Random House, New York, 1969.

Tunnard, Christopher: *The City of Man,* Scribner, New York, 1953.

Walton, John, and Donald E. Carns (eds.): *Cities in Change,* Allyn and Bacon, Boston, 1973.

Zeisel, John: "Symbolic Meaning of Space and the Physical Dimension of Social Relations," in John Walton and Donald E. Carns (eds.), *Cities in Change,* Allyn and Bacon, Boston, 1973.

## CHAPTER 12

"Cars and Cities on a Collision Course," *Fortune,* February 1970.

Clapp, J.: *New Towns and Urban Policy—Planning Metropolitan Growth,* Dunellen, New York, 1971.

Collins, John: "Lusaka: The Myth of the Garden City," *Zambian Urban Studies,* University of Zambia, 1969.

Downs, Anthony: "Private Investment and the Public Weal," *Saturday Review,* May 5, 1971.

Fried, Joseph P.: *Housing Crisis U.S.A.,* Praeger, New York, 1971.

Gabree, John (ed.): *Surviving the City,* Ballantine Books, New York, 1973.

Gans, Herbert J.: *Levittowners,* Pantheon, New York, 1967.

Heraud, B. J.: "Social Class and the New Towns," *Urban Studies,* vol. 5, 1968.

Howard, Ebenezer: *Garden Cities of To-morrow,* Faber and Faber, London, 1902.

Merlin, Pierre: *New Towns,* Methuen, London, 1971.

National Committee on Urban Growth Policy: *The New City,* Praeger, New York, 1969.

Osborn, Frederick J.: *Green-Belt Cities,* Schocken, New York, 1969.

Owen, Wilfred: *The Metropolitan Transportation Problem,* The Brookings Institute, Washington, D.C., 1956.

Pell, Claiborne: *Megalopolis Unbound,* Praeger, New York, 1966.

Ray, John B.: *The Road and the Car in American Life,* M.I.T. Press, Cambridge, Mass., 1971.

Rodwin, Lloyd: *The British New Towns Policy,* Harvard University Press, Cambridge, Mass., 1956.

Schaffer, Frank: *The New Town Story,* MacGibbon and Kee, London, 1970.

Senior, Derek (ed.): *The Regional City,* Aldine, Chicago, 1966.

Sidenbladh, Goran: "Stockholm: A Planned City," in *Cities: A Scientific American Book,* Knopf, New York, 1965.

Tass, Leslie: *Modern Rapid Transit,* Carlton Press, New York, 1971.

Taylor, Lord, and Sidney Chave: *Mental Health and Environment in a New Town,* Longmans, London, 1964.

Thomas, Wyndham: "Implementation: New Towns," in Derek Senior (ed.), *The Regional City,* Aldine, Chicago, 1966.

Von Eckard, Wolf: "A Fresh Scene in the Clean Dream," *Saturday Review,* May 15, 1971.

Weissbourd, Bernard: "Satellite Communities," *Urban Land,* vol. 31, October 1972.

White, Kevin: *Newsweek,* February 12, 1973, p. 32.

Whyte, Jr., William H.: *The Organization Man,* Doubleday Anchor, Garden City, New York, 1956.

Willmott, Peter: "East Kilbride and Stevenage," *Town Planning Review,* vol. 34, January 1964.

———: "Social Research and New Communities," in John Gabree (ed.), *Surviving in the City,* Ballantine Books, New York, 1973.

## CHAPTER 13

Berry, Brian J.: "City Size Distribution and Economic Development," *Economic Development and Cultural Change,* vol. 9, July 1961.

Breese, Gerald (ed.): *The City in Newly Developing Countries,* Prentice-Hall, Englewood Cliffs, N. J., 1969.

Coale, Ansley J.: "Population and Economic Development," in Philip Hauser (ed.), *The Population Dilemma,* Prentice-Hall, Englewood Cliffs, N. J., 1969.

Davis, Kingsley: "Burgeoning Cities in Rural Countries," in *Scientific American, Cities: Their Origin, Growth, and Human Impact,* Freeman, San Francisco, 1973.

———, and Anna Casis: "Urbanization in Latin America," *The Milbank Memorial Fund Quarterly,* vol. 24, April 1946.

———, and Hilda Hertz Golden: "Urbanization and the Development of Pre-Industrial Areas," in *Economic Development and Cultural Change,* vol. 3, October 1954.

Hauser, Philip M.: *The Population Dilemma,* Prentice-Hall, Englewood Cliffs, N.J., 1969.

Hoselitz, Bert F.: "The City, the Factory, and Economic Growth," *American Economic Review,* vol. 45, May 1955.

———: "Urbanization and Economic Growth in Asia," *Economic Development and Cultural Change,* vol. 6, October 1957.

Isennberg, Irwin: *The Developing Nations: Poverty and Progress,* Columbia University Press, New York, 1969.

Jefferson, Mark: "The Law of the Primate Cities," *Geographical Review,* vol. 29, April 1939.

Linsky, Arnold S.: "Some Generalizations Concerning Primate Cities," *Annals of the Association of American Geographers,* vol. 55, September 1965.

Myrdal, Gunnar: *Asian Drama,* vol. 2, Pantheon, New York, 1968.

Proceedings of the Joint UN/UNESCO Seminar Held in Bangkok, August 8–18, 1956: *Urbanization in Asia and the Far East,* UNESCO, Calcutta, 1957.

"Some Regional Development Problems in Latin America Linked to Metropolitanization," in *Economic Bulletin for Latin America,* United Nations, New York, vol. 17, 1972.

Sovani, N. V.: "The Analysis of Over-Urbanization," *Economic Development and Cultural Change,* vol. 12, January 1964.

Taeuber, Irene B.: "Population Growth in Less Developed Countries," in Philip M. Hauser, *The Population Dilemma,* Prentice-Hall, Englewood Cliffs, N.J., 1969.

United Nations Commission for Latin America: "Urbanization and Distribution of Population by Size of Locality," in Gerald Breese (ed.), *The City in Newly Developing Countries,* Prentice-Hall, Englewood Cliffs, N. J., 1969.

## CHAPTER 14

Barraclough, Solon L.: "Rural Development and Employment Prospects in Latin America," in Arthur J. Field (ed.), *City and Country in the Third World,* Schenkman, Cambridge, Mass., 1970.

Beyer, Glen H. (ed.): *The Urban Explosion in Latin America,* Cornell University Press, Ithaca, N. Y., 1967.

Breese, Gerald: *Urbanization in Newly Developing Countries,* Prentice-Hall, Englewood Cliffs, N. J., 1966.

———: *The City in Newly Developing Countries,* Prentice-Hall, Englewood Cliffs, N. J., 1969.

Ducoff, Louis J.: "The Role of Migration in the Demographic Development of Latin America," *The Milbank Memorial Fund Quarterly,* vol. 43, October 1965.

Durand, John D., and Cesar A. Palaez: "Patterns of Urbanization in Latin America," in Gerald Breese, *The City in Newly Developing Countries,* Prentice-Hall, Englewood Cliffs, N. J., 1969.

Estimates from Peruvian national figures, 1970.

Estudio Economico para America Latina, ECLA: United Nations, 1966.

Field, Arthur J. (ed.): *City and Country in the Third World,* Schenkman, Cambridge, Mass., 1970.

Frank, Andrew C.: "Urban Poverty in Latin America," in *Studies in Comparative International Development,* vol. 2, 1966.

Gakenheimer, Ralph A.: "The Peruvian City of the Sixteenth Century," in Glen H. Beyer (ed.), *The Urban Explosion in Latin America,* Cornell University Press, Ithaca, N. Y., 1967.

Goldrich, Daniel: "Toward the Comparative Study of Politicalization in Latin America," in D. Heath and R. N. Adams (eds.), *Contemporary Cultures and Societies in Latin America,* Random House, New York, 1965.

Hauser, Philip M. (ed.): *Urbanization in Latin America,* UNESCO, Paris, 1961.

———, and Leo F. Schnore (eds.): *The Study of Urbanization,* Wiley, New York, 1965.

Heath, Dwight B., and Richard N. Adams (eds.): *Contemporary Cultures and Societies in Latin America,* Random House, New York, 1965.

Heberle, Rudolf: "Social Consequence of the Industrialization of Southern Cities," *Social Forces,* October 1940.

Hoselitz, Bert F., and Wilber E. Moore (eds.): *Industrialization and Society,* UNESCO-Mouton, Paris, 1963.

Leeds, Anthony, and Elizabeth Leeds: "Brazil and the Myth of Urban Rurality: Urban Experience Work, and Values in 'Squatments' of Rio De Janeiro and Lima," in Arthur J. Field (ed.), *City and Country in the Third World,* Schenkman, Cambridge, Mass., 1970.

Lewis, Oscar: "The Culture of Poverty," *Scientific American,* vol. 215, no. 4, 1966.

———: "The Folk-Urban Ideal Types," in Philip Hauser and Leo F. Schnore, *The Study of Urbanization,* Wiley, New York, 1965.

———: "Urbanization Without Breakdown: A Case Study," *The Scientific Monthly,* vol. 75, 1952.

Mangin, William P.: "Mental Health and Migration to Cities: A Peruvian Case," *Annals of New York Academy of Sciences,* vol. 84, 1960.

Miro, Carmen A.: "The Population of Latin America," *Demography,* vol. 1, 1964.

Moore, Wilber E.: "Industrialization and Social Change," in Bert F. Hoselitz and Wilber E. Moore (eds.), *Industrialization and Society,* UNESCO-Mouton, Paris, 1963.

Morris, James: *Cities,* Harcourt, Brace and World, New York, 1964.

Moynihan, Daniel P. (ed.): *Toward a National Urban Policy,* Basic Books, New York, 1970.

Smith, T. Lynn: "The Changing Functions of Latin American Cities," *The Americas,* vol. 25, July 1968.

Schnore, Leo F.: "On the Spatial Structure of Cities in the Two Americas," in Philip Hauser and Leo F. Schnore (eds.), *The Study of Urbanization,* Wiley, New York, 1965.

Shook, Edwin M., and Tatiana Proskouriakoff: "Settlement Patterns in Meso-America and the Sequency in the Guatemalan Highlands," in Gordon R. Willey (ed.), *Prehistoric Settlement Patterns in the New World,* Wenner-Gren Foundation for Anthropological Research, New York, 1956.

Sjoberg, Gideon: *The Preindustrial City: Past and Present,* Free Press, Glencoe, Ill., 1960.

St. Clair, David (trans.): *Child of the Dark: The Diary of Carolina Maria De Jesus,* Dutton, New York, 1962.

Theodorson, George A. (ed.): *Studies in Human Ecology,* Row, Peterson, Evanston, Ill., 1961.

Turner, John F. C.: "Squatter Settlements in Developing Countries," in Daniel P. Moynihan (ed.), *Toward a National Urban Policy,* Basic Books, New York, 1970.

Willey, Gordon R. (ed.): *Prehistoric Settlement Patterns in the New World,* Wenner-Gren Foundation for Anthropological Research, New York, 1956.

## CHAPTER 15

*Africa Social Situation: 1960–1970,* prepared for the African Population Conference, Accra, Ghana, by the Economic Commission for Africa, December 1971.

Banton, M.: "Social Alignment and Identity in a West African City," in Hilda Kuper (ed.), *Urbanization and Migration in West Africa,* University of California Press, Berkeley, 1966.

Bienen, Henry: *Tanzania: Party Transformation and Economic Development,* Princeton University Press, Princeton, N. J., 1970.

Cameron, J., and W. A. Dodd: *Society, Schools and Progress in Tanzania,* Pergamon Press, Oxford, 1970.

Clower, Robert W., et al.: *Growth without Development: An Economic Survey of Liberia,* Northwestern University Press, Evanston, Ill., 1966.

*Demographic Handbook for Africa,* United Nations Economic Commission for Africa, Addis Ababa, 1971.

Etho-Swedish Institute of Building and Technology: "Survey of Housing Conditions I and II: Totals and Average," mimeograph, May and July, 1962.

Foster, George, and Robert Kemper (eds.): *Anthropologists in Cities,* Little, Brown, Boston, 1974.

Gutkind, Peter C.: "The African Urban Milieu: A Force for Rapid Change," *Civilizations,* vol. 12, 1962.

Hamdan, G.: "Capitals of the New Africa," *Economic Geography,* vol. 40, July 1964.

Hance, William A.: *Population, Migration, and Urbanization in Africa,* Columbia University Press, New York, 1970.

Hanna, William John, and Judith Lynne Hanna: *Urban Dynamics in Black Africa,* Aldine-Atherton, Chicago, 1971.

Hauser, Philip M., and Leo F. Schnore: *The Study of Urbanization,* Wiley, New York, 1965.

Hodgkin, T.: *Nationalism in Colonial Africa,* Muller, London, 1958.

Kuper, Hilda (ed.): *Urbanization and Migration in West Africa,* University of California Press, Berkeley, 1966.

Kuper, Leo, Hilstan Watts, and Ronald Davies: *Durban: A Study in Racial Ecology,* Jonathan Cape, London, 1958.

Leslie, J. A. K.: *A Social Survey of Dar es Salaam,* Oxford University Press—The East African Institute, London, 1963.

Lloyd, P. C.: *Africa in Social Change,* Penguin Books, Baltimore, 1967.

Lowy, Michael J.: "Me Ko Court: The Impact of Urbanization on Conflict Resolution in a Ghanaian Town," in George Foster and Robert Kemper (eds.), *Anthropologists in Cities,* Little, Brown, Boston, 1974.

Merab, Docteur: *Impressions d'Ethiopie,* vol. II, Leroux, Paris, 1921–1923.

Oloo, Dick (ed.): *Urbanization: Its Social Problems and Consequences,* Kenya National Council of Social Service, Nairobi, 1969.

Palen, J. John: "The Volume and Implication of Migration Into Addis Ababa," paper read at VIII World Congress of Sociology, Toronto, Canada, 1974.

Pankhurst, Richard: "Notes on the Demographic History of Ethiopian Towns and Villages," *The Ethiopian Observer,* vol. 9, 1965.

Pons, V. G., cited by A. L. Epstein, "Urbanization and Social Change in Africa," *Current Anthropology,* vol. 8, no. 4, 1967.

Robertson, H. M.: *South Africa,* Cambridge University Press, London, 1957.

Sjoberg, Gideon: "Cities in Developing and in Industrial Societies: A Cross-Cultural Analysis," in Philip M. Hauser and Leo F. Schnore, (eds.) *The Study of Urbanization,* Wiley, New York, 1965.

*World Population Prospects 1965–1980,* Working Paper no. 30, United Nations Economic Commission for Africa, Addis Ababa, 1969.

*The World Population Situation in 1970,* United Nations, New York, 1971.

## CHAPTER 16

Abu-Lughod, Janet: "Migrant Adjustment to City Life: The Egyptian Case," *American Journal of Sociology,* vol. 67, July 1961.

———: "Testing the Theory of Social Area Analysis: The Ecology of Cairo, Egypt," *American Sociological Review,* vol. 34, April, 1969.

———: "Varieties of Urban Experience: Contrast, Coexistence, and Coalescence in Cairo," in Ira M. Lapidus, *Middle Eastern Cities.* University of California Press, Berkeley, 1969.

Davis, Kingsley, and Hilda Hertz Golden: "Urbanization and the Development of Pre-Industrial Areas," in Paul K. Hatt and Albert J. Reiss, Jr. (eds.), *Cities and Society,* Free Press, New York, 1957.

Hassan, S. S.: "The Ecology and Characteristics of Employed Females in Cairo City," paper presented at the Seminar on Demographic Factors in Manpower Planning in Arab Countries held at the Cairo Demographic Center, November 1971.

Hatt, Paul K., and Albert J. Reiss, Jr. (eds.): *Cities and Society,* Free Press, New York, 1957.

Hourani, A. H., and S. M. Stern (eds.): *The Islamic City,* Cassirer, Oxford, 1970.

Issawi, Charles: *The Economic History of the Middle East,* University of Chicago Press, Chicago, 1966.

Lapidus, Ira M.: *Middle Eastern Cities,* University of California Press, Berkeley, 1969.

Stern, S. M.: "The Constitution of the Islamic City," in A. H. Hourani and S. M. Stern (eds.), *The Islamic City,* Cassirer, Oxford, 1970.

Weber, Max: *The City,* D. Martindale and G. Neuwirth (trans.), Free Press, Glencoe, Ill., 1958.

## CHAPTER 17

Aird, John S.: "The Size, Composition and Growth of the Population of Mainland China," *International Population Reports,* ser. P–90, Department of Commerce, Bureau of the Census, Washington, D.C., 1961.

Ando, Hikotaro: *Peking,* Dodansha International, Tokyo, 1968.

Bose, Nirmal Kumar: "Calcutta: A Premature Metropolis," in *Scientific American, Cities: Their Origin, Growth and Human Impact,* Freeman, San Francisco, 1973.

Breese, Gerald: *Urbanization in Newly Developing Countries,* Prentice-Hall, Englewood Cliffs, N. J., 1966.

Chen, Pi-chao: "Overurbanization, Rustication of Urban-Educated Youths, and Politics of Rural Transformation," *Comparative Politics,* April 1972.

Fryer, D. W.: "The Million City in Southeast Asia," *Geographical Review,* vol. 43, October 1953.

Galston, Arthur: "Peking Man (and Woman) Today," *Natural History,* November, 1972.

Ginsburg, Norton S.: "The Great City in Southeast Asia," *American Journal of Sociology,* vol. 60, March 1955.

———: "Urban Geography and 'Non-Western' Areas," in Philip M. Hauser and Leo F. Schnore, *The Study of Urbanization,* Wiley, New York, 1965.

Gist, Noel P.: "The Ecology of Bangalore, India: An East-West Comparison," *Social Forces,* vol. 35, May 1957.

Hall, J. W.: "The Castle Town and Japan's Modern Urbanization," *Far Eastern Quarterly,* 1955.

Hauser, Philip M., and Leo F. Schnore: *The Study of Urbanization,* Wiley, New York, 1965.

Kar, N. R.: "Urban Characteristics of the City of Calcutta," *Indian Population Bulletin,* April 1960.

Murphey, Rhoads: *Shanghai—Key to Modern China,* Harvard University Press, Cambridge, Mass., 1953.

———: "Urbanization in Asia," *Ekistics,* vol. 21, January 1966.

*Scientific American: Cities: Their Origin, Growth and Human Impact,* Freeman, San Francisco, 1973.

Tien, Hung-Mao: "Shanghai: China's Huge 'Model City,'" *Milwaukee Journal,* December 16, 1973.

Ullman, M. B.: "Cities of Mainland China: 1953 and 1958," *International Population Reports,* ser. P-95, U. S. Government Printing Office, Washington, D.C., 1961.

U.S. Department of Commerce, Bureau of the Census: *Estimates and Projections of the Population of Mainland China: 1953–1986,* International Population Report, ser. P-91, no. 17, U.S. Government Printing Office, Washington, D.C., 1968.

Vogel, Ezra: *Canton Under Communism,* Harvard University Press, Cambridge, Mass., 1969.

*The World Population Situation in 1970,* United Nations, New York, 1971.

## CHAPTER 18

Banfield, Edward G.: *The Unheavenly City Revisited,* Little, Brown, Boston, 1974.

Dantzig, George B., and Thomas L. Saatz: *Compact City: A Plan for a Liveable Urban Environment,* Freeman, San Francisco, 1973.

Davis, Kingsley: "The Origin and Growth of Urbanization in the World," *American Journal of Sociology,* vol. 60, March 1955.

Downs, Anthony: "Squeezing Spread City," *The New York Times Magazine,* March 17, 1974.

Doxiadis, C. A.: "The Coming Era of Ecumenopolis," *Saturday Review,* March 18, 1967.

———: *Ekistics,* Hutchinson, London, 1968, p. 430.

Fogelson, R. M.: *The Fragmented Metropolis: Los Angeles 1850–1930,* Harvard University Press, Cambridge, Mass., 1967.

Greer, Scott: *The Urbane View,* Oxford University Press, New York, 1972.

Hodge, Patricia Leavey, and Philip M. Hauser: *The Challenge of America's Metropolitan Population Outlook 1960 to 1985,* prepared for National Commission on Urban Problems, Praeger, New York, 1968.

Jacobs, Jane: *The Death and Life of Great American Cities,* Vintage—Random House, New York, 1961.

Le Corbusier: *The Radiant City,* Part I, Pamela Knight (trans.), Parts II and VI, Eleanor Levieux (trans.), Parts III, IV, V, VII, and VIII, Derek Coltman (trans.), Grossman-Orion, New York, 1967. Translation of *La Ville Radieuse,* 1933.

Machiavelli, Niccolo: *The Prince,* W. K. Marriott (trans.), Dent, London, 1958.

Moynihan, Daniel P. (ed.): *Toward a National Urban Policy,* Basic Books, New York, 1970.

———: "Toward a National Urban Policy," *The Public Interest,* Fall, 1969.

Mumford, Lewis: *The Urban Prospect,* Harcourt, Brace and World, New York, 1968.

National Commission on the Causes and Prevention of Violence: *Violent Crime: The Challenge to Our Cities,* Braziller, New York, 1969.

Palen, J. John: "Belief in Government Control and the Displaced Worker," *Administrative Science Quarterly,* vol. 14, December 1969.

———, and Karl H. Flaming (eds.): *Urban America,* Holt, Rinehart and Winston, New York, 1972.

Ryder, Norman B.: "The Future Growth of the American Population," in Charles F. Westoff (ed.), *Toward the End of Growth,* Spectrum Books, Prentice-Hall, Englewood Cliffs, N. J., 1973.

Schmandt, Henry J.: "Solutions for the City as a Social Crisis," in J. John Palen and Karl H. Flaming (eds.), *Urban America,* Holt, Rinehart and Winston, New York, 1972.

Seeley, John R.: "Remaking the Urban Scene: New Youth In an Old Environment," *Daedalus,* vol. 97, no. 4, Fall 1968.

Soleri, Paolo: *Arcology, The City in the Image of Man,* M.I.T. Press, Cambridge, Mass., 1969.

Tilly, Charles: "Migration to American Cities," in Daniel P. Moynihan (ed.), *Toward a National Urban Policy,* Basic Books, New York, 1970.

Von Eckardt, Wolf: "Urban Design," in Daniel P. Moynihan (ed.), *Toward a National Urban Policy,* Basic Books, New York, 1970.

Waldman, Elizabeth: "Changes in the Labor Force Activity of Women," in *Monthly Labor Review,"* U.S. Department of Labor, Bureau of Labor Statistics, June 1970.
Webber, Melvin W.: "The Postcity Age," *Daedalus,* vol. 97, no. 4, Fall 1968.
Westoff, Charles F. (ed.): *Toward the End of Growth,* Spectrum Books, Prentice-Hall, Englewood Cliffs, N. J., 1973.
Wright, Frank Lloyd: *The Living City,* Mentor-Horizon, New York, 1958.

# Index